# RECREATING PARTNERSHIP

# RECREATING PARTNERSHIP

❖◆❖◆❖

## A Solution-Oriented, Collaborative Approach to Couples Therapy

PHILLIP ZIEGLER
TOBEY HILLER

W. W. Norton & Company
New York • London

For information about permission to reproduce
selections from this book, write to
Permissions, W. W. Norton & Company, Inc.,
500 Fifth Avenue, New York, NY 10110

Composition by Bytheway Publishing Services
Manufacturing by Haddon Craftsmen
Production manager: Leeann Graham

**Library of Congress Cataloging-in-Publication Data**

Ziegler, Phillip
    Recreating partnership : a solution-oriented, collaborative approach to couples
therapy / Phillip Ziegler, Tobey Hiller
        p.    cm.
"A Norton professional book."
Includes bibliographical references and index.
**ISBN 0-393-70349-5**
1. Marital psychotherapy.    I. Hiller, Tobey.    II. Title.

RC488.5 .Z537 2001
616.89'156—dc21            2001030352

W. W. Norton & Company, Inc., 500 Fifth Avenue, New York, N.Y. 10110
www.wwnorton.com

W. W. Norton & Company Ltd., Castle House, 75/76 Wells Street,
London W1T 3QT

1  2  3  4  5  6  7  8  9  0

This book is dedicated to three
couples who make a difference

*Sam and Emma*
*Ethan and Lisa*
*Josh and Jan*

# Contents

# Acknowledgments

There are, of course, many people who have played a part in the realization of this book—far too many to acknowledge here. But some cannot go without mention. We want to express our thanks to:

Supportive friends and colleagues: Pepper Schwartz, Ph.D., Michael Hoyt, Ph.D., Scott Miller, Ph.D., Kim Chernin, and Renate Stendhal;

Former teachers: Ike Sofaer, Dick Korn, and Eva and Al Leveton, M.D.;

Clinicians and theoreticians who, through workshops and books, have influenced our ideas and practices: Insoo Kim Berg and Steve de Shazer, John Walter and Jane Peller, Harlene Anderson, Michael White, David Epston, and Karl Tomm;

Participants on the SFT-L listserv from whom Phil picked up enough good ideas to justify the time on-line stolen from working on this book;

Our editors at W. W. Norton, Deborah Malmud and Casey Ruble, who made sure we said it right so what we said might make a difference;

Workshop participants and trainees, whose enthusiasm inspires us and who keep us on our toes by asking good questions;

All of our friends, especially those at Hurd's Gulch, who forbore;

The couples, our most important teachers, who have let us into their lives and taught us how to be of help;

And finally and most of all: each other, for all the wonderful stories.

# Introduction

During the more than 45 combined years we have been practicing therapy, we've been impressed and fascinated with the variety of ways couples manage to make relationships[1] work (and amazed at some of the creative ways they can also find to make them *not* work). We question Leo Tolstoy's famous opening sentence in *Anna Karenina,* "Happy families are all alike, every unhappy family is unhappy in its own way" (Tolstoy, 1965, p. 1). We have come to a different conclusion. Regardless of their commonalities, all couples, happy or not, have their own unique ways of living their life stories. In fact, it is much easier to identify commonalities among couples whose relationships will fail than it is to predict which relationships will survive or thrive.

In our experience, knowledge about what is common to successful and unsuccessful marriages—which interpersonal practices are harmful and which foster trust, intimacy, and mutual satisfaction—isn't what seems to make the real difference. Most couples have read enough self-help books, attended enough workshops, and seen enough infomercials to know what types of communication practices and interpersonal behaviors supposedly cause relationships to thrive. They are the same practices and behaviors couples will learn and practice in most couples therapy. Unfortunately, simply teaching couples these general practices is too often like giving people who want to lose weight lists of nutritious foods and telling them that all they need to do is eat less and exercise more. It doesn't work very well in the long term.

More people today seek professional help for marital and relationship problems than for any other reason (Veroff, Kulka, & Donovan, 1981, as cited in Gottman, 1999, p. 4). It has been estimated that 40% of mental health referrals involve marital conflict (Budman & Gurman, 1988). Marital counseling and couples therapy are major industries—and they're growing.

The number of professionals—psychologists, social workers, marriage and family therapists, pastoral counselors, substance abuse counselors, and others—offering help to troubled couples, and the number of clinical models used to guide them, have dramatically increased since the early 1960s (Jacobson & Gurman, 1995). But is all this couples counseling doing any good? Has our profession been fulfilling its promise—are we collectively making a difference in the lives of couples turning to us for help? The evidence is disturbing.

An examination of the research on the effectiveness of couples counseling and marital therapy reveals that our profession's reliance on supposed expertise about how people should behave in intimate relationships is failing to equip us to help couples rebuild happy and satisfying relationship lives. James Bray and Ernest Jouriles (1995), reviewing a large body of research on the effectiveness of various traditional approaches to marital therapy, concluded that there was only the merest statistical evidence that marital therapy was helping to prevent separation and divorce. Even more disturbing, Bray and Jouriles observed that follow-up studies revealed that the majority of couples who remain together following marital therapy are not happy in their marriages (1995, p. 465). They found that regardless of the clinician's theoretical orientation, the techniques used, and the duration of treatment, no more than half the couples entering marital therapy reported significant increases in their happiness together. And when later follow-up inquiries were made, 30% of this satisfied half reported that they were again having serious troubles. This means that in the long term, only 35% of all couples who sought marital therapy felt their relationships were happier and more satisfying than before entering therapy.

John Gottman (1999) draws an even more disheartening conclusion from his review of research on the effectiveness of current methods of couples therapy. He estimates that "about 35% of couples marital therapy is effective in terms of clinically significant, immediate changes, but that after a year about 30–50% of the lucky couples who made initial gains relapse. This means that all we can claim is that in the best studies, conducted in universities with careful supervision, only between 11% and 18% of couples maintain clinically meaningful initial gains when treated by our best marital therapies" (1999, p. 5). We find these statistics alarming. They make clear that our profession has no right to be complacent about our effectiveness in helping couples save their marriages or in helping people improve the quality of their relationship life. These statistics constitute a call for our profession to reconsider assumptions and methods.[2] If no one method proves more effective than any other, and most turn out to be relatively ineffective, we need to ask ourselves: Can we do better? Shouldn't we, as a profession, be rethinking our assumptions about what works in couples therapy? Are there clinical ideas and practices that can increase our effectiveness? The framework we present in Recreating Partnership Therapy (RPT) is our affirmative answer to these questions.

For many years, we practiced couples therapy guided by the belief that the issues troubling most couples could be solved by identifying dysfunctional communication patterns, teaching couples communication skills, and fostering insight into their individual and systemic dynamics. We helped couples to talk more effectively and intimately about their experiences, hopes, needs, feelings, and perceptions, so that each partner could gain greater understanding and empathy for the other person. We pointed out interpersonal dynamics that fostered hostile conflict, mistrust, hurt, and negative expectations and tried to interrupt them. While we emphasized the systemic nature of marital problems and chronic conflicts, we also gave some attention to the effects of people's individual psychological histories. Even at this time in our careers, however, we were interested in identifying the particular assets and resources our clients possessed—and in how they used or failed to use them in their intimacies. While we had not yet developed a systematic way of talking about and highlighting these competencies, we saw them as a potential focal point for producing change.

In those years, we helped many couples. But improvements often came very slowly or turned out to be temporary, with a disheartening return to the original destructive patterns. While we were thinking a lot about the various rhythms of change, we were still focusing on trying to understand what seemed to cause some marriages to thrive while others failed or remained deeply dissatisfying. Though we had general and coherent ideas about what led to marital failure and success, we were often not particularly systematic about what we did from moment to moment in the consulting room. At some point we stopped trying to determine what produces relationship success or failure and instead began asking what distinguishes successful couples *therapy*—the therapeutic work that couples said made a significant positive difference—from therapy that either failed or had little impact.

Eventually our reflections began to reveal replicable patterns of success in the conduct of couples therapy. We noticed that success or failure could not be predicted on the basis of what we initially perceived to be the couple's skill deficits, individual personality flaws, or dysfunctional interpersonal patterns. The best predictor of success seemed to be whether, early on, both partners began to identify their individual and relationship strengths and became motivated to work hard together to bring about mutually desired changes. These changes took place if we were able to help the couple turn themselves into a solution-building team capable of tapping their own assets in a way that raised their hopes that things could be better. Recreated partnership and increased hopefulness seemed to work together. We noticed that as partners felt themselves to be working as solution-building teams toward common goals, their hope, motivation, and effectiveness in making changes increased. And as they felt more hopeful about the future they became more able to work collaboratively both in therapy and in their everyday worlds.

As we repeatedly observed this pattern in our successful work with couples, we came to the conclusion that partnership, creativity, and hope grew from conversations that generated these conditions. Couples, it became clear to us, come to therapy with a history of destructive, painful interactions, experiencing themselves as unable to work together to solve certain problems; therefore, they have little reason to hope the future will be brighter than the past. We realized that it was critical not to perpetuate this sense of failure, inadequacy, blame, and hopelessness by focusing on what people were doing wrong. Instead of continuing to explore a couple's destructive interactions in the past and present, we began to shift the focus of inquiry, observation, and comment away from what supported each partner's adversarial, blaming position. Rather, we explored future possibilities, past successes, and strengths and resources. We began to see things in terms of positive and negative narrative frames. When our conversations with people oriented them and us around positive, preferred narrative frames, people were able to work collaboratively and hope grew. In such an atmosphere, the therapeutic enterprise had a greater chance of success. And, when couples in subsequent sessions talked more about what was working, what was better, and changes that were both pleasing and hope-generating, before long they were reporting that their relationship was thriving.

As we were making these clinical observations and developing these ideas, we began hearing and reading about other clinicians thinking and working along similar lines.[3] Most notably, we became interested in solution-focused brief therapy (Berg, 1994; De Jong & Berg, 1998; de Shazer, 1985, 1988, 1991, 1994), narrative therapy (Epston, 1993b; White & Epston, 1990), and collaborative language therapy (Anderson, 1997). This book reflects the conjunction of our clinical experiences, our encounters with these innovative approaches, and our own reflections about the process of effective couples therapy. It is both theoretical and practical. We hope that in reading this book and beginning to experiment with the ideas and techniques described in its pages, readers will find themselves becoming more proficient in helping couples to change.

Writing a book is itself a transformative experience. It will become clear to our readers that one of the central ways we view therapeutic dialogue is as a transformative context where desired changes are articulated and set in motion. There's always an interaction between the concrete practice and the narrative of change that constitutes therapy. Writing this book has also been a process in which the very act of trying to articulate the what and how precisely has produced new understandings of what we are doing with clients, leading us to new possibilities. The book we started is not the book we finished, and even the book we finished is in some respects not the book we would start now. We have tried to convey the importance of openness, curiosity, and an interest in how to use the ubiquity of change. We hope that embracing the ideas and practices in this book will be part of a process of evolution and ongoing development for you as well.

A few words about the transcripts in this book: For reasons of confidentiality, we altered the names and some of the background facts of all the case examples. In most cases we edited transcripts to make them more concise and thus useful for demonstrating particular points. This can leave the impression that our sessions follow a predictable course in an economical, unmessy fashion. However, that's not the way it is. Although we regularly ask certain specific questions in our work with most couples, each therapy enterprise, every session, every hour, and every conversation is unique. Also, our descriptions of the techniques may not convey the emotional power and depth this apparently simple work often has. No transcript, no matter how complete, captures the subtle shifts, nonverbal events, and emotional and dialogic ebbs and flows that take place in a clinical hour. The playfulness and humor and the moving human encounters that often occur in our sessions with couples cannot be adequately conveyed in this form. Many things we do and say during the course of therapy arise from the context of a given moment and, although important, are too evanescent to be considered part of a method. You, too, of course, will bring your own rich spectrum of creative and personal gifts to the practice of therapy.

# RECREATING
# PARTNERSHIP

# Stories Couples Live: Narrative, Perception, and Meaning-Making in Relationship Life

In all intimacies, people seem to hold several versions or "stories" of their relationship. It is through these differing stories that day-to-day relationship life is experienced. The perceptions, memory streams, and assumptions people hold regarding their relationship in these various versions can be markedly different, and consequently can support or invigorate very different dyadic climates. These narratives, however, are not static, but fluid and evolving, always under construction as couples move through their lives together, making and remaking the meanings of their individual and collective experience. But over time, some versions tend to gather weight as a couple lives more often within those stories' terms; as this happens, those stories begin to exert greater influence than the others.

## Good Stories, Bad Stories, and the Narrative Continuum

In both the profession and its literature, the terms *narrative* and *story* tend to be used interchangeably. However, in general *narrative* refers to the larger, overarching construct in which various stories, accounts, and subnarratives play a contributory part. The *stories* contribute to the larger mosaic. While it might be possible to delineate quite a number of "stories of relationship" in varying editions across a spectrum of pleasing to displeasing for any given couple, those that seem to have the greatest impact fall at the two ends of the relationship-story narrative continuum. These versions of relationship are what we call the *good story* and *bad story* narratives. We use the terms *good* and *bad story narratives* and *the narrative continuum* as shorthand ways of talking about the varied (and often contrasting) perceptual, interpretive lenses through which the partners in a couple story and live their lives together. We recognize, of course, that the *good story/bad story* concept is itself a construct, a story. Just as some stories serve in the building and maintaining of good relationships, some stories are more helpful than others as orienting frameworks for the therapist.[1] We've found, both in our clinical practices and in teaching, that the *good story/bad story* dichotomy can help guide the couples therapist in the co-construction of contexts productive for tapping a couple's unique resources for positive change.

How can these different narratives be recognized? The *good story* narrative refers to the set of stories and experiences the partners in a couple would, if asked to think about it, view as stories of success and satisfaction. In these stories the self, the other, and the relationship are viewed and experienced in a largely positive light. The hallmark of these narratives is their ability to express and generate a sense of partnership (collaboration and mutuality) for the couple, along with a sense of pleasure or satisfaction in the recognition of the particular strengths and desirable qualities of each person and the relationship itself. While *good story* narratives often contain elements of the romantic, they are different from unrealistic fantasies about how the relationship could or should be; they are versions of the relationship both partners have felt actual at one time or another and are therefore more likely to see as plausible for the future. When experiencing themselves within the *good story* narrative framework, the partners see the relationship as a loving, uniquely desirable partnership and as a context for successfully handling life's problems (regardless of whether they hold their views for the same reasons or from the same perspective).

The *bad story* narrative is the set of stories and experiences that coalesce at the other end of the continuum. These stories, individually and/or collectively constructed, reflect and generate feelings of alienation, disappointment, frustration, unhappiness, and personal and relationship failure. Couples chronically living under the perceptual and interpretive cloud of the *bad story* narrative often feel trapped, tricked, defeated, and incompetent. The *bad story* narrative, of course, is not confined to relationships that are unsuccessful or come to an end. Couples whose *good story* narrative is strong and prevailing also have *bad stories*. The *bad story* narrative (at least elements that can contribute to its development and flow) enters as soon as disappointments, disagreements, and/or conflict arise in a relationship—and this happens, in some measure, in all relationships. However, when these narratives are dominant, people see themselves, their partners, and/or the relationship in a negative, dissatisfied, and mistrustful light; a sense of collaboration, both in addressing problems and in enjoying good times, has broken down.

We want to clarify that our concept of the *good story/bad story* narratives and the narrative continuum on which they lie are meant to be general and cover a host of possible experiences, attributes, and unique formulations. We also want to emphasize that it is the partners in a couple, not the therapist, who assess where a given experience, encounter, or story falls on this narrative continuum—one end or the other, or somewhere in between. Although part of the therapist's job is to take advantage of the fluid nature of both the narratives and the assessments, the weight and placement along the narrative continuum that individuals and couples give to various events in their lives are particular and personal. For example, a couple that lives part of the time separately on two different coasts might report that when they're together they often have passionate arguments, yet describe themselves as successful and happy and view their partnership as satisfying. Another couple might report that they rarely fight and spend most of their free time doing things together, but one or both partners say they are very unhappy with the relationship, describing it as boring, lonely, and without passion. Recipes for relationship satisfaction are custom-made; ingredients one couple might see as essential another might leave out entirely. Research confirms that style differences between successful couples make it hard to establish a single blueprint for satisfying intimacy (Gottman, 1994, 1999). Thus the terms *good story* and *bad story* have no diagnostic or moral flavor: what is "good" or "bad" in particular instances depends upon the accounts of couples themselves. Nor do *good story* narratives consist of trouble-free stories or refer only to times of ease and comfort in a couple's life. The *good story* narrative may be in force for a couple during times of profound adversity or sorrow: what is "good" is the positive ability of the couple to rely on their partnership as a source of strength and comfort in moving through difficult times, including those posed by the challenges of relationship itself. In fact, it is often during hard times that the most powerful *good stories* are constructed.

We want to emphasize that the *good story/bad story* narrative concept is not a causal theory about why problems develop in a relationship or what maintains them, nor is it a teaching tool for educating couples about how to view their relationships. (We will discuss if, when, and how we talk about the *good story/bad story* dichotomy with couples a little later.) It is not a "technique" but a framework assumption about how couples work. We aren't interested in "getting rid of" certain stories, or in discovering the origin of the *bad story*. We believe not that *bad stories* will disappear in successful relationships, but that couples will learn how to exit their *bad story* narratives more quickly and frequently than dissatisfied couples, so that the *bad stories* do not become the dominant narrative for the relationship. We do not seek to impose new and "better" stories about the couple's relationship. We use the *good story/bad story* concept to help us better understand and utilize, in therapeutic dialogue, the evolving narratives and clusters of idea (already existing for each couple) that affect behavior and perception in relational life. The concept helps us know when and how to pursue particular lines of inquiry, to encourage couples to talk to each other in session, and to bypass some of the common difficulties encountered in relationship counseling.

Quoted in Freedman and Combs (1996), Michael White, the developer of narrative therapy, has this to say about how particular narratives—regardless of how they might be viewed from the outside—function in people's lives:

> Not only do these stories determine the meaning that persons give to experience, . . . but these stories also largely determine which aspects of experience persons select out for expression. And, as well, inasmuch as action is prefigured on meaning-making, these stories determine real effects in terms of the shaping of people's lives. (p. 21)

While White does not consider himself either a constructionist or a constructivist, this statement serves as a good starting point for talking about some of the philosophical and epistemological ideas we have brought together in our concept of the *good story/bad story* narrative. Constructivism and constructionism are related philosophical paradigms. While differences between these two need not concern us for long, we do want to clarify that radical constructivists such as Paul Watzlawick (1984) assume objective reality does not exist; critical constructivists such as Michael Mahoney (Neimeyer & Mahoney, 1995) argue that while objective reality exists, we cannot can verify its existence; and social constructivists such as Kenneth Gergen (1991, 1994; Gergen & Kaye, 1992) emphasize that social reality, at least, is always shaped by social discourse and language. For our purposes, what's important to understand is that reality is always to some degree invented—constructed within and between persons in the context of a social community from a blend of perception, memory, assumption, interpretation, and behavior—rather than discovered as an objective presence perceived through the senses. Michael Hoyt (1996) says it well:

> The doors of therapeutic perception and possibility have been opened wide by the recognition that we are actively constructing our mental realities rather than simply uncovering or coping with an objective "truth." What makes us most human is not our opposable thumbs nor our use of tools but, rather, our capacity to conceive a future, recall a past, construct meanings, and make choices. How we choose to conceive and pattern the present, the past and the future profoundly influences our course. (p. 1)

Social constructionism, the branch of constructionist thought that has had the greatest impact on our thinking, shares the view that life is experienced through stories, but shifts the locus of story-making from within people to the interpersonal space between them. Thus, emphasis is directed specifically toward the role of language and conversation in shaping people's social realities. Kenneth Gergen (Gergen & Gergen, 1991), a principal architect of social constructionism, explains that this epistemology:

> draws attention to the manner in which conventions of language and other social processes (negotiation, persuasion, power, etc.) influence the accounts rendered of the "objective" world. The emphasis is thus not on the individual mind but on the meanings of people as they collectively generate descriptions and explanations in language. (p. 81)

Steve de Shazer, writing about the philosophical underpinnings of his solution-focused approach, sometimes refers to social constructionism, but prefers to place his ideas on a different philosophical foundation. Rather than concerning himself with the possible theoretical differences between constructivism and constructionism, he is more interested in the distinction between two major influences in the twentieth-century philosophy of language: structuralism and post-structuralism. In *Putting Difference to Work* (1991), de Shazer explains that "for the structuralist, meanings are stable and knowable through transformation, but for the post-structuralist, meaning is seen as known through social interaction and negotiation; meaning here is always open to view since it lies between people rather than hidden away inside the individual" (p. 45).

While the differences in these various epistemological positions are interesting to us intellectually, we find what is common among them more useful as guides in the daily conduct of couples therapy—they remind us that the relational "house" couples build, maintain, and live in, is constructed, to a significant degree, in language and through conversation. In other words, it is through the couple's interactions and conversations, especially those with each other and with significant others (family members, good friends, even the "voices" of the media) that their "couple" reality is constantly shaped and changed for better or worse. Over time, various versions of the relationship stories thicken, gathering detail and resonance, while others thin or shift character.

Of course, this co-constructive influence of dialogue and relational interaction applies to what takes place in the therapeutic consulting room as well. In the conduct of couples therapy, a social-constructionist focus guides the therapist in the use of specific conversational processes capable of positively transforming people's perceptions of each other, their actions, and the quality, tone, and life of their relationship. As Harlene Anderson (1997) puts it, "Some conversations enhance possibility; others diminish it. When possibility is enhanced, we have a sense of self-agency, a sense that we can take the necessary action to address what concerns or troubles us; our dilemmas, problems, pains, and frustrations, and to accomplish what we want; our ambitions, hopes, intentions, and actions" (p. xvii). Our concept of the *good story/bad story* dichotomy gives us a framework for making effective use of constructionist ideas by providing us with a continuing sense of what we can ask or say in our meetings with couples that will further possibility-enhancing conversations.

# The Role of Relationship Climate

The creation of the narratives (whether satisfying or dissatisfying, bonded or alienating, shared or divisive, or anything in between) in which a couple lives their life is a complex but also very natural social process that requires no particular conscious effort. In this process, the two people co-construct their experiences, memories, and expectations into a mutual language and narrative(s)[2] that are codified and fleshed out in various idiosyncratic and private ways. Most events and experiences and the stories people make of them fall somewhere in the middle of the narrative spectrum. They do not support either a relationship-sustaining environment or an alienating atmosphere, nor do they play a significant role in maintaining or reinforcing either the *good* or *bad story* narratives. But when the *good* or *bad story* narratives begin to exercise a perceptual and interpretive hold over one or both partners, more and more experiences begin reinforcing the dominant narrative.

What causes relationships to deteriorate, from a constructionist perspective, is the fact that the *bad story* narrative has gained a significant hold over the partners. Regardless of their specific content, or how long they have been influencing the partners' perceptions and interactions, certain stories have woven together into relationship-destructive constructs: the *bad story* narratives. These *bad stories* have led to a cumulative, regenerating perception and experience of events that results in an increasing loss of a sense of partnership. Under these conditions, the couple experiences increasing difficulty viewing themselves as a team through good times and bad, a unit working together for a mutually defined common good. As a *bad story* narrative thickens and takes on perceptual "mass," people become less and less able to draw upon their shared *good story,* the narrative that keeps goodwill and feelings of love alive even during challenging times.

Conversely, when couples experience themselves living in the realm of their relationship-supportive *good story* narrative, they will be able to draw on some level of partnership and collaboration. Looking back into the past and forward into an imagined future can then provide them with a sufficient sense of confidence, comfort, and pleasure in their "we-ness" and inspire feelings of hope about the future. Attention to how the *good story/bad story* distinction affects the "weather" of relationship interactions is important in

RPT because it helps the clinician better understand how to help a couple tap the resources that will make it possible for them to recreate partnership.

By the time couples come into a therapist's office, most are bringing well-developed *bad stories* about their relationship. Usually both partners have developed ideas about the sources of the trouble, marshaled evidence of its influence on their lives, and tried out problem-solving or change-promoting tactics based on their theories about what needs to change and how to do it. People have defined a stream of incident and experience (the *bad story* narrative) to express what has gone wrong and explain why their efforts to improve the situation haven't worked. At this point, they see evidence of the negative story in the past and present, and expect it for the future, so that hope is at a nadir. This narrative frame constricts possibility and opportunity for positive movement in the relationship and, most importantly, for partnership.

However, alternative *good story* versions of the relationship are available for almost all couples. When questioned (in the right way, and at the right time), most couples in therapy can come up with a more positive narrative of their relationship—the shaping of events and experiences, mutual and individual, that brought them together and that they share as a perception of themselves, their history, and their intimacy when the relationship seems more the way they want it to be. One often says, colloquially, that a new couple is "building a life together." This phrase deftly names what couples do to form a relationship—they construct their life together on the basis of an evolving narrative, beginning with their meeting (or even preceding it) and continuing through the present into a future they envision and shape together. Even when their individual meanings for these visions or histories differ, the narrative is cooperatively built and experienced as bonding and companionable. Couples generally marry or commit themselves in some way to a life together on the basis of a shared feeling of goodwill, excitement, and trust—trust not only in each other, but also in this evolving story of togetherness.[3]

So a version of a *good story* narrative—containing an implicit future, ideas about who each person is to the other and in the world, and features of interaction that both partners recognize and enjoy—is the basic territory in which most couples begin living their emotional lives together. If it remains viable, this *good story* narrative functions to keep disagreements and disappointments within a manageable or acceptable realm. It is also the basis on which people make concrete life decisions with both short- and long-term consequences—decisions regarding where to live, what job to take, whether or not to have children, and many other smaller and daily acts. Even for couples caught up in strong *bad story* narratives, this *good story* narrative is usually potentially present as a source of energy, affection, relationship skill-building, and mutuality, and therapists who know when and how to draw out its elements can help couples begin to reinvigorate it. It is in the particular details and flow of these competing narratives that both problems and unique solutions develop.

Although most relationships do begin with the co-construction of a mutually bonding positive narrative, not all relationships begin with a strong *good story* in place. Some couples start the construction of a negative relationship landscape quite early; sometimes the very inception of the relationship becomes an element, for one or both partners, of the *bad story* narrative. This may occur, for instance, when one partner sees him- or herself as entering the relationship out of guilt or as a way out of a painful, lonely, or troubled life situation, or when an individual feels trapped, reluctant, or doubtful in the relationship. In such situations, where the *good story* narrative has never been vigorous for one or both partners, or where the *bad story* narrative is part of the intimacy's formulation, satisfying partnership may be difficult or impossible to achieve. Even here, however, if there are some elements of satisfying partnership a couple can co-construct (remember, build, or imagine for the future), people may find ways to move toward a sufficiently pleasing future (a largely *good story* narrative).

In any case, when couples enter therapy, the *good story* narrative has lost influence in the life of the relationship. It no longer has enough vigor to provide the couple with a feeling of partnership and an abiding trust in a desirable and secure future. Whatever evidence might be found for the *good story* is being regularly overlooked and lacks sufficient weight to overcome the informing presence of the *bad story*. A study by Robinson and Price (1980) supports the power of this kind of perceptual frame: Unhappily married couples underdetect their partner's positive interaction by 50%. In this situation, acts intended to heal disagreement or solve problems and gestures of reconciliation or kindness do not have positive effects on the emotional climate of the marriage. This is a vivid indicator, we think, of the power of the *bad story* to block the efforts a couple may make to turn their relationship around.

In interpersonal relationships, meaning and perception shifts facilitate behavioral changes. Cumulative and lasting behavioral change will be blocked if perception and meaning shifts do not occur. Since the dominance of one of these relationship narratives affects people's perceptions of themselves and each other, conversation during the course of therapy about elements of these narratives will strongly influence the possibility of change. Narrative thickens and is reinforced as people give it detail, history, and structure in a therapy session. Use of the *good story/bad story* concept is consonant with our belief that work in the area of perception and meaning-making is the key to facilitating relational change. The more rich, varied, and dense the *good stories* become through therapeutic conversation, the more influential they will be outside the consulting room. Because the *good story* narrative functions to keep disagreements and disappointments within a manageable or tolerable realm, it makes the partners more open to each other's efforts to solve problems, conciliate, or move back into warm relationship. This means that when bits and pieces of the *bad story* narrative can be absorbed or transformed into a *good story* context, they become evidence of problems solved or ways a couple's union can accept difference. Failure to reinvigorate the *good story* narrative will render the therapist's and couple's efforts to solve problems and achieve desired change useless, and ultimately will produce only short-term progress, or worse, actually be counterproductive.

## Self-Sense and Mutuality

One way to explain the power of the *good story/bad story* narrative process lies in the way we respond to the social indicators about self we pick up from others.[4] One of the most powerful aspects of falling in love is the experience of feeling that another person accurately sees or understands us in a way that renews a sense of pleasure and excitement about being ourselves. One way to see the process of falling in love is as the mutual experience of giving and receiving a very positive reflection of the self. Unlike some theorists, we don't see "falling in love" as all dream and illusion or, as psychoanalytic couples therapists argue, as an unconscious mate selection replicating early childhood experiences and developmental deficits (Bader & Pearson, 1988; Hendrix, 1988; Solomon, 1989). Like all elements of relationship, the experience of falling in love is to varying degrees constructed, but what we think is most important is the way it can form a powerful beginning to the *good story* narrative a couple forges and carries forward into the future.

The process of giving and receiving a positive sense of self increases the likelihood that, at least temporarily, people will, in fact, enact the positive aspects of self being reflected back to them from the other. Being seen as a preferred self (the way one likes to be seen) tends to support action and behavior that validates that version (Eron & Lund, 1996). Thus, falling in love enhances aspects of the self that are intimacy-competent, growth-relevant, and empowering. Other people's reactions to and ideas about us, as well as the notions we carry culturally, familially, and historically about ourselves strongly influence our self-sense; seeing oneself through the eyes of the beloved during the bonding time has profound positive power for the forming intimacy and provides an important element of the *good story* narrative couples carry, even through periods of disappointment.

People experience varying (and sometimes opposing) self-senses in the different *good* and *bad stories*. When the *bad story* narratives gain influence in the life of a couple, the partners' self-senses suffer a loss of positive reflection, and the individuals will often not only feel unhappy with their partners but also experience themselves as unsuccessful, ineffective, or unlovable. The negative self-sense that arises under the influence of the *bad story* narrative makes it harder for people to perceive, believe in, and tap their own talents, skills, and resources. When people live in lively, rich *good story* narratives, in which they order their experiences mostly around a positive expectation and perception of their intimacy, they are more apt to experience both themselves and the other as lovable, interesting, competent, creative, and effective. This is true even when social, economic, and other life conditions are difficult or challenging. This positive experience of self encourages behavior supporting these senses of self and the relationship, which enhances will, energy, creativity, and optimism. Thus, there is a generative and evolving process in which the self-sense and the framing relationship narrative give each other form, substance, and vigor.

It is, of course, possible for only one person in a relationship to experience a positive self-sense. This may happen, for instance, when one partner sees an event as proof of mutuality and a positive self-sense while the other partner privately experiences the same event as alienating (an example of this might be a relationship in which one partner, an outdoor person, feels satisfied in self and relationship when she and her partner are kayaking on challenging white water, while the other person, less enthusiastic about these undertakings, feels she must comply with her partner's version of fun but experiences the white-water trips as stressful and scary). But in relationships where partnership in various different interactions is strong, both individuals experience a sense of expansion and stability of the competent and desirable self. Couples who are able to live in a shared, long-term, durable *good story* have evolving access to capacities and skills in themselves that are recreative of satisfying intimacy; these capacities support a sense of self that reflects a personalized version of pleasure and competence in nurturing and maintaining a loving relationship. In addition, successful negotiation of the inevitable *bad story* territory, when it comes up, gives partners in successful couples a heightened sense of trust, both about their shared ability to negotiate conflict and about the disclosure of significant feelings, ideas, and aspects of self they may otherwise experience as outside their preferred self-sense. In this way, a vigorous *good story* narrative can support the development of self-awareness and self-acceptance.

## Thickening the Good Story, Loosening the Bad Story

Before we discuss specific ways the *good story/bad story* concept helps in the conduct of couples therapy, we want to emphasize an important structural difference between the roles the *good story* and the *bad story* narratives play in intimate life. As already noted, the *good story* is generally to some significant degree a shared narrative, in which events and experiences are viewed or described congruently, with mutually recognized positive effects. The partners seem to be telling essentially the same tale, with individual embellishments. These embellishments or differences in perspective are seen as welcome elaborations to the story by the other partner, rather than as arguments about the reality being described. Of course, partners hold distinct, individual *good stories* about the relationship as well, and a significant part of couples work is to flesh these stories out, making each partner more aware of the details and meanings of the other's positive story. Learning about what each values in the relationship and the other that's different or individual helps to strengthen the partners' bond by building new links between private meanings or stories and a shared narrative. The *good story* narrative is, in the telling, both an *experience* and *expression* of partnership. It is, in a sense, partnership in action (and partnership in consciousness), as the couple shares a shoulder-to-shoulder framing and articulation of their reality, with some individual glossing that is seen as exciting rather than divisive.

*Bad story* narratives, however, are individual and often divergent or conflictual. The couple presents two divided views of how things happened, what experiences mean, and who did or said what. Because there has often been a good deal of argument about whose version is right, some parts of the stories are usually very well known to both partners, but many aspects are disputed and disclosure and honesty have often suffered. Various elements of *bad story* narratives are often held privately by each partner, either uncommunicated or codified in language no longer mutually transparent. Members of a couple caught in a *bad story* narrative will often tell friends or family members things they won't tell their partner. They may secretly hold ideas such as "if he does that one more time, it's proof he doesn't love me," or "I'm only staying because of the kids," or "I'm out of here as soon as I can get a better job." Partnership has broken up. Meanings have diverged. As two (often mutually exclusive) *bad stories* have gained power to influence perception, meaning-making, and behavior in the relationship, the couple's ability to work together on problems and develop shared plans has deteriorated.

Obviously, this difference between the two kinds of narrative is quite important with respect to a couple's ability to work collaboratively in therapy to solve specific problems. Couples living in *bad story* territory predominately experience division and separation. As soon as they enter the *good story* territory, even briefly, they're experiencing some form of mutuality, some sense of togetherness. As soon as the partners begin experiencing success in collaborating to solve their presenting problems in therapy, they enter and invigorate their shared *good story*, so that the process in play is circularly generative. A sense of alliance in perception and purpose becomes possible. This means that in any discovery, exploration, or utilization of a couple's *good story* narrative, the therapist and couple are beginning to reconstruct or reaffirm the potential for recreating partnership. Even when the relationship is not going to last, forming an amicable team for dealing with whatever experiences come up around parting becomes more plausible.

Obversely, therapeutic exploration of the *bad story* territory may have a regressive influence, supporting its dominance in the couple's perceptual life. This is not to say that the airing of concerns and dissatisfactions and the pursuit of disclosure and honesty in the relationship dialogue should be avoided in couples counseling. However, it does suggest that the clinician's decision to participate in conversations that highlight *bad story* narratives must be very purposeful.

As noted earlier, the *good story/bad story* concept is not simply a tool or set of techniques. Nor is it an attempt to find or define some objective relational truth. It is also not a narrative we seek to impose on our clients. The *good story/bad story* dichotomy is a useful framework, a way of looking at and talking about dyadic relationship that helps provide direction and focus in the therapeutic dialogue. Following is a summary of five ways the *good story/bad story* concept can work as an important structural underpinning (perceptual framework) for effective couples therapy.

## 1. Normalizing difference, conflict, and disappointment.

Conveying to people that elements of the *bad story*—the streams of experience containing a couple's conflicts, disappointments, and inevitable differences—are common to all relationships can help people feel less angry or alone in a culture where the idealized pictures of relationship often lack verisimilitude. The disappointment people experience when they "fall out of" the *good story* and into conflict and trouble often makes them think of themselves as well off the beaten path of the normal and acceptable. This can heighten the sense of anger, disappointment, and even shame that accompanies the experience of being caught in this painful situation. While it's not necessary to talk explicitly with people about the *good story/bad story* concept, many couples find it helpful to hear that in most intimate relationships people carry around some alternative versions of their lives together. Just talking about how hard it can be for most people to remember positive aspects of their relationships when things are difficult can be comforting to a couple in distress.

## 2. The *good story* as a ground for discovery of resources.

As soon as couples begin to recall or describe what motivates them to want to improve their relationship, what brought them together in the first place, or how they bypassed the worst scenario in their most recent fight, they are beginning to recover pieces of the *good story* narrative. In this process they will naturally begin exploring and describing their strengths, capabilities, and talents in intimacy. This is when the therapist's curious questions are crucial in opening the pathway toward what works and feels helpful. An assumption on the part of the therapist that an exploration of what is strong, workable, and bonding in the relationship produces a different course than scrutiny of what has gone wrong and why. As the therapist guides the conversation toward the wellspring of the *good story*, each partner can discover (and make available for future use) particular ways of being, doing, and seeing that contribute to well-being and satisfaction in the relationship.

### 3. Supporting the development of well-formed goals for therapy.

Only when we enter the territory of the *good story* does productive goal-building become possible. In order to develop well-defined and clinically useful goals for therapy (therapeutically well-formed goals), couples must find and enter some shared territory where they see things in similar ways and are able to share preferred future pictures. Otherwise, the goal discussion itself often becomes part of the *bad story*, with each member of the couple pointing to changes the other needs to make or with each disagreeing vehemently on what is important or how to achieve it. This kind of scenario, where partners can't even agree on what the problem is, is familiar to all couples counselors. Sniffing out aspects of the *good story* and highlighting them recreates partnership and sets up a climate for collaborative goal-building.

Students often ask us whether we talk explicitly about the *good story/bad story* dichotomy with couples. We conceive of our clinical job, which is collaborative in nature, as one of evoking, not of teaching. Consequently, we're not specifically interested in "teaching" couples to recognize and/or interpret the kind of narrative they are living in together at some moment; we are interested in inviting people to find and thicken the aspects of behavior, perception, and meaning that they say moves them toward their preferred futures. In RPT we use the *good story/bad story* narrative concept to help us, as clinicians, better recognize when and how to evoke elements, details, and attitudes that exist in a couple's relationship-enhancing narrative. Occasionally we do share our ideas about the power of *good story* and *bad story* versions of relationship with couples. Some couples prefer structural explanations or invite conversation about the ways their varying perceptions can affect their relationship lives. But generally we find most couples benefit from constructing *good story* narratives rather than learning about them as concepts. Lectures on narrative or constructionism or the role of perceptions in framing reality obviously aren't necessary in the conduct of therapy; however, when we are asked or if it seems useful, we will explain anything we are doing in therapy—any tool, technique, or informing idea we have. But we do keep in mind that there are occasions when too much explanation impedes the natural flow of a creative dialogue or flattens the excitement and motion of change.

What is crucially important and must occur one way or another if partnership is to be recreated, is for a couple to move far enough into *good story* territory that shared and mutually understood goals can be envisioned and fleshed out, even if the couple continues to hold conflicting versions of some events. For example, as we explore the times a couple has experienced as more pleasing and satisfying, they might tell us that recently they had a relaxing, fun time together at the zoo with their children. They tell us that it pleased them to be together as a family and see their children having fun. They felt close. By building on this *good story* event, we can clarify what kinds of future experiences will make up this couple's goals. The very act of having this kind of dialogue in front of a receptive witness helps them to solidify their *good story* narrative, making partnership in the therapy hour possible.

### 4. Pinpointing means of interpersonal repair.

The *good story/bad story* concept provides an important orientation for the therapist in helping couples to find and make use of the unique and concrete "how to's" of interpersonal repair and self-soothing activities. Research comparing successful and unsuccessful marriages makes clear that couples who effectively engage in such activities are far more likely to describe their marriages as satisfying, even when they acknowledge problems and conflicts. John Gottman (1999) talks about the importance of effective "repair" or soothing efforts during or after conflict:

> In all marriages people display the behaviors that are predictive of marital dissolution. They occur significantly less in stable, happy marriages than in marriages headed for divorce. However, the reason for this reduced frequency was that repair attempts were made, and they were effective. . . . Families who are ailing not only show patterns that are dysfunctional, but also display mechanisms of health, and the therapist can become allied with these mechanisms in treatment. (p. 36)

He suggests that the therapist's role in this is to educate couples—particularly during fights, when they are in states of excitation—to do a better job of soothing and repair. We feel that in investigating and fleshing out the *good story* with a particular couple, we will find with them the unique methods of relationship repair, self-soothing, and refreshing of the *good story* that work for them. Because it is a custom-made prescription, it is more likely to be utilized and to work. These couple-specific behaviors, thoughts, and perceptions are what help each couple to exit their *bad stories* and move into their *good story* narratives. Helping couples access and cultivate these particular assets gives them a sense of empowerment about their ability to increase their own and each other's satisfaction, resolve difficulties, and return to a satisfying relationship.

While in RPT the therapist and couple collaborate in finding ways to refresh and amplify the *good story* narrative, they also mark—sort of like putting up legible road signs—the behavioral and perceptual return paths the couple can use to return to the *good story* when the *bad story* arises.

One way to erect these markers is through competency-oriented conversations about past successes—encounters and experiences that stand out as different from the current frustrations, impasses, and struggles. These kinds of conversations[5]—where the couple and the therapist are talking about times when a *bad story* experience didn't happen or was less problematic— lead directly to bits and pieces of the *good story* narrative, which can then be fleshed out by further questioning about what each partner was doing differently at those times. These exceptions or success narratives often contain exchanges between partners that de-escalate hostility and tension. They offer examples of soothing and repair gestures that worked but may have gone unnoticed. These examples can be identified and underscored in therapeutic conversation and made available for future use.

It's relevant to note here that couples therapy itself can be seen as a process of interpersonal repair in which pinpointing the bridges between *bad story* and *good story* plays an important role. The experience of therapy itself need not be painful, emotionally intense, and/or frightening to be effective. Emotionality may or may not occur for people in couples counseling; what is important is establishing a context in which emotion, discovered resources, and storying will contribute to the positivity that makes desired change outside the session more likely. Using positivity in the therapy hour to support change is not the same as engaging in pep talks, slurring over problems and difficulties, or lecturing about a positive attitude. It is a process of finding and mining the assets, sense of agency, and points of view of the *good story* context, fueling effective efforts toward change. Gottman (1999) writes:

> The best and most consistent correlate of marital satisfaction and dissatisfaction across research laboratories . . . has turned out to be a construct researchers have called "negative affect reciprocity." This term refers to the increased probability that a person's emotions will be negative (anger, belligerence, sadness, contempt, and so on) right after his or her partner has exhibited negativity. . . . Negative affect reciprocity has been the most consistent discriminator between happily and unhappily married couples. It is far better a measurement even than the amount of negative affect. (p. 37)

This suggests that one should avoid making the therapy hour itself a negative-affect-reciprocity workshop. If a therapist pursues supposed causes, facts, and evidence of dysfunction and pathology, a process of *bad story* thickening will likely occur. On the other hand, when clients are encouraged to talk about successes and competencies, the *good story* gains ground and what might be called positive affect reciprocity increases. In highlighting exceptions to problems like prolonged fights or lack of companionability, couples can begin to identify and construct what each partner did (and could do more often) to stop the downward spiral into *bad story* territory. Usually people can identify something they thought or did differently that stopped the cycle of what Gottman is calling negative affect reciprocity.

Interestingly, Gottman says that in distressed marriages there are more repair attempts than in happy ones, but that they fail to make a difference. We think this is because when the influence of the *bad story* narrative is strong, leading people to perceive the relationship as unsafe, dissatisfying, and threatening, the meaning of repair attempts will either not be read as positive or go unnoticed. Suppose, for instance, that a husband's *bad story*, which includes the perception that his wife is "a constant nag," is strongly in force. The wife, in a spirit of conciliation, suggests that they go away for a weekend together. But because he is seeing her as constantly nagging, he perceives this as an allusion to her past complaint that he doesn't do enough to make her happy or take care of the relationship, and he withdraws. This instantly gives the wife evidence for her *bad story*, which is that her husband is unresponsive and uninterested in intimacy. What might have been a successful repair attempt backfires under the influence of the *bad story*.

Most couples therapists are familiar with the frustrating experience of witnessing one partner reject what seems to be the other's good-faith attempt to reestablish trust or intimacy, perhaps by offering a concession, explaining an act in an unthreatening way, or expressing personal responsibility for a current problem or difficulty. The repair attempt is treated as another foray in the battle. When one partner reacts to the other's caring or conciliatory gesture negatively or with hostility, as though the other is manipulating, lying, or negotiating in bad faith, we assume it is because the *bad story* context frames any positive gesture as suspicious or untrustworthy. In our experience, a reinterpretation of these acts as soothing and reparative is unlikely to occur until the *good story* narrative lens is in place. Therefore, some reinvigoration, remembering, and refreshing of the *good story* context must precede or accompany repair attempts if they are to be successful. This is why, in RPT, the practitioner collaborates with the clients in "reacquainting" them with their own *good story* elements, with particular attention to highlighting their occasionally effective repair techniques.

## 5. Viewing difference creatively and realistically.

We hope to stimulate couples' curiosity and interest regarding the various ways their multiple attitudes and perceptions influence their relationship. When partners in a couple can tolerate multiplicity and begin talking about varying perceptions, assumptions, and points of view rather than disputed facts or right and wrong, they are usually on their way toward bridging their differences and finding a way to accomplish their goals. The *good story/bad story* concept creates a context in which difference can be seen and handled (by both therapist and couple) as inevitable and a potentially useful, enriching, and/or tolerable experience rather than an irritating, divisive, and destructive one. Any success in moving from *bad story* to *good story* allows people to feel more tolerant of differences and less afraid of disunion.

In the process of negotiating goals, differences often transform themselves into varied or interlocking assets. People can begin to see arguments or differing perspectives as a context for the practice of their creativity, flexibility, and empathy. It has been our experience that when couples realize that some *bad story* experiences are simply part of relationship life, and as they gain confidence about finding their way back toward harmony, they tend to alter their views of their own conflicts and disagreements and sometimes even enjoy certain aspects of differences they once found abrasive. Over time, as repair and soothing attempts work effectively and the *good story* predominates, the presence of their disagreements loses its destabilizing power and doesn't seem the inevitable precursor of disharmony.

Research suggests many of the differences couples have in the beginning of their relationship will be long-standing or permanent (Gottman, 1999). If many of the differences couples have are never resolved, it is important that therapy helps the couple to achieve some acceptance of division and find ways to reduce the harmful effects of conflict. It is problematic for couples to believe they can resolve all their differences; achieving acceptance of difference is crucial to durability and satisfaction in a relationship (Jacobson & Christensen, 1996). It is also problematic for therapists to assume it's their job to help people resolve all their differences or that therapy can create some idealized version of an appropriate intimate relationship. The *good story/bad story* concept helps here. It supports a realistic view of relationship life and fosters an acceptance of the differences and disappointments that are endemic to it.

Our job as therapists, then, is to help people learn to see, do, and say things that will reinvigorate their shared *good story*. We are not trying to teach couples how to act like other couples who are successful, nor do we use our model to decide when the couple is conforming to a preferred interactional style. In RPT, the clinician hosts conversations that allow couples to co-construct unique tools and then provides a context for them to engage in conversations that invigorate the *good-story* narrative, both in conflict and nonconflict areas. These tailor-made tools give people a broader sense of their own competence and their relationship's resilience. This, in turn, supports an increase both in the vigor of the *good story* and in the actual time spent in satisfying partnership.

What works in marriages works in therapy also. Most couples caught in the *bad story* narrative work on a theory similar to that of traditional modes of therapy—that is, that finding and articulating what is wrong will cause positive change. Each partner in the unhappy couple continually points out to the other what he or she is doing wrong, with the hope the other will see the error of his or her ways and correct the faulty behavior. This doesn't seem to work very well in unhappy relationships. It doesn't work very well in therapy, either. While it's very important to acknowledge the pains and difficulties people need to share in couples counseling, in RPT we believe the way to help people turn troubled relationships around (or, alternatively, bring a relationship to a resolved and noncombative end) is through the empowerment of finding and using their competencies. Focusing on and pointing out dysfunction, deficits, or problematic patterns of behavior is equal to giving weight and substance to the *bad story* narrative.

What we believe is helpful, in therapy as in intimate relationships, is finding and enlivening a useful *and effective* positive frame for the development, with our clients, of satisfying futures. And here the *good story* concept is pivotal, because in each relationship the positivity available in this narrative will be specific to, and therefore effective for, that couple and their situation. The *good story/bad story* narrative dichotomy offers solid ground for the therapist to co-construct with the couple a uniquely useful frame for the reparative and creative process that therapy can be, drawing on the particular modes and abilities each couple has for noticing, learning, changing, growing, and imagining—all the rich and varied resources people can bring to changing their lives for the better.

# CHAPTER 2

# Recreating Partnership Therapy: Basic Working Assumptions

*Learn about the pines from the pine,*
*And about bamboo from the bamboo.*
    —Matsuo Bashō

Suppose a couple comes to therapy because the wife has recently begun suffering anxiety attacks whenever her husband goes out in the evening with his friends. She's been losing sleep because of frightening nightmares in which he's having sex with other women. During the day she ruminates about his leaving her. The husband says he loves his wife very much and has no interest in other women. But nothing he says or does seems to reassure her, and he has become increasingly worried. The wife says that "in her head" she knows her husband loves her and isn't thinking about leaving her for another woman. Nonetheless she feels driven by what she knows are irrational fears, panicking whenever he's about to leave the house to join his buddies for an evening of racquetball and a few beers.

What sense are we to make of this situation? How are we to understand the nature of this couple's "real" problems? Who "has" the problem—the wife, the husband, or the couple? Who should be seen in therapy? The wife alone? The couple in conjoint sessions? Should each partner be seen individually by separate therapists while a third sees them together? Should they be seen by a male/female co-therapy team? By a therapist with an observing/reflecting team behind a one-way mirror? Once it is decided how and by whom these people will be seen, more questions must be answered. The therapist must decide what information she needs about the couple and how much she must learn about their individual and relationship history and the history of the presenting symptoms. Should the focus of treatment be on talking about and changing the couple's feelings, cognitions, or behaviors? How active should she be in directing the therapy, both with respect to what is talked about during the therapy hours and what people are expected to do between sessions? Should she give homework assignments, and if so, what kinds?

How therapists answer these questions depends, to a large extent, on their theoretical orientation and clinical assumptions about what makes people tick, what causes relationship difficulties, how change happens, how people generally solve problems, and how therapy works. Regardless of how eclectic a therapist might be, his theoretical orientation, assumptions, and presumed expertise will determine the process and much of the content of therapy. Whether the therapist adheres strictly to one modality or blends a number of them, a couple is, in a sense, educated for therapy in the mode preferred by the therapist.

In our example, for instance, a psychodynamic couples therapist might assume this wife has unresolved abandonment issues—that she suffers from separation anxiety related to developmental failures during the separation-individuation phase of infancy. She might recommend that the wife begin individual treatment, where the transference relationship with the therapist could serve to highlight and resolve these unconscious issues and underlying psychological problems. She might, if she blends analytic and systems thinking, prefer to see this couple in conjoint sessions where she would address what she views as the regulatory function of the wife's symptoms around issues of autonomy and independence for both partners.

An emotionally focused couples therapist, relying on attachment theory, begins by assessing the partners' affective states and their influence on the couple's ability to bond satisfactorily. With this couple she might focus treatment on identifying, exploring, and modifying both the husband's and wife's interactional styles regarding the wife's emotional insecurities. She might begin by listening to and validating the wife's fears and insecurities, and proceed to help the husband recognize his own bonding and attachment needs. She would then go on to help the partners develop their capacities for emotional engagement as a foundation for a more secure and durable bonding.

If this couple arrived at the door of a behavioral therapist, treatment would look quite different. The therapist might see the wife alone, but rather than exploring the wife's childhood experiences in search of root causes for her current anxieties, he might rely on behavioral techniques such as systematic desensitization to bring about changes in how she responds to events and fears in her current life. Or he might meet with the couple in conjoint sessions and assign both husband and wife behavioral tasks designed to reinforce greater relaxation and confidence in the wife. In order to strengthen the marital bond and increase the couple's capacity for intimacy, he might also teach the partners communication skills, focusing on how to talk about feelings and how to manage conflict.

A cognitive therapist treating this couple would assume the wife's anxiety derives from faulty thinking, most likely a set of unreasonable assumptions about people, relationships, and life in general. These problematic ideas would be the targets of her interventions. As she identified the specific cognitive errors influencing the wife's fears, she would set about challenging them, helping the wife replace them with more reasonable, functional ideas.

A therapist trained in the brief-therapy approach of the Mental Research Institute in Palo Alto would assume that what the partners were doing to address their problem was in fact maintaining it. Her goal would be to find ways to get the partners to do something different in their effort to solve the problem of the wife's anxieties. Once the MRI strategic brief therapist identified the specific problem-maintaining actions the couple has been using to solve their problems, she would offer homework assignments designed to disrupt these failing problem-solving efforts.

Outcome research on the effectiveness of therapy has failed to establish that any one theory, technique, or school is significantly more effective than any other (Miller, Duncan, & Hubble, 1997), and this includes couples therapy (Bray & Jouriles, 1995; Gottman, 1999). These findings suggest that the couples therapist might do better to be eclectic, blending ideas and practices from different schools, rather than working within the confines of a particular theoretical model. All too often, however, an eclectic approach to couples therapy is a patchwork and catch-as-catch-can process, with no consistent, overarching orientation. For instance, failing to appreciate the theoretical incompatibilities of systems theory and psychodynamic theory, many practitioners assess couples without being clear whether they are viewing a dyadic system driven by cybernetic forces, two individuals driven by unconscious psychic forces, or some combination of both. In our view, an eclectic approach that blends a number of appealing theories and techniques that are randomly applied with all couples is not as effective as an approach that guides the therapist in custom-tailoring the therapy for each couple. An eclectic approach will be more effective if it is based on certain consistent guiding assumptions about how therapy works best and how people naturally change and solve problems in living.

Most traditional approaches to therapy, whether purist or eclectic, have certain common elements. First, they are therapist-theory-driven, meaning the therapist brings to the therapeutic enterprise a theory about the cause of relationship problems and this theory then dictates what must be done to alleviate them. Second, they are hierarchical, casting the therapist in the role of expert designer of the therapy, while the couple receives the ministration. The therapeutic milieu is one in which the couple is examined, as in a medical model, for dysfunction, deficit, or developmental problems, and then moved toward health (cured) by means of professional intervention and consequent growth/change of the partners in the couple. Third, the goals of treatment are established by the practitioner, reflecting what the therapist believes is wrong with the way the partners think, feel, and interact and how they should change. The unique capacities, resources, and capabilities possessed by the individual partners and the couple as a team are not specifically targeted in this process. Finally, in all these traditional models of marital or couples therapy, the temporal focus is either on the past, where the couple's problems are thought to have originated, or on the present, where the therapist hopes to identify forces maintaining the troubles.

We have found that effective couples therapy needs to rest on a different set of assumptions about the nature of the therapeutic process and the relationship between couples and their therapists. Our views are based on our clinical experience, our familiarity with research in the field of couples therapy, and our encounters with other theoreticians and clinicians who are moving outside the bounds of traditional therapeutic paradigms.

In his review of 40 years of outcome research literature, Michael Lambert (1992) identified four principal factors that clients report played a significant role in the success of their therapy (see also Miller et al., 1997). The most significant factors, according to Lambert, are what he calls extra-therapeutic variables. He found that approximately 40% of what clients report contributed to therapy success relates to factors having nothing to do with the therapeutic process or the therapist. Included in this category are the personal and social resources of the client, as well as fortuitous events and experiences unrelated to therapy that occurred in the client's life while he or she was in therapy.

The second most significant factor (30%) is the client's perception and experience of the therapeutic relationship. Since the time of Carl Rogers our profession has rightly assumed that therapy success depends on a strong therapeutic alliance—a rapport or fit that maintains what Rogers called the "core conditions" for effective therapy (Rogers, 1951). Most therapists know that the therapeutic alliance depends on the client's perception of the therapist as genuinely caring, empathically understanding, and respectful of the client. Therapists in general know how to use active listening techniques in order to convey empathic understanding and build and maintain rapport. Unfortunately many clinicians working with couples rely almost exclusively on active listening techniques, spending most of their time reflecting back to the partners their understanding of the emotional aspects of the experiences under discussion. Active listening techniques are all too often the fallback activity when a therapist doesn't know what else to do.

Lambert's third common factor, which he says accounts for 15% of what contributes to therapy success, is the placebo effect—the client's hope and belief that a trained professional can help, that therapy will work. In a sense, this factor is related to the quality and strength of the therapeutic alliance. While clients come to therapy with varying degrees of confidence in the therapeutic process, their confidence in the therapist and what he offers will increase or decrease very quickly. Part of building a strong working alliance is promoting realistic hope that things can be made better, that therapy will make a difference. One of the most significant research findings in this regard is that the client's active participation early in therapy is the best predictor of a successful therapeutic outcome (Miller et al., 1997). Naturally, when people believe what they're doing can make a difference (personal efficacy), when they're hopeful about the future (optimism), and believe the therapist can help (confidence), they are likely to participate more actively in the therapy process.

The fourth factor is the particular technique or set of techniques used by the therapist. Clients give this factor about 15% of the credit—equal to that of the placebo effect. We do not take this to mean techniques are minor in their effects, or that becoming skilled in the use of a wide variety of therapeutic tools does not make one a more effective clinician. This finding simply tells us that, in most cases, techniques are more important to the therapist than to the client and clients reflecting on their experiences in therapy rarely cite specific techniques as pivotal. In fact, many clients may not even notice them. We have interpreted these findings in the following way: Specific techniques make a difference to the degree they foster and utilize the other three factors—extratherapeutic variables (especially the strengths and resources clients already possess), a strong therapeutic alliance, and the client's feelings of hope and confidence. In addition, we think the more transparent the therapist's use of specific techniques and tools, the better.

A number of innovative approaches to therapy, whose developers variously refer to their work under the rubric of terms like *constructionist, postobjective, poststructural,* and sometimes *postmodernist,*[1] have emerged in different places around the world. Clinicians and theoreticians in northern and southern Europe, Canada, the South Pacific, and in various parts of the U.S. have been developing a set of notions about the roles of therapist and client, the nature of the therapeutic undertaking, and the elements important to a helping milieu different than those of traditional therapies, and more compatible, in our view, with the factors research suggests can promote change in therapy.

Compared to the more traditional modes of approach we sampled in our example at the beginning of the chapter, these constructionist therapies tend to be collaborative, rest on a narrative view of human experience, eschew cause and effect theories, put a central focus on the future as the locus of therapeutic work, and emphasize, in the therapeutic enterprise, the positive capacities and resources of the client(s) in building solutions. They encourage a reexamination of therapeutic practice in terms of the role and nature of expertise, the place of concepts such as normalcy, the effects of hierarchical practice versus a more egalitarian relationship between practitioner and client, and the role of perception and meaning in the construction of relational reality (Gergen & McNamee, 1992).

We locate the practice of RPT within the arena of this kind of thinking. More specifically, in the course of developing our way of working we have drawn primarily from three approaches: solution-focused brief therapy (Berg, 1994; De Jong & Berg, 1998; de Shazer, 1985, 1988, 1991, 1994), narrative therapy (Epston, 1993; White & Epston, 1990), and collaborative language therapy (Anderson 1997).[2] The assumptions on which we base RPT arise from the formulations about human social behavior and therapy shared by these approaches. We will refer to these three models throughout our discussion of these assumptions and the various RPT techniques we use in our work with couples.

By using the constructionist *good story/bad story* framework as an overarching guide in the conduct of couples therapy, we seek to bring about three interrelated outcomes: (1) the promotion of collaborative solution-building, (2) the identification and highlighting of the partners' resources and assets, and (3) the reinvigoration of the couple's shared *good story* narratives. We'll be discussing in detail how to accomplish these outcomes throughout this book, but before any technical questions can be addressed, we feel it is essential to lay out the foundation on which we base our practice. These working assumptions organize our thinking and orient us in conversations with clients.[3] Without an understanding of these assumptions, any application of particular techniques will become muddied, confusing, and/or ineffective. It is hard to help, deliver services, or make choices about hosting conversation unless you are clear about what you are doing (as well as what you're *not* doing), why you think you should be doing it, and how to do it.

## 1. Couples therapy should be future-oriented, not past-oriented.

In RPT, we invite people into conversations about future possibilities about what will be different when they can say therapy has been successful (Berg & Miller, 1992; De Jong & Berg, 1998; de Shazer, 1985, 1988, 1991, 1994; Friedman & Lipchick,1999; Furman & Ahola; 1992; Hoyt, in press). Some focus on the past occurs because people want to tell their stories and voice their concerns to an interested, helpful professional, but we do not actively investigate the past in search of possible causes of the couple's troubles. We prefer to explore and develop in detail what will be different when each partner can say "things are better," when both feel they're working together successfully in solving their current problems, and when it appears to us that their *good story* narrative is in force.

We therefore invite couples into future-focused conversations about how things will be different when they are more the way they want them to be. Couples therapy will be more effective and efficient when conversational time is spent clarifying where people want to go and what will tell everyone they are moving in the desired direction than if it is spent exploring the nature, extent, and effect of their current and past complaints and dissatisfactions (their *bad story* narratives). When a couple is able to imagine (and flesh out in some detail) realistic, satisfying future experiences together, they are already taking important steps toward moving beyond the confines of their current problems. Hope and possibilities expand as people envision futures that reflect their *good story* narratives, and these future pictures are implicit with solution—they suggest paths toward their realization.

RPT's future focus is in contrast to the traditional emphasis in psychology on the power of the past as an irrevocable shaper of the present. We assume that the future is as powerful a force as the past in shaping the present, sometimes more so.[4] It is clear that what people want, hope, fear, and expect to happen strongly influence their present actions. Consider the college student who, expecting a future in which she will become a doctor, studies medicine in the present. Or the wife whose expectation that her husband will fail to meet her needs for intimate conversation leads her to say little or nothing to him in the evening when he comes home. The imagined future is as powerful a formative influence on the present as the remembered past; thus, developing and amplifying satisfying future pictures can help start a distressed couple on the road to desired change.

Finally, the future, or people's conception of it—their hopes, intentions, and imagined pathways forward—can affect their perspective on the past, too. Because people have multiple versions of their histories, when a couple is able to find a *good story* future, they can begin noticing features of this narrative of their relationship in the present and remember it (bring it back into prominence) when they look back at the past. A future focus can therefore help people to mine the past as well as the present for what is effective in building a more satisfying relationship.

## 2. Couples therapy should be strength-based, not deficiency-based.

We assume that regardless of the nature, extent, or duration of their problems, people coming to us for help have the necessary resources to make changes that will make a difference in their lives. In other words, we maintain a competency-based stance (Thomas & Cockburn, 1998). We see our clients not simply as people with problems but as people who are temporarily unable to utilize competencies they already possess (or can readily develop) to resolve their present difficulties. This assumption, like all our assumptions, is a working assumption—it's where we start. If it turns out that a particular couple lacks the resources or assets needed to make the changes they wish, therapy may become a mutual project of helping them develop the skills and locate the resources they need. Ours is a facilitating role, designed to help couples identify, clarify, tap, or develop their own particular resources so they can work together as a team to deal with what's troubling them in custom-made ways. This means that from the first encounter to the final good-bye, from our initial conversations about what brings the couple to therapy to our final conversations about how the couple can keep things moving in a desired direction, we listen for indications about strengths, abilities, capacities, talents, and knowledge (De Jong & Miller, 1995).

This does not mean we ignore or trivialize the effects of people's problems on their lives or dismiss the impact of stressful and traumatic life events or conditions such as poverty, chronic illness, or loss. Our emphasis on strengths does not mean we confine therapeutic conversation to the positive or ignore the impact of harmful or problematic behaviors on people's lives. In fact, our competency orientation helps us to be more effective in dealing compassionately and effectively with challenging or intractable life situations and problems, such as domestic violence, substance abuse, infidelity, and destructive parenting practices. In all our cases, we approach issues and problems assuming that people want to find their way out of painful and destructive patterns, that they have assets and resources to accomplish that goal, and that when they find the means that fit their situation, they will change in desirable ways.

Working from a strengths perspective is more than simply using a certain set of strategies or having a positive attitude. It requires a reorientation in perspective about people, the therapeutic process, relationship problems, and how change happens. Proposing a strengths perspective in social work practice, Dennis Saleebey (1997) says:

> Rather than focusing on problems, your eye turns toward possibilities. In the thicket of trauma, pain, and trouble you can see blooms of hope and transformation. The formula is simple: Mobilize clients' strengths (talents, knowledge, capacities, resources) in the service of achieving their goals and visions and the clients will have a better quality of life on their terms. (pp. 3–4)

It is in success that the key to change lies; we're trying to *catch people being successful*. When viewed as competent, people are better able to mobilize their energy, will, desire, and creativity for making the changes they want. The focus of the clinical lens on dysfunction and deficit can be demeaning to the client, foster a sense of disempowerment, and, as a perceptual framework, prevent the therapist from being alert to the client's creative capacities—the wide range of functionalities and assets people of all types bring to challenging situations and times in their lives. Change occurs most readily when people feel competent and hopeful—in control of the means of making things different. We have found it much more consistently helpful to focus on the unique ways couples who come to see us are resourceful, capable people who want help in bringing their talents and skills to bear in addressing their relationship problems.

### 3. The couples therapist should assume couples are temporarily stuck rather than dysfunctional.

Related to our belief that the power to change, solve problems, and rebuild partnership resides within the resources of a given relationship is our assumption that couples coming for therapy are simply currently stuck, rather than dysfunctional or pathological (Durrant, 1993; Friedman, 1996; Shoham, Rohrbaugh, & Patterson, 1995). Certain problems and conflicts have taken on a central role in the life of the couple and, as a result, the partners are caught in a complex web of behavior, perception, and meaning-making (the *bad stories*) that is impeding their ability to work together effectively to tackle their problems and conflicts. The point of therapy is not to solve all a couple's problems, and it certainly is not to find and name problems the couple has not presented. Our role is to help them get unstuck by assisting them in working collaboratively to achieve common goals. Once people tell us they see themselves on the road toward these goals, they're ready to begin exploring how to keep things moving in that direction without further assistance from us. If they find themselves running into problems in the future, they are, of course, free to come back for as few or as many sessions as they might need to get themselves unstuck once more. In other words, we assume therapy can be brief and/or intermittent (Johnson, 1995).

Couples who have recreated partnership and reinvigorated their *good story* narratives may no longer need our help in meeting future challenges they'll encounter. We do not assume meaningful and lasting change (whatever that means to the particular couple before us) has to take a particular course, requires a certain duration of treatment, or entails consideration of a particular list of issues. Nor do we assume the process of change necessarily has to be painful, a struggle, or a "two steps forward and one step back" experience. Simply stated: People get stuck; we help them get unstuck one way or another, and they move on.

Consider, by way of comparison, the following advice author and couples therapist Phil Deluca (1996) gives to people trying to change a relationship:

- This is the challenge you must face when you decide to resolve your relationship problems: there is no pain-free solution.

- Change, by its very nature, causes everyone involved to be hurt and angry. Those who want their troubled relationship to improve, but also expect to avoid further hurt will go to their graves waiting for something that will never happen.
- Because of its nature, and the turmoil it causes to all parties involved, changing one's behavior is an individual, painful, and therefore lonely undertaking. You will need to remember that initially your partner is more likely to attempt to undo your efforts than to join you. (pp. 6–7)

These are strong, brook-no-disagreement opinions about the nature of change—and they are commonly held by helping professionals. But on what basis are these opinions held? We can all name experiences of change in our personal and professional lives that challenge these supposed truths. While change may be painful and/or arduous (in or out of therapy), it just as well may not be. Viewing change as inevitably painful makes it more likely to be so. In our experience, it often seems that when people change and feel responsible for those changes, both they and others are pleased and receptive. We frequently get excited and enthusiastic reports from couples about their joy and satisfaction when they see themselves making positive changes in their relationship.

The idea of people being stuck rather than dysfunctional is one of the central tenets of brief therapy and it is related to the notion that once people begin moving toward solution they can leave therapy and be independently successful (Cade & O'Hanlon, 1993; Durrant, 1993). We do not define ourselves as either brief *or* long-term therapists (Ziegler, 1998). Because we are collaborative, it is our clients (not our model, theories, or preferences) who determine the duration and extent of our work together. We are sensitive to the time and money therapy consumes, and we believe therapy should be carried out as efficiently as possible. At the same time, we take care not to rush clients out of therapy before they feel ready; this means duration is co-constructed with our clients and varies from instance to instance.

Since we assume it is sufficient for therapy to help couples get unstuck rather than to resolve underlying or long-standing relationship dysfunction, character defects, or pathology, we work toward a trend (a movement toward more positive and satisfying experiences), not an outcome. This means that therapy, regardless of its duration (brief, mid-range, or long) ends when people feel they are moving forward and ready to go it on their own.

**4. Talking about solutions leads to their discovery; talking about problems often only perpetuates them.**

Problem-solving conversation makes sense when you are talking about the physical world. What's wrong with the toilet has bearing on what you do to fix it. However, in the area of human relations, where problems are subjectively defined and socially constructed in language and between people, talking about problems in certain ways can have the effect of thickening their influence as shapers of the parameters of action and thought. Traditional models of therapy are based on a problem-solving paradigm (De Jong & Berg, 1998). This paradigm, which is basically the medical model of approaching disease, requires that the therapist clarify the nature of the problem (assessment), determine its causes (diagnosis), and design steps (interventions) that will alleviate or remove the causes (cure). It is assumed that presenting symptoms are signs of underlying pathology or deeper problems, which are the target of intervention.

Solution-building (De Jong & Berg, 1998; de Shazer, 1985, 1988, 1991, 1994), on the other hand, is a radically different paradigm. In this way of thinking, focusing on couples' strengths and coauthoring the partners' future goals are viewed as more important than trying to identify causes of problems and discussing the possible etiology of dysfunction. To construct solutions, we talk with clients about satisfying pictures of relationship and exceptions to their problems rather than examples of their problems. We want to thicken and enhance their *good story* narratives. The construction of viable solutions need not involve a discussion or understanding of the client's problems and difficulties (de Shazer, 1988, 1991, 1994).

However, as we noted earlier, this does not mean that in RPT, we never talk with people about their problems. Even though we do not initiate problem-focused conversation, we believe talking with our clients about their problem experiences, hearing their concerns with respect and sensitivity, and engaging with them about their *bad story* narratives can be helpful. But we do not do this to establish a root cause or source and then take clinical measures on that basis. We participate in these sorts of conversations for three reasons: (1) to establish and maintain rapport, (2) to explore our clients' theories of change, and (3) to identify possible exits from the *bad story* to the *good story* narrative.

People have strong and viable needs to talk about what's bothering them and about the pain or struggle in their lives and to feel validated regarding their theories about how their present difficulties have come about. In couples therapy, there is a "warming-up" period where each partner wants to make sure that their difficult, often long-standing circumstances matter to the therapist and are clearly understood. Some room, therefore, can and should be given to people's concerns. However, it is especially important in couples therapy, where partners often say things that trigger hostile and combative reactions in the other, to find ways of engaging in such conversations that are not regressive. The main point is to host conversations that help people move toward solution talk. A process focused on solution-building invites the partners to begin working together as early as possible to construct a mutually meaningful future, find shared goals, and rediscover and solidify their *good story* narrative.

## 5. The most effective point of entry into the phenomenological world of the couple is through the doors of perception.

It can be useful to think of experience as a wheel with several interconnected elements: (1) cognitions (memories, meaning constructions, expectations, attitudes, beliefs, values, assumptions, etc.); (2) perceptions (what is noticed and viewed as significant and what is overlooked); (3) emotions (subjective feeling states); and (4) behaviors (actions—voluntary, involuntary, and habitual). These are not discrete elements; they perpetually influence each other and are always interwoven. How we react behaviorally to someone smiling at us depends on our perceptions, cognitions, and emotions—whether we noticed the gesture and what meaning we made of it (a construct influenced by our memories, expectations, and assumptions regarding smiling people in general and this person in particular) and what emotional responses this perception occasioned in us. A kiss is never just a kiss, and a smile isn't just a smile.

In our work, perception—how people see things—is the primary entry point into our clients' phenomenological world. We believe that we are best able to build rapport and generate possibilities for positive change by engaging our clients in conversations about what they notice and have failed to notice about events, other people, themselves, and their relationships with others and the world around them. When people explore their perceptions with us, we gain direct entry into the world of their subjective experience. This world encompasses thought, values, feelings, meaning constructions, attitudes, and perceptions of past behaviors, both of the client and others in the client's life. Therefore, in developing a context for change, we ask people about their particular perceptions related to their problems, what they observed when attempting to solve those problems, what will look different to them when the problems are solved, and what they will notice is different about their partners when things seem better in the relationship.

In RPT, we focus our inquiries from the beginning less on what partners do than on how each partner perceives and interprets the other's actions. We are especially interested in the power of these interpretations to generate and inform action and reaction. As we learn in these exploratory dialogues about the frames of reference, theories of change,[5] and guiding stories that influence people's experiences, we can see potential exits from the *bad story* narrative. When we ask people what they will notice is different about their lives when their problems have been solved, we have a starting point for building solutions. These kinds of inquiries, which focus on perception and meaning-making, encourage both therapist and couple to pay attention to the perspectives and attitudes surrounding positive aspects of relationship experiences, and, in doing so, they influence how our clients' attention is directed in the future. This helps us participate with a couple in rebuilding, revising, and refreshing the *good story* narrative, both past and future.

## 6. Couples therapy should be a collaborative, consultive process.

As important as our solution orientation (reflected in the first five assumptions) is the collaborative, consultive stance we take with our clients. Most couples come for help in solving problems and addressing issues that are only vaguely defined. Part of our job is to help them frame and define their concerns and desires in therapeutically useful ways by clarifying with them what specific changes will make a difference. We assume the partners know what changes will make a difference (although they may not know they know), and it is our job to help them tap that knowledge. Clients possess important, unique, and expert knowledge on their lives and how they want them to change. In this regard we share the nonexpert stance of other constructionist therapies, assuming that clients are the best judges with respect to outcome and goals.

In RPT we believe not only that the clients are experts with respect to their own lives, hopes, and desires, but also that they have important ideas about how therapy can be most useful to them (Duncan et al., 1997; Duncan, Solovey, & Rusk, 1992; Johnson, 1995; O'Hanlon, 1998). Until we explore those ideas about what needs to happen in therapy and what we can do to help, they may be only vaguely recognized by the clients. We also tap this knowledge. From the initial encounter to the final good-bye, we continually call on the couple to serve as our consulting team. We ask their opinion about what we can do together that would further the ends of therapy, and we regularly check out whether the directions we are pursuing are helpful and whether what we are doing together serves their needs. For example, we often ask clients questions like "Was this conversation helpful?" or "What else do you think I should know about your situation?" or "Are we on the right page here?" Knowing when and how to conduct such inquiries and how to use the information we glean from them as we move through the therapeutic enterprise are extremely important skills. Duncan, Hubble, and Miller (1997) say this about the importance of a collaborative mode in therapy:

> research suggests that successful outcome occurs by creating a space for clients to use their resources, ensuring clients' positive experience of the alliance, and accommodating therapy to clients' views of what is relevant. *Each client, therefore, presents the therapist with a new theory to learn and a different course to pursue.* (p. 34, their emphasis).

We carry these research findings into practice by using our clients as our consulting team. In order to do this, we must enter into each partner's experiential world to see things from his or her perspective, and this means setting aside, at least temporarily, our own. This does not require, however, abandoning our own knowledge, experience, or common sense—or acting as though we have no ideas, experience, and opinions of our own. After all, many clients come to therapy wanting input and suggestions from someone who has spent his or her professional life helping people solve their problems. So while we assume we and our clients each have important contributions to make to the therapy enterprise, we make decisions in concert with our clients, on a case-by-case basis, about how much to share of our personal experiences, values, and ideas and whether or not to offer suggestions or advice.

It isn't easy to abandon the expert role—it's a rather sticky slot. Setting aside our various elegant and intricate models of normalcy/abnormalcy can be quite difficult. It's hard not to think, given our years of clinical training and experience, that, at least with respect to the process of therapy, we know best. We have found, in practicing RPT, that the most effective way to keep the couple in the driver's seat is by adopting, as best we can, a stance and attitude of curiosity and not-knowing. Anderson and Goolishian (1992), who are credited with having coined the term *not-knowing,* describe the position as one that entails:

> a general attitude or stance in which the therapist's actions communicate an abundant, genuine curiosity. That is, the therapist's actions and attitudes express a need to know more about what has been said, rather than convey preconceived opinions and expectations about the client, the problem, or what must be changed. The therapist, therefore, positions himself or herself in such a way as always to be in a state of "being informed" by the client. . . . Such a position allows the therapist always to maintain continuity with the client's position and to grant primary importance to the client's world views, meanings, and understandings. (p. 29)

In collaborating to set a course for the couple's therapy, the therapist, curious, interested, and open to discovery, follows her clients into their territory. The map of this unique territory is drawn collectively. Among other things, this collaborative stance on the part of the therapist tends to help establish a more welcoming, excited, supportive, and energetic tone in the couples session. After the first session, people are often eager to come back, leaving sessions buoyed by a positive experience and feeling better about themselves and each other. Laughter, an enthusiastic reception of people's ideas and stories, and a feeling of hopefulness, energetic discovery, and excitement about the couple's shared capacities are more characteristic of this way of collaborative working than a sense of crisis, difficulty, and toil.

Taken together, these six assumptions provide the framework for our practice, creating the matrix from which our techniques (organically, we hope) arise. They reflect certain fundamental points of view about human experience, about how people make meaning of events and turn them into subjective experiences, and about how we all encounter change. They comprise a way of looking at relationships that applies both to the intimate dyad of a couple and to the relationship of therapist and couple. These interlocking assumptions serve as a set of orienting ideas that help us, moment by moment and in the overall course of therapy, decide what to do, say, and ask that will foster a reinvigoration of the couple's *good story* narrative and help them recreate a sense of partnership, common purpose, and personal empowerment. When these working assumptions guide us in our daily encounters with clients, we can do a wide variety of technical things and be successful in helping. And we can better understand why, in a given instance, a particular technique or way of conversing has been helpful. The complex and subtle flow of the therapeutic enterprise becomes easier to "see." In this way, our working assumptions clarify what the sometimes rather amorphous-seeming practice of therapy can and cannot do in the way of helping.

To illustrate how the assumptions we discussed above work in practice and generate these kinds of exciting therapeutic encounters, we want to close this chapter with a partial transcript of an initial interview with a couple we'll call Judy and Jerry.

THERAPIST: Welcome, folks. How can I help? (*Client as knowledgeable; collaboration in the therapeutic process.*)

JERRY: Things have gotten pretty bad. We want to save our marriage if possible, but it seems like it's just been getting worse and worse lately. Judy's threatening to leave. And sometimes I feel, fine, let her go. The fact is, I think we still love each other and don't want to break up. But I can't stand all the fighting. And she can't either, I know that. But we just can't seem to talk about stuff without getting into big fights. Too big.

THERAPIST: Judy, is that the way you see things too?

JUDY: Pretty much, yeah. I'm just about at the end of my rope, actually. I really don't want to leave Jerry, but he's got to learn how to control his temper. I'm hoping you can help somehow.

THERAPIST: Okay. So it sounds like there's been a lot of fighting, and both of you sometimes feel you're kind of at the end of the line, and Judy you're concerned about Jerry's temper. But you do love each other and want to make a go of it if you can. (*Acknowledging and validating clients' experience, which includes pieces of both the* bad *and* good *stories.*) So I wonder how you think I might be able to help you two work together to turn things around? (*Client as knowledgeable; invitation to solution talk; emphasis on building a team.*)

JUDY: Well, gee, I don't know. But we've just got to do something about this fighting, this constant horrible atmosphere.

THERAPIST: Okay. Maybe a good place to start is this: Could each of you tell me how things will be different when both of you could come in here and say, "Wow, we've done it. We've solved our problems, and our marriage is getting better. We like the way things are going, and we feel like we don't need to come here anymore"? What will be different, what will be happening between you, when you can tell me that? (*Focus on the future, on solution, developing the client's theory of change, and on the* good *story; stance of curiosity.*)

Both partners are silent for a while. Finally Judy speaks.

JUDY: Well, like we said, it's the fighting all the time. About money, and Jerry's drinking, mostly. So first of all, if things were better, Jerry wouldn't be drinking anymore. And if we had a fight about something, we'd just be able to talk about it like regular people—you know, calmly—without all the screaming and door slamming. (*Client begins to construct her future goal picture, which includes elements of her* good *story narrative.*)

JERRY: Well, it would really help if you could just get Judy to stop nagging me all the time. That'd be well worth the entrance fee, as far as I'm concerned. And maybe explain to her that she's got to be more careful about spending money on stuff we don't really need. That'd help. (*Clients often invite us into conversations about their* bad *stories even as we invite them into* good *story conversations. Both partners have mentioned changes they'd like to see in the other person; an asset orientation on the part of the therapist usually means these invitations to solution by the client are declined in favor of teasing out the resources implied in* good *story pictures.*)

THERAPIST: Okay. I'm starting to get a sense about what each of you does that doesn't feel so good to the other person. But can we go back to what Judy was starting to say? I want to hear more about how things will be when your problems are solved, about what will be different, what will be happening between you that tells each of you that things are getting better. (*Future focus; declining client's invitation into problem-focused conversation.*)

JUDY: Well, as I said we won't be fighting so much. And Jerry wouldn't be drinking.

THERAPIST: Well, I see. That's what wouldn't be happening, I guess. But, let's see, if I had a video camera and was filming what was different, what would be happening instead, I wonder? What would I be getting on film, in other words? When I looked through the camera lens, what would I see and hear that *is* happening? (*Future focus; collaborative co-*

*construction of therapeutically well-defined client goals. This latter process will be discussed in detail in chapter 5.)*

JUDY: Huh. I need to think about that. . . . Give me a minute here. . . . Oh, yes. Jerry's home, and we're doing stuff together in Nicki's room. *(Smiles, as she begins envisioning this desired future picture involving their daughter.)* I can see it, we're all playing and laughing together. You know, having fun as a family, fooling around, being close. *(Thinks a bit longer.)* And when a fight starts, things don't go from bad to worse. (*Collaboration is happening. Client accepts the therapist's invitation to explore and amplify her goal pictures. Notice that these pictures are no longer simply an absence of the problem experience. The good story appears in bits and pieces. Note that therapist is working with the client's perceptions of a desirable future.)*

THERAPIST: Okay, I see. So when things are better, you're all together having fun as a family. And when fights start, they go differently. Tell me more about this, about how things go differently when the disagreement starts. Not so much about what isn't happening, but about what *is* happening that tells you that the two of you have really changed things. *(Future focus. The wife has presented two emerging desired future pictures—playing as a family in Nicki's bedroom, and successfully handling a conflict. Either might be focused on, but the therapist chooses the latter because they've been talking about fighting as an issue. This is further invitation to talk about partnership and develop the good story narrative.)*

JUDY: *(Eyes looking into the distance, as if watching an imagined scene.)* We're, you know, . . . uh . . . sort of looking at each other. Actually looking. We look somewhat upset, but not like we hate each other. (*Judy looks tentatively at Jerry now and finds he's watching her attentively. He smiles at her. Even though he hasn't been talking in this part of the interview, he has been listening closely. Now they're smiling at each other. He moves his hand closer to hers on the couch.)*

THERAPIST: More like what? How are you looking instead? (*Strengths focus. Desired future post-problem experiences are now being talked about and "made real" in talk. They are entering a good story narrative and beginning to feel the stirrings of partnership.)*

JUDY: Oh my gosh. I can really see it. *(Laughs, glancing warmly at Jerry.)* Sort of like we are right now, here. We look like we still care about each other, and we're sure about that, even though we don't agree. We're mad, but we both know we still love each other and don't want to hurt each other. Wow, that's amazing. *(She starts to tear up as she talks about this imagined scene, which clearly means a lot to her. Jerry has moved closer on the couch, and now, cautiously, takes hold of her hand.)*

JERRY: You know, this is how we used to be, remember? Most of the time. Maybe there's some hope for us after all. *(Smiles at Judy. Jerry has entered the world of the* good story *as well, and both husband and wife are sharing a positive perception of their relationship life, extending from a satisfying past into a desired future.)*

THERAPIST: (*Turning to Jerry.*) Jerry, I wonder if you could think back a little and tell me about a time when something like what Judy's talking about happened recently? When the two of you disagreed about something, but you treated each other like friends, more the way she just described. (*Search for assumed client success, competencies, and strengths; inviting greater sense of partnership; "thickening" the* good story.)

JERRY: Well, I can't think of anything like that, really. (*Therapist waits without commenting. Because therapist doesn't speak, Jerry takes more time to think.*) Oh. Hmm. That's funny. Now that you mention it, we did start to get into a fight just this morning, actually. You know, just before coming to see you. I don't know why I didn't think of that right away. (*This experience in which clients suddenly remember successes and exceptions shows how solutions are co-constructed in conversation, that memory is fluid and creative, and that, when the* good story *context is in some measure available, competencies can be found.*) We started arguing about how much it was going to cost us to be in therapy. I said we couldn't afford it, and Judy said if we didn't get help she was going to leave. That hurt. And things could've really gotten bad right then . . . but then somehow we didn't end up in a shouting match as usual. Huh!

THERAPIST: So, now that you're remembering this, tell me what you can recall that got the two of you out of that fight. (*Further invitation to co-construct a* good story *of success and find potential client competencies.*) Suppose I'd been a fly on the wall this morning—what would I have seen each of you doing that might have contributed to the way you accomplished that? (*Exploring the clients' potential resources and strengths from the point of view that this couple is simply stuck rather than dysfunctional.*)

JERRY: Well, I started talking about how therapy could go on for a long time. How we couldn't afford to keep coming week after week, like some friends of ours do. They've been in couples therapy for, I don't know, 2 or 3 years, and they don't seem to be getting any better. They still fight all the time and complain about each other constantly. Judy got really upset all at once and said that thing about leaving. Both of us got pretty hot under the collar, and it seemed like we were going to end up in the same old fight. . . . Then things kind of cooled off. I don't really know how—I guess, even though we were both really angry, we sort of backed off, both of us. Maybe we were on good behavior because we knew we were coming here. To tell you the truth, I don't really know how it happened, actually. (*Notice the husband is talking about a* good story *experience but has not yet identified any elements of individual or shared agency.*)

THERAPIST: That's pretty amazing. Here the two of you were set up for a big explosion, but it didn't happen. That sounds important. You were primed for a fight, and instead you did what you want to be able to do—turn away from potential blowups—and I'm really intrigued. (*Jerry and Judy nod enthusiastically. By complimenting the couple, the therapist highlights the clients' competencies, points to and shows curiosity about a potential set of assets.*) It sounds like it would be useful for us to make sure we understand how you did it, how the two of you were able to talk about a hot topic, even start down the road to an explosion, but somehow make it go differently. Could each of you think a little more about that scene this morning so you can tell me what you did that led to that success? (*Inviting client discovery and construction of client agency and competency. This conversation orients the couple toward attending to experiences that fit within their* good story *narrative rather than those that reconfirm and solidify their* bad stories. *As their perceptions of their experience shift to the* good story *narrative, the meanings they make of their encounters and the other partner's actions will change, producing new behavioral responses. In the loop of perception, meaning-making, and behavior, we entered at the point of perception.*)

JERRY: Well, I looked at Judy and thought to myself, I don't want to get into a big fight just before coming to see you. That would definitely start us off on the wrong foot. So I guess I just decided I wasn't going to let anything she did or say set me off right then.

JUDY: Well, and I remember that when Jerry kept on talking about how much therapy was going to cost I decided maybe I'd just back up and listen. I wanted to argue with him and remind him how important coming here would be. In fact, I even began by telling him I'd leave if we didn't come. But then I realized it wouldn't help to talk like that—I saw he was hurt. So I just decided to be quiet and listen to him. I guess I just figured there was no point in going down the usual road.

JERRY: Yes, I remember that now. After that first lousy thing you said, and I said, "Well, that's sure a helpful thing to say!" and you didn't say anything, I just decided not to let it get me, and when I kept talking, you didn't keep at it. I was surprised. You began to just listen. So I started to feel you weren't spending your time just getting ready to argue with me. I expected an argument, I did, but instead you just listened. That's interesting. I never would have thought about that if we weren't talking about it now. Once I said my piece, and you just listened, I felt there wasn't anything more to say. And I didn't feel so upset anymore. I even thought to myself, I almost hate to admit it, that I knew you were probably worried about the expense too. (*They're looking at each other and smiling quite warmly now. At this point, in the context of some* good story *material, a couple's conversation has naturally evolved. We'll talk about the importance of these kinds of dialogues in chapter 9.*) I even felt kind of bad bringing up the issue just before we were going to come here, you know, to work on our problems, because I knew how important this is to you. And to me. (*Judy begins to look teary again at this point. The language of teamwork is entering both their statements, evidence that they are beginning to recreate partnership.*)

THERAPIST: Well, this is really interesting. It sounds as though each of you already has some ideas about what you can do to make a difference. Things you can do and say and ways you can react, when you have disagreements and problems in the future, so they won't get the best of you. Do you folks suppose that if you're able to do more of what you did this morning it will make a difference? that it will be a good start to turning your relationship around? (*They nod assent. They're sitting close and touching, both smiling broadly. The reinvigoration of the good story and future orientation have created some basis for hope and a beginning sense of partnership.*)

# CHAPTER 3

# Active Neutrality: Building a Working Alliance With Both Partners

All major schools of psychotherapy recognize the importance and power of the therapeutic relationship itself in providing help to clients. It is the firm ground on which the work of counseling takes place. Various terms have been used to describe its active elements or process, including *rapport, interpersonal fit, safe container,* and *therapeutic alliance.* Carl Rogers (1951) was the first to define the therapist attitudes and qualities on which a strong therapeutic relationship could be built. He called them *core conditions* and said they were both *necessary and sufficient* for successful therapy. Since Rogers, the importance of the following three conditions has been more or less universally accepted: unconditional positive regard (consistent demonstration of caring, honoring, and respect toward the client); accurate empathic understanding (communicated understanding of the client's subjective, phenomenological experiences); and therapeutic genuineness (authenticity on the part of the therapist).

However, while most practitioners would agree with Rogers that these conditions are *necessary* for building and maintaining an effective therapeutic alliance, many do not see them as *sufficient.* The history of psychotherapy entails an ongoing search for change-generating interventions to supplement this framework and meet the goals of clients more completely. We believe that the conditions listed above are necessary but not necessarily enough to bring about change effectively and efficiently.[1] This chapter and the one that follows make quite clear how essential we think building and maintaining a strong therapeutic alliance with clients is—this is indeed the core and basic condition for effective therapy. However, the various techniques and interviewing questions used in RPT serve a dual function—they both create a strong working alliance with both partners in a couple and at the same time serve as change-generating interventions.

As any practitioner knows, trying to establish a working alliance with two antagonistic partners in couples therapy can be quite a challenge. People usually bring a host of complaints about their partner to an initial session. They come in the door strongly wedded to their theories regarding the source and nature of their troubles, and these theories often call for the other partner to make changes, start the ball rolling by changing first, or admit responsibility for the troubled state of the relationship. These initial complaints, perceptions, and theories are part of the individual partners' *bad story* narratives. They are not easily dismissed or revised.

The way to establish a good working relationship with both partners (and establish a context for potential collaboration) is by maintaining a stance of *active neutrality* (Anderson, 1997). This concept is complex. It refers both to a therapist's ability to build an effective rapport and working alliance with both members of a (sometimes warring) dyad, as well as to the overall stance a therapist must maintain throughout the course of therapy. *Active neutrality* is initiated and sustained by all the practices of RPT; in this chapter we briefly touch on techniques and tools we discuss more fully in later chapters. We do not view this concept as separate from the other practices of our approach, but as woven into each one.

Throughout the life of the therapeutic enterprise with couples, we try to reduce the influence of the individual partners' *bad story* narratives while highlighting and reinvigorating the couple's individual and shared *good stories*. Establishing active neutrality is the first step in creating a climate in which partners in a relationship can transform and revise their problem narratives. We don't do this by analysis, scrutiny, or directives, however. From the beginning we hope to recreate capacity for partnership through narrative-loosening and narrative-changing conversations. This helps turn partners who have become adversaries into creative solution-building teams. This transformation requires that we immediately establish and maintain a strong therapeutic alliance with each partner.

How can the therapist successfully convey the sense of being on both partner's sides when they are at odds about what is going wrong in their marriage and who is principally to blame? How can we acknowledge and validate what each partner tells us in the presence of the other without running the risk that one or both will see us as taking sides? Family and couples therapy literature usually offers this general advice: The clinician must maintain a posture of neutrality in which the therapist appears objective and impartial.

We think it is unrealistic to assume that therapists can remain perfectly impartial and objective. And even if we could, we would be surprised if partners in couples therapy could always perceive us as impartial when we say things that seem sympathetic to their partners. This is where the posture of *active neutrality* comes in. This stance requires two things of the therapist. The first is a demonstrated, ongoing belief that the experience of reality is perspectival and involves multiple—and sometimes conflicting—perceptions, meanings, and orderings of events. The second is a continuing commitment to the posture of curious not-knowing.

Let's look at these elements one by one. First, in order to demonstrate an active neutrality, we continually communicate to our clients that we understand and recognize the validity of all points of view. Because we consistently convey our intention to see things through everyone's eyes, and because we take an interest in, honor, and confirm competing theories and narratives, we are in effect taking everyone's side. Rather than trying to appear on no one's side—an "impartial" or "objective" stance—we sympathize in whatever way we can with all experiences and validate everyone's perspective. We are not listening for right and wrong or some objective truth, nor do we look for symptoms, signs of problematic ways of thinking or being, or interpersonal dysfunction. We validate everyone's version of what's "really" happening. In this kind of listening, arguments about what happened or who is right no longer appear so compelling; no one has to change anyone's mind or be convinced to accept only one view of things. Clients' theories of how and why things happened are accepted as expert testimony and treated as making sense instead of as flawed. Our intention is not to position either partner as wrong by challenging anyone's point of view or experiences. This means that the judicial stance in which some clients try to cast a therapist is declined. We also do not try to reconcile conflicting points of view or encourage either partner to see the problems and conflicts from the other's point of view; instead we want to help clients discover and thicken a shared *good story*, without imposing our views upon them.

Harlene Anderson (1997) uses the term *multipartiality* for this therapeutic stance:

> A therapist wants each person in the conversation to feel that his or her version is as important as any other. It is a position of *multipartiality*, one in which a therapist takes all sides simultaneously. This is in contrast to neutrality, in which a therapist strives not to take any one person's side. In my experience, such neutrality usually leads the people we work with to wonder, to suspect, and sometimes feel assured of whose side we are on and which version we believe. When this happens people can easily plunge into competing efforts to lure a therapist to their side. (pp. 95–96, her italics)

A second and related aspect of active neutrality is the therapist's commitment to maintaining an attitude of curious not-knowing. We try to set aside our own personal and professional assumptions and values (which we assure readers we have in abundance) in order to follow the threads of each person's thoughts and experiences. We want to flesh out each partner's models, theories, and perspectives. To do this, we must first and foremost be curious to learn. This means we must resist the temptation to regard clients as objects of assessment or the focus of analysis and instead continually assume they are expert witnesses of their own lives, who can impart valuable knowledge to us, if we know how to ask the right questions.

As we noted earlier, working from a stance of curious not-knowing does not mean we regard ourselves as knowing nothing or that we abandon common sense or personal beliefs about what kinds of behavior foster success or failure in intimate relationships. It is instead a matter of putting our own frames of reference second (bracketing them) as best we can, so that we can enter the experiential world of each partner with an enthusiastic eagerness to learn and understand. This makes it possible to discover meanings, associations, and frames of reference we might otherwise miss. Both these elements—an acceptance of multiple perspectives and a stance of curious not-knowing—bypass the "problem" of client resistance because they establish a climate of acceptance, credence, and respect around both partners' feelings and reported experiences. In fact, when one or both partners appears to resist the therapist or the therapeutic process, we take it as a sign that we are doing or saying something that violates one of these two tenets.

Practically speaking, especially in initial interviews, active neutrality is best accomplished through partner-to-therapist dialogues rather than by encouraging dialogue between the partners. This gives each person an experience of having the therapist's full attention and lessens the opportunity for regressive argument between partners about what "really" happened. This often requires that the therapist use tactful means of holding the observing partner at bay and blocking efforts to interrupt or argue. For example, suppose a husband is describing what he experiences as his wife's domineering behavior. As he's describing his perceptions to the therapist, the wife jumps in, saying, "But for God's sake, George, I wouldn't act like that if you ever got off the stick—you procrastinate about everything." At this point the therapist might simply say, "Hold on, Alice, we'll get to you in a moment. I just want to make sure I fully understand George first. And then we'll come right back to you." It is important, of course, to make sure to return to Alice so she has the opportunity to share her perceptions and theories with an interested and respectful listener.

As we acknowledge and validate each partner's version of his or her experience, crediting meanings and detailing perceptions and how they came about, the fact that we are open and curious about everyone's stories and seem able to honor multiple perspectives makes it possible for clients to begin doing the same. In this way, active neutrality can help to establish a context that invites the couple to see their problems as arising, at least in part, from the fact that they are living in two different perceptual worlds. This realization prepares the way for later conversations in which the couple redefines their difficulties as a complex of harmful external forces or experiences that distress them both, damage their relationship, and hamper their efforts to have a satisfying future.[2] It also opens the possibility for the first glimmers of a shared perspective to emerge, beginning the process of recreating partnership. In maintaining active neutrality, the therapist invites the couple to shift from viewing her as an outsider and/or a judge and instead see her as an active co-collaborator who will serve as resource, consultant, facilitator, and coach to help them form a solution-building team.

It must be emphasized that working from a stance of active neutrality is not simply a matter of using clever interviewing techniques for building alliances. It requires an ongoing and authentic commitment to the idea that there is no one truth in the field of human relationships and that experience is strongly affected by our subjectivity (our histories, perceptions, meanings, opinions, desires for the future, etc.). Active neutrality means, first and foremost, that we come into our work with an abiding interest in our clients' ideas about growth, relationship, and change. But, while we don't challenge or confront our clients based on a collected body of knowledge about what is normal, appropriate, or functional in a relationship, in certain situations we do ask questions that may create doubt or provide opportunities for new ways of thinking about things, especially when it may be hard for us to understand how certain behaviors and points of view interact for an individual or when we feel an enlarged perspective might help to invigorate a *good story* climate. It is in conversations that "loosen" or enlarge people's perspectives about their concerns and problems that they are most likely to come up with creative and innovative ways of being and doing.

It is considerably easier to grasp the concept of active neutrality than it is to hold on to it in the consulting room. For instance, remaining open, curious, and validating to multiple viewpoints can be extremely difficult when one partner exhibits behavior or expresses ideas repugnant to the practitioner. How does one remain actively neutral in the face of abusive, violent, or repellant behaviors? We don't turn a blind eye to the things people say and do that seem cruel and harmful, nor do we ignore our own feelings and ideas about what is outside the bounds of ethical behavior and human decency. However, we address such issues through the entry points (theory of change, *good story/bad story* dichotomy, perceptual hinges) the particular couple offers. Discussions around issues like these begin with attention to what the partners tell us they want from therapy. They develop, in other words, from the goals couples frame for themselves as we talk about their situation.

Rather than confronting what we see as objectionable behavior or trying to convince people to change how they talk or act, we begin by assuming that somewhere in a person's experiences, theories, and meaning-making this form of behavior (the means) is intended to produce some reasonable desired result (the ends), and we want to bring this intention out in conversation. We do not condone physical or emotional abuse, nor do we skirt such issues. Rather, we want to do what might be most useful in creating genuine safety for both partners.[3] In our experience, an atmosphere and context of safety is best established when it is addressed and created for and with both partners. We try to develop a dialogue in which the partners can gain a shared sense of what could create safety; in this context people are more likely to be able to frame goals based on an acceptance of responsibility for changing abusive and relationship-destructive behaviors and attitudes. One route we can take toward the development of agency (the acceptance of responsibility for change) in such cases is to examine the clients' theories of change. Again, this requires that we have genuine curiosity about the meanings that generate even repugnant behavior.

For instance, suppose a client tells us that her husband often shouts obscenities at her and makes threatening gestures whenever they have an argument. At this point we might ask him what his goal is in talking to her in that way. He responds that it is the only way he knows to get his wife to "shut up and listen for a change." This statement prompts us to ask further questions. We still do not know what subjective experience (the end) he is after, and we remain guided by our assumption that sooner or later he will tell us about human relational needs. Getting his wife to "shut up and listen" is, we assume, a means to a still unarticulated end. Ends, or *meta-solutions* (Walter & Peller, 1988), rarely come forth in the first pass. So we would continue this line of inquiry until he and we have a better sense of what is at stake. (The same process of exploring ends and means will be undertaken with the wife when we ask her about her goals.) We might ask him, for instance, how her doing that—being quiet and listening to him—would make a difference to him. Suppose, after several passes, he says, "If she would just listen sometimes and say, 'Joe, that's a great idea,' I'd feel she respected me." Now we're getting to his real end, his wife "respecting" him, an experience that would make a positive difference to him. We've begun to enter the territory of this man's desired *good story*. Up to now, his theory of change, which has been that shouting and threatening is the best way to get his wife to show respect for him, has prevented him (and her) from experiencing that preferred narrative. In fact, his behavior may get her to be quiet, but it's not producing respect, which is what he really wants from her. At this point, it is not hard for a therapist to introduce some doubt about his means and look with him for other ways to accomplish his desired end. Obviously, this will involve talking with his wife and allows for possibly dovetailing goals she may have with his, thereby creating a shared *good story* narrative.

Both in these types of cases and those less challenging, the process remains the same. We are looking for entryways into a *good story* narrative that is satisfying to both partners, as well as for what each partner might do differently that would aid its reinvigoration. In this way, active neutrality naturally focuses each partner's attention on his or her own behaviors. We're helping people find good reasons—reasons generated by and meaningful to the partners in the particular couple—for abandoning ideas and behavior that are causing trouble in favor of those that move the couple toward their desired future. This desired future contains a preferred picture of the self, the other, and the relationship. Therefore, we work to highlight the ideas of self and other that make it likely people will shift some behaviors and attitudes, helping them find entryways into the *good story* (and exits from the *bad story*). We accomplish this from a genuine position of curiosity and respect when we are able to stay, in our questions and responses, inside the client's frame of reference. This, of course, is the essence of active neutrality.

Once started, the processes of validating multiple viewpoints and maintaining a not-knowing stance tend to be regenerative, because they foster such a creative matrix for therapeutic conversation. Active neutrality requires—and at the same time supports and rewards—the therapist's efforts to remain curious about and interested in everyone's point of view. The ease with which the therapist holds and validates conflicting narratives and theories helps partners back away from a stance of anxiety and combativeness about differing points of view and move into a creative mode.

Most therapists are extensively schooled in the idea that one of their main functions is interpretive. The act of listening and observing without adding an interpretive gloss or looking "behind," "beneath," or even more deeply "into," is a difficult one. It takes a good deal of practice to subtract the constant interpretive voice from one's observations, but this practice provides rich rewards: It makes true collaboration with our clients possible. If the therapist-as-expert is looking for pathology, if she is waiting for signs of dysfunctional interactions or confirming her preferred causal theory, she will lose her position of active neutrality, tend to do and say things people will experience as fault-finding and side-taking, and make it impossible to use the couple as a consulting team in their mutual endeavor. The not-knowing stance is at the other end of the spectrum from the interpretive one.

Not-knowing is communicated by asking questions like "Is there more you can tell me about how you see this?" "What else do you think is important for me to know and understand about what you're telling me?" "Can you tell me more about that?" These questions, of course, must express a real interest in, curiosity about, and respect for the client's experience and ideas. Giving this kind of credence to clients' expert knowledge is the beginning of tapping their considerable resources for generating change. If we are willing to learn from our clients, and have a genuine confidence and interest in their potential ability to solve their problems, we'll be in the best position to help them access and utilize their unique caches of knowledge, skill, and resource and, at the same time, draw on our own funds of knowledge and resource purposefully in conjunction with theirs.

Two common challenges often arise at the beginning of couples therapy. The first is when each partner recognizes that he or she has a part in the problem and needs to change, but believes the other should change first. The second is when each partner agrees there is a problem but views the other partner's behavior, personality, or attitudes as the source of the couple's trouble. In both these situations, each partner naturally wants the therapist to take the "right" side, which obviously is his or her own. Active neutrality can be helpful to clinicians facing these situations.

In cases where both partners in a couple admit they have some part in the problem, they often are in conflict over who should start the ball rolling—that is, disagreeing about precedence. This insistence that the other partner change first may be an attempt to force him or her to accept responsibility, both for the trouble and the needed changes. In such a case, each person has developed a solution story in which it is only fair, reasonable, logical, etc., that the other should go first. For example, a husband says he will gladly spend more time with his wife (something she wants) if she would only stop organizing their activities the way she wants them. Or a wife says she would be willing to clean off her desk and pay the bills more regularly (something he wants) if her husband would help more with the weekend chores. Since each partner believes his or her changes should (even must) be preceded by a change made by the other, it is understandable that each has been holding back and trying to convince the other to behave differently. This situation leaves both feeling frustrated and powerless. Neither has been effective in producing change in the other *or* in showing the more desirable self each feels he or she would be living out if all were well. In this situation people feel prevented from a positive experience of the relationship by the other person, and they usually feel disappointed in themselves, as their own sense of competency and efficacy is challenged by this deadlock. It can be a challenging situation for their therapist as well.

The following is an example of the use of active neutrality in these "you go first" types of cases. Liz and Tamara came in saying they wanted to begin living together, but before they could do that, they had to resolve some serious issues. The most important was how to "see intimacy" (Liz's phrase). Each of them acknowledged that they had to make changes in how they interacted about designing shared time, but each felt the other did and said things that started a negative cycle; each believed the other person needed to change first. Liz said Tamara was always withdrawing and, to Liz's mind, unpredictably needed long periods of time on her own; Tamara would opt out of particular conversations or retreat to her own apartment and not return phone calls. This made Liz feel abandoned and insecure, and although she was willing to make changes in her own ideas about spending time together and make room for "more distance" between them, she felt they wouldn't make any real progress on this issue until Tamara examined her "isolating." Tamara, on the other hand, explained the situation like this: "Because she's so anxious about this, I guess, Liz can't seem to accept the ways—and there are a lot of them—that we're different, and she's always accusing me of things I'm not feeling and motives I don't have. It makes me feel confused about what I'm doing—I start thinking maybe it's true, I'm not any good at having a relationship. Until she stops doing that, always telling me I'm doing it wrong, I won't feel safe enough, listened to enough, to spend more time with her." It was tempting to the therapist, in this case Tobey, to go right into a discussion of the differing meanings each partner attributed to their behaviors and to look for a shared perspective on "seeing intimacy." However, these two people had already spent a lot of time talking about their perceptions and processing what was going on, so Tobey chose to begin by addressing the who-goes-first issue. Notice how she remains actively neutral, maintaining a curious, not-knowing posture throughout the interchange. In offering a narrative that might open up new possibilities, she is not investigating or suggesting any causal theories about change, but simply inviting the couple to consider a perspective, if they choose, that might help them develop possible solutions to their current differences.

TOBEY: Okay, so it sounds like both of you are willing to make some changes, but each of you feels the other should take the first step. And, while you both make a good argument for the other going first and you each understand a lot about why this issue presents difficulties for both of you, it does seem that this waiting approach hasn't worked, at least so far. So let me ask a few questions that might help us find a way for both of you to get some of the changes you're talking about here—a better, more relaxed way of being together that makes you both, in your differing styles and needs, feel better about the ways you're coming and going and being together. I'm wondering, is it reasonable for both of you to assume that if the other one started making some changes around this, you'd be likely to follow suit?

BOTH: Yes. Uh huh.

TOBEY: Well, then (*addressing both*) . . . suppose one of you did go first, making these changes you've been thinking about. And the other made some changes in how she dealt with things as a result. Do you think the one who went first would be more likely to continue changing, or go back to the old ways?

LIZ: Continue to change, of course. That's an easy one.

TAMARA: No. I think Liz would go back to her old ways, just to be contrary. (*Tamara laughs and smiles at Liz, who doesn't look entirely amused.*) Just kidding, I'm sure she'd continue changing.

TOBEY: And if it were you, Tamara, who went first, would you be likely to continue changing if Liz responded with some changes?

TAMARA: Yeah, I think so, if I . . . well, yeah, of course I would.

TOBEY: That's interesting. Because if you're both right about this, it means regardless of which of you goes first, if one of you begins to change, the other will too, and this will encourage the first one to continue doing her different stuff. Once the positive changes are happening, regardless of who went first, you'll both see the other person making changes that feel good to you, and then you'll be on the way to interacting differently about how to be together—because you both have good ideas about how to make some changes, seems like, once you get started. So, do you suppose if either one of you just started out, you know as sort of an experiment, a goodwill gesture, do you think the other person would begin making changes too, knowing that would keep the ball rolling? (*By offering this idea, Tobey adds a new element: the idea of "keeping the ball rolling," a future picture of a continuing good story where the current impasse is already solved. Notice that she offers the idea in the form of an inquiry, from a stance of curiosity, and that she emphasized the fact that both Tamara and Liz have implied they have ideas about what will help.*)

TAMARA: Well, maybe. It seems likely.

LIZ: I think so.

TOBEY: Well, I imagine this isn't exactly a new idea (*giving them both credit*), but for one reason or another you haven't been able to act on it up to now. (*In the course of fleshing out a preferred future picture, Tobey will maintain an actively neutral posture about who should go first. The establishment of a future picture in which the ball has already been started rolling opens the frame past the you-go-first argument. Note that Tobey has not confronted or advised about the you-go-first stasis but instead given them implicit credit for the partnership they both want to create.*) So I'm wondering, now that we're talking about it, how each of you could do this, maybe with little steps? What would be a first small step each of you could make in working your side of the fence, even though you haven't seen changes on the other side yet? (*Curious posture presupposes they have an answer and that the answer will be useful.*) And, maybe just as important, how will you let the other person know that you notice she's doing things you wanted?

LIZ: Well, I guess I could be welcoming—be warm, you know—when Tamara comes back from one of her times away. Rather than talking about how hurt I am or being cold. I guess I could ask her what happened for her while she was gone, what it meant for her, not why she felt she had to leave me. Be interested. She's told me before she likes that.

TAMARA: (*Jumping in.*) Okay, hmm, yeah. And what I'd be doing, I wouldn't be going creeping in feeling all ready to be blown up at. I'd hug her, I'd let her know I was glad to see her.

TOBEY: (*Speaking to Tamara.*) And so when you came back you'd be warm and outgoing, show her you're glad to see her, and she'd notice that difference. And what about other times, if, say, Liz wanted more time together and the two of you had started to make some good changes around that, what would she see you doing differently? (*The line of inquiry fleshes out positive signs Liz will notice, no matter who's gone first.*)

TAMARA: Hmm. (*Thinks for a minute.*) Well, I'd be coming to her and letting her know specific things I wanted to do together, I guess. Like suggesting we take Pooch for a walk. Or telling her I wanted to plan the day so we had definite time together. She feels good when I'm the one to get us to do that. (*The clients have bypassed the who-goes-first argument and entered the arena of a potentially shared good story. By validating and not contravening each partner's need to make change only in response to the other person's changes, Tobey has helped them each begin to visualize more satisfying ways of interacting around separation/togetherness.*)

TOBEY: (*Turning to Liz.*) And if Tamara did that, would that tell you she was making some of the changes you want, steps that would keep you making the changes she wants?

LIZ: Definitely. That's how it is when we're really connected, when things are good between us. We're glad to be together, and the tension goes away.

TOBEY: And how would she know, what would tell her in what you were doing, that you noticed her changes?

LIZ: Well, I'd be calmer, I guess, when she came and went. I'd know we were going to have our time together, and I wouldn't have to ask her over and over again when we were going to see each other.

Rather than mediating who should go first, or suggesting that each partner should concentrate on her own responsibility, or investigating each partner's differing needs, Tobey maintains a stance of curiosity about what each will notice once a cycle of change has already started. This validates both partners' mutually exclusive positions but does not adjudicate between them and at the same time helps the couple move past their focus on who is responsible for initiating change. Tobey also does not point out how they've come to an impasse and urge one or both to act first. She works within their frame of "you first," loosening it up a bit until the partners in the couple bypass the question of precedence as pivotal and concentrate instead on small steps they can both see as reciprocally meaningful. Tobey's lack of intensity or pressure (which is replaced by a relaxed curiosity) around this detente makes it more possible for the couple to begin developing attainable and mutually satisfying solutions. We've found this approach to be much more effective in breaking these deadlocks than telling partners they need to stop trying to change each other, investigating the past for how or why this impasse came about, or labeling people's behavior as codependent, passive–aggressive, or in some other way dysfunctional. Instead we host conversations like the one above as a way of inviting couples to revise their ideas and try something different (or even something they may have previously thought about but not felt willing or confident enough to attempt).

If one or both partners rejected our theory that either could start a change cycle, we wouldn't press the issue. We might return to working within their theories, asking, for example, a series of questions that would cast doubt on the utility of continuing to try to get the other partner to go first. Or we might follow whatever leads we found toward bits and pieces of the *good story*, for instance asking Tamara and Liz to flesh out the *good story* scenario of the two of them planning when and how to spend time (or the picture of both of them greeting each other warmly when Tamara comes home from an absence), so that the feeling of alliance available there could lead us into conversation about preferred future pictures that bypassed the going-first problem. Or, since both parties are interested in change and are ready to make some changes of their own (though up to now only if the other goes first) we might ask: "What will tell each of you that you're working in partnership to solve this problem?" When we come, by one route or another, to explore with each partner what initial small changes she might make, the focus of conversation is on what changes can make a difference, not who is to blame or who should go first.

Another common challenging situation for the couples therapist hoping to maintain active neutrality is the couple with competing and/or incompatible causal and change theories. The following is a case from Phil's practice that demonstrates the power of maintaining a stance of active neutrality and not-knowing with a couple who is presenting with what might be viewed by some as very serious, deep, long-standing problems. This couple fits the description of what Duncan and colleagues (1997) refer to as "therapy veterans"—clients who have seen a number of therapists and have adopted many psychological ideas about what is wrong with them but who have not been helped to make significant improvements in their lives. As becomes clear during the session, the psychological ideas they have learned in previous therapies have become the basis of their competing theories, and each partner places the problems and responsibility for their solution at the other person's door. The couple was referred to Phil by their 7-year-old son's therapist, who was treating the boy for ADHD. The referring therapist felt that, in addition to receiving individual therapy and medication, the boy could be helped if the parent's marriage improved. The parents came to the first session saying they knew that if they got along better their son would be under less stress and family life in general would be more satisfying and happier. Each had, however, a well-developed, sophisticated theory explaining how the other partner needed to change how he or she parented.

Phil began by acknowledging each partner's experiences and validating each one's theories of change. The father's theory was that the mother was overinvolved with their son, that she was unconsciously trying to prevent him from having a close relationship with his son, and so he, the father, felt excluded much of the time. He explained that all his life he had been plagued by deep feelings of shame and fears of abandonment. And, while he had undergone therapy several times to work on these issues, he believed that unless his wife faced up to her "anxiety and overprotectiveness," nothing was likely to improve. He explained that when he felt excluded by his wife and son he withdrew in anger and shame and did things he knew made matters worse, things that upset his wife and caused his son a good deal of distress. However, he felt that given what he perceived as an impenetrable exclusionary bond between mother and child, he was powerless to do anything but succumb to his feelings of shame and abandonment fears. He wanted Phil's help in getting his wife to see how controlling she was, and how her anxieties and overprotection of her son were causing their family problems. He also wanted Phil to explain to his wife the importance of letting their son handle his own problems without her interference, especially problems the boy had related to his father.

The mother had her side of the story and specific ideas about the nature and roots of their problems. According to her, the father, for the psychological reasons he had named—deep shame issues and fear of abandonment—behaved in ways that called upon her to protect her son. Her husband, she said, would often become irritable and rejecting of their son, and she felt that in those situations the boy needed her protection. She also felt that when the son spent too much time with his father, his father's moods made the boy anxious and depressed. Because of this, she had convinced the father to agree that she and the boy should spend most evenings alone together, while he either remained in some other part of the house or went out. Unfortunately, on nights when all three were together or the father and son were alone, according to the wife, things inevitably took a turn for the worse. The son might do or say something that the oversensitive father would experience as emotionally wounding, and the father would get nasty, withdraw in angry silence, or do or say something that provoked anxiety in the boy, requiring the mother to step in to protect him. She wanted her husband to agree to work on his "shame issues" and his "fear of abandonment issues" so he could be a better father.

After exploring with each spouse their views and theories, Phil began asking questions that invited the couple to see their difficulties as problems not for each of them individually but for them together, as a couple and parenting team. They agreed that a common goal, despite their differing points of view, was to become better partners, both as spouses and parents. This gave Phil the opportunity to begin the process of developing a solution-building team by coauthoring a problem definition that might encompass both partners' theories and experiences without invalidating either. To articulate some other specific common goals, he drew out that both wanted their son to grow up emotionally healthy and strong. Both wanted family life to support the well-being and self-esteem of all family members. When Phil asked about their hopes regarding their own marital relationship, both talked about wishing it could be more intimate and satisfying. Throughout the interview, Phil maintained the stance of multipartiality, including both partners' points of view and theories of causation and change.

At this point, the wife made a comment about how she thought there was some connection between her husband's shame and abandonment issues and her overprotectiveness issues. Sensing a possible entry point for coauthoring a team-building, *good story* narrative that could include every-one's theories and problem definitions, Phil asked both the wife and the husband if they thought that figuring out what that link was would give them a starting point for making positive changes in family life. Both said yes. The idea for this suggested link did not grow out of any general theory of Phil's regarding interlocking pathologies or the unconscious forces at play in mate selection. It grew out of something offered by one member of the couple, a comment that Phil sensed might be developed into a useful and shared *good story* narrative of intimacy and success particular to this couple's sense of themselves. Had either partner rejected his invitation to coauthor a *good story* and collaborative solution-building narrative from the wife's comment, he would have dropped it and waited for another opportunity, another possible invitation to coauthor new narratives or revisions of old ones that might be useful.

The husband then began talking about his feeling that he would be powerless to make things better as long as he saw the problem in terms of his wife's overprotectiveness (over which he had no control) or in terms of his own deep-seated unconscious shame and abandonment issues (over which he also felt no sense of control). Viewing the problem in this way, he was realizing, made it hard for him to contemplate actions that might reduce the emotional, perceptual, and behavioral consequences of his feelings of vulnerability.[4]

The mother then began talking about the fact that it had been easier for her to focus attention on her husband's problematic behavior than to work to change what she knew to be an attitude of overprotectiveness toward her son. When Phil asked what they thought would be a helpful way to proceed at this point, both agreed that each of them would find it difficult to make the kinds of changes in themselves that might make a difference. This gave Phil the opportunity to offer a problem definition that put the couple on the same side against a common problem. He suggested that both partners wanted to make certain changes but were not confident they could make them. This redefinition, which both partners agreed fit their situation, no longer put them on opposing sides. No one needed to defend or blame. Each could begin talking about how hard such changes would be to make, at least alone. In further conversation with Phil, they began to realize the task might be less onerous if somehow each could make some small but significant changes that would help and support the other in making changes as well. By the end of the first session, the mother and father had defined a number of small steps each felt able and willing to take. Both agreed these steps would move them in the right direction toward transforming their relationship as a marital partnership and parenting team.

Phil saw this couple for a total of six sessions spread over about six months. When therapy ended the father was doing things with his son in the evenings as well as on the weekends. The mother had become involved in a book club and the church choir and was participating in these and other activities in the evening. The son was no longer on medication and, according to his teachers and his parents, seemed less anxious, more adventuresome, and generally happier.

# Loosening the Hold of the *Bad Story* Narrative: Problem Talk That Makes a Difference

Conversation is the field in which therapy takes place. We want to begin this chapter, which addresses ways to soften the solidity of the *bad story* narratives people bring to couples therapy, with some attention to this medium in which storying and dialogue happen.

We view therapeutic dialogue as invitational and co-constructive. In RPT, what clients and therapists address (the content) during each therapy hour and how they address it (process) is negotiated through an ongoing verbal interaction, in a constant offering and declining or accepting of conversational flows and gambits. In this process, both therapist and clients establish together what is important to talk about and how to talk about it, as all partners in the dialogue participate in a joint project that establishes the direction, tone, and content of their interaction. In effect, they teach each other, through invitation and response, how to be together.

The questions a therapist asks or does not ask, what his comments and body language indicate, and how he responds to clients' invitations to talk about various subjects reveal what he thinks is and is not important. The selectivity inherent in a particular line of questioning, for instance, can quite clearly convey a therapist's theory of change or transmit his model of a compliant and appropriate client. For example, when a therapist asks many questions about how a problem or issue began, he is inviting a couple to pursue a causal theory as the basis for therapy. Alternatively, when he turns the conversation away from talk about the problem, even without any explicit reference to what is or is not important, clients learn that talk about the problem is not encouraged. Conversational cues also let the therapist know what the client thinks is important to talk about and indicate the clients' method of approach to the issues at hand. An informed attention to these features of conversation helps the clinician understand how to co-construct with his clients an open and enriching therapeutic dialogue.

# Distinguishing Therapeutic Conversations: Role Relationships

Instead of viewing our clients as motivated or resistant, or the therapeutic relationship as fixed, we prefer to think in terms of characterizing conversational roles. We distinguish three types of therapeutic conversation, based on the respective and interdependent roles maintained by the client and therapist during a given interaction. These roles materially affect the content and direction of the conversations, and awareness of them makes it possible for a clinician to participate more effectively in the conversation at hand or invite the client into another type that might be more productive. It should be noted that this is a classification of conversations and roles, not a labeling of clients or types of therapeutic relationships.[1] This perspective on the invitational and fluid nature of conversation helps us make purposeful choices about how to participate.

The three types of therapeutic conversation are: (1) visitor/host, (2) complainant/sympathizer, and (3) customer/consultant.

### Visitor/Host Conversations

Sometimes a partner comes to therapy, whether alone or with the other partner, expressing the belief that therapy is inappropriate or unnecessary. The person has usually come because of some pressure or threat from the other partner rather than a desire to work on a relationship problem in this context. Such a person usually begins by telling us (1) there is no problem, or (2) if there is one, she or he has no part in causing or maintaining it, and/or (3) she or he does not think therapy will be a useful forum for addressing whatever problems exist. This person doesn't need our help, isn't asking for it, and doesn't want it. A husband, for example, might come to a first session with or without his wife and explain that he doesn't believe in therapy and has come only because his wife is threatening to leave him if he refuses to seek professional help. We view the husband's comments as an honest, heartfelt invitation to join him in a visitor/host conversation. It may turn out—and a major therapeutic task is to explore and promote this possibility—that this reluctant visitor will come to identify changes in his life he would like to make. If that happens, he may begin to think therapy could help, at which point our conversation with him will take the form of customer/consultant.

When partners come together they often are not equally motivated for therapy. One partner is the moving force in seeking therapy; the other person may come willingly, be mildly motivated, reluctant, or quite unwilling. This disparity, when it occurs, is not in itself problematic. What is problematic is the therapist's failure to recognize and address the disparity in a therapeutically useful way. In these cases, we are being invited into different roles with respect to each partner in the couple. Without an active awareness of this, we may find it difficult to establish and maintain active neutrality, and we can have no real understanding of how to proceed toward co-constructing effective partnership.

Whether a reluctant partner[2] comes alone or accompanied, it is important to accept the client's invitation into a visitor/host conversation and begin here, rather than assuming at this point that the person is ready to engage in solution-oriented conversation. Things can change, of course, and they often do. We want to do what we can to encourage an active participation in other types of conversations. At this point, however, what is helpful—clarifying, respectful, and productive of understanding—is simply to serve as a good host, providing sympathetic, respectful attention. This means welcoming the client, and acknowledging and validating his or her experiences and feelings about the relationship and his or her feelings and attitudes toward therapy. When we sense that the client feels met on his or her own terms (i.e., we have accepted his or her invitation and explored the relationship he or she invites), we will in turn initiate some possible shifts in role. Once (and if) the client begins identifying some desired changes, our conversations are shifting in type from visitor/host to customer/consultant.

### Complainant/Sympathizer Conversations

It happens fairly often that both partners begin therapy by inviting us into complainant/sympathizer conversations. When people seek therapy for help in solving their problems they frequently expect and need to spend some time talking about what is troubling them. As we noted in the last chapter, building rapport is crucial—both partners need to feel welcome to talk about their concerns as they see them, and the clinician must respond in ways that foster therapeutic alliance. So we begin by meeting both partners where they are and by taking in, with respect and openness, the life stories they bring. Of course, if one or both partners never moves out of the complainant/sympathizer mode, it will be hard to exit the *bad story* context and therapy will not be very effective. Nonetheless, when there are antagonistic, adversarial postures, it is counterproductive to make immediate efforts to point them out, shift the type of conversation, or decline the kind of dialogue the couple is initiating. Instead, we begin by accepting each partner's invitation to enter into complainant/sympathizer conversations. We acknowledge and validate what each tells us, without becoming involved in a search for "objective" truth or accepting the role of arbiter of right and wrong. This is the active neutrality we spoke of in the last chapter. We don't try to force a particular conversational direction, and if our own invitations to move in a different direction are declined, we follow our clients' cues. A posture of curiosity and alertness helps in the threefold task of establishing active neutrality, maintaining awareness of the kind of conversational flow we're involved in, and picking up possible cues for the resources available in the *good story* narrative. While engaging in complainant/sympathizer dialogue, we remain alert for opportunities to exit the *bad story* narratives and enter customer/consultant conversations.

### Customer/Consultant Conversations

Customer/consultant conversations occur when couples have begun to identify changes they desire and the therapist is engaging with them in ways that will help them move toward that preferred future. Over time, these conversations tend to reinforce the *good story* narrative. Both partners naturally move toward an acknowledgment and recognition of their individual contribution to the couple's problems and solutions, and each is becoming increasingly motivated to work collaboratively for changes and goals desirable to both partners. Couples rarely come into therapy prepared to have such conversations with us. (It would seem that couples who approach their problems and conflicts in this way don't seek outside intervention or professional help.) However, regardless of how they first appear, our working assumption is that every couple and every client is a potential customer. Once the process of loosening the hold of the alienating *bad story* begins, we are on the way to engaging in customer/consultant conversations. The process of building future pictures and constructing goals, which we discuss in the next chapter, brings people readily into a responsible role with regard to change and ensures that customer/consultant conversations will prevail.

## Distinguishing Conversational Content: Bad Story vs. Good Story Talk

We have been characterizing therapeutic conversation on the basis of the varying roles played by therapists and clients. A related way to distinguish types of therapy conversation, central to the solution-focused brief therapy approach, defines the content of conversation in therapy as either problem or solution talk (Berg & Miller, 1992; De Jong & Berg, 1998; de Shazer, 1985, 1988, 1991, 1994). Problem talk, as the name suggests, focuses on causes, concerns, difficulties, symptoms, underlying problems, who is to blame, and other details of the problem narrative. Solution talk, on the other hand, focuses on preferred futures and past successes, along with strengths, resources, and skills. This distinction is crucial for traditional solution-focused brief therapists because they believe only solution talk is progressive and therefore useful in generating solutions.[3]

As social constructionist therapists, we assume what we talk about with people in troubled relationships, as well as how we talk about it, influences how couples view their problems and what needs to be done to solve them. We are less concerned about whether the content of conversation is strictly problem- or solution-centered than we are about how we are talking together and whether we are oriented toward finding ways out of the couple's alienating *bad story* narratives in favor of the relationship-enhancing and generative *good story* narratives. We agree with Harlene Anderson (1997) when she suggests the therapist should not consider "one category useful conversation and the other non-useful. . . . The distinguishing factor is the way something is talked about, not its problem or solution focus or content" (p. 73). This is why, in RPT, we prefer to differentiate conversational content according to the *good story/bad story* dichotomy rather than on the basis of its solution or problem orientation. Therapeutic conversation will be most generative and transformative, we find, when what we are talking about serves to potentiate, clarify, and reinforce a couple's shared *good story*. Thus, we rarely take the initiative in inviting people into conversations about the details of their fights, the histories of their troubles, or the possible roots and causes of their difficulties. However, some kinds of talk about the problem, when that is what evolves in our conversations with couples, can lead toward *good story* territory and help to bridge the couple's relational gap. In such cases, the therapist can ask questions and make comments that both loosen the hold of the *bad story* narratives and make it possible for couples to locate doorways into the *good story*. Talking about how fights come to an end, or what partners do to make some fights shorter (milder, etc.), is an example of this kind of productive therapeutic talk about problems.

Problem talk initiated by clients can be an opportunity for: (1) developing rapport; (2) increasing our own understanding of what matters to people, and of their concerns, overarching desires, and theories of change; and (3) softening the hold the *bad story* has on the context for individual perception. In participating in conversation about the *bad story*, the clinician must maintain an interest in the assets and resources of each person's preferred self (how each wants to see him- or herself reflected in the other's words and actions), a curiosity about the hopes and wishes hidden within the *bad story* glossing of events, and an alertness to potential exit routes from the *bad story* narrative. These ways of participating in the dialogue increase the possibility that conversation will shift from complainant/sympathizer and problem-focused to customer/consultant and solution-oriented.

# Techniques for Loosening the Hold of the Bad Story

To help us decide when, where, and how to use the techniques that loosen the *bad story* during problem-focused conversations, we ask ourselves the following questions: Where is the thread to a loosening of this story? What clues to competency, skill, strength, or resource lie hidden in this problem-saturated narrative? How might I draw out an articulation of how things are different when they are better? How might the problem be redefined so that it is less of a problem and/or easier to solve? How could I help the partners to find a way of seeing the problem as shared? What parts of this *bad story* point to an exit? And what questions and comments can I make to refresh and reinvigorate the couple's *good story*? What we are often thinking about in these conversations is the *how*: how to do our part in the conversation to foster a renewed sense of partnership and possibility, how to find the resources for partnership and hope in what a partner is saying, how to shift the narrative context.

There are a number of ways we answer these questions. When we participate in *bad story* or problem-focused conversations initiated by our clients in order to loosen the *bad story's* hold, we (1) identify exits from the *bad story*; (2) use reframing techniques, including normalizing, mutualizing, and coping questions to offer alternative definitions and perspectives on elements of the *bad story*; and (3) invite couples into externalizing and relative influence conversations (which we view as forms of mutualizing).

### *Identifying Exits from the Bad Story: Reflecting Partnership, Highlighting the Preferred Self, and Noticing Larger Goals*

When a therapist engages in conversation about the troubles, feelings, and opinions housed in a person's *bad story* narrative, it is important is to combine sympathetic reflection with a reference to the *desire and possibility for change*. This opens up potential exits from the *bad story* and highlights the first glimmers of partnership. We suggest, therefore, that reflection of the person's *bad story* concerns and feelings about the couple's situation should include both the problem aspect and the desire for change aspect. An example of this would be, "I can understand why you're feeling pretty discouraged, Rachel, and cautious about believing Tom's statements that he wants to stop fighting about how to handle the kids and take care of things like the morning rush to school. At the same time I can see, since you're both here talking about this problem and about your different ways of thinking about it, that you do share a common goal: figuring out what you can both do about it, together. Up to now, you haven't been able to find a way to get at the problem as a team, but it seems like you both want to go in the same direction here and turn things around. Does that sound right to you?"

This reflection acknowledges the problem and Rachel's discouragement and doubt, but highlights, in framing her concerns, the shared goal that has brought the couple to therapy. In this kind of reflection, the therapist is listening, as though with a third ear, for the clues that signal potential partnership in the *bad story* material. This softens the combative atmosphere and establishes ground for collaboration. Finding clues to effective partnership in these stories can lead people away from blame and fear and make it possible for each person to begin to understand the other's meanings—their hopes, wishes, desires—in more positive and empathic ways, which re-establishes a basis for hopefulness about change. Hidden in most *bad story* narratives, clouded by its history of disappointment, struggle, and accusation, is an element of a potential shared *good story*: the desire for things to be different and better so that the relationship will be more satisfying (Parry & Doan, 1994).

Conversation should always lean toward emerging exit routes, which will be particular to each individual and his or her ideas about both self and change. Clues about the particular exits from the *bad story* narrative begin to appear when a therapist invites dialogue that enlarges the participants' understanding of ideas of preferred self (Eron & Lund, 1996, 1999) and larger goals. It is important to note that the *bad story* contains a frustrated preferred self—the person trying to fix the relationship (in behalf of the overarching shared goal of better relations) and desiring to be seen in certain ways by the partner. In exploring this a clinician might ask, for instance, "So, given that sometimes you don't feel appreciated, George, in the way that would make a difference for you, for the work you do in the garden and around the house on the weekends (the *bad story*, problem focus), let me ask you a question: What do you think you're showing Vivian about yourself, and about the way you think about the relationship, when you're doing this work around the house, the way you're talking about? (the preferred self, larger goals)." When the client says, "I'm trying to show her that I really care, the way I know she does, too, about our house, that it's important to have it be nice for us, and that I want to feel like I'm pleasing both of us, that she likes what I'm doing," the clinician can take the opportunity to frame an exit from the *bad story* narrative by highlighting a larger goal this client has—wanting their environment to be pleasing and wanting a feeling of togetherness about that—that will most probably be shared, a potential element of the *good story* narrative they can both recognize. Once the conversation highlights such elements, other means to achieving a future picture containing these bits and pieces of the *good story* narrative, things both partners can see themselves doing, will emerge in the subsequent goaling conversation (see next chapter).

This kind of inquiry about the self, which makes it possible to draw out potentially shared couple goals, is an exit point from the *bad story*. The emphasis of the conversation is not on causes of the trouble, nor does it assign blame or thicken the *bad story* context; rather it establishes a meaning, on the part of the husband, that may contribute to rebuilding partnership. And this kind of inquiry about the preferred self hidden in the complaint gives the wife a view of the husband's concerns that is a better basis for empathy or mutuality than having to defend herself against the charge of being unappreciative or complaints that she never pays any attention to what he does around the house. Developing these individual meanings and linking them to shared *good story* narratives can help people, as they experience new ways of seeing each other's concerns and distresses, find "escape routes" in the future when *bad story* material comes up—shared pathways of shifted perception they can take out of familiar wrangles or disagreements. These exits are important for establishing the ways and means of relationship repair.

As the clinician begins, in these kinds of discussions, (1) to highlight potentially shared goals, co-constructing a partnership scenario; (2) to focus positively on individual assets (misapplied or unused because of the *bad story* context) that could work to increase partnership in a *good story* context; and (3) to emphasize the mutual desire for movement toward a preferred future, the *bad story's* influence will diminish. As conversation focuses on how the partners want their relationship to be different from the current state of affairs and how that will look and feel in the future, or how that has happened in the past, the therapist can initiate movement into the couple's *good story* territory (customer/consultant conversation) and the work of goal development can begin. In this way, conversation that begins with the *bad story* narrative can serve a transformative and generative function. (The case we presented at the end of the previous chapter, of the couple with the 7-year-old boy, provides a vivid example of how problem talk, given attention to a particular couple's theory of change, can be productive. If Phil had tried to move the couple toward solution talk too early, no partnership, either between the parents or with the therapist, would have been established, resulting in premature termination.)

Problem talk is always transitional. What we are mainly interested in is developing a context for recreating partnership and tapping a couple's potential for positive change. Working with a couple to build a context that fosters partnership is what it's all about. To that end, we look to loosen and break up the narratives of powerlessness and defeat that make up defining *bad story* contexts, move into dialogue that will heighten a sense of shared concerns, and begin building bridges toward the *good story* context. When this kind of turnaround is happening, we can observe a transformation begin to take place in the office. As a couple, with our help, rediscovers remembered and imagined elements of their shared *good story* and finds exits from the *bad story* narratives into an alternative reality, the partners almost invariably become visibly warmer, more attentive, and respectful toward each other. The loosening of the *bad story* and the move toward solution talk in this context establish both a public (in front of the therapist) and private (between themselves) sense of the couple's alliance and competence for change. Even when the *bad stories* remain strong, or the relationship's longevity remains in question, clues to a potential or remembered *good story* make alliance around establishing shared goals possible. Thus, by engaging in problem talk that loosens the hold of the *bad story* perspective, we can assist in the re-establishment of a relationship team.

## Reframing

Reframing offers clients a redefinition of their problems in order to change "the conceptual and/or emotional setting or viewpoint in relation to which a situation was experienced and to place it in another frame which fits the 'facts' of the same concrete situation equally well or better" (Watzlawick, Weakland, & Fisch, 1974, p. 95). Brief/strategic therapists like Watzlawick, Weakland, Haley, and Madanes use reframing for very specific therapeutic purposes—to put a spin on the client's current problems so that it will seem reasonable to carry out the paradoxical homework assignments the therapist gives at the end of the therapy hour. The task assignment, not the therapist's reframing of the problem, is the principal intervention in these approaches.

In our work, we use reframing to generate with a couple multiple ways of perceiving and interpreting events, which can make it easier for them to solve the problems they are bringing to therapy. We assume that when people are able to entertain multiple perspectives, they will be more likely to tap assets and resources for moving toward their desired goals. During problem-focused conversations, we engage in what narrative therapists Jill Freedman and Gene Combs (1996) describe as deconstructive listening, "a special kind of listening required for accepting and understanding people's stories without reifying or intensifying the powerless, painful, and pathological aspects of those stories" (p. 46). If we listen in this way, asking certain questions and offering comments that suggest new ways of narrating people's experiences, our conversations will loosen the perceptual and interpretive grip of each partner's *bad story* narrative and help to re-establish their shared *good story*.

There are three principal types of reframing conversations and questions we use in RPT: normalizing, mutualizing, and coping.

## Normalizing Problem Definitions

Many clients perceive the problems they bring to therapy as unique or as signs of abnormality. In normalizing conversation, the therapist either suggests or implies by her questions that these problems might be simply the normal difficulties of relationship life. This expressed attitude makes the problem, whatever it may be, seem less like an indictment of the couple and their competence. Sometimes we normalize simply by our choice of language in responding to a couple's descriptions of their problems, making it clear that we do not see what the couple is describing as unusual or overwhelming. Examples of normalizing comments are : "Naturally," "Of course, I'm not surprised that . . . ," "That sounds pretty typical to me," "You'd be surprised how many people have struggled with this issue," "It's a tough one, but solvable." Sometimes we normalize by telling stories about ourselves that show how we or other people we know have faced similar problems. These kinds of "down-home" disclosures can convey that most couples, even supposedly "expert" therapists, face and have to work through the difficulties and disappointments of relationship life.

The following is an example of normalizing conversation used to help a couple redefine a problem. Some might assume, as this couple did, that a problem such as theirs would require extensive treatment; in fact, the couple was seen only three times.

Gary and Roberta came to Tobey explaining that they had a serious problem: "sexual incompatibility." Tobey began by saying, "It's pretty common, in my experience, for couples to get into difficulties in trying to deal with differing sexual needs and styles. I wonder if, perhaps, the real problem here might be that the two of you as a couple haven't been able to figure out how to handle the ways you each see things differently in this area." Thus, Tobey normalized the problem of "sexual incompatibility," which certainly sounds very difficult and intractable, and redefined it as a "negotiation problem"—that is, a problem of working together as a team to find shared ways to approach their different sexual needs. This normalizing reframe (emphasizing partnership), which the couple readily accepted, made them both relax visibly, and Gary said jokingly, "Oh, you mean there's hope for us?" "Sure," said Tobey. Then she asked Gary and Roberta to give examples of this newly-defined team problem.

Roberta spoke first. Gary, she explained, wanted sex all the time, usually more than once a day. This was much more than she wanted. She felt pressured by him, but also said she was worried that there might be something wrong with her. She explained that in the past she'd always enjoyed their sex life, but after the birth of her first child she found she was not as interested in making love as before. More recently, because they were arguing over their sex life, both she and Gary were tense and anxious when they tried making love, and she hadn't been enjoying it at all.

When he took his turn, Gary explained that one of the reasons he initially was drawn to Roberta was because of the "electricity" of their sexual connection. When they were first together their physical intimacy had been a wonderful part of their relationship, he said, and this lasted well into the first years of their marriage. He had loved Roberta's sexual spontaneity and enthusiasm, as well as her willingness to experiment. But now, he explained, she rarely seemed interested. She never initiated lovemaking and whenever he did, he sensed that he was imposing on her. Eventually he, too, lost interest in keeping their sex life alive, and nowadays he rarely initiated anything. They were down to once or twice a month, and it was fairly mechanical and not very satisfying for him, either.

Tobey began asking questions intended to loosen the hold of the *bad story* narrative, "sexual incompatibility." Reframing the problem had already helped Gary and Roberta relax and begin opening up space for new perspectives on what was happening. Tobey continued by inviting Gary and Roberta to coauthor a mutual definition of the problem that might help recreate partnership and make the problem easier to solve. First she inquired about the meanings the changes in their sexual feelings and interactions held for both of them. These conversations revealed that after the birth of their first child, Roberta had begun feeling less attractive. During her pregnancy, she had gained some weight and hadn't been able to take it off after the baby was born. She felt self-conscious when her husband looked at her and when he touched what she described as her "dumpy body." Because she had felt too shy to talk straightforwardly about this before, Gary was somewhat surprised to learn Roberta felt this way. He had not thought of her as fat. He said he still found her sexy and desirable. Roberta questioned this. She said she had assumed Gary wanted sex with her simply because he always wanted sex, not because he desired her.

As the conversation continued, Gary and Roberta's perspectives evolved. What had been "sexual incompatibility" changed into "a communication problem." To Gary and Roberta this communication problem seemed soluble, at least in part, if Gary could find new ways to let Roberta know that he found her desirable, instead of communicating this only by initiating sex. In the weeks between sessions, Gary agreed to tell Roberta about all the ways he found her attractive and interesting. Roberta responded quite quickly to his comments and compliments by discovering a renewed interest in sex. By the third and final session (about six weeks after their first visit) Gary and Roberta reported that their sex life had improved dramatically and said they felt ready to end therapy.

While many therapists might assume that communication problems usually underlie sexual problems, Tobey did not begin her work with this couple with this assumption or initiate a move toward this kind of investigation. First she suggested a redefinition of the problem, normalizing it as the partners' differing needs and ideas about sex. This helped to loosen the hold of the *bad story* narrative they both shared about this aspect of their lives. As opportunity arose in the session and as the couple talked about their concerns, meanings, and experiences, the problem definition evolved, and, using the cues they offered, Tobey helped Gary and Roberta normalize and redefine their problem as a "communication problem," which they fairly quickly resolved.[4] Because this problem could be seen in terms of partnership, it could be absorbed into a *good story* narrative they shared about resolving sexual differences and working together on a "communication" problem.

## Mutualizing Problem Definitions

Mutualizing is another form of reframing or redefining a couple's problem that is particularly useful in helping couples recreate partnership. Couples usually come to therapy presenting conflicting points of view. Nonetheless, we assume they hold overarching meta-goals, which are currently clouded by the *bad story* frame. Mutualizing is a conversational process of coauthoring a narrative of shared goals and common concerns within the conflictual territory of the alienating problem narrative.

As we have indicated above, we use questions to help people discover aspects of mutuality in how they view and approach problems. We want to help them define differences and aspects of the *bad story* narrative in ways that may make it possible for them to experience a sense of collaboration, despite their differences. Through our questions, we invite partners to reframe the situation as one in which they both face the same problem: How can they, together, find mutually satisfying solutions in the face of their competing/differing needs and perspectives? For example, let's say a couple is arguing about the way they interact about the husband's desire for time alone in his study. The wife feels the husband, who closes his door, is being uncaring and dismissive of her by closeting himself away from her. The husband says that his wife's inability to be independent and tolerate his need for solitude means she is insecure and intrusive. The therapist (checking along the way that this description fits for them) says that it seems that they are finding themselves stuck because they have been reading each other's gestures, which simply represent differing styles of "we-ness" and "I-ness," as signs of dysfunction and a lack of care. Both partners, he suggests, have been trying to solve the problem by convincing each other of the reasonableness of their own position and the irrationality of the other's. This approach hasn't been working, and in fact it has damaged their sense of partnership. He asks, "Do you guys think it would be helpful to say that the real problem you two are having as a couple is to find mutually acceptable and satisfying ways to live together, making room for both your styles and needs and keeping your sense of partnership strong?" By reframing the problem in this way, the therapist has made it possible for the couple to see a solution in terms of re-establishing partnership rather than changing the other. This makes it possible for the couple to attribute new meanings to each other's gestures (seeing them as stylistic differences rather than evidence of dysfunction or a lack of caring) and, on that basis, to come up with a mutually satisfying set of ideas about different ways to handle these moments. We want to offer or co-construct with our clients different problem or "trouble" definitions that can help to generate an increased sense of collaboration.

A particularly effective way to reframe a problem in mutual terms is through externalizing conversation, a technique developed by Michael White and David Epston (1990). These narrative therapists point out that often those of us in the helping professions view those who turn to us with their problems as somehow defective or deficient, and their relationships as dysfunctional. In other words, the people themselves are treated *as the problem* rather than as *having* a problem.

Externalizing questions influence couples to begin thinking of their problem as a force or presence that is external to themselves. These questions are effective with couples because they generate a shift from antagonistic, blaming, and guilt-inducing ideas about the problem's source to a shared, shoulder-to-shoulder perspective. In other words, externalizing conversations mutualize problems, producing a sense of teamwork in approaching solutions and facilitating new ways of being together. As White and Epston (1990) explain:

> At times, when families or couples present for therapy, persons are in considerable dispute over the definition of the problem. These disputes make it difficult for them to work cooperatively in any attempt to challenge the effects of problems in their lives and relationships. In these circumstances, externalizing can establish a mutually acceptable definition of the problem and facilitates conditions under which persons can work effectively together to resolve their problems. (p. 54)

We agree with White and Epston that when problems begin dominating a couple's life, the stories partners tell about themselves, each other, and their relationship become increasingly negative, alienating, and oppressive. These *bad stories* influence each partner to view the other as the cause of the problem or even as the problem. In other words, a strong, chronic, and/or long-lasting *bad story* narrative often leads to the perception that the partner and the problem are synonymous. We want to host conversations in which the story of *partner-is-the-problem* is replaced by one in which *the partners face the problem together*. This shift of perspective is the function of externalizing questions.

In externalizing conversations the partners can be asked to reflect on how the problem is influencing their thinking, perceptions, and actions, and in addition, to consider how they are influencing the problem. White and Epston (1990) call this conversational process of asking people about how the problem is influencing them and how they are influencing the problem "relative influence" inquiry:

> Relative influence questioning is comprised of two sets of questions. The first set encourages persons to map the influence of the problem in their lives and relationships. The second set encourages persons to map their own influence in the "life" of the problem. (p. 42)

When the partners are able to describe how the problem has been influencing them in ways that are harmful to their relationship, the therapist can begin to explore how each partner's thinking and behavior might be serving the problem—extending its life and power in their lives. By asking each partner, for instance, to consider how he or she might be inadvertently "helping the problem do its dirty work" (Zimmerman & Dickerson, 1996) or inviting them to explore how each of them might have been "recruited by the problem" (White & Epston, 1990), the therapist helps to create a climate in which the partners feel freer to consider and acknowledge ways they may be contributing to the problem, without having to accept blame. No one is forced to see him- or herself as the destructive cause of the marital trouble, which makes it easier for people to begin accepting responsibility and working collaboratively to create solution. The idea that the *bad story* narrative depicts an unalterable reality in which the couple is helpless fades, and is replaced by a sense of potential personal and shared efficacy in dealing with a malign or destructive force.

As any couples therapist knows, it can be quite hard—sometimes impossible—to engage couples successfully in solution-building conversations when the partners continually set each other off in the session, renewing their *bad stories*. Whatever steps the therapist takes to move the conversation beyond blaming, fault-finding, or withdrawal, the couple repeatedly returns to arguing over who is to blame for their troubles, who caused the last fight, what the facts of the matter are, and who needs to change. For many such couples, the *bad story* is so gripping that little change is possible without some shift in point of view. Externalizing conversation can gently lead such couples out of the *bad story* context and make it plausible for them to imagine—and feel in action—cooperation; this lays the general groundwork for them to begin developing mutualized solutions.

We might ask how the adversarial positions—the "need-to-win" impulses, for instance—are influencing the partners' perceptions of each other and their relationship, as well as their actions and reactions. "What does this need-to-win voice get each of you to do that is probably making it harder for you to solve the problems threatening your relationship?" Once the partners are talking in terms of how each is being influenced to behave in ways that are harmful or unproductive of understanding or intimacy etc., they can be asked if they would want to be doing things differently if they could. That is, if they felt they had a choice, would they want to think and act in ways that are not adversarial? These kinds of questions invite people to see themselves as capable of alternative, creative acts with positive implications for the relationship.

While we sometimes find value in reconstructing causal stories with clients when they repeatedly decline our invitations to enter into progressive, solution-oriented conversations, we rarely engage people in lengthy "recruitment" conversations or ask specifically how people are "being used by the problem to carry out its dirty work." Rather than using such inquiries to cultivate new, improved causal narratives to replace partners' blaming practices, we prefer to identify and magnify both partners' motivation to work collaboratively to make things different.[5] Once the couple begins talking about "the problem" as external to themselves, we can begin asking how they imagine they will be thinking and acting differently when they are gaining freedom from the influence of these practices and patterns.

We want to mention one very useful practice we have developed that externalizes problems and allows us, at the same time, to share information from John Gottman's research findings regarding what interpersonal processes support and hinder intimate relationships.[6] When a couple has been telling one of us about their problems and conflicts and repeatedly declines our invitations into solution talk, we often make the following intervention: "You know, as I've been listening to what each of you has been telling me, I keep thinking about something I read recently written by John Gottman. He's been studying married couples for many years trying to find out if there was anything he could observe about these couples that would predict which marriages would survive and which would end in separation and divorce. He's made some interesting discoveries. And he claims that he can now predict—with 94% accuracy!—which couples will make it and which won't, based on only a few observable patterns. Would you folks be interested in hearing what those patterns are?" Couples, of course, do not say no to this question; by now the partners are usually responding with considerable interest. We continue: "Well, this is how he summarizes it. Most couples fight—it's a natural and healthy part of marital life. So whether and how often a couple fights is not the main factor." (Note that this normalizes the fact that this couple fights a lot, easing any concern that their marriage is a failure because of this frequent conflict.) "What is more important—the key, according to Gottman, to what makes or breaks a marriage—is *how* those conflicts are resolved, especially whether the resolution leaves people feeling close, safe, and caring again. And no matter what style a couple has for dealing with conflict, couples who last have at least five times as many positive as negative moments together. This means that for every negative, painful comment, action, and encounter, each of you needs to experience five positive ones. So I'm wondering whether you think these findings and ideas might be useful to you in developing solutions? Do you think it would be helpful to take a look at your current ratio, as you see it, and figure out how to improve it? And figure out what the two of you need to do—and what you need each other to do—in order to improve this ratio for your relationship?" Again, when we ask couples these question, we invariably get enthusiastic affirmatives in reply. We've made the ratio the problem, not the partners and what they do or do not do. The issue becomes one of figuring out together what the couple has already done that works, and what they could agree to do in the future to influence the ratio positively.

Many kinds of externalizing and relative influence questions and interventions can be useful. Here are some examples of other kinds of relative influence and externalizing questions, mostly drawn from narrative therapy, that can help couples redefine their problems during problem-focused conversations:

- *How has this problem of differing sexual needs kept you from letting Dave know when you're feeling affectionate?*
- *How has this problem of fighting made you feel about yourself? And how do those feelings make it harder for you keep out of the conflicts?*
- *When this problem of divided loyalties first entered your lives how did you respond? How do you remember your partner responding? Looking back now, can you see ways that your responses might have unintentionally played into the hands of this destructive force?*
- *What are some of the ways you've been influenced by this problem of money chaos? How has your thinking (feeling, assumptions, attitudes, behaviors) been a reaction to its presence and influence?*
- *How has the problem of needing to be right used you—gotten each of you to do things that make it harder for you to work together?*
- *How does the problem get you to overlook the times your partner is trying to make things better between you, trying to restore the goodwill and love between you?*
- *How has the problem prevented you from staying in touch with the things about your partner that you liked when you first got together (decided to marry)? What are those things? Do you suppose if you could keep those things in mind it would make it easier for you to work to make things better?*
- *What helps you the most to keep the problem of your critical inner voice from getting you to do or say things that drive your partner away?*

- *Who would be the least surprised to find out about how the two of you are turning things around in your relationship? What do they know about you that would keep them from being surprised?*

The following dialogue is part of an interview in which Phil successfully used externalizing and relative influence questions. Jim and Linda were used to engaging in heated battles. In fact, both were highly successful litigation attorneys.[8] In the first few minutes of the first session they began arguing. As one would answer a question posed by Phil, the other would begin a challenging cross-examination. Immediately, shouting and name-calling would erupt. As the transcript reveals, Phil tried several times to acknowledge the feelings, experiences, and perspectives of each partner. But he could not engage the couple in solution-building conversations. Guided by the principle that you can't push a river, he chose instead to try to introduce some complexity and doubt into each partner's *bad story* narrative. This portion of the transcript begins after Phil has asked how he could help.

JIM: We could just start with the fight we had in the car on the way over here. That's as good a place as any, don't you think? Linda? (*Turns to her.*) Tell him what you said in the car. . . . Go ahead, you know, about this whole therapy thing being a waste of time. Go ahead. Maybe tell him the names you called me, too. (*Turns to Phil, waves his hand in Linda's direction without looking at her.*) She waits 'til we're coming here to tell me she really doesn't want to try therapy again. She thinks we should just get a divorce. So I don't really know why we even bothered to come.

LINDA: That's not what I said. Jesus, Jim you twist everything! I said I don't have much hope for therapy, and that if this doesn't help, I don't want to keep working on our marriage. And you *know* that's what I said. Why do you always put words in my mouth?

PHIL: You know, most couples come here feeling pretty much at the end of their rope. (*Normalizing.*) I get it that both of you are pretty upset with each other—from what just happened it looks like you both probably have a pretty short fuse these days. And I can understand both of you might have your doubts about whether therapy can make a difference. (*Acknowledging and validating.*) But I wonder if we could for the moment talk about how you both think I might be helpful to you. Maybe you could begin by telling me how that argument might go differently when things are better between you? (*Inviting conversation about goals and the future rather than asking about their feelings about the fight or the issues that led up to the fight.*)

LINDA: (*Ignoring Phil's questions, staring angrily at Jim.*) I can't stand the way you talk to me. You know, you really are a bastard. A total pig. Here

I am in a therapist's office, where we're supposed to be trying to do something about things, and you start right in by accusing me of stuff I never even said! This is why I don't see any point in this. You don't want to change, I don't know why I even get up any hope. You're just going to act reasonable and nice in front of the therapist the way you always do, but at home you're a complete jerk, you won't do it one iota differently. I just can't go through this anymore. (*She gathers her bag and sweater as though she's preparing to leave the session, but doesn't get up, though she's clearly very agitated and on the verge of leaving.*)

PHIL: Wow. I can see how upset you both are. Linda, it seems like you're pretty convinced nothing much can come from therapy at this point and maybe you'll turn out to be right. But hold on a minute. (*Linda sits still, waiting to see what Phil will say.*) Maybe, before you decide things are hopeless, I wonder if it would make sense to use this hour to see if we can begin turning things around just a little. What do you have to lose? (*Linda and Jim still look grim, but Linda puts her purse back down on the couch.*) Could we take a few minutes to figure out how these fighting patterns you're bringing with you got such a powerful grip on the two of you? (*"Fighting patterns"—the beginning of externalizing the problem. Phil has shifted away from working toward collaboration to engaging in problem talk with an externalizing intent. Both partners, looking a bit intrigued by what Phil just said, nod in assent*). Okay. I'd like to ask you both to think about how these battlefield scenes came to play such a powerful role in your marriage.

JIM: It's been like this a long time. Much, much too long, I think.

LINDA: Go to hell. It's always my fault, I suppose. It's never you, is it?

JIM: I didn't say it was all your fault. (*To Phil*) See what I mean? Did I say it was all her fault?

PHIL: Can you guys help me out here? Let's slow down a bit so we can figure out what we need to do so this session is useful to you. My guess is that you have fights like this a lot. I'm getting a pretty good sense of how unpleasant they are for both of you. I want to try and go in a different direction here to see if something better could happen for you both. So, Linda, I'd like to start with you—I'll ask Jim the same questions in a minute—tell me how these fighting patterns that have gotten a grip on you both get you to do stuff you might not otherwise want to do? (*Externalizing the problem again as "fighting patterns" that influence people. Phil is also starting to introduce relative influence.*)

LINDA: I never thought about it that way. I don't know. (*Phil waits.*) Well, I guess when I hear Jim say something I don't think is right I get pretty angry and want to set the record straight immediately. I can't stand the idea that he's going around thinking something happened a certain way when it didn't. When he says I did or said something I know I didn't, it just drives me nuts. It's so unfair, and there's no way to get him to see it any other way. (*Note the significance here of preferred-self material, which Phil chooses not to pursue at this point in favor of externalizing.*)

PHIL: Okay. So if I understand you, you're saying that the courtroom pattern can start up in you when you hear Jim say something that seems wrong to you or puts you in a bad light.

LINDA: Yes. Exactly.

PHIL: And then under the influence of this force you respond in ways that, if you were to step outside the situation and observe the interactions, might appear to be harmful to your relationship.

LINDA: Maybe so. Really I'm just trying to set the record straight. That's what I mean to do.

JIM: (*Breaks in.*) I would say the screaming and yelling, that's the problem, and Linda's constant criticism of me.

PHIL: Okay. So it seems like you could both agree that if the fighting was reduced, if the adversarial pattern wasn't affecting your marriage, that would be a sign of improvement. (*Clarifying a piece of the shared goal picture.*) Naturally, like most couples who come here, each of you has a different theory about why you're fighting. (*Normalizing.*) But I keep wondering how *fighting* has managed to work its way into your lives and how it's been so successful in driving a wedge between the two of you. (*Externalizing.*) Turning people who once fell in love and chose to make a life and raise a family together into enemies. It sounds as if the fighting stuff comes into your marriage and works you both over and makes each of you do and say things you wouldn't otherwise do or say. (*Developing relative influence perspective.*) How do you suppose it gets each of you to do its dirty work, so to speak, making you enemies?

JIM: Well, that's not the way I think of it, but the constant fighting makes me not like Linda. Sometimes it even makes me want to hurt her. I'm sure I wouldn't say some of the things I do if we weren't fighting.

PHIL: So "fighting" gets you to say and do things that hurt Linda.

JIM: Yeah, I'd have to say that's true.

PHIL: If you felt you had a choice, would you want to find ways the fighting wouldn't have so much power over you? So that even when Linda did or said something you didn't like, you wouldn't do things that cause her pain?

JIM: Well, sure. But she's got to work at it too.

At this point, Jim is moving toward a customer/consultant conversation, just as Linda did earlier in the conversation. Although the couple kept sliding back into the *bad story*, as the session developed the focus shifted toward building partnership around dealing with the fighting problem, and exits to the problem narrative became easier to find. Phil proceeded by expanding this line of inquiry with them, asking them how fighting prompted them to do and say things they might otherwise not want to do or say. Once both partners were able to talk about how anger and fighting (now the external problem) got them to do things that hurt their relationship, a foundation of partnership in viewing the problem and its effects was laid. Phil next asked them about times when they were able to influence the fighting problem in positive ways, bringing fights to an early close or avoiding them. This kind of conversation is a rich source of potential exits from the *bad story*. Continued therapy with this couple, which lasted for close to a year, was marked by arguments and uproar during and between sessions, with periods of progress and setbacks. At a certain point, however, a noticeable shift took place. Although they continued to argue a good deal, there was a visible softening in the way they related, and their fights became less painful. They reported that both they and their friends noticed a sense of connection and warmth between them—evidence of partnership. When they left therapy, they agreed that the need on both their parts to "be right" was something they would always have to keep an eye on together. But they felt confident they could now do this most of the time and that they were on the right path together.

## Coping Questions

Coping questions, an interviewing technique we have adopted from solution-focused brief therapy (Berg, 1994; De Jong & Berg, 1998) are another way of reframing problem situations. "Coping questions are a form of solution talk that has been tailored so as to make sense to clients who are feeling overwhelmed" (De Jong & Berg, 1998, p. 173). Coping questions both validate the partners' experiences and perceptions (building rapport by conveying understanding and respect) and simultaneously convey that, since the situation could be worse, the couple has been using some strength or resource that has been making a difference (opening an exit from the *bad story*). When a clinician asks a couple, "How are you managing to cope with this situation, given all the difficulties you've been facing?" she is letting them know not only that she understands how bad things seem, but also that she notices something else—something they have not been paying attention to—that is also implied by their *bad story* narrative. Why, she wonders aloud, are things not even worse? More specifically, what are the partners doing, thinking, and feeling that has helped them to cope?

As the partners reflect on these questions, they begin to see their situation in new ways, ways that point toward assets and competencies and could lead toward their *good story* narrative. Thus, coping questions function as an effective way to develop an exit from the *bad story* by identifying (constructing) a fragment of the *good story*. They loosen the hold of a *bad story* narrative, especially when people present with multiple, entrenched, and

seemingly overwhelming problems, while still conveying respect and concern for people's current sense of futility. The therapist should not ask
coping questions in a way that downplays the couple's pain or suggests they
need to "look on the bright side." She's not implying: "Hey look, things
could be worse." Instead, it is a matter of expressing curiosity about small
but very generative details that hint at desirable human qualities—usually
forms of persistence and courage in the face of adversity.

Consider this example. A husband and wife have given the therapist a
long list of complaints and examples of seemingly insoluble and painful
problems. They have serious financial difficulties. The husband's teenage
son (the wife's stepson) has been using drugs and was recently arrested for
malicious mischief and suspended from school. They have frequent arguments about how to handle parenting. The husband accuses the wife of
having a drinking problem, and they both say they are having a hard
time liking each other these days. Each accuses the other of being abusive
whenever they try to deal with any contentious issue. When they give their
respective histories, the husband says he grew up in an alcoholic household
with a physically abusive father, and he believes that's why he ended up
with an alcoholic partner who refuses to "work with me on anything."
The wife reports that she grew up with a neglectful and preoccupied single
mother, and although she has worked on various issues in individual therapy,
she remains unable to shake loose the feeling that life is dangerous and
relationships are unreliable. The couple has separated several times, and
though they want to stay together, they are always on the verge of the next
walk-out. Whenever the therapist tries to engage them in dialogue that
might tease out pieces of a shared *good story* or highlight a success, exception,
or competency, the couple launches into another intense and protracted
argument, and the sense of pain and desperation in the room is palpable.

A therapist might introduce and ask a coping question like this (notice
the numerous overt and covert compliments embedded in these comments):
"Wow, I can tell from what you've both been telling me that things have
really been hard, pretty overwhelming, for some time. There's an awful lot
of stuff going on that's difficult and painful enough to make anyone want
to throw in the towel. But in listening to both of you, I've been wondering
something. As bad as things have been, both of you keep trying to make
things better and looking for ways to make a go of your marriage and keep
your family together. Given all you've been telling me about how things
have been in your lives, I'm wondering how you've managed to cope and
keep your family going through some pretty hard times?"

The therapist expresses that she sees this couple's ability to cope and
keep striving as a sign of strength. The fact that they are coping, especially
given how difficult they say things have been, is framed as commendable
and as a sign that the partners have certain resources and strengths that have

helped them survive as a couple. Further inquiry will produce (construct) the details of their coping strategies, which constitute *bad story* exit points. In this case, the husband explained that he coped by telling himself he'd be a better father, no matter what, than his own; the wife talked about remembering that things felt worse when they were apart than when they were together. The therapist's coping inquiries brought out positive strategies, assets, and helpful perspectives particular to this couple that would be detailed and fleshed out in further conversation.

In summary, while RPT is a solution-oriented approach, we recognize that there are often times we must be willing to accept clients' invitations into problem-focused conversation. We do not want to be solution-forced or appear dismissive of people's concerns, feelings, and experiences (Nyland & Corsiglia, 1994)—flexibility and sensitivity are essential qualities of an effective couples therapist. However, when we engage in problem talk in RPT, we want to do so in ways that can make a difference and serve therapeutic ends. We work within couples' problem-saturated narratives looking for exits into more satisfying and potentially useful ones; thus, problem-focused conversations are always transitional, bridging from the couple's *bad stories* to their shared *good story* narratives.

# Co-Constructing Therapeutically Well-Defined Goals: Targets and Transformation

We are convinced that the project of therapy will be more effective, efficient, and articulate if the couple and therapist establish the goals of their enterprise early on. Early outcome definition is important to the work of therapy because it orients all the participants in the therapeutic process, provides purpose and direction, and lets everyone know when and if therapy has been successful. When conducted without clearly defined outcomes, therapy becomes a series of meetings in which couples report examples of their troubles and/or replay their recent disagreements without much direction or change, which leaves both the couple and therapist discouraged and frustrated. On the other hand, when a couple comes in reporting improvements, neither the couple nor the therapist may know exactly what to do or talk about. Both the couple and the therapist may view the good week as "uneventful" in terms of therapy, as though the only events worth attending to are problematic. This means that the positive happenings (important signs of the *good story's* influence and vigor), while warmly received, remain uninvestigated, and eventually one member of the couple will bring up some "little" problem or the therapist will ask a few probing questions that lead back into *bad story* territory.

Though we do not define ourselves as brief therapists, we take a cue from them about the importance of having clear, well-defined goals for treatment. In almost all cases, during the first session we engage the partners in a process of mutual goal-building that establishes what will be different, and what will be happening, when they can say they got what they came for and are ready to say good-bye. We call this function of goal-building *establishing the target,* a function graphically articulated by brief therapist Michael Hoyt (2000) with this golfing metaphor: "It's a long day on the course if you don't know where the hole is" (p. 6).

In RPT, however, the conversational process of goal-building is more than simply a means for developing a set of outcomes for therapy. A second function, the *narrative function,* is equally important in furthering the therapeutic enterprise. Engaging with partners about their goals and guiding them in talking to each other about how they want things to be different in the future is itself transformative (Walter & Peller, 2000). Positive change happens during goal-constructing conversations as people begin to see each other and their problems in new ways. They begin to realize that they possess strengths and resources that have been unrecognized and underutilized, and these realizations create new possibilities. In short, in their narrative function, goal-building conversations reinvigorate the couple's *good story* narrative. Thus, in these kinds of conversation we have a dual purpose: to generate specific targets and outcomes for therapy and to influence the perceptual and interpretive lenses through which the partners view each other, their actions, and their life together. These two functions are interrelated. When hosting goal-building conversations to establish therapeutic outcomes (target function), RPT therapists are also participating in a process of narrative revision. Keeping the criteria for therapeutically well-defined goals (goals that are "well-formed" in therapeutic terms) in mind during these conversations is the key to fulfilling both functions. All the criteria of well-formed goals serve to move the conversation toward a consideration of desired, realistic, and tailor-made outcomes and narratives that free up the couple's creativity for positive change and solution. Goal building, properly conducted, helps clients and therapists make use of a constructive optimism. When the therapist is attentive to fulfilling the specific criteria, the conversation will naturally tend to generate hope and energy for a newly-envisioned and satisfying future.

## Criteria for Therapeutically Well-formed Goals

Let's start with de Shazer's (1991) definition of well-formed goals:

[T]hey are small rather than large; salient to the clients; articulated in specific, concrete behavioral terms; achievable within the practical contexts of clients' lives; perceived by clients as involving their own hard work; seen as the "start of something" and not as the "end of something"; and treated as involving new behavior rather than the absence or cessation of existing behavior. (p. 112)

Cast in RPT terms, the purpose of goal construction is to develop a set of experiential signs characterizing each partner's model of the *good story* narrative. In articulating a grouping of such signs, goal-building defines outcomes that (1) all parties recognize as valid and mutually desirable, and (2) are therapeutically utilitarian. Thus, the therapist will know where to go next in terms of inquiry, how to formulate helpful questions, and what will move the dialogue toward a context supportive of partnership. The following list identifies the criteria for developing well-formed therapy goals.

### 1. The goals must be salient to both partners individually and as a couple.

Perhaps the most important characteristic of well-defined therapeutic goals in couples therapy is that they speak to the relationship desires and concerns of both partners. The phenomenological signs that things are getting better must detail a *good story* narrative that both partners can recognize as in some way their own. Goal development is an initial and pivotal step in recreating partnership. Discovering and articulating a future picture they both want can give partners a feeling of sharing they may not have experienced in a long time. By giving space and time to the discussion of what is meaningful to each individual—and why and how certain changes would make a difference—the therapist can help them develop empathy, exit their *bad story* narratives, and, crucially, begin to see how some of their individual desires or needs, which may have seemed at odds with those of the other partner, can lead toward a commonly desired future.

It is important to note that while the partners' goals cannot be mutually exclusive, each individual can have differing perspectives and highlight or "see" different pieces of the outcome scenarios. Sometimes, each partner's version of the *good story* is markedly different from the other's, but a bridge between the two can be built by finding commonly desired experiences (such as collaborating around helping their kids with homework, spending time together in fun pursuits, or supporting each other in enjoying individual interests and hobbies). Often, individuals with different pictures can begin to see the meaning and significance of their partner's picture as well as how their two pictures may be related. This new understanding helps to create a shared commitment to work for aspects of both goals, which in turn enlarges the common ground.

Envisioning a compelling future picture has strong emotional resonance. Goal development is often an emotionally moving process, eliciting feelings of closeness, vulnerability, and tenderness between the partners in a couple, even when there has been a lot of conflict or disaffection. It is frequently during the exploration of the meanings of these future pictures that the partners experience the first stirrings of hope and renewed feelings of openness toward each other. Obviously, the feeling that they are undergoing discoveries that will make a significant, emotionally satisfying difference in their lives helps to engage people fully in a therapeutic process and increases the likelihood that they will utilize their creative resources fully.

## 2. Goals must be stated in positive terms.

When we first ask couples about their goals they often begin by telling us what is wrong with their relationships and/or their partners. They seem to be experts mainly on what they don't want and what they don't like. And, typically, when we ask the individual partners what the first signs that things are getting better will be, they describe activities or experiences they hope will end or occur less often: "He won't be watching as much TV"; "He won't interrupt me all the time"; "She won't yell at the kids so much"; "She won't act like she's bored when we're spending time together." We want to invite people to reframe negatives like these (the "absence of" pictures, still focused on the *bad story*) into descriptions of what will be happening *instead* that will feel more satisfying and signify positive changes (the "presence of" pictures, evidence of the *good story*). In other words, what do the partners want *more* of rather than *less* of? This is a productive framing of change because it lays the groundwork for the altering of perceptions and selection of evidence. Because we want people to refocus their attention on happenings that match their *good stories,* we want them to define goals in terms that prompt them to look for bits and pieces of the *good story* narrative, rather than watch for the elimination of some element of the *bad story.*

We often invite clients to redefine negatives, to turn them into signifiers of positive change, simply by asking an "instead" question: "When your wife isn't always worrying about work in the evening, what will she be doing instead?" We are moving toward well-defined goals if the husband responds with, "Oh, she'll come and ask me to go for a walk with her a couple evenings a week." It will be easier for this husband to notice and give significance to his wife's invitations to go for a walk than to notice that she is worrying less about work in the evening. (And, of course, it is possible she might take these actions without putting aside some evening attention to work.) By framing this goal in a positive form we highlight meanings and desires—meanings particular to him and his needs and daily life. If we asked him how it would make a difference for him if she were to pay less attention to work in the evenings and go out for more walks with him, he might tell us that these would be signs that she's interested in him, enjoys doing things with him, wants closeness, etc. He is more likely to feel satisfied in these needs if she asks him to go for walks than if he monitors her evening preoccupations with work to see if she's thinking and talking about it less. In addition, when and if the wife does these things, she will experience herself taking active steps to rebuild their *good story* narrative as he has begun to articulate it, rather than steps to erase (and validate) his *bad story* picture of her. Thus, each partner can experience a preferred self sense (loved in his case, responsive in hers) in this kind of positive scenario. For both partners, these positive signs and signals are building blocks of the potential *good story* narrative as it is embodied in the husband's goal picture.

### 3. Goals should be stated as concrete, observable behaviors rather than feelings, moods, or attitudes.

Goals, in this context, are outward measures; when they are happening others will see observable signs, and it is the signs that are the goals *because they signify the desired shift in meaning.* This does not mean we discourage conversation about feelings, moods, and attitudes in goal conversations. Many goals are initially stated in these terms, and what people have to say about their needs, wishes, and desires is quite important to the project of therapy. However, we must help people to convert inner experience into signals, cues, and signs that can be observed so that both the individual and the partner have a handle on what change is occurring and how it will be expressed and where it will be seen in relational life. These conversations, in which people articulate the observable signs of a feeling, mood, or attitude change, often highlight personal and relational meanings that have gone undiscovered or unformulated; such discoveries create important empathic connections between partners and simultaneously serve to transform the narrative. Even when people do not talk about meaning or their attitudes and formulations, the way these observable signs are coauthored in the collaborative dialogue between therapist and clients naturally takes account of feelings, cognitions, and desires, which do not necessarily have to be made explicit.

We assume that people seeking therapy have the power and resources to change at least some things for the better, but that what they want may not always be completely clear to them. It is our job to guide conversation so that clients can clarify the changes they want and become able to identify and utilize competencies they already possess to make those changes happen. So we are talking about defining *happenings*. These happenings can then be defined in ways that serve therapeutic ends. Bill O'Hanlon (Hudson & O'Hanlon, 1992; O'Hanlon & Weiner-Davis, 1989) uses the term *video talk* to convey that the client's goals should be framed as happenings that both the client and others could observe—what will people, especially the client, be saying and doing when things are different and better and his goals are achieved (i.e., when he is feeling more the way he wants to feel)? For instance, suppose a husband tells us that because of his wife's affair he no longer trusts her, and that his goal is to be able to trust her again. This goal formulation, while meaningful to him, must be concretized before it will be therapeutically useful. We need some way of determining what observable changes in his behavior will tell him, his wife, and us that he trusts her sufficiently to say this is no longer a problem. We might ask him questions like: "What will your wife (your kids, friends, I) notice different about you that shows you're feeling more trusting toward your wife?" As he identifies these observable signs of his emerging state of trustfulness, they create a pathway toward change. Because behavior, perception, and meaning-making form a loop, defining these behavioral signifiers opens the doors of perception to change. This husband might identify the following signs: "I'll be laughing wholeheartedly at her jokes instead of frowning and wondering if she's making fun of me." "I'll go off and do my own thing when she goes out rather than waiting at home for her, worrying about where she is and when she's coming back." "I'll let her know, spontaneously, when I first see her at night, how glad I am to see her instead of waiting for her to go first." As we continue the conversation with them, we can ask what the wife will be doing in these video scenes that interacts with (and thickens) this experience of increased trustfulness.

This imagining of an outcome picture carries with it a whiff of the accomplished (the narrative-transforming function in play). The mystery of "how" has already been solved, and that shaping of the future reorganizes present behavior to trend toward it. The concretized description of the future helps him, his wife, and us to identify ways and means toward that state. The very seeing of it as a possibility helps to mobilize both partners' hopes and new behaviors, perceptions, and attitudes.[1]

Goals must be concrete. Suppose a wife tells us her goal is "better communication" with her husband. This goal is too vague for us to know precisely what she means. "Better communication" is what we call a "suitcase term"—until it is "unpacked" and the contents laid out and identified, it tells us very little that is therapeutically useful about what she really wants. We can ask her to tell us exactly what she and others will notice that tells her and every one else that the conditions of better communication are met. From this starting point, we might ask what her husband or her children will notice is different about her when she and her husband are "communicating better." This leads us to the next criterion.

### 4. Goals must be stated in terms of an interpersonal framework.

When we explore the interpersonal framework of goals (Hoyt, in press; Walter & Peller, 1992), we clarify and amplify with each partner what others—spouse, children, other family members, friends—will notice that is different when their goals are achieved. In the example above (about the wife who wants better communication), the therapist helps her flesh out the variety and richness of the details of her goal of "better communication" by asking her to imagine herself in her preferred situation and see the scene through the eyes of others.[2] In addition, asking her to imagine the impact these changes will have on others adds more to the perspectival complexity of her preferred narrative.

Suppose she tells us her husband will see her being calm when they discuss the children's school situation and homework. We will ask what exactly he would see that tells him she is calm. The details are what we're after. She might reply that he would see her smiling, that her tone would be warm and relaxed, indicating her confidence that they both felt the dialogue was important, and that she would listen with interest to what he had to say. Her children, she says, would notice their mom and dad being nice to each other at the dinner table. "What will they see different that tells them this?" we might ask. While being very concrete about the specific details of change, inviting her to imagine observable gestures and actions, we are casting these details in terms of relationship. "They'd see us laughing, joking back and forth, the way we used to do, listening to each other. Being affectionate." This highlighting of behaviors that can be seen and noticed ("symptoms of happiness," you might call them) that tell her and others she is living in her *good story* goal picture puts in motion a possibility for these changes to "happen." They are being made real in the conversation itself.

### 5. Goals should be broken down into small steps: change as process rather than event.

Goals that are initially stated in terms of global pictures requiring sweeping changes (again, suitcase words or phrases like "happier," "closer," "having more fun," "being more cooperative," "being more thoughtful," etc.) are often divisive or difficult to achieve; they should be revised collaboratively into smaller, step-by-step pieces. Frequently couples come for counseling hoping therapy will erase their problems. After what has usually been a long-term struggle with what is troubling them, people want an end to the distress and frustration. Consequently, people may state as their goal the complete removal of the painful problem, condition, or conflict. This type of all-or-nothing mindset, however, leaves no room for incremental changes or the natural ups and downs that may occur. Global expectations can make it difficult for people to see the small signs that indicate an entrance into or a thickening of the *good story* narrative. One important way to begin the process of influencing the perceptual and interpretive lenses through which the partners view their relationship encounters is by helping them shift from either/or thinking to both/and thinking (Lipchick & Kubicki, 1996). In other words, we want people to begin thinking about their goals not in terms of desired events or fixed conditions, but in terms of positively evolving processes (Walter & Peller, 1992), so they can start to be on the lookout for signs of change. For example, the goal of "making a decision" is broken down to "taking the first steps to deciding"; "having good communication" becomes "improving communication."

To accomplish this, we help people re-vision problems, solutions, and goals along a continuum. This entails identifying what small changes will signify step-by-step movement along a pathway toward the goal. We ask questions that encourage people to imagine small, concrete shifts that can serve as signs that they are moving from the problem picture at its worst toward the solution picture at its best and most realistic. To encourage the framing of goals in terms of a trend rather than a complete switch from one state to another, we often ask the partners to imagine and describe "the first small steps" that will mean progress is happening.

### 6. The goals must be achievable by the partners.

Some couples come to therapy wanting unrealistic changes or assuming that therapy can magically solve an intractable problem. In such cases we may want to explore what gives people reason to believe such changes can happen, in or out of therapy. For example, suppose a wife wants a baby with her husband, who has two children from a prior marriage. When married before, he had a vasectomy and does not want to have it reversed. He says he has already raised two children and isn't interested in having any more. The wife's goal is obviously to change her husband's mind. But if he is unwilling to change, unless the wife can be helped to develop goals other than convincing her husband to reverse his vasectomy, there is little likelihood therapy will be beneficial for her. Similarly, the goal he brings to therapy may be to change her mind, and if she is unwilling to give up the desire and intention to have a child, the therapy may not offer a way to achieve his goal either. It is possible this couple's goals could be refashioned into therapeutically well-formed ones, but given their present form, it would be a mistake for the therapist to agree to help the couple achieve them. As both partners come to recognize that their goals, as presently defined, are, by their own admission, unlikely to come about (either in or outside therapy), we can begin exploring what related or overarching goals might be attainable instead.

Therapists faced with client goals that seem unachievable by client effort and/or through therapy may find it helpful to view such goals as the client's current means to an as yet undefined end or meta-goal hidden behind the initial statements of wants and desires (Walter & Peller, 2000). *Meta-goal* has a rather dry sound, but it points to a profoundly important area of meaning and emotion for people, where strong and lifelong yearnings often float unarticulated within the client's currently stated desires or goals. When explored, these ends (the meta-goals) embedded in a client's particularized goals reveal significant and emotionally resonant desires or needs that have become associated, for this client, with the one imagined outcome he or she has presented. As the client is helped to clarify these core desires it becomes possible for him or her to conceive of multiple means for satisfying them. Thus, meta-goals are, in a sense, the ends surrounding or embracing the client's initially stated goals—pictures of self, other, and relationship that have central and driving meanings in people's lives. When this is kept in mind, the therapist can see client goals that are initially presented in overspecified ways as means to "larger," more inclusive goal pictures not yet explored or discovered.

For example, suppose a wife wants her husband to attend AA meetings; he adamantly refuses. She says her husband is alcoholic and, unless he stops drinking, their marriage will not improve. Achievement of the changes she desires is not within her control. However, we assume this specific goal reflects other unarticulated but meaningful changes that might be important to her. As we explore with her how her husband's going to AA and becoming clean and sober will make a difference to her, we learn (and she may be articulating this for the first time) that her larger goal—which will be reflected in her husband making these changes—is to feel that her husband "really cares about the marriage," that he's "really serious about getting his life back on track," and that she can "count on him in the future." So, while it is possible her husband might not be willing (or at least not yet willing) to do the things she wants, he might be willing to do other things she identifies that would tell her that he "really cares about the marriage," "that he's really serious about getting his life on track" and that she could "count on him in the future."[3]

## 7. Goals developed at the beginning of therapy evolve throughout the life of the therapeutic enterprise.

Change is constant and ubiquitous in human life. People daily undergo alterations in mood, circumstances, conditions, attitude, etc., and all of us meet challenges and solve problems constantly. What people want and intend also undergo constant readjustment and evolution. Goal development in the form of generating desirable future pictures makes use of this universal experience of constant change and creative adjustment. When asking couples about outcome pictures (detailed future scenarios of solution and success), we are not seeking descriptions of static, singular states or conditions; we participate in the coauthoring of numerous, interwoven scenes of satisfying, desirable future encounters that will become part of their ongoing narrative (Walter & Peller, 2000). Throughout therapy, the clinician must keep abreast of the evolving nature of these pictures, making use of the natural capacity people have to see things in new ways and continually re-vision and refashion their lives together. Goal definition begins early in therapy and it continues, in one form or another, throughout the entire therapeutic enterprise.

The very process of goal clarification generates a flow of imagination and creativity that affects the way people think about what they want. New perceptions and behaviors, as well as a growing sense of partnership as people work together on future pictures of success, bring about new experiences, intentions, confidence—and these in turn produce new picturings of how things are and could be. Goal definitions are built piece by piece, in the flow of dialogue. From week to week in therapy—or sometimes in the same hour—people can change their ideas about where they are going. De Shazer (1994) puts it this way: "Whether clients can know what they wish for before their wish is fulfilled cannot be known. . . . For therapists to expect clients to know at the beginning of therapy exactly where they want to go is unrealistic; if they did, they probably would not need therapy" (p. 273).

## Hosting Goal-Building Conversations

Goal-building is collaborative and client-centered. In our goal-building interviews, we ask questions that invite the partners to move into their *good story* frame. Then we begin, collaboratively, to fill in the details. Together we explore, test, revise, and amplify each partner's future picture until it takes on form and credibility and meets the test of being therapeutically well-formed. These pictures of how things will be different when couples are living in a more satisfying way—where experiences other than those related to the problem are prominent in their lives—are the framework into which we fit the various specific experiential pieces. As people imagine and fill out the details of their *good story* narrative, they are already beginning to live with the meanings and behaviors that can contribute to its invigoration (the narrative-transforming function of goal-building). During this conversational process, the therapist's role is to conduct helpful inquiry and give responsive feedback within the framework of the clients' concerns, ideas, theories, intentions, and desires. We like what Duncan and Miller (2000) say about this kind of process in *The Heroic Client,* when they explain that the questions they ask clients:

> impose minimal therapist content and allow maximum space for the client to find new connections, distinctions and meanings. Questions are not designed to influence particular meanings or other theory-based realities, but rather to invite the client's reactions to and descriptions of the concerns that initiated therapy. A candid exchange evolves, resulting in a collaborative formulation of what will be addressed, criteria for successful resolution, and how therapy will proceed. (pp. 150–151)

It can be all too easy to overlook some aspects of collaboration. In the following example, under the influence of his initial enthusiasm for solution-oriented work, Phil forgot to attend to the clients' theory of change. This couple, Helen and Louis, had lived together for 15 years. Helen opened by saying that Louis was a "rage-aholic" and that she didn't know if she could continue to live with him. Louis admitted he was a moody person but said their troubles were due to a combination of his own "biochemical imbalance" and Helen's perpetual complaining and criticizing. They were agreed in describing their fights as quite abusive and violent, but said they didn't know how to stop them and were at their wits' end. They had seen several couples therapists in the past, but to no avail. They were convinced that any solution would involve hard work and struggle.

Phil, flushed with his recent (and rapid) successes, failed to acknowledge the importance of what this couple was saying—that their problem was difficult, long-standing, and complex, and that solving it would be a huge challenge for them and for any therapist working with them. Rather than validating and honoring what they were saying and using this as a basis for talking together about the hard work any changes would require, collaborating with their theory of change he said, "Well, you know, it might be easier than you think to make the changes you want. After all, sometimes, in the right situation, couples can turn things around in a flash." This misguided effort to instill hope invited the following exchange:

HELEN: Are you talking about an epiphany?

PHIL: Well, I guess you could say that.

HELEN: Epiphanies happen when someone is about to die.

PHIL: (*Somewhat nonplussed*) Well, I didn't know that. I thought it just meant a change that took place in the blink of an eye.

LOUIS: Well, Helen is right. The original Greek word referred to realizations that came at the moment of death. (*Sarcastically*) I'm not sure that's what we want.

HELEN: (*To Phil*) I can't believe you're suggesting such a thing.

PHIL: (*Now completely at a loss.*) Of course not, I was only trying to suggest that we might be able to turn things around more quickly than you think, even though the problems have been around for so long and have caused you both so much grief.

HELEN: I can't imagine how you could think that. We've been to four different therapists, and nothing has helped.

LOUIS: (*At least they are on the same side for the moment.*) I completely agree with Helen. Suggesting that things could change fast in our case, especially before we've had a chance to describe just how bad things are, seems pretty damned insensitive.

PHIL: Well, you're right about that. I apologize. I meant to say that in some cases things can shift fairly quickly, but it sounds like in your case we're facing a difficult challenge you've worked on a lot before, and it would take a lot of hard work (*trying to recoup*). But I'm willing to do what I can to help you two turn things around.

At the end of the hour, Phil asked if they would like to make another appointment and was rather surprised when they agreed to come again. The following day, however, he received a voicemail message from the husband saying he and his wife wanted to check out a few other therapists before making a final choice. Phil never heard from them again.

In RPT, goals are drawn out through a process of inquiry and negotiation in which the couple and therapist together build a credible version of the couple's desired future. But how does the clinician know whether or not he is on track in guiding this collaborative process? How can he be sure that he is effectively balancing respect and consideration for the clients' perspectives and theories while also orienting the process toward the evolution of goal definitions that aid the therapy enterprise? His continuing attention to whether the emerging goal pictures meet the criteria of being therapeutically well-formed guides him from moment to moment in knowing what questions to ask and how and when to ask them in order to bring forth the unique experiences, histories, talents, models, and theories of change of each couple (De Jong & Berg, 1998; de Shazer, 1991; Walter & Peller, 1992).

A principal tool for hosting goal-building conversations in RPT is the preferred-future-picture or outcome question.[4] These questions clarify a future *good story* picture by focusing on what will be different when the problems the couple brings to therapy are a thing of the past, or the couple feels they are making some progress in putting the problems behind them. In order to answer our questions and imagine these preferred experiential scenarios, each partner must construct mental images that may include some reference to past desirable experiences or may be entirely imagined. In either case, as the partners develop these scenarios and talk with us about them in each other's presence, we are moving into the territory of the *good story* narrative.

As the partners answer goal-building questions, the therapist continues to ask herself what elements and aspects of well-formedness have yet to be fleshed out or built into the goal definitions. If the current goal is general, questions are asked to make it more specific. If the goal is stated in terms of what won't be happening, the therapist asks what will be happening instead. If it is stated as an unchanging condition or an end state, she asks about what might be the first step or sign. In this way, every answer by the client invites another specific question that can move the goal definition toward meeting all the criteria and, as goals become well-formed and outcome targets for therapy, the conversation serves as a means of transforming the predominant narrative that is shaping the couple's perceptions and interpretations.

Following are some general examples of questions we typically ask in beginning the process of co-constructing outcome pictures:

- *What will be the first things each of you will notice that will tell you that you're on track to solving this problem?*
- *When we've been meeting for a while and we solve this problem and you're ready to end therapy, what will be different?*
- *If I had a video camera and followed the two of you around when things are more the way you want them to be, what will I see and hear that tells me you've solved this problem?*

Once the partners begin answering our initial questions, we follow up with amplifying questions (De Jong & Berg, 1998). Amplifying questions give detail and life to the meanings inherent in goals. They make scenarios out of summaries. The simplest and often most effective amplifying question is "What else?": "What else will you notice?" "What else will be different?" "What else will your children notice?" "What else will tell you that . . . ?"

All of these goal-building questions and conversations are based on the working assumption that each partner has unformed but potentially mean-ingful images of how they would like their relationship life to be different. The process of fleshing out these images influences the partners' thinking and perceptions, encouraging hopefulness, agency, and mutuality. In the ongoing give and take between the therapist and each partner, the couple become less bound by their antagonistic points of view, theories, and formu-lations and begin embracing pictures of self, other, and relationship that can promote a renewed sense of working shoulder-to-shoulder on a shared vision.

In goal-building dialogues, people often hear themselves or their partners saying things they have never said, thought, or heard before. This is because, in order to answer the questions we put to them, they must think in unfamiliar ways, imagining possibilities not considered before. This is a central reason for pressing people to meet the criteria for well-formed goals. For example, simply asking someone to convert an "absence of" wish into a "presence of" statement often produces a new perspective for both partners, speaker and listener. Asking what a partner "will be doing instead" alters both partners' perceptions of possibility. The proof that this can be a powerful tool for altering perceptions is the fact that many people answer such questions initially by saying either, "I don't know; I need to think about that" or "That's a good question."

Well-conducted goal-developing conversations give the therapist a clear sense of her role in the therapy hour. If you are concentrating on the criteria for well-formed goals and on fleshing out outcome pictures that meet these criteria, you will be helping your clients to move immediately toward solution, clarity, and partnership, when that is possible. Instead of casting about in an improvisational manner for how to conduct a helpful session on the theory that all roads lead to Rome, the clinician can use this form of inquiry and set of questions to guide her and the couple toward a successful conclusion of the therapeutic enterprise while refreshing the positive narrative.

## The Miracle Question

The miracle question, developed by Insoo Kim Berg and Steve de Shazer, is the basic interviewing technique used in solution-focused brief therapy for initiating goal-building conversations. Here is one formulation:

> Now I want to ask you a strange question. Suppose that tonight after the two of you go home, have dinner and go to sleep, a miracle happens. The miracle is this—the problems which brought you here today are solved. However, because you're asleep, you don't know a miracle has happened. When you wake up tomorrow morning, the day after the miracle, what will be the first things you'll notice that will tell you the miracle has happened and the problems which brought you here are solved? (de Shazer, 1988, p. 5)

The miracle question is a very effective intervention because it accomplishes a number of important things all at once. The question disconnects people from a focus on the problem and redirects attention to their solutions—from what's wrong to how they would prefer things to be in the future. By asking people to imagine how things will be different when the problem is solved without regard to *how* it was solved, the miracle question requires them to temporarily set aside their theories about who or what needs to change. Because the question talks about miracles or wild possibilities, it gives people permission to set aside the constraints of their current formulations of experience and the limits of reason so they can tap their creative imaginations. It fulfills the narrative function of good goal-building by moving the focus to one end of the storying continuum. And the miracle question blends both the end-point question and the first-sign-of-change question in one intervention, providing a starting point for developing the details of this miracle picture through amplifying questions.

For instance, as a wife begins to describe her post-miracle morning, we can ask questions that flesh out and amplify her goal picture. What will be the *first thing* she notices that's different—about herself, about her husband? What does she imagine is the first thing he will notice is different the morning after the miracle (about himself, about her, about what's happening between them)? What will the kids notice that's different when they see their folks? As the day proceeds, what signs will tell her things are different, and later, after both she and her husband come home from work, what will they both notice that will tell them things are different, that their problems have been solved? The more imaginally vivid this post–miracle day becomes, the more possible perceptual and behavioral change becomes for both partners. All these details become fleshed-out bits and pieces of the *good story*; then, when people experience them happening in their post-session daily life, they identify them as evidence that things are getting better.

It should be pointed out that this question has nothing to do with miracles or magic. The miracle question is simply a clinical device that leaps the fence of the present problem into a future of solution by positing a "miracle," an unexplained transformative event that has already happened. It thus begins a generative imaginative process between the therapist and the partners that leads to the development of a list of therapeutically well-defined goals, while clarifying the first signs of progress. As de Shazer (1994) points out:

> The miracle question was not designed to create or prompt miracles. All the miracle question is designed to do is to allow clients to describe what it is they want out of therapy without having to concern them-selves with the problem and the traditional assumption that the solution is somehow connected with understanding and eliminating the prob-lem. (p. 273)

We want to end this discussion of goal-building with the following transcripts of portions of two initial sessions. These transcripts demonstrate goal development and give a sense of the unfolding, constructive nature of conversations concerning future pictures. We want to emphasize, in present-ing these two cases, that while the development of goals and future pictures are always the first order of business, the route must vary with individual cases. Goal-building does not consist of asking a few simple questions in a recipe-like fashion, and goal-building interviews cannot be successfully car-ried out in a formulaic way. How the partners answer each question deter-mines what question the therapist will ask next; the process evolves moment by moment. Using this form of inquiry takes practice; an interview that flows well rests on the therapist's understanding of the assumptions and tools we have been discussing.

The first case is a good example of how the therapist orients the conversa-tion so that it serves both to clarify what specific behavioral changes will make a difference to both parties and as a context in which the couple recreate partnership. Both June and Carl have been telling Phil how each wants the other to change. Phil, hoping to engage the partners in *customer/ consultant* conversation, begins asking goal-development questions.

PHIL: So, June, can you tell me what you'll notice different about Carl when the two of you have turned your relationship around? (*"What you'll notice" implies that her noticing, not just her partner's changing, is important, which places emphasis on the perceptual in the loop of perception-behavior-meaning. The use of "when" rather than "if" carries the presupposition that this couple will successfully turn their relationship around. The focus is on small, observable behaviors.*)

JUNE: First off, he won't always be looking for ways to avoid doing stuff with me. (*At this point her answer lacks specificity, refers to an action outside her control, and is stated in the negative. The therapist's job is to help her shape this initial solution picture into one that is therapeutically well-formed.*)

PHIL: What will he be doing instead when he lets you know that he wants to do things with you? (*An "instead" question reframes the goal in positive terms.*)

JUNE: Well, for one thing, maybe when Carl comes home from work and I'm in the kitchen making dinner—because I get home earlier, so I'm usually the one who's cooking and cleaning up from the morning, and I don't think he even notices that—he would come in and give me a little kiss. Say hello in a warm way. You know, let me know he's glad to see me, and that he appreciates what I'm doing. (*Here there is movement toward an experiential goal picture that meets the criteria of observable changes that are salient to her. Although June is still describing changes outside her control, she's beginning to generate details of her preferred future picture, changes that will make a difference to her. At this point Phil is wondering (1) how these changes will make a difference to her, (2) what other experiences (things she might notice her husband doing) would have a similar meaning for her—that her husband is being more attentive, and (3) how her husband will know his actions are making a difference. This is the interpersonal context from which we can begin constructing the possible links between desired changes on the part of one partner and desired changes on the part of the other.*)

JUNE: (*Adding spontaneously*) Or he'd come sit next to me on the couch after dinner, snuggle up close, ask me what's on my mind, or start a conversation about how our days went.

PHIL: Uh huh. So when he comes home and walks into the kitchen and gives you that kiss and tells you he's glad to see you, or he snuggles up on the couch and talks with you that way, how will that make a difference for you? (*Phil chooses to explore the personal meaning of these experiences, to establish the meta-goal. This provides a foundation for exploring other things June might see Carl doing that would have the same meaning for her, and it helps her identify things she might do differently that could possibly influence those changes in him.*)

JUNE: (*Thinks in silence for a while.*) I would feel like I matter to him. That he's still glad to be married to me. Maybe he'd even notice once in a while how much I do to make him happy. Most of the time, I get the message that I'm some kind of a pain in the neck to him, kind of an intrusion in his life, and he'd rather just be on his own. Or maybe with someone else. (*She looks a bit teary. Note that she is presenting both her good story* and *her bad story. Phil wants to acknowledge her concerns, but he is interested in finding exits from the* bad story.)

PHIL: That must be pretty hard on you. It sounds like it's been pretty painful for you not to get the message from Carl that he values all that you do to please him, to feel he isn't happy being with you. So, if I understand you, when he does what you just described, and you feel his attentiveness, this will help you to feel appreciated, wanted, and loved. Have I got that right? (*Summarizing, acknowledging, and validating. Also building the bridge between what June wants her partner to do and the immediate and larger meaning his action will have for her.*)

JUNE: Yes, exactly.

PHIL: Now that I have that pretty clear in my mind let me ask you this: What will you be doing differently when Carl is being more attentive that will let him know you notice he's changing? (*Calls on the wife to begin thinking about what changes she will make as part of a preferred future picture and as part of a circular interpersonal process of change. This is an example of a perspective-shifting question. We discuss this kind of inquiry fully in chapter 8.*)

JUNE: (*Says several times that she doesn't know. Phil responds each time either with silence or by asking her to give it a little more thought.*) I guess he'd notice me acting nicer. Not so grumpy. Being friendlier. Oh, and no doubt wanting to be closer physically—that too. (*She grins rather mischievously, and Carl smiles at her.*)

PHIL: What else? (*Phil seeks more details of the preferred future picture by using an amplifying question to gather more details.*)

JUNE: Well, he'll see me being nicer about going to see his brother Joe and his family. I don't really care for them. They drink a lot and their lives are, well, messy. But if things were better between me and Carl, I'd put on a good face and go, for his sake. He'd see that.

PHIL: Okay, June. I want to ask you one more question before I ask Carl a few. You've been telling me some changes both you and Carl will be making when things are better between you. But see if you can tell me what the first signs will be that the two of you are turning things around. You know, what stands out to you right away, something you'd notice that tells you things are getting better? (*Now Phil is building into the goal picture a description of the first small steps. This conveys that change will happen incrementally and orients the partners to watch for the small changes.*)

JUNE: Well, like now. I'm noticing something right now, actually. Carl is looking at me with those soft brown eyes of his. It's a way he has of

... (*To Carl*) I haven't seen that look for a while. (*To Phil*) Looks kinda cute, doesn't he? (*Both June and Carl are smiling at each other in a tender, flirtatious way.*)

PHIL: Yeah, he's certainly looking better than when he came in! (*All laugh.*) So now I want to ask Carl a few questions—is that okay with both of you? (*Checking in with the couple about whether what Phil wants to do is agreeable and seems helpful.*)

BOTH: Uh huh.

PHIL: (*To Carl*) So Carl, you've been listening to June answer my questions. Is she right? Would it make a difference to you, in the ways she said, if she showed you those signs that your changes mattered to her?

CARL: As a matter of fact, she hit the nail on the head. If she did some of that stuff, things between us would get a lot better fast. All I ever hear about is what a mistake it was for her to marry me. It's always I don't know the first thing about being married, or about love. If she saw more how I really felt, if she said nice things again—because she used to, you know—if that could happen it'd make a big difference. I do love her. And I want our marriage to work. For us, and for the kids.

PHIL: Does it make sense to you, then, from what she says, that if you did some of the things she mentioned, and she did some of the things that would tell you what you were doing made a difference, that together you would turn things around here?

CARL: I really think so, yeah.

PHIL: Well, then. It sounds as though both of you want and need to feel the other loves you and is glad to be married to you. (*Highlighting shared goal and preferred self.*) And, from our conversations here today, we're getting a pretty good sense of what each of you could do to help the other have the kinds of feelings you both want. Am I right about this? (*Both Carl and June nod in assent.*)

PHIL: Do you both think it would be useful for us, before we end today, to keep trying to figure out what each of you can do, like June just began to do, to give the other person the feeling that they're loved? (*Prepares for collaborative solution-building, stressing couple expertise in knowing what will be helpful in therapy.*)

CARL and JUNE agree.

PHIL: Okay then, let's do that. Carl, let me ask you . . .

In the remainder of the session, Phil went on to amplify their outcome pictures.

Tobey was the therapist in the second case. Her emphasis was on meta-goals and meanings because one partner's goals initially were overly specific; her initial goals reflect the sense that only very specific actions on her partner's part would satisfy her. Such goals, which fail to meet the criterion of being within the person's control, are often experienced by the other partner as attacks or criticism. In investigating Christa's larger goals (her meta-goals), Tobey helps her develop new and multiple means to her desired ends.

Tobey has been asking what will be different in the future when the partners are "being more thoughtful with each other," the goal the couple first named.

CHRISTA: She won't be interrupting me. She'll let me finish what I'm saying without going off on some tangent. (*Stated in the negative; goal outside of her control.*)

TOBEY: When she's not interrupting you, what will she be doing instead? How will the conversation go differently? (*An "instead" question, intended to produce a positively framed goal. Because Tobey is working with an overspecified goal, she intends to find out more about meta-goals and meanings.*)

CHRISTA: She'll be quiet while I'm talking. She'll seem more interested in me and what I have to say.

REBECCA: But I *am* interested, that's what she doesn't understand. We just have different styles of carrying on a conversation. This has been a problem for a long time.

CHRISTA: See? She just did it again.

TOBEY: Maybe we could back up a little here. I can see both of you have things you want and things that are bothering you, and I'm not surprised you have some different ideas about what feels good in conversations. I've noticed that happens a lot. (*Acknowledging, normalizing, actively neutral reflection of partners' feelings.*) But I'm interested in something for you both. Let me start with Christa. Christa, I'm curious about something we haven't talked about yet. What would it mean to you—that is, what kind of a difference would it make for you—if Rebecca was more quiet while you were talking, making it seem more to you like she was interested in what you had to say? (*Tobey is looking for a meta-goal, so that later they can take a look at other means to accomplish her ends. Also, this will help amplify ways for Rebecca to understand Christa's goals differently. Notice that these "being more thoughtful" goals are emerging from the clients rather than being imposed by the therapist.*)

CHRISTA: Well, like I said, I'd feel she was really interested in me, that I wasn't always the one that had to listen. I get flustered and pissed off when she interrupts me.

TOBEY: Tell me a little more about that, about what kind of difference it would make to get the feeling she was interested in you, how it would be if you weren't in the flustered and pissed-off place. (*Tobey uses a bad story piece to point toward a not-problem scenario and asks for further amplification of the meta-goal.*)

CHRISTA: Well, you know, I think I'd feel more loved, I'd feel comforted and important, like she was eager to hear about me and what happened to me. Like it was an equal partnership, where we both get a chance to let off steam about our days and how they went.

TOBEY: So, okay, Christa, if you were feeling more like that, more comforted and loved, what would Rebecca notice about you that would tell her that what she was doing was making a difference, that you were feeling more loved and important? (*While looking for observable detail, Tobey is beginning to build a relational bridge that could refresh a shared good story picture.*)

CHRISTA: (*Glancing over at Rebecca, as if for verification*) She'd notice me being nicer, I guess, not so grumpy. I get angry.

REBECCA: (*Nodding*) Yes. She does. She's angry pretty much all the time now, it seems like. I mean, that's a problem, too.

CHRISTA: (*Immediately irritated*) Well, I don't think I'm the only one with an anger problem here. Rebecca's got an edge a lot, too. She's been working on expressing her feelings more, and that just means, as far as I can tell, that I get it in the neck more. (*Clients have returned to the bad story, in a complainant/sympathizer mode; Tobey responds to their concerns about anger before returning to the goal-building process.*)

TOBEY: So I see that anger's probably something that bothers you both in the relationship, and that maybe we'll need to figure out what things would look like for you both if it weren't so much of a presence in things. (*Acknowledging, externalizing, referring to a possible future preferred picture. Now Tobey returns to Christa's positive future picture.*) So could we work on this bit by bit, starting with what we were talking about? (*Both nod.*) So Christa—and Rebecca, you'll probably be thinking about this picture too, because it's something that makes a difference for both of you—you said a minute ago that if you were feeling more loved and comforted Rebecca would notice you being nicer. I think you said "not so grumpy." What would you be, then, instead of grumpy? How would Rebecca be able to tell that you were feeling like being nicer? (*Further fleshing out of the future picture in positive terms. Tobey has declined the invitation into bad story territory but makes note of its importance, as it could be necessary to incorporate this "problem talk" later and because it suggests a not-problem future picture to fill out.*)

CHRISTA: (*Thinks for a bit while it's quiet.*) Well I'd do more stuff like make her tea in the morning. More thoughtful, the way I'd like us both to be. I'd stop what I was doing when she came in and take time to talk to her. I'd be calmer, probably joke more, laugh more. I'd talk to her about her garden—she's an avid gardener—if it weren't for her, I probably wouldn't pay much attention to it myself, but when things are okay I'm into talking about the tomatoes and stuff. (*Rebecca smiles.*)

TOBEY: And if that kind of stuff was happening, if you were making her tea, joking more, talking to her about the garden—the stuff that showed you were feeling more loved and comforted—what would you notice about Rebecca that would tell you she was seeing the difference, that it was making a difference to her?

CHRISTA: Oh, well, she'd probably be more relaxed too, laughing more. She'd be slowing down, maybe, and spending more time with me. She starts rushing around, getting really busy when things aren't good. Then I feel like she's there, but not really there.

TOBEY: But when she is? (*Another "instead" question.*)

CHRISTA: Oh, we hang out more. Sometimes we cook together, and we help each other a lot on projects around the house. (*By looking at meta-goals and then moving back to specifics, the clients have begun to build a* good story *picture that at the moment is unrelated to goals around conversational style.*)

TOBEY: Okay. That's pretty clear. Thanks a lot, Christa. Rebecca, now I'd like to ask you whether Christa pretty much got that right. Would those be some of the ways you'd show how a change between you was making a difference?

REBECCA: Absolutely. Relaxed is a big thing. In fact, if I were more relaxed, not so anxious about getting on her wrong side, I think our conversations would go differently—I wouldn't try to squeeze everything in so fast, to get her attention and avoid a blowup. I'd be enjoying what both of us had to say.

At this point, there are several ways to go, all related to developing the *good story* narrative and making sure goals are utilitarian. Tobey chose to examine Rebecca's meta-goals in turn, by asking her about how being more relaxed would make a difference to her in the relationship. It turned out Rebecca's goals were quite similar to Christa's and concerned being attended to and loved. Since both of them had a shared end, a new set of specific means, as well as a reworking of the old ones, could be developed on the basis of a shared and fleshed-out *good story* picture of feeling loved and attended to. Tobey began to examine exceptions to the problem (past successes), but Christa said that she really felt they needed to examine their angry interactions more, and Rebecca agreed. In some subsequent sessions, Tobey followed this lead and talked with them about the meanings, some of them related to their experiences in their families of origin, each gave to their interactions when they were at odds. This led Christa and Rebecca to construct and detail an outcome picture they called a "harmony" scenario and come up with some specific ideas about how each person could lead them out of angry interactions. After about 10 sessions, they reported that their life together was much calmer and they were arguing less. Though they still had "edgy" moments, both were enjoying their relationship more, and each felt more confident of being loved and attended to. At this point they decided they had other issues they wanted to work on, including how to "say yes and no to each other" and how to become more physically intimate again. The goaling process, in other words, continued and evolved throughout their work, which lasted about five months. It is worth noting that when they finished therapy Christa and Rebecca still had quite different conversational styles, and each found the other person's style sometimes nettlesome, but they reported that they were better able to accept these differences and work around them on their own terms once their partnership, and the *good story* of their relationship, was strong and lively again.

# Reinvigorating the *Good Story* Narrative: Coauthoring Success Stories and Exceptions

In the last chapter we focused on the imagined preferred future. In this chapter, we shift the temporal focus to the present and recent past—from how people want their lives to be different in the future to how they have already been different at some times. This means we focus on successes and positive experiences. Solution-focused therapists call these "exceptions"— times when the problem could have happened but didn't or was somehow less of a problem (Berg, 1994; Berg & Miller, 1992; de Shazer, 1988, 1985; Walter & Peller, 1992); narrative therapists refer to them as "unique outcomes" or "sparkling moments" (Freedman & Combs, 1996; White & Epston, 1990). Conversations about recent and present exceptions and successes are rich contexts for mining couple-specific solutions. It's in the stories we coauthor with the couple about these preferred experiences that their unique strengths and resources are identified, making it possible for them to employ these assets purposefully to make such experiences happen more often.

Like future-focused goal-building conversations, success and exceptions conversations serve several therapeutic functions. First, they tell the partners and the therapist what kinds of experiences will signify that the couple has reached their goals (target function). Second, when conversation explores what people were doing, thinking, feeling, saying, and seeing when things were more the way they want them to be, it clarifies and highlights the couple's individual and relationship strengths and resources (agency function). Third, when couples are talking with us and each other about these better times, they do so from within the narrative world of their *good story*, giving it life and vigor (narrative function). And finally, when couples are talking about recent exceptions and successes, they perceive that change is already happening, experiencing themselves already in the process of solving their problems (hope-generating function).

When hosting present and/or past-centered conversations, we continually listen for and ask amplifying questions about: (1) presession changes, that is, positive changes that occurred after the call for the first appointment was made or since the last session, (2) successes, and (3) exceptions. Before addressing how to host these conversations, we want to note again our working assumption that people's social realities—their subjective experiences in relationship to others—are socially constructed. Keeping this perspective in mind will clarify certain technical matters concerning what to ask and how and when to ask it.

It is fairly obvious that the imagined relationship scenarios developed in future-focused conversations are constructed by clients and therapist—built up in a process of imagining in dialogue—and consist of a sort of mutual story-making. But it might not be as obvious that conversation about the present and recent past is also an imaginative and creative process, in which experiences are reconstructed. A reauthoring takes place. Memories of the past and perceptions of present events are fluid and malleable, subject to influence by inquiry and dialogue. Consequently, conversations about past and present experiences can change how people remember events and the meanings they give to the shaping of these events. In these terms, exceptions and past successes are stories constructed in conversation, not simply reports of objectively remembered events.

In solution-focused brief therapy, the term *exception* has been used both to refer to recollected events and to narratives constructed in therapeutic conversation. Exceptions are frequently defined as actual past occurrences. For example, Klar and Berg (1999) seem to suggest that the therapist is looking for actual remembered exceptional events:

> Once the therapist and client develop a mutual understanding of what the client wants in the future, their focus turns to constructing a desirable outcome based on identifying exceptions. Solution-focused brief therapy defines these exceptions as times when some aspects of the client's life are going as the client would want. It assumes that all problematic situations, even ones as chronic or serious as drug and alcohol abuse, feature times when the problem could have occurred but did not. Clarifying what the client is doing different at those times and building on those differences toward the outcome the client wishes from therapy is the core of solution-focused therapy. (p. 233)

Exceptions conversation can help clients recall events that for one reason or another have escaped their notice, or have somehow been forgotten. We agree that conversations about actual exceptional times are extremely useful; bringing people's attention to these preferred experiences can help to develop solutions and reinvigorate the couple's *good story*. But it is important not to assume that exceptions are a set of facts set in stone; this definition is confining because it prevents therapist and clients from taking advantage of the constructed, pliable nature of experience (Walter & Peller, 1996).

What if a couple says they can't remember any successful experience with the problems bringing them to therapy? If the therapist thinks of successes as either having happened or not, inquiry comes to an end. However, the therapist who thinks of exceptions and successes as constructed narratives still has conversational options; he can pursue coauthored bits and pieces of experience that can be built into a positive, competency-rich story, when none seemed to exist before the conversation began. If we keep in mind that we are talking about subjective formulations constructed from personal perceptions, attitudes, and meanings—complex shapes capable of revision and reformulation through dialogue and reflection—we will not be stumped when people initially fail to come up with any success stories. Unexpected exceptions and then competencies will bloom in the midst of our conversations—resources that might be a surprise, or seem newly minted, to both clients and therapist. Consider, in this regard, the value of the following definition of exceptions offered by de Shazer (1990), which emphasizes a constructionist perspective:

> It is important to remember that exceptions do not exist out there in the "real world"; they are cooperatively invented or constructed by the therapist and client talking together. Before the therapist and client talk about exceptions, these times are simply seen as "flukes" or differences that do not make a difference. It is the therapist's task to help clients make flukes into differences that make a difference. (p. 96)

When we ask couples about exceptions, we invite them to draw new experiential and perceptual distinctions around various events and interactions. We view these dialogues as a means to coauthor success stories within the space of problem-focused narratives rather than as data-gathering inquiries about actual events. Therefore, we assume, even when people initially tell us they can recall no recent exceptions or successes, that possibilities exist for discovering exceptions in fact and/or coauthoring exceptions in the story.

Having established that successes and exceptions are often a blend of memory and invention, we are in a better position to understand how conversation about the recent past can serve the therapeutic functions described at the beginning of this chapter, that is, the target function of goal-building; the narrative function of loosening the hold of the couple's *bad story* and reinvigorating their *good story*; the agency-highlighting function, through which couples identify their unique strengths and resources; and the hope-generating function, in which couples see that they are already on track to solving their problems.

# Goal Development

Like future-focused conversations, conversations about past and current not-problem experiences serve to build outcome pictures, clarify preferences, and develop well-formed therapeutic goals. Inquiry about presession change, successes, and exceptions provides an alternative route to customer/consultant conversation. These conversations allow us to define signs of significant relational change. When clients engaged in problem-focused conversations are able to identify when and how things went better in the past—more the way they would like them to go in the future—we are moving toward clarifying goals.

Whether goals can best be developed by future-focused or past-focused conversations, or by some blending of both, depends on the context of each case. In RPT, we usually begin with future-focused conversations. Asking people who are explaining how painful or frustrating their situation is to tell us about exceptions to their problems can sometimes be too jarring or seem disrespectful and dismissive. Asking how they would like things to be different in the future is a more graceful and receptive way to invite people out of complainant/sympathizer conversations into customer/consultant ones. But, if we are sensitive and respectful, even when people come in with a global sense that their relationship life is utterly terrible, carefully and patiently teasing out bits and pieces of exceptions and successes can provide a starting point for developing goals. As a general rule, however, we use exceptions as the starting point when people can easily recall not-problem experiences, using these concrete experiences as the foundation for goal-building. Building from actual recent successes is easier for many couples than using imagined future pictures. There is no formula for this, because each couple, each session, each conversation, and interchange is unique.

# Narrative Reauthoring

Asking people to talk about recent successes and exceptions and about what has gone better since they called to set up the first appointment or since the last session invites them to step outside the familiar problem-saturated *bad story*. When couples are encouraged to talk about successes or exceptions, they begin identifying exit points from their alienating *bad story* narratives. And the telling itself is a *good story* experience. This narrative function is a central feature of narrative therapy (Freedman & Combs, 1996; White & Epston, 1990). Narrative therapists cultivate these alternative stories in conversation with their clients to help clients deconstruct frozen, problem-saturated narratives and to assist them in authoring preferred ones. They ask about exceptional times in order to help people rewrite and develop stories in which they become heroes, not victims—resourceful and competent rather than deficient and flawed. In RPT, when people talk to us and each other about exceptional times, sparkling moments, etc., the gripping *bad story* narratives of their lives together begin to lose their interpretive power to organize experience. On the flip side of the narrative coin, we use these conversations about past successes and exceptions to bring attention, liveliness, and weight to the couple's shared *good story* narrative and recreate a sense of togetherness, bondedness, and collaboration. As the partners talk about what we sometimes call "pearls on the necklace" (the precious moments couples can string together), they amplify the *good story* presence in their relational life.

## Building Agency

Once stories about recent past successes and exceptions are taking shape, we invite clients to take the next step, constructing agency. By "agency" we mean the important link between people's preferred experiences and the actions or attitudes on their own part(s) that each can come to see as a significant contributor to that experience. This might be called the empowerment process in therapy. When people feel capable of bringing about their preferred experiences, their sense of personal power and responsibility is enhanced. Agency is developed by asking questions about what each partner thought and did differently and what steps he or she took in those exceptional times (Berg & Miller, 1992; Walter & Peller, 1992). Such questions presuppose that each partner had a hand in making the satisfying experience happen, and that what each did and how each decided to do it arose from competencies (strengths, skills, capabilities, attitudes, and knowledge) they already have. Once discovered and articulated, these competencies can be used to make the changes the couple seeks in therapy; partners can intentionally think and do the same things in the future. In most cases, it is easier for couples to repeat already successful behavior patterns than to try and stop or change existing problematic ones (Berg, 1994). For each partner, this process enhances self-esteem and a sense of authority in guiding his or her own life.

In agency development the individual and collective competencies of the couple can be constructed and fleshed out. As the partners answer our agency questions—"How did you get that to happen?" "What do you suppose you were telling yourself that led you to respond the way you did that time?" "How could you get yourself to do that again in the future?"—they identify elements of their own preferred selves and bits and pieces of their *good story* sense of the relationship. Recall Michael Lambert's conclusion that 40% of what contributes to therapy success is related to extratherapeutic variables—factors that include people's unique histories, capabilities, and ideas (Lambert, 1992; Miller et al., 1997). In constructing agency, these extratherapeutic variables can be exploited as useful resources. By asking about such variables in the context of talking about exceptions—by naming them and complimenting people for possessing them—we help to change the way people see themselves, each other, and their relationship.

## Exceptions and Successes As Examples of Change Already in Progress

Talking about exceptions and successes leads to conversations about how couples are *already* changing or on the way toward achieving their goals (though they may not have seen it this way before). One of the most significant discoveries made by de Shazer, Berg, and their associates is that quite often things got better for clients between the time they called for an appointment and the time of their first session (Weiner-Davis, de Shazer, & Gingerich, 1987). They found that 80% of the clients, when asked, reported positive changes between the time they called for an appointment and their first session. Since it is often easier to help people continue to move in a direction they already see themselves taking than it is to get them to change direction, talking about presession changes, recent successes, and exceptions establishes that *change is already happening*. Then, all that is needed is to figure out how to keep it going. "Exceptions are seen by us as signs and/or signals and/or indications and/or behavior(s) and/or thinking and/or talk that indicate that *a solution has already begun*" (de Shazer, 1993, p. 117). When, early in therapy (even in the first session), couples see themselves as already on track toward solving their problems and reaching their goals, they begin to feel effective and hopeful. They immediately view themselves as able, purposeful, and resourceful and feel more optimistic about the future (more "psychically muscular," one might say), and this positive self-sense is helpful in strengthening energy and will for change.

In the following case example, Tobey demonstrates how conversation about a recent exception serves the functions we discussed above. Larry and Karen came to therapy saying they were unhappy about their sex life and that whenever they tried to talk about the issue, they ended up feeling angry, hurt, and estranged. This portion of the transcript begins about ten minutes into the first session.

TOBEY: Larry, can you tell me about a time recently when you and Karen were able to talk about sex without ending up hurt and mad at each other? (*Rather than focusing directly on the "sex problem," Tobey focuses on the difficulties they have in approaching this problem collaboratively. To begin building a preferred outcome picture, she asks for a recent exception to this difficulty.*)

LARRY: (*Thinks for a while.*) Not really. We've tried to talk about it maybe twice, three times recently and every time it went badly. We just can't do it. That's why we came—maybe we'll be able to do it here. (*As is common when we ask people about exceptions, Larry's first response is to tell Tobey he can't think of any. Assuming he can't think of any exceptions yet, Tobey remains quiet.*)

LARRY: Well, maybe during our week in Hawaii, I guess there's that time. God, I hope we don't have to come here or go to Hawaii for the rest of our lives just so we can talk about sex without ending up in a mess with each other. (*Smiles.*)

TOBEY: (*Laughs.*) Well, maybe we can do something about that awful prospect. But maybe there's something worth learning about this Hawaii experience. Let's talk a bit about the conversations you two had there. If that's what you're telling me, that you had a good conversation about sex—what was different about it? (*Tobey asks for details about the exception.*)

LARRY: (*Smiles at Karen, who smiles back but quickly lowers her head.*) Well, for one thing, instead of ending up mad or hurt we made love, and I think I can safely say we both enjoyed it. That was certainly a big difference. (*To Karen*) Wouldn't you say so, Karen?

KAREN: (*To Larry*) Yes, I agree, but there were lots of other things about that afternoon that made it go that way. For one thing, you and I went for a long walk together and talked about some really nice stuff, about how it was when we were first together, the kind of talk we hadn't had in a long time. You didn't talk about the cases you were working on—you were just focusing on us, on being together. That made a big difference.

TOBEY: Ah. I'd like to hear more about this, Karen, but first I want to check something out with both of you. Was this a better experience because your conversation ended up with sex, or because you were able to talk about a difficult issue and stay close and connected? Or both? (*Tobey seeks to find out what is important to the couple about this exceptional experience, rather than assuming she knows; she is clarifying their goal picture.*)

LARRY: For me it's both.

KAREN: Both for me, too, but we can't end every discussion about sex in bed. Although, knowing Larry, that would be fine with him. (*Smiles at Larry and gives him a playful little push.*) Seriously, though, that's part of the problem. Whenever the topic comes up, I assume Larry will be unhappy with me if we don't end up in bed.

LARRY: *(Responding to Karen's humor)* That would be great with me, we could cut out the talk about sex altogether and just have sex. But what I think we really need is to be able to talk about sex and not immediately get into a bad place. Maybe just have sex every other time the topic comes up. *(All three laugh.)*

KAREN: Well actually, the talk part, feeling connected when we talk, that's really important.

TOBEY: Okay, so let's go back to this time in Hawaii, when you were able to talk about sex and you both say it went better. Let's see if we can find out how the two of you made that happen. *(Tobey invites conversation that will identify agency and enhance partnership.)* Karen says it made a difference, Larry, that you talked with her about your relationship and not about your work, and that you were walking, spending relaxed time together. What else can each of you recall about that experience that could tell us something about how you made it happen? *(Tobey continues to amplify agency, what each now recalls doing differently in that exceptional experience, an action or thought that could help make such experiences happen more in the future. This has a narrative function as well.)*

LARRY: Well, for one thing when I said isn't this a perfect day to spend the afternoon making love Karen didn't give me that look, that look like I'm some kind of oversexed monster.

TOBEY: What look did she give you? *(Eliciting a statement of what did happen, rather than what didn't, fulfilling one of the criteria of goal-building. Tobey fleshes out the exception.)*

LARRY: Well, she has this wonderful smile. You know. See that dimple there? She smiled in that certain way. Like receptive. Then somehow we started talking about our feelings about what was happening or maybe it's better to say what *wasn't* happening, in our sex life.

TOBEY: What else can you tell me, both of you, about this experience and what you did differently? Thinking about it now, Larry, what do you recall doing that might have made a difference to Karen, and Karen, what do you remember doing that might have made a difference to Larry? *(Tobey is helping them to reconstruct (story) their experience so that it is useful for developing signs and signals of change-producing behaviors and attitudes.)*

Larry and Karen then had an opportunity to articulate a number of ways each of them had behaved differently when the issue of sex came up in Hawaii. These included Larry's listening, staying receptive to the "wandering" quality of the conversation, not seeming so eager to rush sex, and Karen's smiling at Larry's jokes and teasing him back. Note that most of these details do not directly relate to their sex life; they flesh out a scenario in which the two of them are having interactions they regard as pleasing. In talking about an exception, this couple is beginning to elaborate ways of being together that solve the problem not only of their differences about sex, but also of communicating about it. By the end of the session, Larry and Karen agreed that an important goal for their therapy would be the ability to have conversations like the one they had in Hawaii more often. In addition, they realized, with some delight, possibly because they were recalling this successful interaction, that both were optimistic about reaching this goal.

# The Pragmatics of Hosting Exceptions and Successes Conversations

When clients and therapist construct stories of exceptions and successes, it is as though they're fitting together the pieces of a *good story* jigsaw puzzle. Each piece of the puzzle is another bit of experience that is meaningless or without significance until it is organized into a coherent whole. Until the therapist and couple fit these puzzle pieces together into a *good story* narrative, they remain isolated fragments, easily forgotten or overlooked. But once these pieces of experience are identified and fit into a coherent whole, this desirable "picture" of things becomes a narrative frame that can be used as a guide for where people want to go (outcomes).

In RPT, conversations about exceptions and success usually involve five to six more or less predictable stages. While it is important to be flexible and responsive to the demands of each therapeutic context, in most cases our competency-building conversations follow this step-by-step process.

### 1. Identifying exceptions and successes.

We can begin conversations about exceptions and success passively or actively. For example, as we listen to each partner tell us about their problems, conflicts, and troubles, we can keep our ears open for any mention of pleasant, desired experiences or times the couple's difficulties were somehow not as problematic. When one partner mentions a nice evening the previous week, the therapist might ask for details about other similar times or about how the couple came to have this experience—what each did to make it happen. Or, the therapist can work more actively by asking the partners to describe a recent exception or success. For example, we might ask the partners in a couple whose presenting problem is "chronic fighting" (either at the beginning of the session or soon after) to tell us about a recent time when they had a disagreement that might have led to a big fight but somehow the fight didn't happen or was less severe. The following are some questions we use:

- *I'm wondering if either of you can tell me about times since you made the call for this appointment when things happened between the two of you that you'd both like to see happen more?* (Using presession successful experiences as a first step in goal-building.)
- *I'd like you to tell me about a recent time when the two of you were at least somewhat successful in working together against the problem.* (Highlights success in working collaboratively.)
- *Can you tell me about a recent time when this problem could have happened but didn't or was in some way less of a problem?* (Focuses conversation on not-problem narratives, that is, exceptions.)

## 2. Clarifying personal meanings.

Once we have coauthored stories of success, we begin fleshing out the personal meaning element of these preferred stories. We want to find out *how these experiences make a difference*—what particular meanings they hold for each partner and what self-sense is involved in experiencing them. This bridge between encounter and meaning creates a narrative framework in which each partner discovers the unique, personal significance of these happenings. We believe that couples who understand these personal meanings, for themselves and each other, are more successful at resolving difference and maintaining the *good story* construct of their lives. Here are some questions we ask couples to bring out the meanings in these *good story* narratives.

- *When your spouse is less angry (less depressed, happier, warmer, more patient), how does this make a difference for you?*
- *How do you treat your partner differently when you are feeling less frightened (worried, guilty, burdened, hopeless)?*
- *When the two of you have experiences like this (when your partner is acting more the way you want), what does it tell you about yourself (your partner, your relationship, the possibilities for the future)?*
- *What would you say is the most important part of this experience? What makes it so important for you?*
- *What do you suppose your partner would say makes this kind of experience so important to him/her?*
- *What is different about you when you the two of you are having this kind of experience? What does that difference mean to you?*

## 3. Establishing agency: making exceptions the rule.

Exceptions and successes, when first identified by couples, will be described either as deliberate and intentional or as accidental, spontaneous, or random (Berg & Miller, 1992; De Jong & Berg, 1998). When an exception or success is perceived as intentional, people can usually describe in step-by-step fashion (with help from the therapist) how they contributed to making it happen. The second type, the accidental or random success or exception, includes instances in which something positive has happened but clients, at least at first, can't explain the steps they took to make it happen. Frequently people ascribe desired changes, successes, and exceptions to some change the other person has made. In such cases, they experience the successes as outside their own control. Stories of success that do not include the element of agency are as yet incomplete—they're stories of luck, not success—and it's the therapist's job to start the ball rolling toward coauthoring agency, which is an essential component if these stories are going to be a field for discovering competency and contribute to ongoing change.

We ask questions that help people establish causal links between the desirable occurrences and what each person was thinking and doing when these exceptions and successes happened, teasing out and developing what both partners did in new or different ways.[1] Turning what seems like accidental success into deliberate occurrence has two positive results: First, it engenders feelings of personal efficacy and competence, and second, it suggests what specifically each partner can do in the future as part of the couple's custom-made, collaborative action plan for turning their relationship around. Even if what a person did differently in these instances was in response to seeing some change on the part of the other partner, these are changes people can own and replicate. We want to help both partners cast themselves as active participants in these satisfying *good story* scenarios.

The easiest way to construct agency is by asking people how they made an exception, success, or positive change happen. When you think about it, this is an odd question, and it almost always sounds odd to our clients when we ask it. Their first response is often "I don't know" or "It just happened" or "My partner changed for some reason." But people have available to them a very powerful story-making, data-shaping ability, along with a self-sense (when people are in a context in which they can view themselves positively) that contains many resources for imagining solutions, accomplishing change, and taking effective action. If we encourage clients to remember exceptions, they will almost always recall something after a bit of rumination. A husband might say, regarding an exception to the rule of fighting with his wife about his stepson, "Well, when I saw we were about to have another one of our same old arguments about the way Nick talks back, I told her she should go ahead and handle it the way she wanted—I'd step out of it for now. But then I wanted to sit down, after he went to bed, and talk about it, maybe over a cup of tea, when we could have time for a real conversation. And she agreed, and even thanked me for the suggestion. Later she told me she could be a lot more interested in my point of view if she didn't feel it came at her right away, in the heat of things. And things did calm down, so we managed to have a conversation that wasn't so tense, even though we still disagree about how to handle Nick's back-talking."

Here are some questions we ask couples to amplify agency:

- *How did you (the two of you) get that to happen?*
- *What do you recall doing differently in that situation that helped make things go more the way you wanted them to?*
- *In reflecting on that success, what can you recall you did or said that might have made a difference to your partner? How do you suppose what you did made a difference to him/her?* (The individual, who must reflect both on what he or she did and how it affected the other, is invited to view the success or exception through the other partner's eyes as a way to "identify" a causal or influential factor.)
- *Suppose I had two videotapes. One tape shows a scene where the two of you are working well together in dealing with a problem, and the other shows a time when the problems are still getting the better of you. What differences would I notice between the two videos?*
- *Mike, what do you suppose Lynn would say you were doing differently at that time that made it a positive experience?* (Asks the respondent to imagine the influential factors the partner would name.)
- *Janet, what would Al say you could do that would get him to do more joking around and laughing (communicating, helping with the dishes, listening calmly), the things you're saying he did then that made a positive difference for you?*

## 4. Clarifying useful self-talk.

The next (and related) step is clarifying agency-enhancing self-talk. We are interested in having clients tell us what they might have been thinking that made it possible for them to act in ways that made a difference. (Again, it makes no difference whether people remember or construct answers to our self-talk inquiries.) Here are some self-talk questions:

- *How did you decide to do that?*
- *What were you thinking that helped you take that step?*
- *What did you tell yourself to get that to happen?*
- *What do you suppose you could say to yourself in those situations that would help you do that again?*

Clarifying useful self-talk is another aspect of establishing agency. These types of questions encourage people to focus on an inner field that contributes to an empowered sense of self and, by extension, to *good story* development, which we consider next.

## 5. Influencing perception in favor of *good story* experiences.

Exceptions and success stories are part of a process of adjusting perceptual lenses. "Seeing" these kinds of experiences, and gathering memory, intention, and meaning around them, gives them enough weight to begin to shift expectation. As couples begin to see the (already existing) potential for having satisfying experiences together, the opportunity for a shift in perspective opens. As this happens, the therapist can help the partners move away from focusing on what confirms their individual *bad stories* and become more alert to evidence confirming the *good story* narrative. We do this in two ways. The first is quite direct. We simply ask people to be on the lookout for examples of exceptions and successes between the current session and the next: *Between now and the next time we meet I'd like you both to notice the times when you're feeling better about the way you made decisions together—times when that process was a little more the way you'd like it to be.* Secondly, we ask questions that increase each partner's recognition of the validity and power of the couple's shared *good story* narrative as it is revealed in the conversation about exceptions and/or successes. We want the desired future and the remembered past to overlap. Here are some questions that can lead to this:

- *What does your ability to make experiences like these happen say about you two as a couple?*
- *Let's say you met another couple facing the same problems. Based on these successes you've had, what would you advise them to do? As you see yourselves working successfully to overcome and solve this problem, what will you be saying about yourselves (to each other, to others)?*
- *What do you suppose people who know the two of you at your best would say about your ability to work together to make these kinds of successes happen more in the future?*
- *Who, among your friends and family, would be the least surprised to hear how well you two handled that situation? What is it they know about you that would lead them to feel that way?*
- *When you've put these problems behind you, what will you want your partner to think and say about you and your efforts to bring about the changes that have made the difference?*
- *What would it take for you to be able to pay more attention to the times when your partner is doing things more the way you want? How would he/she know that you noticed?*
- *When your children are grown up and talking to their own partners about the two of you and how you turned your relationship around, what do you want them to be able to say about you?* (This, by the way, is a very effective perspective-shifting question for couples with children.)

In some cases, people are unable to come up with any exceptions or success stories at all, making it seem impossible to move toward *good story* territory. We have already noted how, in such cases, we might gently persist in our inquiries, waiting and listening for opportunities to ask about exceptions, or how we might shift to asking future-focused questions. But there is a third possibility. We can also ask people to employ their imaginations to reconstruct the past—to "make up" a scenario of a past success.[2] We might say something like this: "I see you're both having a hard time recalling a recent time when you folks were successful in dealing with this problem, so I'd like to try something. Would you both be willing to use your imaginations to answer some odd-sounding questions? Just as an experiment, could you both imagine a recent time when this problem happened, but see the scene with things going more the way you want? Try as best you can to see yourselves as if you were watching a videotape, and tell me what's happening. What do you see yourselves doing in this picture?"

For example, suppose a couple wants help in finding ways to work better together around getting their daughter to do her homework: "Well, imagine, just for now, that during the last few days Robin was playing her guitar and calling her friends instead of doing her homework—you know the kind of thing that you've been telling me can trigger a fight between the two of you. Only this time, instead of things going badly, with you having one of your fights about the different ways you each want to handle it, somehow things go differently. Now watch the video scene, letting things go more the way you would like them to go and tell me what you see and hear happening that's different." As each partner imagines this "past success" and we ask questions to fill in the details of what each partner is doing differently, the conversation will produce solutions, elements of agency, and a *good story* narrative.

## 6. Making an action plan for further change.

The final stage in exceptions/success conversations is attending to what both partners can do to keep things moving in this *good story* direction. This step involves thickening and solidifying the constructed blend of meaning-making, perception, behavior, and agency so that it will continue past the endpoint of therapy. Now that the clients have identified the specific actions that have occurred during exceptional and successful times and articulated the unique personal meanings of the experiences of self, other, and the relationship they were having, we can help them develop future plans for change—action programs that will make these past and current exceptions the rule in the future. The following are some questions we might ask to help the partners develop these future-change strategies:

- *What can your partner do that will make it easier for you to do more of the things he/she says will make a difference to him/her?*
- *What do you suppose your partner would tell me are the things you could do differently that would make the biggest difference to him/her and do the most to improve your relationship?*
- *How will knowing what these changes mean to your partner—how they*

*help him/her to feel closer to you (better about the relationship, more hopeful about the future)—help you continue doing these things that matter?*

- *What are some of the things you could continue to tell yourself (do differently, notice) that will make a difference to you in improving your relationship?*
- *What are some of the things you could do to make sure you experience more of that way of being connected (calm, relaxed, serene, tender, trusting) in the relationship in the future?*
- *What do you think your partner would say you could do to contribute to his/her experiencing more of that way of being (connected, calm, independent, adventuresome) in the future?*

Notice that while some of our questions are about what the respondent can do, we often rely on perspective-shifting (and empathy-building) questions that ask partners to imagine a reaction on the part of the other. This is partly because these questions help to recreate partnership by asking people to demonstrate their connection to the other. We discuss these kinds of questions in detail in chapter 8.

If a couple is feeling ready to end therapy and proceed on their own, the following questions are useful at the point of termination to foster the flow of positive movement.

- *What do you suppose you could do after therapy ends that will keep the ball rolling in the right direction?*
- *After you two stop coming here, what do you suppose you'll be doing that will tell your partner (your kids, your friends) that you're still trying to do your part to make your relationship a success?*
- *What's the most important thing for each of you to remember to do so these things have the best chance of happening more in the future? What's the next most important?*
- *What will you have to keep in mind in the future, during the inevitable challenging times, so you'll be able to do what you've been telling me makes a difference?*

## Putting the Pieces Together

Questions that focus on successful or exceptional times help both therapist and clients to choose from multiple perceptions of reality and begin building a satisfying relational story by defining desirable elements (actions, thoughts, and memories) of that story. This solidifies the details of a goal picture and highlights the means people can use (and have already used) to move toward that picture; in other words, people can develop an action plan based on these successful experiences. At the same time, this process immediately puts people into a frame where solutions are already happening. For instance, suppose the therapist asks his client, Miles, to describe a recent time when he and his partner, Justin, spent time together in a way that made a difference for him—when they were, in his words, "closer, living in the same emotional space." After first saying he can't think of anything, he pauses for a moment, and then, expressing some surprise at his realization, says they "were actually pretty close about a week ago." He turns to Justin, smiling—Justin smiles back—and remarks that it's funny he didn't remember that right away. The therapist follows up by asking what Miles recalls doing differently before and during the desired experience. Miles says, "I don't really know; it just sort of happened." The therapist, wanting to co-construct agency, asks him to give the question some more thought, adding that if he can remember something he did differently, it might help in figuring out how to have that experience more often.

Miles ponders, probably searching his memory for something he did or thought. He is reconstructing events, assembling them into a somewhat altered narrative, remembering, revising, redefining, and adding to the many bits and pieces of the evening's experience. He looks surprised and pleased. He says that when Justin went to put on his headphones and listen to music right after dinner, instead of starting to clean up the kitchen on his own, or telling Justin he was tired of having him rush off after dinner, he went and joined him on the couch. He says, at first, that he can't remember exactly why he did that—maybe he was just too tired to be interested in cleaning up the kitchen and wanted to sit down. Then Miles adds another piece. He now recalls feeling "protective" of Justin during dinner. During their conversation, Justin had been talking about how he used to play the guitar a lot when he was younger and, in passing, he had mentioned the death of a good friend of his, a musician, and this made Miles think Justin was probably feeling kind of sad. Miles now remembers that he went into the living room to be with Justin because he thought Justin needed cheering up. Here's how the conversation continues: "Oh yeah, and when I sat down I kind of snuggled up, and he took off his headphones and put one against my ear to show me what he was listening to. So then I told him that I liked it that music was so important in his life. And he said it felt good to him, having me in there next to him. And also that he felt better after talking to me in the kitchen. That felt really good. And not long after that he kinda lost interest in his headphones." Miles, Justin, and the therapist all start laughing. Miles says "Well, we were making pretty good music ourselves." After this description of a success/exception, the therapist went on to explore and amplify with Miles and Justin the bits and pieces of interaction and meaning-making that generated this close and affectionate evening together—specifically what each of them did, what they noticed about the other's actions, and how that made a difference for both of them. The focus was on how, together, they participated in making this *good story* event happen, and from this discussion they developed together an action plan for making more such events happen in the future.

# CHAPTER 7

# Scaling Questions: Numbers Can Make a Difference

The types of questions and conversations we have covered so far tend to have a kind of flow or implied sequence to them. Thus, it might appear that we conduct therapy in a kind of cookbook fashion, beginning with establishing rapport, moving on to conversations that loosen the hold of the *bad story,* then asking questions about goals and preferred future pictures, and finally inquiring about recent successes and exceptions. We have presented RPT in a step-by-step fashion not because this sequence is the "right" one to follow, but to make it possible for readers to understand, piece by piece, the various conversational processes and questions we use. As we have tried to make clear, the tasks of the couples therapist are manifold, and the conversational ebbs and flows in which the couple and therapist co-construct solutions and future pictures aren't part of a straightforward, linear sequence. Rather, the therapeutic process is complex, weaving back and forth in multiple directions; direction is established moment by moment, leaving room for the creativity, styles, and personal rhythms of both therapist and clients.

In RPT, regardless of how conversations unfold, we intend to orient people toward signs of progressive difference that will be seen as evidence of their *good story* narratives. Scaling questions, developed in solution-focused brief therapy, are well suited for accomplishing these ends (Berg, 1995; Berg & Miller, 1992; Berg & de Shazer, 1993; De Jong & Berg, 1998; de Shazer, 1994; O'Hanlon & Weiner-Davis, 1989; Walter & Peller, 1992). Berg and de Shazer (1993) explain that scaling questions:

allow both therapist and client to use the way language works naturally by agreeing upon terms (i.e., numbers) and a concept (a scale where 10 stands for the goal and zero stands for an absence of progress toward that goal) that is obviously multiple and flexible. Since neither therapist nor client can be absolutely certain what others mean by the use of a particular word or concept, scaling questions allow them to jointly construct a way of talking about things that are hard to describe, including progress toward goal(s). (p. 19)

Before going into a full discussion of the nature of scaling questions and the various ways we use them in RPT, let's look at a simple example to see how they work. Scaling conversation begins when we invite one or both partners in a couple to place themselves on a continuum from one to ten[1] with respect to some subjective state or condition, that is, progress toward solving their problem, motivation to work hard to solve it, confidence that it can be solved, etc. Once this "baseline" placement has been identified, we ask further questions intended to clarify signs of difference—small, concrete, observable happenings that tell respondents that movement is taking place along this continuum.

Suppose a couple tells us their goal is "better communication." In its present form the couple's goal is not therapeutically well-formed because it lacks specificity, is not stated in observable terms, and suggests a fixed state or final endpoint rather than steps in a process. In this case, instead of using the types of goal-building questions described in earlier chapters, we decide to use scaling questions to help the partners identify and clarify what observable changes will tell them they have "better communication." We begin by explaining to the couple that we are going to ask some odd questions involving numbers and ask if they would be willing to try and answer them. After the couple indicates their willingness, we ask: "On a scale of 1 to 10, where 1 stands for times your communication was at its worst and 10 stands for how you'll be communicating when you are ready to leave therapy (both of you are satisfied with your communication, your communication is as good as it could realistically become), where would each of you say you are right now?"

Suppose the husband says "4" and the wife says "3½." We have no idea what these numbers mean to either of them. Nor is it necessary to determine what led them to choose their numbers. The numbers are *only* important because they establish in each partner's mind a baseline from which perceptions of difference will be constructed in further conversation (de Shazer, 1994). We have taken a first step together in making small differences salient for a preferred future picture.

We are now ready to take the next step, which is to ask one of the partners what specific, observable change will signify that he or she has moved up one number on the continuum. When people begin imagining and describing what will be different when they have moved up on the scale, we have already begun coauthoring a narrative of positive difference (an element of the partner's *good story*). Now it's a matter of fleshing out and amplifying the details of these scenarios of difference. The stock question here is, "What else will tell you that you've moved up from a 3 to a 4?" or "And, what else will you notice?" Note that these questions do not ask people about what they will have to *do* to move, but rather *what they will notice* when they have already moved; the focus is on perception, not action.

Having identified and amplified the signs of difference, we are ready to take the last step in the scaling process—identifying the personal meta-goals and meanings these perceived differences hold for each partner. We invite the partners to reflect on and talk about the emotional and interpersonal significance these imagined scenarios have for each of them. We ask: "When you notice that (whatever the signs of change are) happening, how will it make a difference for you?" As each partner talks with us, in the other's presence, about the personal significance of these changes, about their hopes, desires, and emotional needs, a noticeable softening and warming often occurs. The partners may begin spontaneously glancing and smiling at each other, perhaps reaching out and touching, and the feeling of bonding is palpable. At this point, we often begin to feel that we're becoming a third wheel. (A nice feeling, in contrast to feeling like a deflector shield.) It takes little or no encouragement from us for the partners to enter into a conversation that enhances the couple's *good story*,[2] as they begin to see their goals in terms of small, discrete steps on a continuum of change. Talking about positive changes, personal meanings, and meta-goals through the medium of these scaling inquiries, the partners have grown more hopeful, willing, and confident.

## Scaling Progress

We can scale progress on a number of issues—toward solving problems, reaching goals, rebuilding a sense of partnership, increasing hope, and motivation to work for changes. This helps in clarifying the details of movement, defining small but meaningful steps in a desired direction, and the process identifies bits and pieces of goal pictures. In scaling progress toward a couple's overall goals for therapy, we would begin with a question that establishes today's story on a continuum: "On a scale from 1 to 10, with 1 representing when things were at their worst and 10 how they will be when your problems have been solved, where would each of you place the state of the problems today?" If both partners offer the same number in answer to our initial scaling question, we can note their mutuality and compliment them for having a shared sense of where they are currently with respect to reaching their goals. If they give different numbers, we acknowledge and normalize the fact that they have differing ideas about where they are with respect to reaching a desired future state. We can ask the partner giving the lower number to guess what the one with the higher number knows, sees, or believes that tells him or her that things are better. This will help to build a bridge between the partners' differing perceptions and bring out a potential shared sense of optimism. We can also do this by asking the higher-number partner questions about where this greater sense of optimism comes from. Sometimes we ask people to guess what number their partner will give, following up by exploring various aspects of how it happens that they came up with the same or different numbers. Such inquiry fosters empathy and creates partnership.

Once the partners have identified their base numbers—how they see things presently—and any discussion about these numbers is complete, we begin asking about what the partners will notice when they've moved up a notch on the progress scale. *What will be the first thing that tells you you've moved up to a higher number?* Or *What do you think your partner will notice that's different when you've moved up a number on the scale?* There are many creative ways scaling questions can be used to heighten, amplify, and trigger people's imaginal pictures about progress. Because they jog people out of their usual channels in thinking about their problems, they can bring into immediate play new ideas, energy, and commitment for change as they clarify individual and mutual meanings.

## Scaling Hope and Confidence: Building Constructive Optimism

Earlier we referred to Michael Lambert's conclusions regarding the relative importance of various factors that contribute to success in therapy (Lambert, 1992; Lambert & Bergin, 1994; Miller et al., 1997). Among these factors, hope, expectancy, and confidence in the therapist and the therapeutic process contribute about 15%. Based on both our successes and failures in working with couples, we have come to the conclusion that whatever the overall importance of hope in therapy is, if one partner leaves the first session less hopeful than when he or she walked in, there's a high probability the couple will not return. A failure on the part of the therapist to help increase both partners' hope during the first session is likely to be the kiss of death for couples therapy. Here, even more than in individual or family therapy, there is little room for lingering doubts about the usefulness of the therapy.

Hope-scaling conversations begin with the therapist's asking the partners to identify where they are on a scale of 1 to 10, with 1 representing no hope at all (or their level of hope when things looked their worst) and 10 representing complete confidence (or the highest level of confidence they can imagine having) that, with the help of therapy, they can solve their problems. Once they identify their current level of hope, we ask some variation of the follow-up question: "What will be different, what will be the first change you notice, when your hope has moved up a notch?" The answer will serve both to initiate a possible goal-building process, clarifying a concrete step that will identify forward progress, and at the same time to help build hopefulness as it grounds signs of increased hope in (imagined) observed behavior. Thus, scaling questions about hope can actually increase a couple's hopefulness as they elicit a couple's potential resources for actualizing change. Frequently, scaling a couple's hopefulness at the beginning and then at the end of an hour can reveal a substantial change in the numbers, vividly emphasizing an experience of rapid forward progress.

While it is important to generate hope early in treatment, we are mindful of the danger of fostering false optimism. In our conversations with couples we want to generate what we referred to earlier as constructive optimism— hope with reason. In cases where one partner has made innumerable past promises and false starts, that partner often comes to therapy expressing more optimism than the other, giving higher numbers for hope and progress. In these cases it is not wise to try to influence the other partner to share the first person's stated optimism. Having heard it all before and endured numerous disappointments, the more dubious partner has good reasons for assigning low numbers. The skeptical partner needs acknowledgment and validation for his or her initial unwillingness to be inspired by the optimism of the other partner, otherwise the individual's hopefulness about the therapy itself may plummet or remain at a nadir. At the same time, we want to be careful not to convey that we personally mistrust the sincerity of the optimistic partner's hopefulness and commitment to change. The therapist might say, "Well, Sharon, I can understand how you might give this a 1—taking a cautious stance here makes a lot of sense, since the changes you want will require a lot of hard work and persistence, and it hasn't always worked out in the past. And Stan's giving it a 5 or 6 is important, because he's starting out with a lot of energy. Maybe both caution and enthusiasm are good ingredients as we get started." This stance acknowledges that past experience dictates caution and a wait-and-see attitude on the part of the pessimistic partner but also allows room to develop the signs that will justify more optimism. In other words, we want to explore with the cautious partner what signs of difference he or she can realistically use in deciding things have moved up one number. What the cautious partner tells us in this regard is an important message to the other partner.

We sometimes use confidence- and hope-scaling conversations in situations when people initially describe goals that appear unrealistic or that are outside their control. For example, when a wife tells us her goal is to persuade her husband to stop smoking and to take better care of himself physically, we might ask her to scale her confidence as follows: "Without your husband's willingness and active participation, where on a scale from 1 to 10 would you place your current level of confidence that you can get your husband to make these changes?" We can then ask what would cause that number to go up. At this point the client will usually admit that there's little likelihood that anything other than changes in her husband's motivation (which is out of her control) could lead her to have more hope of achieving this goal. Now we are better situated to invite her to begin thinking about other possible goals that might be within her control—for instance, how she might better take care of herself, or what choices she might want to make if her husband continues to smoke and ignore his health issues.

The following are examples of hope-generating and reality-testing questions:

- *What will each of you notice you are doing or thinking differently that will tell you that your hope has moved up one number?* (Self-reflective.)
- *How realistic would your partner (friends, family, others) say it is for you to place your hope at this level on this issue? What do you suppose he/ she (they) knows that causes him/her (them) to believe you might be overly optimistic?* (Reality check, useful especially when one partner is optimistic that the other will make certain changes but other appears unmotivated.)
- *What do you suppose will be the first things you notice about your partner that will tell you he/she has moved up one number on this hope scale?* (Perception of partner.)
- *Do you think your partner knows what he/she could do differently that would move you up one number on your hope scale?* (Role-reversal question, putting oneself in the other's shoes. Note that we do not ask what the other partner can do to raise the respondent's number. Such a question tends to reinforce a theory of change that assumes things will improve only when the other partner does something different. This question gives room for an empathic connection around meanings and perspective. See the next chapter for a discussion of these kinds of questions.)
- *If I were to ask your partner, what do you suppose he/she would tell me you could do that would cause him/her to be more hopeful, that would move him/her up one notch on the hope scale?* (Another perspective-shifting question.)

- *What will be the first sign that both of you are feeling more hopeful about the future and more confident that, working together with me, you'll turn your relationship around?* (Reinvigorating the shared *good story* by developing interpersonal signs of greater hope.)

The following is a transcript of a hope-generating scaling conversation from Tobey's work with a couple presenting with what at first seems like an insoluble problem. Note how Tobey words her questions to highlight and induce small, incremental changes. Carlos, who had been employed part-time while looking for full-time work, had recently been offered a good position as an associate attorney in a law firm located in another part of the state. Linda did not want to move. She had a successful private therapy practice that had taken her years to build. She wanted to stay close to her parents and lifelong friends and didn't want to uproot their 7-year-old daughter. Neither of them wanted to live separately, but Carlos very much wanted to take the position.

Tension and arguments over this issue had escalated since Carlos received the job offer, which was about two weeks before this session. As a result of their conflict and frustration over this issue and their inability to find a solution, Carlos and Linda had begun talking about living separately. However, they were both concerned that if they did separate, their marriage might not survive. The transcript starts at a point in the session when Tobey decided to scale the couple's hope that, with her help, they could collaboratively resolve this issue and preserve their marriage.

TOBEY: On a scale of 1 to 10, with 1 representing that you have no hope that the two of you can solve this problem, and 10 meaning you're entirely convinced you will, where would each of you put yourself right now?

LINDA: I guess somewhere between 2 and 3.

CARLOS: For me, it's maybe 1½ at the most.

TOBEY: Linda, what do you suppose accounts for your being more optimistic than Carlos? (*Upon reflection, it might have been better for Tobey to have asked Carlos what Linda might know that accounts for her greater degree of hope. Asking Linda to explain why she's given the number she has puts her in the position of having to justify her optimism, which could possibly lead to an argument over whose numbers better reflect reality. In any event, Tobey is trying to use Linda's reasons for giving somewhat higher numbers as a starting place for conversation that might lead to an increase in Carlos's hopefulness.*)

LINDA: (*Frowning*) Well, the real thing is, I guess I assume I can solve it by giving in. I don't want to, and if I do we'll have other problems later on, I know that, so I haven't wanted to talk about this much. But if I agreed to move, this problem, anyway, would be solved. (*Linda recognizes that the problem can be solved, but in a way she doesn't favor and which might cause other problems later. But there is some possibility here—if this turns out to be the solution, Tobey could help Linda and Carlos construct ways to minimize the chances that it will cause future problems.)*

CARLOS: (*To both Linda and Tobey*) I don't want Linda doing something she really doesn't want to do. Something she'll resent me for later. I agree with her completely—for her just to give in isn't a solution. Linda, I know you don't want to move away from the Bay Area, and I don't want to force you into anything. But I do want to take this job. So I think we're stuck.

TOBEY: So this is one possibility—that Linda agrees to move with you. But neither of you wants to go that route because you both believe that if Linda does this, there's trouble ahead. And it sounds like there could be, maybe. Of course we can consider other options before you make any final decisions, but let's just explore this a little more before we move on. Suppose Linda does agree to move, so the family can remain together. And suppose we could figure out a plan to make both of you fairly confident her decision won't come back to haunt you—how hopeful would you guys be that this problem can be solved? What numbers would you give it then?

CARLOS: Well, if we could be pretty sure that Linda could be happy I'd say 7 or 8.

LINDA: It's hard to imagine I'd be happy if I moved, but if we could figure out a way I'd say about the same . . . 7 or 8.

TOBEY: Okay, suppose we start here. Not to say this is what you'll do, but to fully explore this option before deciding about it. Do you both think this would be a productive discussion? (*Notice that Tobey checks in with the couple; she does not assume that this kind of mediation around this particular solution is what the couple wants.*)

BOTH: Uh huh. All right.

TOBEY: Then let me ask you this, Linda. What number would you give your current level of hope that things could work out if you agree to move to San Diego with Carlos, with 1 being no hope at all and 10 being complete confidence?

LINDA: Before we walked in here I would have said 1, but now it's maybe 2½.

TOBEY: So think about this, and tell me, what will you notice different when your confidence has moved up to, say, 3½?

LINDA: (*Thinks for a while.*) That's a good question. I guess at some point we'd have to move so I could see how it actually went. I'm not sure I can tell in advance. But I guess I might be at 3½ when—and if—Carlos and I agreed that I could come up to the Bay Area, with or without the kids, as often as I want or need to. And maybe we'd have to agree I could still maintain my practice for, oh, say three days a week here in Oakland and commute back and forth for six months or so. I mean that'd be hard, it's not the greatest prospect, but I'd want to do it one way or another, if I did make the move. And this one is really important—if I'm really unhappy, after maybe six months or a year, Carlos would agree to look for work back here again. (*Now we're beginning to develop solutions using scaling questions. As the session continued, Carlos and Linda talked about his willingness to support her picture of how things would be if they both moved. Linda reiterated that she still didn't like the idea, but she was beginning to see how it might happen in a way that would make it acceptable. By the end of the session, although no decision was yet reached, both Linda and Carlos said their hope about making this decision together had risen to an 8 during the hour.*)

A few days before the next scheduled appointment, Linda called to cancel. In the voicemail message she left, she said, with some excitement, that a few days after the last session she had agreed to move to San Diego but that Carlos had just gotten a lead on a job in San Francisco, and they wanted to put off the next session until he found out whether he could get the San Francisco job. Linda called again several weeks later to report that Carlos had taken the job in San Francisco—an extratherapeutic factor of random chance that helped out. She thanked Tobey, said she thought they were doing fine now on their own, and said the session had been very helpful in reminding both her and Carlos how much they meant to each and that they could work out even difficult problems together.

## Scaling Motivation

In 1984, de Shazer wrote what is now considered a classic paper entitled *The Death of Resistance*. In that paper, he argued that traditional theories of resistance set therapist and client at odds by assuming that resistance is a characteristic or force within the client that seeks to prevent change. Such a perspective means that when a client is seen as resistant, therapy becomes a battle (against this force in the client) the clinician must win if therapy is to succeed. In psychodynamic models the therapist must overpower or defeat resistance through interpretation and corresponding client insight. In strategic systemic approaches, interventions must be designed to bypass or even utilize the forces of resistance. De Shazer offered a different view of resistance. He began by redefining resistant behavior simply as an indication that, at the moment, the client and therapist were working at cross-purposes. These signs were merely the client's way of telling the therapist to do something different. A second conclusion de Shazer drew in that paper has been a consistent article of faith for him as a brief therapist: To become more effective as an agent of change, it is less important to develop theories about *why* people resist change, and far more important to understand *how* people *do* change.

James Prochaska, working primarily in the addictions field, also questioned the utility of working from theories regarding what keeps people from changing unwanted behaviors (Prochaska, Norcross, & DiClementi, 1994). Like de Shazer, he and his associates thought it would be more fruitful to identify the common factors in cases where someone successfully changed an unwanted behavior or problematic habit. One conclusion they drew from studying people in therapy who successfully made such changes was this: The single most reliable predictor of success, regardless of the therapist's theoretical model or techniques, is the degree to which the person is ready to change. Concomitantly, therapy was more successful to the degree the therapist matched what she did and said to wherever the client currently was along a change-readiness continuum. Prochaska developed such a change-readiness continuum and a model for assessing the client's position on it at any given moment—from precontemplation, to contemplation, to preparation, to action, to maintenance, and finally to termination.

Both Prochaska's and de Shazer's theories of change shift clinical practice from stressing the necessity to overcome client resistance to encouraging negotiation and collaboration around goals and processes acceptable and meaningful to the client. This perspective emphasizes the importance of co-constructing solutions with clients, taking account of their current readiness and motivation to take active steps to change (Hoyt, 2000). Success in therapy requires not the therapist's ability to overpower the client's current reluctance to change, but instead his skill in identifying and matching the client's current readiness to take some small steps toward goals meaningful to him or her.

Miller and Rollnick (1991) and DiClemente (1991) have developed a clinical approach they call "motivational interviewing" based on Prochaska's stages of readiness. They assume people contemplating significant behavioral changes are naturally ambivalent about undertaking such changes. However, by viewing motivation as to some degree interpersonal (capable of being influenced in conversation with others) rather than a solely intrapersonal characteristic or fixed state of mind, motivational interviewers assume that *how* they talk with clients about their readiness to work actively for change can influence this factor for better or worse. Blending Prochaska's readiness continuum with their social-constructionist ideas and motivational interviewing techniques, Miller, Rollnick, and DiClemente offer ways to use therapy conversations to increase client motivation.

In RPT, we recognize that conversation and language can influence people's perceptions regarding their current motivation and that when their perceptions change their motivation also changes. Thus, we use motivation-scaling conversations to increase people's readiness to take active steps for the betterment of their relationship. Phil used this approach during an initial interview with Gerald and Tim, a couple who disagreed about whether they needed therapy. Gerald had been complaining that Tim was no longer emotionally available, they never seemed to do anything but bicker, they were completely losing their bond, and he was feeling very unloved. Finally, after Gerald threatened to leave the relationship, Tim reluctantly agreed to come to one session. When Phil asked how he might be helpful, Tim immediately replied that he didn't believe in therapy and didn't think he and Gerald needed any outside help. He explained that he was there only because Gerald had threatened to move out if he refused to come. Phil began by acknowledging Tim's reluctance and belief that many couples can solve their problems without professional help. Phil agreed therapy wasn't right for every couple and said that before they decided to work together it was important to find out, in fact, whether therapy might possibly be helpful for them. Tim began to relax and expressed appreciation about Phil's understanding.

So far Phil and Tim had been engaged in a visitor/host conversation. Phil, sensing Tim's readiness, invited him into a motivation-building scaling conversation. This, he hoped, would build a foundation for a solid therapeutic relationship based on customer/consultant conversation. Here is an edited transcript of part of this initial session.

PHIL: Not everyone wants or benefits from couples counseling. So, I'm not going to tell you I can guarantee therapy will be helpful or that you should definitely give it a try. But, I wonder if you'd be willing to give some thought to a few questions that might help us figure that out. How about it? Can I ask you a few questions to help you decide whether or not couples counseling might make a difference?

TIM: I guess so.

PHIL: Okay. I want to start with a sort of strange number question. Suppose we say the number 1 stands for your having no interest at all in coming to therapy and 10 stands for you being totally committed to coming and fully confident that with my help the two of you can turn your relationship around. What number between 1 and 10 would you say represents where you stand right now, today?

TIM: Well, first off I want it to be clear that I do want things to get better between me and Gerald. It's just that I think we can do it fine on our own. I don't see why we need to come to a therapist—nothing personal—to deal with our problems. So as far as coming here, I'd have to say I'm at about 1. Maybe 1½.

PHIL: Okay, fair and honest. Just out of curiosity, Tim, what number do you think Gerald would have guessed you'd say?

TIM: (*Thinks for a few seconds.*) Oh, probably minus 5. (*Both laugh.*)

GERALD: That's just about right. Definitely in the minus column. I had to make a lot of threats to get him to come here at all.

PHIL: (*Deciding to use this difference to construct motivation.*) So you have some willingness, some motivation. In fact, it sounds as though you're more motivated to use therapy than Gerald might think.

TIM: I guess so. But don't get me wrong. I don't really want to be here. I think therapy's a waste of time and money. We have friends who've been seeing shrinks, pardon the expression, for years. Their relationships are terrible; I can't see any real changes. I wouldn't want to be in those relationships, even with all the therapy. No way. (*Note that this response suggests a resource—a piece of the good story. Tim is saying that despite the problems he and Gerald are having, he would rather be in this relationship than some other. Phil might have chosen to explore with Tim what it is about their relationship that makes him feel this way. His answers might have provided pieces of the good story and possible strengths and resources Tim already finds in this relationship. But Phil sticks with the theme of scaling motivation.*)

PHIL: I understand you'd want something different to happen for the two of you in therapy. You'd want to see changes, and right away. So let me ask you this: Suppose when you two go home tonight you see some positive changes. (*Embedded suggestion to watch for such changes.*) Some changes that cause you to maybe move up to a solid 1½ or maybe 2 in your feelings that working here with me could really make a difference. (*Notice Phil makes the potential change very small.*) What would you be noticing?

Tim answered by identifying a number of small things he would notice that evening that would move him up in his willingness to participate actively in therapy with Gerald. During the rest of the session, Gerald and Tim had several chances to talk about ways they wanted to improve their relationship. As they talked with Phil and each other, and as each listened to what the other was saying, the atmosphere became noticeably friendlier and warmer. Gerald said it made a big difference to hear that Tim very much wanted to work on rebuilding their relationship, though he wasn't sure they needed therapy. Thus reassured, Gerald was able to use the therapy hour to talk about changes he wanted, and he responded positively to Tim's requests for changes as well. By the end of the hour, Tim had warmed up considerably to the possibility that therapy might be helpful and that changes could occur fairly rapidly. Toward the close of the session, when Phil asked Tim to scale his willingness to come back, Tim almost surprised himself when he said he was now at 6½, possibly 7. Tim and Gerald did return the following week and continued to work with Phil for over two months until their successful termination. The following are some questions we use to scale and amplify motivation:

- *On a scale from 1 to 10, 1 being no motivation and 10 being willingness to go to any length, how motivated would you say you are (your partner is) to make the changes you want (are asking him/her to make)? What number do you think he/she would give himself/herself?*
- *What will your partner notice you doing differently that will tell him/her that your motivation has moved up one number?*
- *What will you see your partner doing differently that will signal you that his/her level of motivation is higher than you thought?*
- *What do you suppose you could do that would cause your partner's motivation to go up a notch?*
- *What has your partner done recently that helped raise your motivation level?*

## Scaling for Safety

We want to return now to the question of how to work effectively with domestic violence in couples therapy. We touched on this in our discussion of active neutrality (chapter 3). Domestic violence is a serious problem,[3] and couples therapists must have effective ways of helping couples dealing with this. At this point in our discussion of scaling we want to show how this method of inquiry can be a powerful tool in dealing with this challenging and, when it arises, central, issue. A great deal has been written about the therapist's role in cases involving domestic violence, and we will briefly survey that literature here. We want to question the common viewpoint that it is always the proper role of the therapist to take a directive, interventionist stance; it is far from clear that such a stance, in the long run, is the best way to address the issue of violence in couples therapy.

Holtzworth-Monroe, Beatty, and Anglin (1995), for example, reflect the interventionist perspective, arguing that all couples should be screened for domestic violence, regardless of the presenting issues. "It is the therapist's responsibility to stress the dangerousness of the violence and the importance of targeting violent behavior for therapeutic intervention. To do so, it is useful to firmly adopt the stance that it is the therapist's 'expert opinion' that the violence is a serious problem, even if the couple does not necessarily agree, and that no violent acts are acceptable within the relationship" (p. 321). Strategic family therapist Cloe Madanes also calls for an active and directive stance for the marital therapist in cases of domestic violence, beginning with the gathering of detailed descriptions of past violent encounters followed up with the use of therapist-instituted interventions such as extracting confessions from the violent spouse/partner, enforcing separation of the spouses/partners, and requiring the violent partner to engage in apology rituals in front of friends and family members (Madanes, 1990; Madanes, Keim, & Smelser, 1995). Many feminist therapists criticize the traditional systemic approaches, arguing that such approaches, because they imply that the abused partner is in some way partly responsible for the problem-dynamic, blame the victim (Margolin & Berman, 1993, as cited in Holtzworth-Monroe et al., 1995). These clinicians prefer to educate and sensitize people to power imbalances and gender issues and help both partners resist the larger social and familial discourses and practices that they believe legitimize male domestic violence (Pence & Paymar, as cited in White & Epston, 1990). Still other couples therapists approach the issue of domestic violence with behavioral-cognitive techniques. In individual, conjoint, and group therapy formats, they teach offending partners anger-management skills and both partners conflict management and improved communication skills (Holtzworth-Monroe et al., 1995). All these approaches work from the assumption that it is the therapist's responsibility to assess domestic violence, convince the couple that if domestic violence is occurring it must be the first and sole issue addressed in therapy, and that the therapist must intervene actively, sometimes going so far as to force the separation of the spouses.

While we share the same concern about the large social harm of domestic violence and its profound destructive effect on all the individuals in families, our approach is quite different. Because RPT is collaborative and solution-oriented, we believe, even with issues as emotionally-loaded and of such large social impact as domestic violence, it is important to keep the focus on what the couple wants to change, on what they think is important, on what they think will help them. That does not mean we leave our own values and responses out of the equation, however.

When it appears that one or both partners behave in physically and/or emotionally abusive ways, we attempt from our position of active neutrality to build a consensus for exploring whether the couple can reach their relationship goals if the violence or potential for violence continues. Rather than focusing on the demarcation or elimination of abusive behavior, we reframe the issue as one of safety (Johnson & Goldman, 1996; Lipchick & Kubicki, 1996; Turnell & Edwards, 1999). We ask if the partners think they can turn their relationship around as long as one or both of them feel emotionally and/or physically unsafe in the relationship. We have never, in our experience, heard a couple answer this in the affirmative. Once a couple, often with some measure of fear, anger, sadness, or anxiety, acknowledges that they will not be able to reach their relationship goals in an unsafe atmosphere, we have laid a foundation for talking about how to build safety into the relationship. If we can do that, other goals can be reached; if we cannot, the partners in the couple will usually begin to consider other options. This process of co-constructed ends and means, as we work on the goal of safety, sometimes results in couples using resources and tools that other clinicians would impose—group therapy for an angry spouse, family dialogue, entering a treatment facility for substance abuse, or separation, but because the couple has decided on and instituted these practices, they are more likely to pursue them. The couple may also come up with practices quite different than these and particular to their own case, but in either situation, any solutions will be developed by the couple themselves, as the therapist talks with them about the goal of establishing safety.

Scaling is an effective technique for exploring safety. Phil worked with a couple in which the husband had a serious cocaine habit and was carrying on a secret affair (which the wife suspected and confirmed during the therapy). One evening the wife came home from work to find her husband high. An argument ensued about the suspected affair and what the husband called the wife's suspicious nature. This escalated beyond their usual screaming and name-calling, and the husband struck the wife, bruising her face and cutting her lip. She called the police, but when they arrived she decided not to press charges. They agreed that night to go into couples therapy, and the next day the wife made an appointment with Phil.

After listening to the wife describe her experiences with her husband's drug use, abusiveness, and possible affair and to the husband's denials and countercharges about his wife's suspicious nature and her "bitchiness," Phil chose to begin by focusing on the potential for further violence by scaling safety. He asked both partners how safe each felt living together under the same roof, with 1 being a complete lack of safety and 10 being completely safe. The husband said 4 and the wife said 1. Phil then asked what each thought the chances were that couples therapy could produce much change in their marriage if these numbers remained where they were. Both admitted the chances were next to none. He then asked if they thought it might be best to begin by seeing whether they could increase the sense of safety at home before tackling other changes. They both agreed this was a good place to start.

Phil asked both the husband and the wife what would make it possible for each of them to move up one number on this safety scale. The husband said he could move up if his wife would stop trying to prove that he was having an affair, if she would stop "poking around in my stuff" looking for evidence of something "that's all in her head." The wife answered by saying she would feel safer if, when she came home from work, her husband hadn't been spending the afternoon getting high. She added that whenever she came into the house and could tell her husband was high, she got scared. When he was straight, she wasn't afraid he would "get crazy and start screaming at me or get violent."

These answers suggested that, for both people, safety would result when the other person changed. Phil considered asking what first changes each would notice if the husband moved up from 4 to 5 and the wife from 1 to 2 in feeling emotionally and physically safe in the marriage. However, he assumed that such a question might further conversation in which no sense of agency could be established. Instead, he asked a perspective-shifting question (see chapter 8), inviting each partner to tell him what he or she thought they could do differently that would move the other up one notch on the safety scale. What did the husband think he could do that would move his wife up from 1 to 2, and what did the wife think she could do that would move her husband up from 4 to 5?

The husband said he thought that if he didn't get high in the afternoon so that his wife wouldn't need to feel afraid when she came home, that would move her up to a 2, maybe even higher. Phil asked him how confident he was that he could do this, with or without outside help. He said he was now very committed to saving his marriage, and that if his wife would feel safer if he didn't "use" in the afternoons, it would be easy for him to cut back. The wife, for her part, agreed not to bring up her suspicions about the possible affair and to leave the issue alone in their conversations, at least for the time being.

Phil was skeptical of the husband's statements of marital commitment and high level of motivation, and his expectation that he could easily control his drug use. However, he did not handle this by confrontational intervention, nor did his questions imply doubt or suspicion. Phil trusted that the truth regarding these matters would emerge in ways that would allow the partners, individually or collectively, to move forward. He ended the session by complimenting the couple for making the decision to seek help and their willingness to try making some difficult changes. He offered the couple the "formula first-session task,"[4] asking them to pay attention to times when safety was present and to look for what was making that happen and how it made a difference in their relationship when both of them felt safer.

When they returned for their next session, the wife reported that her husband "did better the first couple of afternoons after the session" but then returned to his afternoon drug use again. He had also used at night, and they had had several pretty awful and frightening fights. The husband said he'd been much better about his cocaine use and that the fights came about because she "kept bugging me about that affair she thinks I'm having." Phil asked them both to scale their confidence that the husband could bring his drug use under control, which both had agreed was the foundation for building greater safety into their relationship. The wife said her confidence level now, at least if her husband refused to seek outside help for his problem, was "zero to none." The husband argued that his wife was, typically, overly pessimistic. He said he was going to try harder, and this time gave his own confidence level "about a 6½ or 7." Phil helped the wife to explore what she would do if she became, at some particular time, afraid that her husband might become physically violent, and she decided she would leave the apartment if she felt they were past the point of talking without an explosion.

After several more meetings, the husband was still getting high daily. He had many excuses to offer, invariably accusing the wife of causing him somehow to get high and lose his temper and making him feel bad about himself because he was still out of work. His wife reported that her perceived level of safety had not moved above 1, and that it was getting clearer to her that things were not going to improve. When Phil asked what her husband could do, if anything, that would cause her to feel safer in the marriage, she said it would make a difference if he began going regularly to NA or went into a treatment facility. Again the husband said angrily that he didn't need outside help and that she should "just give me time, and stop this constant pressuring."

The wife came to the next session alone. She explained that during the week her husband had gotten very high and drunk one afternoon, and when she came home she could tell he was potentially violent. She immediately left the apartment and went to stay with a girlfriend. Painfully, she recognized that she had not been able even to begin to feel safer during the time they had worked on this in therapy. She decided to file for divorce, and got a restraining order against him. A few days later, several friends who had not wanted to speak up before told her that her husband was indeed having an affair, and in fact had had several others during their marriage. This reconfirmed her intention to leave the relationship. The wife continued to meet with Phil over the next four months as she went through the divorce process. (Phil invited the husband to come in individually, but he declined.) In therapy, she talked about how painful it was to have to face the truth about her husband and her marriage and how much she had stopped taking care of herself over time. Her ex-husband continued to be a difficult presence in her life from time to time, but gradually, as her confidence and pleasure in her own independence continued to increase and she developed new ways to handle these moments, his influence in her life diminished. By the time she ended therapy, she said she was well on her way to rediscovering an old self she really liked and was feeling confident she could continue building a new life on her own.

In this case the goal of safety was achieved, even though the couple's initial goal of saving the marriage was not. When the wife decided that safety was a priority, and when it became obvious that this goal was not going to be met within the relationship, she took steps to change her life by leaving her husband. This case and others like it have led us to confirm what other solution-oriented, collaborative therapists report:

A perhaps unexpected benefit of solution-focused treatment with cases of domestic violence is the influence it can have in supporting a victim of abuse to end the abusive relationship safely and expediently. There is an inaccurate perception among many clinicians working with abused women that couple treatment will, like some evil potion, have the effect of forcing an unwilling woman to override her own better judgment and continue in a relationship that is dangerous and un-changing. (Johnson & Goldman, 1996, pp. 190–191)

Although scaling questions may initially appear overly cerebral or cut-and-dried, or perhaps seem like merely an adjunct tool that is only occasion-ally appropriate, they are actually extremely flexible and useful forms of therapeutic inquiry. They help the therapist avoid certain language traps, shift perspective, deal noncombatively with individually differing points of view, and co-construct with the clients change strategies that are step-by-step, accompanied by concrete, observable signs, and initiate and support narratives of change.

# CHAPTER 8

# Perspective-Shifting Conversations: Building Empathy and Thickening the *Good Story* Narrative

In RPT we seek to help partners generate new and more useful ways of perceiving and making meaning of each other's actions. Interactions between people are circular and mediated by perception and meaning construction. We want to influence what people notice, as well as the meanings they make of these perceptions, because it is their perceptions along with the meanings they attribute to them that will determine their behavior. While there may be an interrelationship (a causal link) between the behavior of one partner and the reactions of the other, what is thus more important for the therapist working with couples is the interrelationship between each partner's *perceptions* of actions and reactions. In all our conversations with couples we aim to reinvigorate their shared *good story* narrative so that each partner sees the other through perceptual and interpretive lenses that are relationship-enhancing. Perspective-shifting conversations are a particularly effective method of doing this.

Because people are motivated by the meanings they make of others' actions, in an intimate relationship where the partners are able to talk about, understand, and modify those meanings, it becomes easier to think and act in ways that support a positive relationship climate. The result is that intimate relationships tend to thrive. This idea informs most communication and feeling-sharing approaches to couples therapy (Gottman, 1999; Greenberg & Johnson, 1988; Heitler, 1990; Hendrix, 1988; Johnson, 1996; Markman, Stanley, & Blumberg, 1994; Notarius & Markman, 1993). However, RPT differs in some important respects from such approaches. There are situations where we teach couples communications skills and help partners to talk about their feelings. But we do not assume that simply having people talk about their feelings will lead to greater intimacy, empathy, and relationship satisfaction, or to perceptual change. The question is this: How can we best conduct therapy so that what people learn about each other promotes relationship satisfaction and contributes to more positive interactions in daily life? Mastering the use of perspective-shifting questions is one way to do this. We use them constantly, in many different forms, because they enhance empathy and clarify meanings as they bring couples into an immediate partnership context. They step people outside the givens of the problem story, and they encourage the partners, with no exhortation or discussion about who is responsible for what, to take steps of their own to produce change.

We have always been interested in the function of meaning in relationship therapy. In our early years of practice, in order to build empathic understanding between partners in a conflictual relationship, we often used the psychodramatic technique of role-reversal to shift people out of their combative, adversarial, villain-hero stances. When Tobey used role-reversal in her psychodrama groups, she found it a powerful tool for helping group members develop insight into the experiences and motives of others in their lives; this often helped people alter their behavior and attitudes in ways that supported change. In these group settings, however, people's partners were not present. When we used this same role-reversal technique in our work with couples—asking partners to physically switch seats and continue their conversation from the point of view of the other person, we found that role-reversal did not function as infallibly to enhance empathy. All too often people simply took the opportunity to "teach" each other something by caricature or exaggeration, representing the other's behaviors and viewpoints in ways designed to show how difficult the partner was to live with. Nevertheless, we continued trying over the years to come up with a way to incorporate the meaning- and perspective-shifting aspects of role-reversal into our work with couples.

We also tried to foster empathic understanding by having the partners talk directly to each other about problems, concerns, and conflicts while we teased out positive feelings and reframed their comments in ways that were less accusatory. In this way we hoped to reduce defensiveness and antagonism and bring about more self-disclosure and mutual understanding. We hoped to make the therapy room a place where people could learn to talk about their concerns and differences in a safe and respectful manner and atmosphere—so that meaning revisions could take place and mutual understanding could increase. The idea was that as couples gained greater mutual empathy and learned to talk about difficult issues in noncombative and nondefensive ways, intimacy would grow and the couple would leave therapy with new communication and conflict-resolution skills they could continue using on their own.

While this communication-coach approach made sense in theory, in practice it didn't quite live up to its promise. When people talked about their conflicts and problems, even with our reframing and redirecting, long-term changes in the relationship often failed to materialize. As we came to understand the role of the *good story/bad story* dichotomy, we understood why. Because most sessions focused on some element of the partners' *bad story* narratives, their *bad stories* continued to serve as the dominant perceptual and interpretive lenses, even if partners momentarily were able to see some merit in the other's point of view. Each week, many couples would come to their sessions and report about the fight they had the other night, and although they might include some reference to their understanding of the other's reasons or thinking, their examples still tended to be descriptions of why the other partner was unreasonable, wrong, or to blame for the trouble-some interaction. It could become discouraging to work hard, session after session, to help a couple express understandings of each other's experience and point of view only to have them return, in the next session, to square one. In addition, some couples saw these sessions as necessary in order to work out their conflicts, and became dependent on the context of therapy and our intervention to deal with their daily ups and downs.

Many of the couples we worked with in this way did in fact make changes. Over time, most reported that their fights diminished in intensity and frequency. They also reported greater closeness and warmth. But we weren't sure the extent to which what we were doing was actually making a difference. It seemed to us that the mere fact that the partners were able to talk about things in the safety of the therapy office, in front of a nonjudgmental third party who responded warmly to their good qualities as individuals and as a couple, helped to ease the hostility, misunderstanding, and mistrust. We came to the conclusion that creating this atmosphere was important, but we felt it wasn't enough. Guiding couples in conversations in order to build empathic understanding could lead to positive change, but only in a hit-or-miss way; we wanted to find a more consistently reliable therapeutic process.

With our development of the *good story/bad story* narrative continuum, we came to realize that perspective-shifting conversations between the partners and us and between the partners themselves could lead to positive and durable changes when those conversations revolved around elements of the couple's *good story* rather than the individual partners' *bad stories*. As our clinical orientation became more solution-oriented and competency-based, we found ourselves asking people more perspective-shifting questions in relation to their *good story* narratives (past exceptions and successes and preferred future scenarios). This helped people to develop more empathy, motivated them to act from their preferred selves and acknowledge the other's preferred self, thickened and solidified the context of the couple's *good story* narrative, and facilitated the couple's collaborative efforts in solution-building.

## Circular and Reflexive Questions: The Milan Family Therapy Center

Some of the earliest perspective-shifting questions were developed by the Systemic Family Therapy Center in Milan, Italy (Boscolo, Cecchin, Hoffman, & Penn, 1987). In their early work with families with severely disturbed children, the group closely followed the ideas and methods of the MRI brief therapy project (Fisch, Weakland, & Segal, 1982; Watzlawick et al., 1974). They used reframing ("positive connotations" placed on problematic behavior) to make subsequent paradoxical task assignments reasonable and then gave these assignments ("rituals") to the families. Over time, some members of the Milan group (Boscolo and Checcin, primarily) became interested in the way the private meaning-making narratives of individual family members seemed to play a significant role in the formation and resolution of family problems. Consequently, they relied less and less on reframing and paradoxical homework assignments and more on the use of what they called "circular questions" to help family members develop multiple perspectives and modify meanings around problematic behavior.

For example, rather than reframing a daughter's anorexia as her way of keeping the heat off the parents' marital troubles (positive connotation), Boscolo and Checcin might ask the daughter's siblings the following circular question: "Which of your parents, your mother or your father, seems most concerned about your sister's eating problems?" As each child answered this question, family members could discover the varying and multiple ways they saw the family and the sister's behavior. As multiple perspectives and meanings emerged in these conversations, the therapist could develop creative ways to solve the problem of the daughter's anorectic behavior.

## Internalized-Other Questions, Bifurcating Questions, and the Preferred View of Self: Narrative Therapy

As constructionist and narrative ideas and practices continued to flourish in the family therapy field, therapists developed new methods of interviewing that fostered generative narratives, multiple perspectives, and helpful meaning reconstructions among family members. These new methods aimed to deconstruct paralyzing, monoperspective narratives so that family members could generate stories that expanded choice and possibility. For example, one role-reversal interviewing technique developed in the narrative therapy approach is called "internalized-other interviewing" (Epston, 1993; Tomm, 1988). David Epston (1993) remarks that internalized-other interviews are especially useful with "those warring couples who construe counseling as a venue to contest their differences. These couples seem to lack any conception of themselves as bound together, for better or worse, in a relationship" (p. 183).

In internalized-other interviewing, the therapist asks one partner to put him- or herself in the shoes of the other partner and be interviewed as this person. (This "interview" style, in which one person speaks to the therapist rather than to the partner, is one way to minimize the exaggerations and caricaturing we used to see in our early efforts to get partners to reverse roles psychodramatically.) Internalized-other interviewing brings forth assumptions and beliefs the partner being interviewed currently holds about the feelings, needs, wants, perceptions, attitudes, etc. of the other partner. Having to answer questions about the subjective experience of the other may increase the interviewee's understanding of the motives, wishes, and feelings of the partner being portrayed. When the interview is completed, the other partner is asked about how accurately his or her partner answered the questions. Rather than fighting over who's right and what really happened, conversation now turns on how closely the interviewed partner reflected the experiences, thoughts, and feelings of the partner he or she was attempting to portray.

Another type of empathy-enhancing question is Karl Tomm's "bifurcating" question (Tomm, 1988, 1993). In chapter 1, we referred to Tomm's theory of the distributed self—that one's self-view is not constant and only sited internally, but is rather multiple and "distributed" in different relationships, in a sense held and reflected by the others in a person's life. This interesting definition suggests that the self is multiple, an agglomerate of all the views and ideas held about a person, distributed over the community in which that person moves, rather than an isolated and single entity carried by the individual into all relationships. So a person's self is "distributed" across a spectrum, carried, for instance, partly by Aunt Mary, who sees Linda as a good, kind niece; Dad, who carries an idea of her as stubborn and ungrateful; Margaret, a friend who sees her as fussy; and Bruce, a coworker for whom she's savvy and funny. In each of these relationships, Linda experiences herself somewhat differently, and in this community, her self is distributed in different aspects among different people. This concept of self gives strong place to perceptions in the formation of meanings about self and relationship. We mentioned this concept of the "distributed self" in connection with the couple's *good* and *bad story* narratives, explaining our assumption that part of what makes a relationship attractive to someone is a sense that the other sees him or her in preferred ways. We reintroduce this term to stress again the social constructionist idea that "self" is not an ego sense or an identity one develops and holds in isolation, but a social construction. Who I think myself to be is in part my experience of "me" as seen through the eyes of various others—an "I" experienced through my experience of your experience of me. Obviously, conversations in which people talk about how they perceive each other, their assumptions about how they think the other perceives them, and how they want to be perceived open up numerous possibilities for reinvigorating a couple's shared *good story*.

Tomm uses bifurcating questions to clarify each partner's preferred ideas of self ("Are you the kind of person who wants to be seen as helpful and willing to go along with others, or are you the kind of person who'd rather get it done a certain way and let the chips fall where they may?") and to clarify which actions on his or her part this person thinks will foster either an undesirable or preferred distributed self. Once the person has clarified that a particular change in behavior or attitude is likely to have a positive impact on the other partner's view of him or her and on the relationship, it becomes possible to explore what the person might do to bring about this desired change.

In a similar vein, Joseph Eron and Thomas Lund (1996) discuss the "preferred view of self" in their narrative solutions approach. They think of this "preferred view" as a representation of self that people seek to maintain and want others to hold of them. Because this preferred view of self is socially constructed (and in part distributed), if a person does not see this preferred view reflected in the things others say and the way others interact with him or her, he or she will have difficulty holding onto this view of self and feel some measure of distress in the relationship.

In RPT, we pay close attention to the indicators of each partner's preferred view of self. We reflect back to people these preferred views of themselves, when we can do so honestly, and we try to see the ways in which they have been enacting these ideas of self. This builds rapport and trust; each person, regardless of the partner's complaints or personal feelings of blameworthiness or failure, experiences the therapist as seeing both self and partner in a favorable light. Then, as we hear about the gaps between how each partner wants to be seen and is currently experiencing being seen, as well as the gaps between how people want to see themselves and those actions of their own that may challenge these preferred views of self, we can ask perspective-shifting questions. These questions often introduce an element of doubt about currently held ideas, so they must be asked from a stance of genuine curiosity and not as rhetorical challenges. For example, if we are exploring what appears to be a gap between a preferred view of self and certain actions a person has taken, we might ask a husband who is verbally abusive to his wife what Eron and Lund (1996) call the "mystery question," a question designed to invite the respondent to join the therapist in a curious exploration of the disjunction. The generic type of the question is this: "How did someone with X preferred attributes wind up in Y situation and being viewed by others in Z ways?" In our example, suppose this particular husband has been telling us he believes himself to be a fair-minded person, and that this is an important quality of his (his preferred view of self). We might ask—and this must be gentle and with genuine openness to his answer: "How did someone who's pretty fair-minded and able to keep his cool in a crisis, a lot of times, wind up in this situation we've been talking about, having a wife who feels unsafe living with him, who says she's terrified by what she's calling your 'rage attacks,' and being seen by your kids as scarey?"

We are interested in fostering agency and in generating people's enthusiasm for taking an active part in change. Inquiring about linkages between meanings and behaviors can be very helpful in this. We have talked about how, in exploring *bad story* narratives, we are mainly attuned to picking up clues to exits, doorways from the *bad story* world to the *good story* world. If we listen well, conversations about problems and the *bad stories* can help us tease out each partner's preferred view of self. We, along with the couple, can learn how each person's actions may be preventing him or her from seeing the preferred self mirrored in the other's actions, and how to reverse this. Perspective-shifting questions help to reveal the links between the specific behavioral changes each partner has been pressing for and the way those changes will serve as signs that each partner can experience him- or herself, the other, and the relationship in preferred ways.

It is interesting to note that behaviorist couples therapist John Gottman (1994, 1999) talks about the fact that a defining characteristic distinguishing successful from unsuccessful marriages is the ratio of positive to negative comments and gestures partners make to and about each other, as well as whether those comments and gestures are noticed and produce observable positive reactions. Gottman's research findings support the idea that an experience of the preferred self plays an important role in satisfying relationship life. When an individual sees a preferred self mirrored in the comments and actions of the other partner, the relationship will thrive; where each sees a self reflected back in undesirable ways, the relationship will cycle downward.

# Relationship Questions:
## Solution-Focused Brief Therapy

Solution-focused brief therapists have also developed interviewing techniques that can expand people's ability to entertain multiple perspectives. In their approach, perspective-shifting questions are called "relationship questions" (Berg & Kelly, 2000; De Jong & Berg, 1998; Hoyt & Berg, 1998). These questions, asked during conversations about past exceptions and preferred futures, call on clients to put themselves in other people's shoes and describe the observable details of the scenarios, especially what they see themselves doing differently. The answers to these questions help to identify resources and develop solutions.

We have drawn from all these models in developing our RPT perspective-shifting questions. They serve us well in our effort to recreate partnership, help couples develop action plans for dealing with problems and concerns, soften the hold of the individual *bad story* narratives, and generate and thicken the couple's shared *good story* narratives. We find it useful to distinguish two types of perspective-shifting inquiries: outside-perspective questions and role-reversal questions.

## Outside-Perspective Questions

Outside-perspective questions are used principally in goal-building conversations where we are coauthoring future pictures and *good story* narratives and concentrating on identifying desired observable behaviors and preferred partner interactions. Outside-perspective questions ask people to see themselves through another person's eyes (usually their partner's) and describe what they notice is different that will tell the other partner things are changing for the better. For example: "You're saying that it's important to you that your wife trust you again. What do you suppose will be the first things she notices you doing differently that will tell her she can begin to trust you again?" or "Suppose it's the morning after the miracle and your wife trusts you again—what will she notice is different about you that tells her it's okay to trust you?" Such questions build detail and actuality into the scenarios we are talking about. This type of question influences the interpersonal field, enhancing partnership, because it requires the respondent to take account of another's point of view in an inclusive way.

Outside-perspective questions focus specifically on actions that can be noticed or observed by others, not on their possible meaning or emotional impact on others. People are simply asked to shift perspective and describe themselves or the details of the preferred future scenario or past exception/success experience through the eyes of another. Observation, not interpretation. The actions described can function as imagined signals of change for the speaker, and this process, in itself, can trigger the line of thought or intention that will lead to change. In a goal-constructing conversation where a husband says he wants to feel less depressed, we might ask, "What will be the first thing your wife will notice is different about you that will tell her you're starting to feel better?" Or, when a wife says she wants to feel closer to her husband again, we might ask, "What will be the first signs your kids will see that will tell them you're feeling closer to Henry again? Maybe they wouldn't talk about (or they're too young to talk about) things in this way, but what will they see?" In a hope-generating scaling conversation we might use this outside-perspective question: "You're telling me that right now you're at a 4 in your confidence that that this marriage can be saved. I'm wondering what your wife will notice is different about you when you've moved up to a 5." (These outside-perspective questions do, of course, entail a kind of role reversal; the husband in this case must pick out signals that might stand out to his wife, but these kinds of shifts in perspective do not necessarily require an increase in empathy.) As the husband tries to construct his answer he must see himself from the outside, as others would, and, in so doing, see differences that can then be signs to him (and to her if she is present in the session) that he is feeling more optimistic about the future of the marriage.

In short, outside-perspective questions ask people to imagine how *others* will answer some form of this change-signifying question: "What will you notice is different when . . . ?"

Here are a few more examples of outside-perspective questions:

- *What will your wife notice is different about you when she's "showing more interest in your point of view"?*
- *What will your friends notice is different about the two of you when you're "starting to get some of the old feelings back"?*

# Role-Reversal Questions

The second type of perspective-shifting question, role-reversal questions, ask people to see themselves through another's eyes, and then to imagine the impact of their behavior on this other person and the possible meanings the other might draw from what he or she observes. We use role-reversal questions only in the context of exceptions and preferred future-picture conversations—in other words, *good story* scenarios. We do not use them to try and show people the negative effect their behavior has on others, but instead to identify the effects of behaviors associated with their preferred scenarios and outcome pictures. For example, we would not ask: "Joe, put yourself in your wife's shoes—how do you think it made Mary feel when you came home late from the office without calling?" Instead we might ask: "Joe, imagine yourself as Mary for a moment, and imagine that Joe, knowing he was going to be late, called you to let you know that. Then, when Joes comes home after the kids are asleep, tell me how you're feeling toward him, even though he's late?"

Role-reversal questions seek to enlarge both a feeling and cognitive understanding of the other's experience; in other words, they build empathy and contribute to the process of developing alternative stories. We usually ask them as a follow-up to outside-perspective questions. Once people are able to tell us what the other partner will see them doing in a preferred scenario, it's an easy next step to ask them *how* what they see makes a difference to them. Once a wife answers the question "What will be the first thing Jack notices different about you when 'your sense of connection' is coming back?" we can ask her how she supposes his seeing her do these things will *make a difference* to him (what it will mean to him). Role-reversal questions ask people to imagine how what they are doing in preferred scenarios will affect the other person, building new links between action, perception, expectation, and meaning.

Here are some sample role-reversal questions that can be used in following up people's answers to outside-perspective questions:

- *How do you suppose seeing these changes in you will make a difference to your partner?*
- *If I were to ask your partner how these changes will help to rebuild your relationship, what do you suppose he/she will say?*
- *How do you think your partner might want to change when he/she sees you doing these things he/she says make a difference to him/her?*
- *When your partner sees these changes in you, what will this tell him/her about you (your commitment to the marriage, your feelings about him/her, whatever words the other partner used to describe his or her meta-goals)?*
- *Jim, see if you can answer this question from your heart of hearts, you know, as you imagine, deep in your heart, Sue would answer it. Speaking as Sue . . . tell me, Sue, how will it make a difference to you to see Jim doing these things?*

These types of questions invite people to reflect on the impact of their own actions on others in the context of the *good story*. They engender an awareness of the preferred selves of both the speaker and the other, and, particularly, of the connection between them. They engage and enlarge the bond between couples that arises when they can understand each other's behavior in a positive light. In other words, role-reversal questions allow one partner to "discover" the other's meanings and, through them, their preferred self. They do not require the other partner to explain his or her own meanings, which can sometimes become a ground for accusation or argument about differing perspectives. Instead, they engage the respondent in reflecting on and showing an imaginal understanding of the partner's views. This is a way of leaving the *bad story* version of the partner behind; thus, these questions serve to elaborate ways each partner can act to modify the distributed self held by the other.

We want to end this chapter with a partial transcript of a session in which Phil uses both perspective-shifting and scaling questions to invigorate a couple's *good story*. Notice how, as the couple answers his questions, their perceptions and meanings shift, enlarge, and evolve. Just as Phil's questions generate their answers, the answers influence Phil's next questions.

PHIL: I'd like each of you to imagine that the number 1 represents your relationship when things were bad enough that one of you made the call setting up this appointment. And the number 10 represents how things will be different when you've successfully changed them and you're feeling satisfied and happy with the way things are between you. What number would each of you give the current state of things?

MIKE: I guess a 2.

DONNA: 4 or 5.

PHIL: Okay. So Donna, for you things have moved up from the worst times all the way to 4 or 5, almost halfway. Mike, you're still seeing things down around 2. Mike, what do you suppose Donna is experiencing in the relationship these days that leads her to rate things 4 or 5? (*Role-reversal question. Notice Phil is not asking about Mike's 2. Instead, he uses this question to invite Mike to reflect on Donna's apparently more positive perspective.*)

MIKE: Maybe you should ask *her*.

PHIL: Well, I might in a bit, but for now it might be helpful, for starters, for you to think about the question and give me your best guess.

MIKE: Well, it could be she's feeling better about it because we've been spending more time together lately. I haven't been going on-line after dinner so much . . . yeah, and we even went out to a movie the other night. That was fun.

PHIL: So you think that because Donna sees the two of you doing more things together, and she notices you're making more time to be with her, these things cause her to feel better about the relationship. I'm wondering how you decided to do those things—you know, things that help her to feel better about the two of you. (*Notice that Phil is beginning to establish agency.*)

MIKE: I didn't really think about it. . . . I guess I do some of that stuff 'cause I want her to be happy. And I like it too, don't get me wrong. I don't like all the complaining, but when she's in a good mood, she's great.

PHIL: Do you think she'd notice your wanting to spend more time with her if she found ways to keep herself in a better mood more of the time?

MIKE: Hey, ask me a hard one. These questions are too easy. (*He laughs.*)

PHIL: Well, okay here's a harder one. How would she know—what would she see is different about you—that will tell her being in a better mood more of the time is making a real difference to you? (*Outside-perspective question.*)

MIKE: Well, first off, she *would* see me spending more time with her. I'd come home, more often, and say let's go out to dinner for a change. Instead of going into the den and turning on the news or getting on the computer. I guess I'd tell her how much I like it when she's being nicer. (*Already imagining ways to be responsive.*)

PHIL: Okay, that's a good start. Now I'd like to ask Donna a few questions. (*Turns to Donna.*) Donna, Mike says he sees things at 2 these days. And as you heard him say, he thinks your numbers are higher than his because lately the two of you have been spending more time together. Is he on the mark there?

DONNA: Yeah. We've done a few more things together. I didn't really think about it, but I guess that might be part of why I'm feeling better than I was, a little better anyway.

PHIL: Apart from you telling us this now, how would Mike have known you've been feeling better, that his showing you he wants to spend more time with you has made a difference? (*Outside-perspective question.*)

DONNA: I guess I probably haven't let him know. Till now. I mean it's pretty new, and there's still a lot of other stuff . . . maybe I'm a little cautious. I could do it now, though. (*Turns to Mike.*) Would it mean something to you if I said I do appreciate it, that we're spending more time together lately?

MIKE: Sure it would. I pretty much get the picture you can't stand me, and don't want to be around me, even though you complain all the time we don't spend enough time together. That's one reason I wasn't as hopeful as you about the way things are going.

PHIL: So Mike, suppose Donna started letting you know when she likes being with you and feels good about you and the relationship, when you show her you want to do things together. If she did that more, would that move you up from the number you gave before?

MIKE: Are you kidding? I might go as high as 7 or 8 if she told me once in a while she sees how hard I'm trying to make things better, instead of always pointing out how I disappoint her, all the ways I'm doing it wrong. We'd go off the chart if she actually told me once in a while that she loves me, or gave me the feeling she was glad we were together. Or even that she was still interested in me physically.

PHIL: Wow. So I'm starting to get the picture that the two of you already have some ideas, and that, sometimes, you're already doing some things that have moved both of you up from where you were when things were at their worst. (*Phil is describing change as already in progress.*) So that if both of you continued to work actively to make time to be together, and express your pleasure about it, you'll have taken some big steps to turn your relationship around. Am I hearing this right? This is pretty exciting.

DONNA: Yeah. But except for the part about me wanting to be physical. I'd have to feel closer to Mike than I do these days before I'd really be into that, into making love. I mean we do have a ways to go.

PHIL: Well, let me ask you this, Donna. If I were to ask Mike to name the first things he'd notice that were different about you, that would tell him you were starting to feel more like being physical with him again, what would he say? (*Outside-perspective question.*)

DONNA: Oh, he'd probably say I wasn't complaining so much. That I was chummier, you know, touching him more, teasing him, stuff like that.

PHIL: And what kind of a difference, if I were to ask him, would he say that would make to him, to see you do that? (*Role-reversal question.*)

DONNA: Hmm. Well, he'd probably say it made him feel more like being with me. Warmer, that I loved him, that I wanted to be close. He'd like it, I know that. (*Turns toward Mike and smiles. Mike smiles back.*)

PHIL: (*Turns to Mike.*) And Mike, if you saw Donna doing that, being chummier, being warmer with you in a physical way—what do you think she'd be thinking, what would she be saying to herself, that would lead her to be doing that? (*Role-reversal question.*)

MIKE: (*Pauses.*) Well, I guess she'd be saying to herself something like, "I feel close to him because I can tell he likes to spend time with me. And we're talking more, he's paying attention." Probably she'd say that means she could trust me, talking more and stuff.

DONNA: Yeah, taking time to talk about things, all kinds of things, is really important. Not just the little stuff. Big stuff, too. (*She pauses.*) The way we're doing it now. You know, maybe we could get back to feeling closer again faster than I thought. If we work on it.

MIKE: Yeah I gotta' say things are looking up here. I'm moving up the scale as we speak!

DONNA: That's really good to hear. I'm feeling better, too.

PHIL: This is exciting to hear. We're almost at the end of the hour, and it sounds like we're getting somewhere. But before we end I want to make sure we're on the right track. Is there anything we need to look at before we end today? Anything you think I should know about or we should talk about?

DONNA: Well, we never really finished talking about our physical relationship. We probably need to spend some time on that.

PHIL: Right. (*Although they have already begun to establish the signs that will indicate positive change in this area, Donna wants to talk more about this, and Phil follows up on her suggestion with a scaling question that may establish movement already in progress.*) Well, maybe we don't have time to complete that today but let me ask you another one of those numbers questions, so we have a starting point for next time. If 1 stands for there being no chance at this point that you're ready to have a physical relationship with Mike and 10 represents that you're ready to have the sexual relationship you both want again, what number would you give your willingness right now? (*It could have been rushing things for Phil to pursue this line of inquiry so late in the session. But since Donna raised the issue again and Phil sensed that the* good story *climate between Mike and Donna was strong, he asked the scaling question, hoping it would result in a positive response and lead to some desirable changes in the couple's interactions between sessions.*)

DONNA: Well, before we came in here today I would have said 1 for sure. But now I guess I would say 4, maybe 5. (*Both Mike and Donna smile and glance warmly at each other. Rather than pursuing the matter further, Phil leaves the positive implication floating here and brings the session to a close.*)

# CHAPTER 9

# Closing the Session

Like beginnings, endings give experiences shape and weight, punctuating what we notice and remember. In the context of therapy, the ending of each session as well as the final session of the therapeutic enterprise are important opportunities for consolidating therapeutic gain. Here we focus on effectively bringing each therapy hour, particularly the initial session, to a close; in the next chapter, we will discuss ways to make the most of the termination session. The closing interactions of each session can forge a link between the experiences of positive change during the therapy hour and the couple's everyday life in the world outside the therapist's office. Even if the session has been a difficult one or it comes to a close before the couple has experienced much positive change, we can use its final moments to set the stage for possible positive between-session experiences. Session closure should not, therefore, be a casual, random affair ending with "See you folks next week." The final moments of the hour should be purposeful, designed to enhance the therapy's utility for the couple: fostering, highlighting, and amplifying whatever feelings of hope, enthusiasm, progress, and partnership have developed earlier. In this chapter we address how we use the session's close to further these therapeutic ends.[1]

As the session begins to wind down, couples are usually feeling more optimistic, relating to each other in a friendlier way, and talking with us and each other in a more relaxed and collaborative way. A good-weather feeling at the end of a session—or an improvement in the weather from bad to clearing—occurs in most cases, whether it is a first, subsequent, or final session. This is no accident. This happens because we work throughout the session to enliven hope, refresh the *good story,* and generate partnership. As the session nears an end, regardless of how large, small, or subtle the changes in the couple's narratives and perceptions of their problems, their relationship, and each other, we highlight and amplify those changes so that the couple can carry forward into their life outside the session whatever has been helpful and positive in the work we have done together.

Not all sessions, however, end on an optimistic note. Sometimes, despite our efforts, people may still be feeling somewhat hostile, disheartened, or distant. In such cases we do not want to appear Pollyanna-ish or overconfident that things will improve. Nonetheless, where the partners are still feeling discouraged and we have seen little evidence of positive change, we do not conclude the session has had no positive impact. Rather, we assume that if we have done our jobs—asked well-chosen questions and helped people find meaningful answers—small, but important perceptual and cognitive changes will probably already have occurred. These changes may bear fruit after the couple leaves the session, and when they return to the next session we can focus on what has been different since we last met.

Though we remain optimistic even when we have seen little evidence of positive change in either partner's attitudes, in the stories they are telling us, or in their desire to engage with us in customer/consultant conversations, we are also mindful of the importance of early positive change in therapy. If a number of sessions pass with no improvement reported by the clients and no change in the couple's readiness to work together toward common goals, we ask the partners whether therapy seems helpful and explore whether we might do something different together that might be more useful to them. We are not trying to force early positive change because we have a need to feel effective. Both our experience and our reading of the research literature tell us that it is crucially important to the success of therapy that the partners experience positive changes early in treatment—ideally by the end of the first session. Therefore, we want every session, especially the initial session, to count.

Research is unequivocal about this: How couples feel about the first few sessions plays a large part in whether they continue in treatment and how hard the partners will work together both in and out of the sessions. As Duncan and Miller (2000) point out: "Early improvement—specifically the *client's* experience of meaningful change in the first few visits—is emerging as one of the best predictors of eventual treatment outcome" (p. 93). In support of this statement, they cite a study of more than 2,000 therapists and thousands of clients where:

> researchers found that therapeutic relationships in which no improvement occurred by the third visit did not on average result in improvement over the entire course of treatment (Brown and others, 1999).

The study also found that clients who worsened by the third visit were twice as likely to drop out than those reporting progress. (pp. 93–94)[2]

One of the most important ways the therapist can maximize the long-term effects of the first few sessions in couples therapy is by being purposeful during the final phase of each session. At the end of the initial session (and, in most cases, at the end of all subsequent sessions), we offer the couple a summary statement, highlighting certain elements of the conversation that has taken place during the hour. In this statement, we reflect what each person has told us about their concerns, but, more importantly, we emphasize whatever elements of the *good story* narrative came to the fore during the session. If at all possible, we want to end on an upbeat note, highlighting whatever changes and movement have taken place during the hour. This is true even when the changes may seem to us subtle and small, because we believe that small changes can lead to big ones. While we acknowledge the partners' concerns and competing perceptions of their difficulties, we highlight competencies and restate stories of success. And when it is clear that positive changes have taken place during the session itself, enlivening the *good story*, we highlight that movement. Finally, we may suggest be-tween-session tasks that might be helpful.

Before we take up the elements of the summary statement more fully, we want to take a detour to discuss two kinds of partner-to partner dialogue that occasionally occur during our sessions. One type often arises spontane-ously in the latter part of a session when positive movement has taken place. The second is a special situation in which the couple tells us they want our help in talking together about a difficult issue they have been unable to resolve alone.[3] Frequently, when couples have made progress in developing mutually shared goals and the emotional atmosphere has become warmer and more relaxed, couples spontaneously begin talking to each other, engag-ing, often without any prompting from the therapist, in a partner-to-partner dialogue we call the "couple's *good story* conversation." These conversations can be an extremely important therapeutic experience, sometimes the most important of the hour, and, while they do not happen in every case, we want to describe their nature and how we guide and sometimes initiate them. In addition, while we rarely suggest such conversations, there are occasions when it is therapeutically useful to guide couples in problem-focused partner-to partner dialogues. When clients tell us they feel stuck because they have been unable to talk to each other about a specific issue— that they have been going round and round about something only to see things worsen—we offer to serve as facilitators. While such work may seem similar to the kind of conversation facilitation commonly practiced in other forms of relationship therapy, we will show how it is our orientation toward solution and collaboration that guides us in this facilitating role.

## The Couple's Good Story Conversation

Most narrative and social constructionist therapists take the position that all conversations during the therapy hour should be between themselves and the individual partners (De Jong & Berg, 1998; Eron & Lund, 1996; Freedman & Combs, 1996; Zimmerman & Dickerson, 1996). They argue that if conversation is be transformative and language is to serve as a means for changing people's experiences, the therapist must always be one of the participants in the therapeutic dialogue. Since the therapist's questions and the client's answers are seen as the primary medium for change, it is ideal for one partner to be engaged in conversation with the therapist while the other listens. We are in general agreement, but the couple's *good story* conversation is an important exception.

For many years before developing RPT, we found that guiding couples in their conversations was often an effective way to help them learn to collaborate and find ways to make desired changes. When partners were able to talk to each other about warm, affectionate, and bonding feelings, experiences that felt pleasing and intimate, and ways things between them were improving, a positive snowball effect took place. More recently, under the influence of social constructionism, we came to understand that our forms of inquiry and the ways we participated in conversations with our clients played a crucial role in whether they could find positive things to say about their experiences. We found that if we devoted the first part of each session to solution- and *good story*-generating conversation between each partner and ourselves, at a certain point toward the end of the session (either spontaneously or with gentle prodding from us) the partners would often begin talking to each other in ways that further thickened their *good story* narrative. So while we abandoned our earlier practice of encouraging partners to talk to each other about whatever was on their minds—a recent fight or their current complaints, for example—we continued to see value in partner-to-partner dialogue once individual and shared *good story* experiences were uppermost in people's minds. Then, when the partners began talking to each other, the content of what they said naturally focused on what was pleasing, what made them happy, what was better, and what made them feel like a team, contributing to further positive narrative re-authoring.

Our guidance, when the couple's conversation is taking place, consists of a gentle leading back to *good story* territory if the couple seems to lose track of it, or support in emphasizing and thickening this context either by some verbal interjection or simply by body language and the tone of our interested silence. There will, of course, sometimes be occasional references to each partner's *bad story* narratives. Sometimes a sort of teasing about issues or problems that have been features of conflict in the past softens and alters a conflictual pattern and, with occasional help from the therapist, the couple can begin a reperception of differences that have had an incendiary quality in the past. Or the partners will offer each other reparative gestures that are not necessarily new, but, in the context of the *good story* warming, are responded to in receptive and enthusiastic ways. So, when things in a particular session have gone well and the partners spontaneously break off conversation with us and begin talking to each other, what triggers this partner-to-partner dialogue is the rejuvenation of the *good story* framework that becomes possible when shared goals bring partnership back into focus, and we want to encourage this in whatever way we can.

## Facilitating Partner-to-Partner Problem-Focused Conversation

There is one exception in RPT to our general rule of supporting *good story* couple conversations and avoiding *bad story* couple conversations. This kind of couple's conversation is not one that spontaneously arises as the emotional atmosphere in a session warms; rather, it is a conversation that one or both parties have been wishing for or even trying to have, but without success. When a couple or one partner in a couple needs to talk about a trust-breaking incident such as an affair, an isolated incident of violence, or an experience like the one we are about to discuss, this type of couple's conversation, guided by the therapist, becomes an essential element in loosening the hold of the *bad story* narrative, rebuilding trust, and moving into *good story* territory.

Usually these conversations have become important because one (or both) partner's movement toward the goal of rebuilding connection and partnership is predicated on a need for the other partner to understand his or her experience more fully. In one of Phil's cases, Katy and David came in soon after David was released from prison, where he had spent two years after being convicted of an embezzling charge. During the first four months since David's release, Katy and David had been fighting a great deal and Katy had been feeling that the marriage might no longer be worth saving. She felt the trust between them had been broken and now that David was home, she wasn't sure she could forgive him and overcome her feelings of betrayal. She explained to Phil that before his arrest David had kept a serious gambling habit a secret. She had not known the extent of the effects of his compulsion, nor had she known he was taking money from his employer to cover his debts. His arrest and trial shocked and disillusioned her, threw both their lives into disarray, and threatened their marriage. During the time he was in prison, she decided to try to make a go of it with him when he got out, but now she felt very angry and hurt, not only by what his actions had done to their lives, but by what she felt was his lack of appreciation of what she had gone through during the two years of his imprisonment in putting their affairs in some order and managing life on her own.

Katy said David "had no clue about how awful it had been for her," and whenever she tried to talk about it and work through her feelings with him, he "shuts me off and gets impatient and angry." She explained that no matter how she introduced the conversation, he claimed she was going over and over the same ground, and he wasn't really very supportive. David, on the other hand, said he had told Katy repeatedly that he was sorry, that he had joined Gamblers Anonymous, and that he intended to conduct his life differently now, and "what more does she want from me?" He couldn't understand why she kept wanting to talk about it, especially when it made both of them feel so bad.

Phil's first concern was to develop goals with each partner for the conversation they were about to have. Using goal-building, scaling, and perspective-shifting questions, Phil helped Katy and David clarify what each needed during and by the end of the conversation in order to feel that talking together had made a positive difference. In exploring goals with Katy, he clarified that what she wanted out of a trust-building conversation with David was simply for him to listen and show in some way that he understood what her experience had been like during those difficult two years and that he appreciated what she had done and was currently doing to support their relationship. She wanted David to listen to her calmly when she described her feelings and experiences and to let her know not just that he was sorry, but also that he appreciated her willingness to stick by him, as well as her efforts in managing their financial affairs and caring for their daughter while he was gone. David said he wanted to experience, at the end of the conversation, that Katy felt closer to him, and that she could take at least a step or two toward forgiving him. He acknowledged that it might be unreasonable to expect Katy to change all at once as a result of one conversation, but he wanted to see certain signs that the conversation was making a difference to her.

Phil thus set the stage for the ensuing conversation by clarifying goals for the conversation with each partner—what needed to be different when they talked about these issues and how talking in this way would make a difference. During the couple's conversation itself, guided by Phil, David told Katy how grateful he was to her for her loyalty and for all she had done for him and their daughter while he was in prison. He said he was impressed by her competence and grateful to her for getting them back on track financially after he left things in such a mess. As they talked together, Katy cried and said how important it was to her to hear from David that he relied on her. David said he hadn't realized how little he had conveyed his feelings of gratitude. He had thought his remorse—saying how sorry he was—would tell her how much he appreciated what she had done. As they talked, they were beginning to experience an altered and satisfying way of talking about feelings in a *good story* context, and in the process, they were rebuilding trust and recreating partnership. At the conclusion of their talk together, Katy and David both said that this had been an "amazing" conversation. When they returned the following week, they began by announcing that they had had several more "amazing" conversations on their own, in which Katy felt David had listened to her in ways she said she had never experienced with him before. David said that for the first time since his release and homecoming he felt more relaxed and open with Katy—he was no longer always on the alert for having to apologize or bent on escaping encounters that felt painful and seemed to be going nowhere.

Note that this conversation was not conducted as an exploration of *bad story* material, nor was it simply an effort to learn better communication techniques. At the outset, Phil collaboratively developed goals with the couple for the conversation itself; these goals were oriented toward solutions (regarding their talking together) the couple themselves detailed and clarified.

## The Therapist's End-of-Session Summarizing Statement

Toward the end of the hour, whether or not we have spent time facilitating partner-to-partner dialogue, we begin gathering our thoughts to make a statement designed to bring together the various themes and accomplishments of the session. The main theme of our summary statement is always the *good story*. We do, of course, begin our closing comments by restating what we have understood to be each partner's concerns, so each person feels understood. However, we usually reframe what people have told us in ways that highlight the meta-goals behind any grievances. Because, throughout the hour, we have been listening for, eliciting, clarifying, amplifying, and weaving together bits and pieces of the couple's *good story* narratives, we are able to offer these coauthored narratives back to the couple, highlighting shared goals and dreams and whatever recent successes, strengths, and resources we have all talked about during the session.

We take care to compliment people's hard work, skills, and capacities. We let them know how impressed and encouraged we are by their commitment to making things better and by what we have learned about their recent successes. We often mention the love and bond we can see and feel between them despite their troubles, when that has been present during the hour. If people have persisted and held on through a painful situation, we note their coping ability. These observations of their goodwill, hard work, and successes have a palpably heartening effect on people. Giving compliments about their gains, skills, and partnership is not simply a matter of buoying people up; we aren't just giving pep talks. We want clients to notice their own particular strengths, individually and relationally, which may have been unnoticed and underutilized till now. Compliments are the end-session expression of our competency-based perspective (Wall, Kleckner, Amendt, & Bryant, 1989). They validate the effort and energy people bring to attempting relationship change, and they are an important notation of the *good story* as it appears to a third party.

Suppose a couple comes to therapy saying they have been feeling distant from one another and want more intimacy and better communication. During the session we have developed goals regarding feeling closer and highlighted some recent times when they felt their communication was better. At the close of the session, we might say:

*When we first began talking together, you told me about how each of you has been feeling quite distant from the other, and how sad you were about this—how you, Joan, have been feeling blue and more like talking to your girlfriends than to Sid, and how you, Sid, have been spending a lot more time on your own even when you're home, outside working in the garden or going out to play racquetball. And you both feel you'd like to be able to talk to each other in more satisfying ways.* (Restating concerns and grievances in a way that softens the *bad story* and refers to an overarching shared goal.) *And I've learned from each of you what changes you'd like to see happen. Joan, you said the first signs that things are improving will be when you and Sid are taking walks together in the evening and spending Sunday mornings cooking breakfast and reading the paper together. Sid, for you the first sign will be when you're eager to get home to Joan to tell her about your day, and you told me you pictured the two of you sitting together in the living room sharing a bottle of wine after a hard day's work, with Joan showing an eagerness to tell you about how she feels about things.* (Restating specific observable experiential signs of goals.)

*I'm impressed to hear both of you saying that these are things you're both willing to do to bring about feeling closer—and I'm encouraged to hear that you've had some satisfying moments during the last few weeks already. You've told me you recently had several conversations you both describe as intimate— the kinds of talks you both want to have more often. And you've identified some of the things you thought and did that made these closer experiences happen. So it seems like you're already beginning to bring the warmth you both want back into your lives, and that's very exciting to hear.* (Compliments as a way of highlighting successes, movement, and competencies; noting agency; narrating the desired future as happening in the present.)

*I can also feel, from being together with you during this session, how much*
*you care about each other. It's easy to see how much you want things to be*
*better, and exciting to see how in small but important ways you've already*
*begun to do that.* (Highlighting the *good story*; therapist enthusiasm.)

While the length and ingredients of the summary statement vary from
session to session and couple to couple, these are the elements we use in
making them.

## Whether to Take an End-of-Session Break

In traditional solution-focused brief therapy, the therapist takes a short break
about 10 minutes before the end of the session to develop the summary
statement (De Jong & Berg, 1998; Walter & Peller, 1992). There are two
principal reasons offered in the literature. First, it offers the clinician a "think
break," a chance to formulate the closing statement (O'Hanlon & Weiner-
Davis, 1989). When the therapist is working with an observing team behind
a one-way mirror, the break affords an opportunity to consult with the
team in developing the summary statement and any task assignments. Even
when working alone, a number of traditional solution-focused brief therapists take this break as an opportunity to think about and formulate their
closing remarks (O'Hanlon & Weiner-Davis, 1989; Walter & Peller, 1992).
The second reason offered for taking the break is as a contextual marker
and a way of creating drama at the session's end. The break "increases
clients' anticipation about what we have to say when we return; they listen
very carefully. Taking a break seems to put an exclamation mark behind
any concluding observations that we might make" (De Jong & Berg, 1998,
p. 108).

Despite these arguments, we have not adopted the practice of taking a
break. There are several reasons for our decision—some practical, some
theoretical, and some temperamental. First and foremost, we think breaking
off contact with a couple, telling them we need some time on our own to
think about their situation, and then returning to deliver feedback to them,
even when our comments are complimentary, suggests a role for the therapist
and defines the therapeutic relationship in terms we eschew. It conveys that
the therapist, regardless of what her role has been up to now, is suddenly
placing herself outside the collaborative relationship and taking the stance
of observing expert who will formulate an opinion and offer advice based
on her insights and wisdom. Even though the feedback statement that
follows the break is complimentary and focuses on people's competencies,
this posturing gesture runs counter to a spirit of parity and collaboration
and establishes the therapist as an authority rather than a facilitating consultant. From a more practical and logistical standpoint, it would be awkward

for us to stop a session and either ask the couple to leave our offices and wait in our waiting room while we gather our thoughts, or leave ourselves while the couple remains in the room awaiting our return. Nor would it work to have everyone sitting silently together in the room while we look at our notes and formulate our statements. We assume that most clinicians in private practice would face this same logistical constraint.

In the end, our decision not to take the think break is mostly a matter of personal style combined with the fact that our professional backgrounds are not within the brief therapy tradition. Those with more experience with brief strategic approaches, where taking a break is part of the tradition, might prefer to adopt it for their work.[4]

## Between-Session Tasks

We also sometimes offer homework assignments during the closing statement. These are offered in a collaborative spirit. They are always in the form of suggestions and experiments, and we make clear that people are free to try, disregard, or modify them. For example, when suggesting a homework task, we may ask if the partners think it's worth trying and whether they can think of ways to make it more useful. We never convey that the couple must do the task in order to improve their relationship, or that their forgetting or not wanting to do the task is a psychological clue to resistance or other problems. In fact, whether or not people carry out the assignment is not important for us. The offering itself is the intervention. While carrying out the suggestion may have positive effects, the snowball effect we're looking for is perceptual and begins at the time the task is discussed.

Our primary intent in offering end-of-session tasks is to highlight aspects of the couple's *good story* that have been fleshed out earlier in the session. The suggestion is intended to produce changes in people's perceptual and interpretive lenses that can begin in the very moment the task is offered. In this respect, RPT task assignments have a quite different purpose than those in most other forms of couples therapy. In behavioral couples therapies, both in operant conditioning and social learning theory models, homework assignments usually take the form of reciprocal contracts in which both partners agree to increase the number of relationship-enhancing behaviors and decrease the number of harmful ones. The targeted behaviors might be those that longitudinal studies of successful and unsuccessful couples suggest lead to greater marital satisfaction (Gottman, 1999; Markman et al., 1994). Or they might be specific behaviors that have been pinpointed in interviews and questionnaires as already in each partner's repertoire, behaviors that the other has indicated have a positive reinforcing effect (Follette &

Jacobson, 1990). In both these approaches, the focus is on behavioral change; therefore, it is essential that the couple carry out the assignments.

In RPT the focus is on changing perceptions and meanings held by each partner in ways that will support the availability of their *good story* experience (which contains relationship-enhancing attitudes and behaviors). Rather than suggesting what the partners should do between sessions that will be pleasing to their partners, we ask each partner to "be on the lookout for" (pay attention to) times the encounters between them are more as they prefer. This perceptual highlighting affects the action-response cycle. We assume that when people look for desired gestures and pleasing encounters, they will see them; by orienting people to watch for and take note of them when they arise, we can have a positive effect on both the perceiver and the relationship—even when the other partner has not actually set out to change his or her behavior.

Our task assignments also have a different function than those used in various forms of strategic brief couples therapies (Haley, 1976; Keim, 1999; Madanes, 1981; Watzlawick et al., 1974). In strategic approaches, the therapist (usually with the help of an observing team) crafts a task assignment intended to break up systemic processes the therapist and team have determined are problem-maintaining. In these approaches, the homework assignment is the principal intervention. During the session, the therapist's role is to find out what he needs to know about how people are currently addressing their problems. This allows him to design interventions that will generate change in the couple's problem-solving strategies; during the hour, he may or may not reframe the problem as a way to motivate the couple to carry out subsequent assignments. According to the theory, when the partners carry out the assignment, the interpersonal context, which is part of the problem, will change. Having people do something different—even exaggerating what they are already doing, doing it under the direction of the therapist, or doing it after the therapist has reframed the activity in a new way—creates a new context in which the clients find their own solutions.[5] But it is important that the couple carry out the current solution-disrupting assignment.

We agree that when people develop new perspectives they discover solutions for themselves—that's why we focus on generating perceptual and interpretive changes. However, we believe that it is the presentation of the suggestion in the therapeutic context, rather than how or whether people actively carry out the task, that begins the perceptual shift that can produce change. This is not to say the process of carrying out assignments (when couples do that) is unimportant or has no effect, but it is the perceptual shift that makes the real difference. Without a change of narrative context, behavioral changes often fail to produce perceived success.

We offer three basic types of assignments in RPT: (1) self-reflection tasks, (2) relational observation tasks, and (3) *good story*-invigorating behavioral tasks. Which type we offer, if any, depends primarily on how motivated people appear to be at the time, how ready they seem to move beyond talking and thinking about their problems, and how prepared they are to take action in behalf of change (i.e., perceptual changes have already begun). There are two principal ways we assess client readiness and motivation: First, we simply ask clients how ready they are to take active steps, and second, we note the types of conversations they have been willing to have with us during the session. Which kinds of conversation—visitor/host, complainant/sympathizer, or customer/consultant—were the partners engaging in during this session, and how much of the dialogue was solution-oriented? When we asked the partners to scale their levels of motivation, where did they place themselves? Was there movement upward on the motivation scales as the session drew to a close? The answers to these questions will let us know whether to offer tasks and what type to offer if we do.

### Self-Reflection Tasks

Self-reflection tasks encourage people to think about what they already have been doing to solve their marital problems, reflect on whether those efforts are making any positive difference, and ask themselves what tells them these actions will produce better results in the future if they are continued. People are also asked to think of (or notice as they go along) other things that might work better in bringing about positive changes. This kind of task suggestion should be made with care and with a sensitivity to its rhetorical impact. We do not want to imply that people are misguided in what they're doing and we're here to straighten them out. The purpose of offering a self-reflection task is to convey that we recognize the partner's positive intent (providing a reflection of an individual's positive self-sense), while highlighting the gap between this positive intent and the current effects or consequences of the actions. These tasks can be a respectful and nondirective way to invite people to be curious about themselves and to think in new ways about what they're doing and the impact of what they're doing, without blaming themselves for failing to live up to their own ideals. Here is how we formulate these self-reflective tasks:

*I'm impressed by how hard each of you has been trying to solve the problems you've told me about. It's clear both of you have been working hard to overcome them. Clearly, it's been frustrating for both of you that these problems keep coming into your lives again and again. And it's been hard to feel your partner isn't working with you, but seems to be working against you. But as we've been talking, you've told me about some times when the two of you managed to team up and keep this (fighting about the kids, mistrust, coldness, etc.) from wrecking your efforts to feel close. I want to learn more about how you're able to join together as a team, at least some of the time. So I'd like to ask each of you to think about some things, so when we meet next time I can get your thoughts on them.*

These are some of the self-reflective questions we commonly use:

- *How confident are you that what you've been doing is going to produce the changes you've been telling me you want?*
- *What small things might you do that would increase the likelihood that your partner will see you in the ways you've said you'd like to be seen?*
- *How do you suppose the problems between you and your partner have been influencing you to act in ways that don't reflect how you like to think about yourself (or how you want your partner to see you)?*
- *What do you suppose your partner would say would be the first small change on your part that would make a difference and motivate him/her to take a small step in return?*
- *Do you suppose that if you went first—took the first step—your partner would be more or less likely to begin making some of the changes you've been wanting him/her to make?*
- *If you think about it, how does your experience of better times—those times when the two of you seem to do better in dealing with this problem—influence the way you feel about yourself, your partner, and the relationship?*

Notice that some of these self-reflective suggestions are in the form of perspective-shifting questions, that others suggest that change is an incremental process of small steps, and that some encourage people to focus outside of the who-goes-first box, all of which are ways of influencing perceptual change.

### Relational Observation Tasks

Because we are interested in orienting people's perception and interpretation of their partner's action toward the couple's *good story*, the most common task assignment we use is asking people to be on the lookout for things their partners do that please them—for experiences that they would like to have more of in the future and that will be signs that things are getting better. While self-reflection tasks ask people to think about themselves and their impact on others and behavioral tasks ask them to take certain actions, observational tasks ask them to notice and give weight to certain aspects of their experience. Again, keep in mind that as people listen to and mull over the suggested observational task, the way they focus on themselves and their relationship is being influenced in that very moment. Just having heard the suggestion leads many people to pick out and remember encounters that are more satisfying and pleasing, interactions that can be construed as indicating that things are getting better. These tasks, like our questions, contain messages.

Observational tasks do not require people to do anything new and different other than watch for what happens in their encounters that they would like to see happen more. (They do not have to "go first" in changing behaviors, they do not have to give up their theories, they do not have to make a move and fear the other will not reciprocate.) These tasks open a doorway to a positive context by encouraging couples to direct attention away from problems and conflicts and toward experiences falling within their *good story* narratives.

When talking about these tasks, we explain that the purpose for our suggestion is to help both people figure out what they are doing differently in successful times, so that during their next session we can use the information to develop ways they can make those positive experiences happen more often. De Shazer (1985) calls this intervention the "formula first session task" (p. 137) because it can be assigned at the end of the first session regardless of the nature or extent of the clients' presenting problems. Here is an example:

> *Between now and the next time we meet, I'd like you to pay attention to the times when things happen between you that you'd like to have happen more, so that when we meet next time you can tell me about them in detail. Try to notice what is different about them—what they tell you about your partner, your relationship, and yourself. And make note of what each of you was doing that was different in those times so we can talk about it when you come back.*

This generic observational assignment has a number of useful functions. By suggesting this task assignment, we are planting a perception-reorienting seed, which contains the following presuppositions: (1) we expect some successes during the coming week; (2) if the partners look for these successes they will notice them; (3) the expected successes will come from the fact that the partners do something different; (4) these successes are worth noting and talking about in therapy; (5) the preferred encounters they observe can be the foundation for developing the goals of the therapeutic enterprise.

Earlier we discussed the situation where both partners agree that changes need to happen and may even describe times when things went better between them, but differ in their theories about why things went better, attributing the better times to something the other partner did differently. In other words, both believe any successes and exceptions resulted from something outside their control. As we explained, we don't find it helpful to challenge partners who attribute past and current successes and exceptions to luck, circumstances, or the other partner's actions. One way we can work within an individual's theory but also invite some re-storying is by acknowledging the idea that the other person's changes have made the difference, but then invite the client to reflect on what he or she has done that may have influenced the partner's changes. In other words, we want to help people who see relationship change as outside their own control to re-story the "causes" of these preferred experiences to include personal agency.

While we occasionally suggest behavioral experiments or tasks (discussed later), in most cases we prefer giving variants of the formula observational task. We take the following factors as signs that, at least for the time being, an observational task would be more appropriate than a behavioral one:

- The partners report low numbers on both willingness and commitment scales.
- Therapeutically well-formed goals have not been developed.
- The partners are currently unable to describe any recent actions on either person's part that are seen to have made a positive difference (i.e., no successes or exceptions).
- Neither partner is able to describe anything he or she has done or could imagine doing that he or she thinks will make a difference to the other and could improve the relationship (i.e., no agency).

We restrict ourselves to offering observational tasks when most of the conversation during the session has been of the complainant/sympathizer type and when the couple has so far declined our invitations to enter into customer/consultant conversation. As long as the partners are coming primarily from their antagonistic *bad story* narratives, any suggested between-session tasks or experiments should be restricted to the self-reflective or observational types.

### Good Story-Invigorating Behavioral Tasks

Behavioral assignments require a higher level of motivation on the part of the couple than self-reflection and observational tasks do. Research supports the therapeutic value of reciprocal behavioral assignments that involve partners doing things (and acknowledging such actions on each other's part) that generate positive feelings between them (Gottman, 1999; Jacobson & Margolin, 1979; Stuart, 1980). But reciprocal positive-behavior reinforcement assignments, a technique used extensively in behavioral couples therapy, are more likely to be carried out and will be more effective when custom-designed with each couple. In RPT, behavioral assignments, in which we ask people to do things designed to contribute to a spiral of positive interactions, are formulated from what the partners have told us about their more satisfying interactions—that is, from reports of successes and exceptions.

As with the self-reflection and observational assignments, these behavioral task assignments are in themselves interventions; it is not important (or advisable) that the therapist check up on them in the following sessions, and it is not necessary that partners carry them out—some do, some don't, and sometimes couples report that they carried out entirely different "tasks" than the ones we assigned, tailor-making something that worked for them. As with the other tasks we offer, suggesting a behavioral experiment is a conversational means of influencing people's perceptual frames—orienting the couple to focus more on individual actions and mutual interactions which can have a positive ripple effect in their relationship, solidifying the *good story*. People may or may not talk about a task assignment when they return; we do not initiate conversation about it or make reference to it. This avoids the problem of people feeling as though they are "bad clients" if they failed to do the task or want to talk about other things.

Readers may be familiar with the difficulty of developing reciprocal behavioral assignments that "fit" the couple or, in the case of strategic therapies, assignments that will break up the systemic problem-solving patterns. The behavioral tasks we use in RPT are always of the same generic type and are based on the idea that progressive change will occur when people do more of what is already working. They do not require the therapist to make up specific, new assignments for every couple. Just as every observational task is a variant of the formula "Look for evidence of the *good story*," every behavioral task is a variant of the formula "Do what you know from experience takes you into the *good story*." When the partners have talked during the session about things each has done or said that were experienced as reflecting and reinforcing the couple's *good story* narratives, we will use those reports to develop the behavioral assignment, encouraging the partners to do more of what they have already done that has had a positive impact. When one partner sees the other do something of this nature at home, he or she is likely to respond with another gesture arising from a *good story* orientation; thus, the *good story* events and interactions accumulate.

This is one way we might offer a behavioral assignment based on what a couple reported doing during specific *good story* encounters:

> *Both of you mentioned a number of things you folks did that seemed to bring you closer together. When Hank agreed to take the kids on Saturday afternoons so you, Marlo, could have some time on your own, that seemed to make a difference to you—telling you that Hank felt it was important that you have some time to yourself, and that he cares about your needs. And Hank, when*

*Marlo asks you questions and shows curiosity when you're talking about what's important to you, that makes a positive difference for you. It tells you she's interested in you and wants to be there for you. So you both know some things you can do that will help make things better in your relationship. Would each of you be willing to do more of these things—both the things you've already done and some of the things you've told me during the session will make a positive difference? Or other things the session has made you think about? Then, when you come in next time, we can talk about what effect these things are having in helping you reach your goals. So each of you should be on the lookout for these gestures to see if you catch them.*

The assignment should leave room for the couple's own invention.

Here is an example of a behavioral task we often use in the common situation where people agree they each must make some changes but each believes the other must change first:

*I want to offer you guys a suggestion, a sort of experiment. Would you both be willing to think about some things you could do or say that you think would make your partner feel better about your relationship?* (They indicate an affirmative response.) *Okay. So then, when you have some things in mind, pick a day or part of a day when you do some of these things without telling your partner what you're up to. At the same time, both of you should be on the lookout to see whether you can catch your partner doing these things. You may have to keep your "antennae" up. When you come in next time, we can talk about what each of you did, what you noticed, and what you learned that might be useful in reaching your goals. Is this something that you think might be useful?*

This task assignment bypasses the problem of who-goes-first and also obviates another common negative side effect of some traditional behavioral assignments, in which one partner continues in a *bad story* frame, monitoring the other partner's failure to perform the assignment "correctly." Because people are watching for positive signs of difference while not announcing their intentions or observations to each other, they will be primed to notice pleasing behaviors and cues from the other person—they may even notice (or construct) positive signs the other person has not set out to perform to fulfill the task. Thus, it is more likely this kind of framing of a behavioral task will alter perceptions toward the positive.

Following is an example of an action task Tobey offered in an initial session with a couple who presented a problem they defined as "growing apart, having no common interests any more except the children." Tobey spent most of the session helping the couple reformulate their complaints and dissatisfactions into therapeutically well-defined goals—clarifying the details of their outcome picture and detailing what first signs each will notice to tell them they are "feeling connected" again and moving toward common pursuits and pleasures. By the end of the first session, in addition to developing a clear set of signifiers of their preferred future, the couple had also identified several recent exceptions. The first was an evening together cleaning out kitchen cabinets when they had found an old kitchen gadget from their early years and spent some enjoyable time reminiscing about moving in and starting a life together. Another was a relaxed Sunday morning they spent in bed while their kids were occupied watching cartoons, when (they discovered in talking in the session) they had both felt close and in touch with common interests as they read the newspaper together and talked and laughed about a film review they both thought was "hilariously wrong." Notice that in framing the task, Tobey links the defined goals, recent exceptions, and the behavioral assignment:

> *You folks have made it pretty clear that you want to be closer again and have more fun doing things together you both enjoy.* (Reflects the couple's shared view of the problem, puts it in positive goal terms.) *You both also agreed that in the past week you've had a few times together that tell you that you do have some of those experiences, and that if you could have more, you'll definitely be on the right track. Your working together on the cabinets and laughing about the old days the other night, and your enjoyable conversation on Sunday morning, pointed up your shared interests and the way you both find the same sorts of things funny, and they sound like the kinds of experiences you both want more of—and that will help you get where you want to go. Because you've been telling me that doing these things can help turn your relationship around—in fact they tell us you're already on the way—I'd like you to try doing more of them, to see what happens. Do you think that would be helpful?*

## Using the Couple as Our Consultants: Getting Feedback

Because RPT is tailored to the theories of the partners in each couple and to the changes and outcomes they desire, we often stop along the way to check whether people feel what we are doing together is helpful (Duncan & Miller, 2000).[6] We do this throughout the session by paying close attention to both verbal and nonverbal signals we get from clients about whether what we are doing is working and enlivens their hope and energy. When people indicate that what we are doing together is not what they want, we negotiate with them about what we might do instead and on that basis try something different. When we get the impression that what we're doing is making a positive difference, we do more of the same. At the ends of sessions we check our assumptions by asking people to tell us whether or not what we're doing together has been helpful. Regular checking-in helps to maintain a strong working alliance and fosters the couple's active participation in the therapeutic process. According to the research, the most significant contributor to a positive outcome is how actively clients participate—collaboration is the key to this (Duncan & Miller, 2000). In our experience, clients who encounter parity in therapist-client relations—who experience the therapist as valuing (and working on the basis of) their input regarding what is happening in therapy—feel respected and work harder.

In addition to asking about what was helpful, we want to invite clients to comment on or ask about anything we have done or said during the session that might have bothered them or left them confused. We think therapist transparency (a feeling on the part of clients that they know and understand whatever they want to about the process of therapy), at least with respect to things that are salient to clients, is essential to effective therapy and consultancy. In pursuit of transparency we make sure our clients have access to all the information they consider important about what we are doing, saying, or thinking in the therapy hour. For instance, if the clients brought up the between-session task suggestions, we might ask, "How helpful was the suggestion we gave you at the end of the last session? Can either of you think of something that might work better?" This, again, is not an assessment of the clients' success in performing a task, but an invitation to collaborate on ways of accomplishing the therapeutic goals. Clients can participate, with positive results, in any number of decisions that therapists have traditionally kept for themselves (e.g., how often to meet, at what interval, what direction to take in a particular session, what has so far been helpful; the list could go on and on). This makes the therapy work better for the people involved and encourages therapists to concentrate on their own area of expertise: conducting helpful conversations that bring out clients' solution-building resources.

These types of end-of-session questions can provide us with helpful feedback and foster a collaborative spirit:

- *Has this session been helpful?*
- *I'd like to know if there was anything we talked about or did today that was particularly helpful.*
- *Is there anything either of you has been trying to tell me today that you feel I don't understand or haven't paid enough attention to?*
- *Is there anything else we should've talked about that you think is important for me to know?*

We do not ask these questions as a matter of course. Whether we ask them at all, and which we ask in a particular instance, depends on the cues and signals we get from the couple we are working with at the moment. We always try to be responsive to the unique contexts of each interaction.

# CHAPTER 10

# From Welcome Back to Good-bye: Subsequent Sessions to Termination

Up to this point, we have focused primarily on how we conduct initial sessions in RPT. We have used the first session as the context for presenting and describing the various elements and techniques of our approach both because of the importance of that initial meeting and because this simplifies the presentation of these practices. Now we want to shift gears and look at how we guide the therapy enterprise as a whole, focusing on what we do from the first session following the initial meeting to the final session. Some of the questions we hope to answer in this chapter include: Does RPT proceed in stages or is each session a more or less complete encounter on its own? Are second and subsequent sessions different from the initial meeting and, if so, in what ways? Are there specific techniques used in RPT at the point of termination that can maximize the long-term positive effects of the couple's experiences in therapy?

Every session, whether first, last, or in between, serves the same basic therapeutic ends: to help the partners in a couple to (1) define and make perceptually salient the specific observable signs of change that will tell them they are making progress toward solving their problems and that therapy can end (target function), (2) identify current and potential individual and relationship strengths and resources (agency function), (3) coauthor and reinvigorate their shared *good story* (narrative function), and (4) develop a sense of positive movement in their relational life—a sense that changes are already happening, that they are already on track toward a preferred future (also narrative function). In this respect, every session can be viewed as if it were the first and/or the last session:

To the extent that you are looking for positives, the exceptions, and solutions, and to the extent that you are promoting change by maintaining rapport and offering positive feedback and encouragement, every session is a first session. To the extent that you are asking what this client (this couple) needs to do differently at the end of every session to be on track toward what he or she (the couple) wants, every session is a last session. (Walter & Peller, 1992, p. 140)

While there are some differences in emphasis and some of the questions we ask throughout the course of therapy reflect the fact that we have met and talked before, every session has the same focus and purpose—to move toward successful termination. This is a list of the interrelated therapeutic themes we pursue to that end:

- *Good story.* In all sessions, we invite clients into conversations that will identify improvements in their experience of relationship life *since the last session*, bringing into the foreground any positive experiences around the couple's presenting problems. Since perceptual orientation and interpretation are central to the experience of movement and to which aspects of experience are remembered and given weight, we engage people in conversations that develop, enrich, and concretize these stories of movement and the perceptual frames that support them. Conversations about positive experiences since the last meeting serve both as means for identifying solutions—what people did since we last met that has made a positive difference—and as contexts for drawing attention to the couple's re-emerging *good story* narrative.

- *Check-in.* We take steps to clarify whether what we did together in the previous session is viewed as useful by our clients. Because RPT is a collaborative, custom-designed approach that takes shape and direction largely from ongoing feedback from our clients, we want to hear from them whether or not what we have been doing together has been helpful and what they think we might be more so. We view our client couples as valuable consulting teams, and we get important guidance from them.

- *Agency.* We explore what each partner did and what the couple did together as a team since the last session to bring about improvements and successes. Conversations about agency are the therapeutic vehicle for articulating what each partner can do to keep the ball rolling; they foster a sense of personal efficacy. Conversations about positive experiences (successes, exceptions, and perceived movement toward goals) since the last time we met are seedbeds for developing stories of possibility and stories containing links between these preferred experiences and future purposeful actions.

- *Partnership.* RPT rests on the assumption that when couples experience themselves successfully working together to solve their problems and address the issues that have been driving them apart, they recreate partnership. As they experience success as a team, they tap into their potential for greater intimacy and joy. So when a couple returns for a subsequent session reporting that they are doing better, we want to focus on the collaborative nature of their successes, highlighting and reinforcing the element of teamwork in moving toward a desirable future.
- *Progress.* Another important element of the evolving *good story* narrative is that even the smallest changes can be sign that the couple has already established a positive trend. By asking about what's better and focusing on successes since the last session, we invite the couple into progressive conversations that can be fertile ground for constructing *good story* narratives in which couples will see themselves as already on track to solving their problems. Once people are talking about the ways in which things are already improving, the stage is set for clarifying whether and when they see enough change to feel ready to go it on their own.

# Initiating Sessions Over the Course of Treatment: Who Sets the Direction?

When clients return after their first session, many traditional solution-focused brief therapists begin by asking "What's different, what's better?" (Berg 1994; De Jong & Berg, 1998; de Shazer et al., 1986; Walter & Peller, 1994). They use this question to give the session an immediate solution/change direction. Because it is assumed that some experiences will be better than others and that talking about preferable experiences is the most direct and effective way to uncover and promote solutions, strict solution-focused brief therapists take this initiative to minimize the possibility that conversation will take a regressive, problem-focused turn (G. Miller, 1997). Steve de Shazer (1991), who always emphasizes the word "brief" in solution-focused brief therapy, explains the reasoning for starting follow-up (subsequent) sessions in this way:

> Progressive narratives are useful in constructing a solution; stability and digressive narratives are not useful, and therefore the therapist wants to open the interview by simply asking the client "What is better?" rather than "How did the homework go?" or some other specific question. In this way, the range of possible progressive narratives in response is expanded to include anything and everything the clients view as making their lives more satisfactory. (p. 130)

De Jong and Berg (1998), offer these reasons for initiating sessions with a "What's better?" inquiry:

> The most fundamental reason for beginning later sessions by asking this question is that once again it reflects the conviction that solutions are primarily built from the perception of exceptions. Given that both problem times and exceptions times will most likely have happened in any client's life since the previous session, why not begin later sessions by asking about what will be the most useful to the client—any perceived exceptions that have occurred? (p. 136)

As we have said throughout this book, RPT is a soft-focused solution approach. Brevity, while often important for various reasons, is not our primary goal. We agree that conversations highlighting and amplifying successes, exceptions, and positive movement are powerful means to therapeutic ends; they are the principal means by which we conduct therapy. However, we are always mindful of the need to balance a solution orientation with our collaborative stance—we do not want to force solution talk on our clients.[1] We have no fixed rules, only useful guidelines, and in any given context we must decide whether to follow those general guidelines or deviate from them in deference to what our clients feel needs to be addressed. Our orientation is toward solutions and conversations that are progressive; whenever we sense an opportunity to move in such a direction we take it. If we have reason to believe at the beginning of a session that the partners are feeling more positive about their relationship and each other, we often begin by asking, "What's better?"

On the other hand, when the partners seem distressed or we can't get a sense of how they're feeling as they enter our offices, we usually begin by asking a question or making a comment that leaves room for people to tell us about whatever is on their minds at the moment. In such cases, rather than forcing "progressive talk" and foreclosing topics that may be important to the partners, our initial comments and questions give people choice. Some "digressive" narratives are well worth pursuing in therapy. We do not want our clients to feel barred in any way from talking about what they want us to hear about and understand, whether it is a recent fight, a complaint against their partner or us, how things seem worse, or reports about things that seem unrelated to the concerns originally bringing the couple to therapy. When we sense that people need room to initiate, we might begin by asking, "Where do you folks think we should begin today?" or "What would you like to get out of today's session?" These opening questions give people a chance to tell us what is on their minds. Most often, however, we begin subsequent sessions in a way that not only gives people room to decide what to talk about but also gently orients conversation toward stories of change and movement. We do this with variations of this invitational comment: "I'd like to start by hearing about what's been better between you two since we last met, what happened that you would like to see happen more often, but I also want to find out if you have other things you think we should talk about first." Or sometimes we reverse the order of this question, suggesting that at some point in the session we would like to hear about what has gone better, but first we want to check in and find out if there's something the couple wants to address now. Both these opening invitations convey our respect for the couple and our interest in their concerns and at the same time encourage people to reflect on their successes and on pieces of the *good story*. Thus, even when people start talking about problems, seeds have been planted for memory scans for exceptions, movement, and change later in the session. If people start by talking about successes and positive happenings, we simply continue on this track.

## EARS: A Guide for Therapists

The Brief Family Therapy Center in Milwaukee (Berg, 1994; De Jong & Berg, 1998; de Shazer, 1985) uses the acronym EARS as a simple aid in teaching trainees to host exceptions/success-constructing conversations in follow-up sessions. In teaching and training contexts we have found this acronym a very helpful tool. Here is how we have adapted it in RPT:

- Eliciting: asking about exceptions and positive movement, that is, what is better and different. While, as we said earlier, we do not always begin follow-up sessions with "What's better?" we continually listen for clues and threads of progressive narratives. If we hear no such threads, we will begin asking exceptions and success-eliciting questions when the time seems right. When people say things are terrible and nothing is getting better, we might, for example, ask how they have managed to prevent things from being worse than they are (coping question), as a way to elicit some strength or resource. When they tell us about the terrible fight they had last night, we might ask how this fight was possibly less intense, came to an end more quickly than usual, or was somehow better or less painful.
- Amplifying: detailing and fleshing out even the smallest bits and pieces of change, movement, and desired experiences. This thickens the *good story* narrative. Once reports of satisfying experiences (successes, exceptions, and positive movement) that occurred since our last meeting begin to emerge, it is our job to help expand and develop these as parts of the mosaic of this bonding narrative. We want to specify details, identify agency, help the partners generate

new perspectives, and construct unexplored solutions. This allows people to begin viewing each other as capable of collaboration and success.

We ask amplifying questions like these: *Can you tell me more about this? How did you decide to do that? How did you get that to happen? How do you think it made a difference to her when she saw you doing that? How did you know doing that would make a difference?* These questions and the conversations they initiate solidify agency, concretize detail, and bring in new perspectives and fresh meanings, creating a relational and narrative context in which further positive changes can keep occurring.

- Reinforcing: highlighting and thickening the possible behavioral, perceptual, and interpretive power of the developing *good story* by our enthusiastic reaction and our compliments. When couples report positive changes and experiences and describe what each has done to turn things around, we compliment them, express our excitement and interest, and ask self-reflective questions. We might ask: *What does this say about the two of you that you were able to make that happen?* Or we might enthusiastically say, *Wow! That's really amazing. You guys were able to make something like that happen, when only a few weeks ago you were both thinking the situation was hopeless.* We often combine humor and enthusiasm. For instance, Phil, who tends to be quite enthusiastic in general, often says to couples, "If you keep this up, we can go on Oprah together!"

- Start again: by asking, *What else is better?* or *What else happened since our last meeting that tells us you folks are turning things around?* These kinds of questions invite couples to go in search of additional *good story* experiences that can nurture feelings of progress, foster hope and a sense of efficacy, recreate partnership, and provide concrete ideas about building solutions.

Deciding when to ask *good story*–eliciting questions, when to begin amplifying and reinforcing, and when to ask starting-again questions requires that the therapist continually take account of the therapeutic context. Knowing when to shift gears, back up, and change direction all require attentiveness to the responses we get from people—in other words, the cues and signals couples give us should guide our every step. Because we do not have a rule that every subsequent session begin by our asking what's better, we have developed some guidelines for deciding whether to initiate progressive conversations or give people room to invite us into conversations about whatever is uppermost in their minds. We take our cues mainly from people's nonverbal messages when we greet them in the waiting room and as they come into our offices, sit down, and start to talk with us.

### When Couples Return Visibly Happier and Closer

Quite frequently couples return to us for a subsequent session reporting that things are much improved. When people tell us on their own initiative or as a result of our inquiries that they are feeling closer and happier and that things are getting better, we immediately begin highlighting, amplifying, and fleshing out these stories of positive change; we explore how the changes made a difference and talk about how the partners, together, can keep the ball rolling. When a couple comes in smiling, talking warmly, holding hands, looking close and affectionate, we might say something like this: "Wow! You both seem a lot different than the last time I saw you. Warmer than a few weeks ago. I'm amazed at the changes I'm seeing here, and I'm dying to hear what's happened. Tell me all about it—what've the two of you been doing behind my back?" This isn't merely a strategic posture. We are glad to see people looking and sounding happier, and we let them know it, each of us in our own style and way. Our clients know how much we enjoy their successes.

### When People Tell us Nothing Has Changed or That Things are Worse

Often couples return thinking to themselves that not much has changed or that no progress has been made since our last meeting. They may look happier and seem closer, but come in prepared to tell us nothing much is different. Or that things are getting worse. A recent argument or the perceived failure of one's partner to do something promised in the last session may be uppermost in their thoughts. In such cases, we begin by acknowledging the partners' feelings and validating both points of view. But still we remain alert for any clues of progressive difference—pieces of experience outside these problem-saturated narratives.

Because we, like all constructionist therapists, assume people have had a variety of experiences since our last meeting—some better and more satisfying than others—if we do not hear about any preferred experiences we will at some point try to elicit some by asking certain questions designed to bring the positive experiences out of this variety and jump us out of the *bad story* box, if possible. We can ask, for example, whether the days on the weekend were better than the weekdays, or which day of all the days since our last meeting was better than others, following with questions about the specifics. We can use scaling questions to inquire about what numbers people would give the best day as compared with the worst day, again following up with questions about what will be happening on a day that is one number higher. We can ask people to take a look at times they could have had an argument or gotten into their problem area, but did not. All these lines of inquiry invite people to draw experiential distinctions that contain preferences, which we amplify into detailed, concrete experiential pictures. Now we're on the road to constructing solutions and mining assets.

The question naturally arises here, again, as to whether the therapist should ask, in the beginning of subsequent sessions, about task assignments given in the previous session. Like traditional solution-focused brief therapists, we do not do this. We do not start follow-up sessions by inquiring specifically about homework assignments (De Jong & Berg, 1998, p. 135). Assignments offered at the end of one session do not forge a link between that session and the next. As we noted in the last chapter, task assignments are intended—at the time they are given—to highlight elements of the couple's shared *good story* narrative and to influence their perceptual and interpretive orientation between sessions. Therefore, when the couple returns for the next hour we do not raise the issue of whether they did the suggested task, though we do intend to make use of it by focusing on *good story* elements.

We do not ask, for example, whether clients paid attention to positive experiences since our last meeting, alluding to a formula first session task assignment. We simply ask what they noticed happening that they want to have happen more, without reference to the "paying-attention" assignment itself. Of course, if a couple initiates conversation about the task assignment and seems eager to tell us how well it went or how they modified it in ways that worked for them, we are delighted to hear all about it. Regardless of whether they carried out the assignment, modified it, or didn't even remember we gave it, our focus is on finding out what's different and what's better, not whether or not they carried it out.

## Ending Therapy: Good-byes That Make a Difference

Most of the time in RPT our work with couples comes to an end when the partners tell us (1) they feel sufficient progress has been made with respect to solving their problems, making their desired changes, and reaching their goals for therapy, and (2) they feel sufficiently confident that they can continue in this positive direction on their own (Walter & Peller, 1994). That is, both partners are experiencing themselves living in their *good story* narrative and believe they can continue on this path without further therapy, at least for the time being. When people report, either on their own initiative or as a result of our various progress-promoting inquiries, that things are getting better and that they are successfully solving the problems that brought them to us, it is time to explore their readiness to end therapy. When progress and confidence in future progress are sufficient signs of success, therapy tends to be relatively brief. We do not assume that presenting problems as well as those that emerge during treatment must be completely solved before termination is appropriate. However, both because of the collaborative nature of our work and because client satisfaction, not brevity, is our watchword, termination decisions belong to our clients. Once they tell us they feel on track to solving the problems that brought them into therapy, the couple gets the final vote on whether we say good-bye, take up other concerns, or continue meeting for a while for support.

The research we note in our introduction (Bray & Jouriles, 1995) points to the high level of erosion over time in the gains people report in couples counseling. It is possible, however, that couples who leave therapy assuming, as a matter of course, that they will face future challenges and that there will be ups and downs in their relationship life might define their relationship with therapy and their levels of satisfaction regarding it differently. In addition, where therapy is viewed by all as relatively brief and oriented toward particular goals/solutions, it is also possible for some couples to return for future couples work on an as-needed basis if other problems arise, without feeling they have failed or their prior therapy has not helped.

### A Good Ending Starts With a Good Beginning

We have adopted two very useful, related ideas from brief therapy (Budman & Gurman, 1988; Cade & O'Hanlon, 1993). The first is that therapy will be more effective and efficient when it begins with clear, well-formed goals. The second is that therapy's transformative effect depends not on the number of sessions that occur but rather on whether the changes made during treatment ripple out into the couple's relational life after therapy ends. For many clinicians trained in traditional forms of therapy, working briefly with couples can be challenging, even counterintuitive. If the therapist brings to couples work ideas and practices she commonly uses in her longer-term work with individual clients, she may find it hard to operate in the focused way we do in RPT. She may be uncomfortable redirecting couples toward clarifying therapeutically well-formed goals when they continually return to engaging in forms of problem talk. While she may see the value of engaging people in conversations that reinvigorate their shared *good story* narratives, because she is uncomfortable purposefully guiding therapy conversation in the ways we have outlined she may find herself falling back on old, familiar interviewing practices when clients begin talking about details of their individual *bad story* narratives. Finally, as Michael Hoyt points out (2000), for both theoretical and practical financial reasons, she may find it difficult, when the signs appear that it is time to begin preparing couples for termination, to begin asking questions that will bring therapy to a rapid (albeit successful) end, knowing that this will result in having to find a replacement referral if she is to keep her caseload full.[2]

A successful ending to therapy requires a purposeful beginning. If the therapist has established well-formed goals with her clients at the outset of therapy and continued to attend to them over its course, the perceptual and experiential signs that constitute these goals will tell clients when their work in therapy is finished. And this may happen quite quickly. We want to keep therapy effective and efficient, and we feel an ethical responsibility to minimize the time and money clients spend in therapy. (This is also a relevant concern for clinicians involved in the managed-care system.) As noted earlier, we believe that therapy should be, in most cases, a relatively brief moment in a couple's life—a turning point after which couples will continue growing and changing on their own, facing challenges and delighting in the pleasures of their ongoing life together. Our contact with them should be a minor interlude in their relationship life—we want therapy to be a watershed, not a lagoon. We expect and intend that the changes made in therapy are a start of something that will have a cumulative effect, resonating in a couple's life beyond the point where we say good-bye, and skillful termination contributes to this. Just as a good beginning makes for a successful ending, an effective ending makes the most of the transformative post-therapeutic influences of the counseling experience.

### How to End in a Collaborative, Solution-Oriented Way

From the beginning to the end of the therapeutic enterprise, we blend a collaborative and solution-oriented stance. Once it appears that a couple is turning their relationship around, that is, they are reporting progress with respect to solving their problems and moving toward their shared goals, it is time to begin asking questions that prepare them for termination—and for life after therapy. These questions address four general issues: (1) whether the partners feel that the positive changes they have been making are adequate to satisfy them that they are on track in solving their problems and reaching their mutual goals; (2) what specific things each partner can do to remind him- or herself to keep things moving in this desired direction; (3) what will give them both sufficient confidence that, together, they can keep the ball rolling on their own and feel comfortable about ending therapy; and (4) what to do when problems and challenges arise in the future.

When one or both partners say the changes they have been making are not enough or that they do not yet feel confident they can make a go of it on their own, we begin by helping them figure out what further signs of change need to happen. This is goal-building, which, as we have pointed out, takes place at every stage of the process. We want to bring out and amplify the signs that tell people sufficient changes have taken place and their confidence levels are high enough to go forward on their own. Here are some questions we use in this effort:

- *What other changes need to happen so that you can both feel we've come far enough that you're ready to end therapy?*
- *What will be different when you can both say you're confident enough that you can keep going on your own and you no longer need to come here on a regular basis?*
- *On a scale of 1 to 10, 1 being you have no confidence that you can stay on track without therapy and 10 being that you're fully confident, what number would you give your level of confidence right now?* After the person answers, we would ask, to tease out the possibility that the partners could be confident enough even if their level is not a 10, *Do you suppose you could be confident enough to leave therapy and continue on your own even if you weren't 100% confident? What number would you give that level of confidence? What will be different that will tell you that you've reached that level?*

As you can see, these questions function both to define goals and to elicit information about what will make people confident in their ability to solve their own problems and manage without therapy. When the couple decides they can keep the ball rolling on their own, it is time to shift into conversations that maximize the long-term effects of their *good story* narrative and the positive changes they have made in therapy.

When the couple, not the therapist, decides when to say good-bye, we have found that most couples are eager to leave therapy once things are getting better. Some, however, are reluctant to leave even after they have made significant changes. These couples want to know that if times get rough, we will be there to help them sort things out. In these cases, we balance respect for the couple's needs and feelings with our responsibility to guide them in preparing to end therapy with confidence, equipped to continue on their own. We take a middle path. When a couple, even when they have accomplished significant positive change, prefers to linger awhile, enjoying the environment of comfort, safety, and warmth we have developed together, we enjoy this basking period with them, as they may feel they need that time to make termination feel solid. But we keep tabs on what will let them know it's time to leave. Some people want to continue meeting with us for a while after achieving satisfying change as a kind of "insurance." For many couples, especially those who have been in therapy for some time and have made significant changes, tapering off the frequency of sessions meets their needs better than stopping all at once. Other couples prefer to schedule one or two follow-up meetings several months down the road. When negotiating a meeting schedule with these couples, we explore what the partners will have to remember and do to be able to report, in these follow-up sessions, that things are still going well. We also ask them to consider what will tell them they might benefit from an unscheduled session. On the other hand, we let them know that if things are going fine and they don't feel the need for a scheduled follow-up session, all they need to do is give us advance notice.

However, just as we want people to feel free about their readiness to terminate, we also want them to feel comfortable raising other issues and concerns or talking about other changes they want to make now that things are getting better. Sometimes people need to experience a certain amount of success in therapy and feel a proven trust in the therapist, their partner, and the relationship before they are ready to reveal and address certain kinds of distress; therefore, we do not want to force a couple out of therapy at the first sign that things are getting better. In some cases, having tested the waters by working successfully on an initial set of problems, clients reveal that they want our help in solving other difficulties. We make room for people to circle back and change direction, even after they are making progress toward their goals. While we do not assume, as some therapists do, that the presenting problem is only the tip of the iceberg or a ticket of admission to therapy, we do remain open and available to help couples address other issues that for one reason or another they chose not to mention earlier.

For instance, in one such case, the wife, after (and only after) she and her husband had begun talking about parenting issues more effectively, wanted to talk about feelings she still had about an affair her husband had had several years before, feelings that made it hard for her to trust him. In another case, a husband reported that his relationship with his wife was getting much better, but now, having gained some confidence in the thera- peutic process, he said he wanted to use the therapist's help to talk to his wife about the fact that he was procrastinating a great deal at work and his job was in jeopardy. In a third example, a wife acknowledged that even though she and her husband were getting along better, she had fallen in love with another woman and was thinking about leaving the marriage to be with her. In all these cases, the presenting problems were stated in terms of communication difficulties. The specific changes defined in goal-building conversations in the first sessions concerned how the couples would handle disagreements in the future and how their intimate conversations could be more satisfying. It was only after things were improving that these couples were ready to talk about other very important concerns and issues. Had we simply congratulated these couples when they reported that things were getting better in their communication and begun preparing them for termi- nation, they might have felt foreclosed from using therapy to deal with painful and significant issues they were now ready to address.

### Therapeutic Endings That Echo

Finishing well both completes and perpetuates the good work that has preceded it. While we can recognize that termination in some ways may be a pseudoevent in that the work continues and formal treatment can be intermittently resumed . . . , it is important to end sessions and a course of therapy well. Done skillfully, we increase the likelihood that, while the therapy may be brief, the benefit may be long term. (Hoyt, 2000, pp. 237–238)

When a couple has been helped to resolve the particular issues that have been driving a wedge between the partners and caused a clouding of their *good story* narrative, the process of termination should set the stage for the couple to continue the relationship-supporting and -enhancing changes on their own. Because we do not expect couples to make all possible significant changes or necessarily completely solve their presenting problems during the time we are working together (and *do* expect that they will meet many challenges and ups and downs on their own), we want to do what we can to prepare couples to continue making changes in the context of a solid, lively *good story* narrative when they are no longer in therapy. When the time comes to say good-bye, therefore, we want to ensure the consolidation of the changes they have been making and perpetuate, to the extent we can, each partner's commitment to continue working for the relationship's well being.

As we do in all phases of our work with couples, at the point of termination we use questions to further therapeutic ends. We inquire of each partner what he or she needs to do and think to keep the ball rolling. We ask people to identify and reflect on possible future challenges and to tell us how they plan to handle those difficult times differently than they might have in the past. In these conversations about what might go wrong, about times when the couple might run into difficulty, get stuck, or backslide, we want to flesh out and amplify what strengths and resources the partners can call on to weather these challenges and quickly get themselves back on course. We want them to approach these inevitable times of trouble with a viable *good story* narrative strongly in place. Here are some of the kinds of questions we ask in a final meeting:

- *What do you imagine you'll be doing to keep things on track after you're no longer coming here?*
- *What do the two of you see as the next steps for you? Do you have some ideas about ways you'd like to change your relationship that you can undertake without therapy?*
- *What have been the most important things you've learned here about your ability to solve difficult problems as a couple? What do the changes you've made here tell you about yourselves and your relationship?*
- *Who among all the people who know you would be the least surprised to find out that you've turned your marriage around this way? What does this person know about you as individuals and as a couple?*
- *What do you suggest I tell other couples who come to me with similar*

*problems (wanting to make similar changes) that might help them do what you two have done?*

- *What do you suppose will be challenges for each of you and what will you need to remember and do as a team to be successful in meeting them?*
- *What will you have to keep in mind to help you remember what you can do to stay on track or get back on track when you have a setback?*
- *What have we done or said here in our meetings that you might call on when times get tough?*
- *Lots of couples we work with who have also been successful in turning their relationship around like to know that they can come back any time for a tune-up. Not everyone comes back, but I want you to know you're always welcome. And you don't have to wait for things to get really bad before calling. So I wonder what signs might tell you that it would be a good idea to come in for a session or two?*

Some of these questions invite people to identify possible future problems and challenges. When helping people at the beginning of therapy to develop solutions and goals, we ask them to imagine preferred future pictures when their problems have been solved. Now, at the point of termination, we want them to imagine possible future challenges so they can identify the unique strengths and resources and custom-made responses that will help them get through these tough times, when and if they happen. Exploring how the couple will handle future problems and setbacks conveys our belief that problems and troubles are inevitable in life—and therefore must be part of the expected future—and that we have come to believe this couple has what it takes to work together in meeting these challenges and building a better future together. If our work together has made a difference, the couple has recreated partnership and this, in the end, is their best resource and their greatest strength.

In the final minutes of our last session we want to leave the couple with a sense of accomplishment and with the knowledge that we have learned from them and seen them at their best. We compliment them on the hard-won, meaningful changes they have made together and savor their progress with them. Sometimes we mention special and unique moments we may have shared together during the therapy or laugh together about mutual jokes. These moments are not stiff or formal. They have the qualities of intimacy, warmth, and collaboration that have developed in the work (no matter how brief) we've done together—a tone particular to each couple, of course. We speak to the couple's individual and collective strengths and resources and convey that in the future, as they face the inevitable new challenges, they will discover and develop new ones. And we let them know, by what we say and by our enthusiasm and pleasure, that we have been honored to have had the opportunity to participate with them in turning their relationship around.

CHAPTER ❖ 11

# Couples Therapy With Only One Partner

Most traditional models of marital therapy have mild to fierce objections to working with only one partner as a form of relationship counseling. However, we have found, in actual practice, that working with a solo partner can be a very effective way to help clients make desired relationship changes (de Shazer & Berg, 1985).

We have not always held this point of view about meeting with solo partners. For many years, influenced by systems thinking, we assumed success in couples therapy could be achieved only if both partners (the dyadic system) actively participated in conjoint sessions. When relationship issues were the presenting problem, we went along with the prevailing idea that it would be a therapeutic error to see only one partner, either initially or during the course of therapy. However, over the years we noticed, in working with individuals, that people often reported increased happiness in their relationships from the work we were doing in their individual hours. So we began to ask ourselves: If this type of relationship improvement could happen in individual therapy for clients initially presenting with nonrelationship problems, why couldn't it happen with individuals who sought therapy specifically for couples issues? We started experimenting with different formats for solo work. Now, after years of experience working with solo partners, we never refuse appointments to callers who say their partners do not want to come—we work with anyone who says they have couple (or family) troubles and who wants to work for change.

What is the basis for the idea that couples therapy should not be undertaken unless both partners agree to participate? One theory is that if one partner is not willing to come for therapy it means he or she is probably not motivated to change or is not committed to the relationship. And, since one partner cannot change another, it is futile for the therapist to try to help a motivated partner influence an absent one to change. According to this theory, the absent partner's refusal to come to therapy is evidence of resistance—an unwillingness to take responsibility for or participate in growth/change—and evidence that he or she will undermine the efforts of the willing partner. We do not think such assumptions are warranted.

People may refuse to participate in therapy for many reasons. Quite often these reasons have nothing to do with either commitment to the relationship or willingness to change. Many people do not think therapy is a useful way to address marital/relationship problems. Some have had bad experiences in previous therapies; others, with good reason, do not want to commit their financial resources to what they fear will be an endless, and possibly unproductive, process. Often people believe there are other, more effective or appropriate ways to make positive changes. These are valid reasons for not pursuing therapy, and they do not indicate a lack of desire to work for relationship change. All we can reasonably conclude when one partner of a couple does not arrive at our door is that this person does not, at the present time at least, want to come to therapy.

Another variation on the resistance argument is that when a caller says the other partner refuses to come to therapy, the caller is, in fact, unconsciously colluding with the partner to prevent therapy from succeeding. In other words, *both* partners are trying to defeat the therapist by this strategic maneuver. The therapist, accordingly, must win an initial battle by refusing to schedule an appointment until both partners agree to come to the first session. As noted earlier, our working assumption is that couples are stuck, not dysfunctional, and that in most cases both partners want to solve their problems. It takes a lot of evidence to the contrary to convince us to abandon this stance. Partners in a couple usually have competing points of view about what needs to change, but we assume both want things to be better and have simply been unable to figure out how to go about accomplishing this. We have been confirmed in these assumptions in an overwhelming percentage of cases. (While it is occasionally true that one partner has an undisclosed desire to end the relationship or is not being honest about his or her commitment to change, it is deleterious to the process of couples therapy and to a collaborative method to assume couples are undercutting or resisting therapy. Clear goal development, including the delineation of behavioral signs, obviates any lack of honesty or commitment.)

A third objection to seeing one partner alone is that one person cannot change another. (This objection can be seen as relevant to the definition of goals and whether or not they are in the client's control.) While it is true that one person cannot force another to change his or her personality or even alter specific behaviors, this does not mean partners in a couple have no influence on each other through what they do and say. In fact, as we have been pointing out in various ways, people are always influencing each other in relationships, in both intended and unintended ways. While the other partner's behavior is outside a client's control, the interactions that support positive change are not—one partner can trip a positive change cycle by shifts in his or her perceptions and behavior. The issue—and this is a central concern in relationship therapy—is *how* people are trying to influence each other to change and whether what they are doing produces desirable or undesirable results.

Another argument against seeing only one partner in a couple is the supposed danger that the therapist, hearing only one side of the relationship-story, will get a distorted view of the couple's difficulties and will not understand the fuller dynamics at play. According to this argument, the therapist must ascertain the "real facts" about a couple's problems in order to design interventions to solve them. Because, however, we work on the assumption that there is no necessary relationship between what causes a couple's problems and what the partners can do to solve them, we are not concerned with ascertaining some objective account of the history of the couple's troubles. Whether we are working conjointly or with a solo partner, we focus on where people want to go and what strengths and resources they will have to muster to bring about a more satisfying future, declining all invitations to adjudicate about the truth or reality of individual *bad stories*.

Another concern about seeing partners separately is that the therapist will become privy to secrets that may set up a collusive alliance between the therapist and one partner—learning about an affair, for instance, or about the fact that a spouse has already decided to separate and has hired a divorce lawyer while saying in the conjoint sessions that he or she wants to work on saving the marriage. Now the therapist is burdened with a decision about what to do with the information and how and if to disclose it. Because the therapist, as a professional, is supposed to know the consequences and effects of clients' secrets and unilateral actions, the responsibility of dealing with this threat to the couple's bond lies with her, and a misstep can have disastrous clinical consequences.

In RPT, our approach is collaborative. It is not normally the point or outcome of solo sessions that we learn secrets our client has not disclosed to the absent partner. However, when we have been made privy to important secrets in an individual session with one partner, we explore with this individual what the likely consequences might be of withholding the secret information instead of sharing it with the other partner. We share our concern that the therapy—and possibly the relationship—will be deterred from positive progress if this secret remains, and we ask the person to reflect on how effective he or she thinks therapy will be if the secret is kept. This often leads the client to decide to bring out the secret information in a session with the partner. If he or she does decide to reveal the withheld information, we can talk together about how to go about doing this, so that the couple's dialogue about it can serve therapeutic ends. If, on the other hand, the individual decides not to disclose the secret and asks us to agree to keep it, we have to make our own personal and professional decision whether or not to continue working with this couple—and part of our consideration in these cases is how comfortable we ourselves feel proceeding under the given circumstances. In most cases, holding secrets is not a good idea. There are times, however, we may choose to hold privy information for a while; but if progress is not occurring in the couple's sessions under these conditions, we renegotiate. Whatever we and the client choose to do, we feel knowing this information is better than working in the dark.

Joel came to see Phil for therapy on his own and explained that he was dissatisfied in his marriage and had been carrying on a secret affair for several years. He said he loved his wife and daughter but also cared deeply for the other woman. He had made several unsuccessful attempts to break off the affair but kept returning to it. He wanted Phil's help to end the affair once and for all, but said that in order to do so he felt he needed to see some changes in his marriage. At a certain point in their conversation about his goals and options, Joel asked whether Phil would see him and his wife in couples therapy. Phil explained that he would be glad to work with them together, but that so long as the affair was continuing he was uncomfortable, professionally and personally, agreeing to see them as a couple. He suggested that perhaps Joel needed to take some time in individual therapy to clarify whether to concentrate on ending the affair or rebuilding his marriage. Phil said that his experience with other clients in similar situations had led him to believe it would very difficult to help Joel and his wife rebuild their relationship so long as Joel continued his affair. Joel said he needed some time to think about what to do next, and he and Phil agreed to meet again in two weeks. When he returned to the next session, Joel announced that he had decided to suspend the affair and concentrate his efforts on saving and rebuilding his marriage. He did not want, however, to tell his wife about the affair and wanted to know if Phil would now see him and his wife, under these conditions, in couples therapy. While Phil was somewhat uncomfortable with this arrangement and talked with Joel about these feelings, they agreed, at least for the time being, to begin marital therapy without talking about the affair with his wife. But Phil made it clear that he might return to this issue, if, as the therapy continued, it seemed necessary to renegotiate the agreement.

As it turned out, Joel decided to reveal the secret of his recently ended affair after several sessions of marital therapy and as positive changes began to happen for the couple. This admission was followed by many months of often emotionally charged sessions. At different times each partner talked about throwing in the towel, but slowly the couple began turning things around. Though the relationship was not ideal for either partner, by the time they ended therapy both had decided this was a marriage worth saving and had found means of enjoying their companionship and rebuilding partnership and enough trust to go forward.

Finally, the most frequently heard argument—and probably the most significant in its effect on the field—against working with a solo partner is the systems-theory argument. Most clinicians, whether psychodynamic, behavioral, or systems-oriented, recognize that relationship problems are to some degree interpersonal—rooted in patterns of interaction between people and, in this respect, functioning like systems. We agree. However, we do not believe that couples and families *are* systems, though they may sometimes behave *like* them. We think the systems-theory idea that couples therapy should only be conducted conjointly is an unnecessary constraint; it derives from a failure to keep in mind that the systems metaphor is simply that—a way of trying to understand couples and families by analogy. When analogies become equivalencies, problems develop (Rosenblatt, 1994). It is one thing to view couples as functioning in some ways like systems and quite another to say that they are equivalent in all respects to information-exchange systems, such as thermostats and radar-guided rockets.[1]

When families or couples are viewed as bona fide systems rather than as functioning in some systemic ways, certain assumptions morph into fact. One such assumption is that couples are subject to homeostatic forces. This means that if one person in a couple changes, the other will change in ways that specifically maintain stasis. A related idea and one that continues to be favored by many strategic, systems-theory family therapists (Haley, 1976; Madanes, 1981), is that symptoms perform stabilizing systemic functions. In other words, a therapist must address the symptomatic or problematic behavior as a system-sustaining function. For example, a child's substance abuse and violent behavior at school might be seen as serving a family-maintaining function of holding the parent's marriage together by providing the one thing the couple can agree on—the need to fix their son. According to this theory, improvement of the son's behavior might result in a breakdown of the marital relationship, which would prompt the partners to do things (unknowingly) to get the child to begin acting out again.

When couples are viewed literally as dyadic cybernetic systems, with all the properties and processes of information-exchange systems, it follows that both partners must participate in treatment together because, as is commonly said, the "marital system itself is the client." This is the essence of the systems-theory argument against working with only one partner in couples therapy. But if this theory is accurate, how can we explain the fact that we and other clinicians are working successfully with solo partners every day? And that changes by one partner often create relationship-enhancing change in the other?

In fact, a close examination of the systems perspective reveals that the theory does provide a basis for working with one partner to change a relationship. While homeostasis works as a conservative force in cybernetic systems (meaning that in order to bring change to dyadic systems, both parties must be directly influenced to change), other characteristics of systems suggest ways that a relationship can be altered by the changes of a single partner. In *Overcoming Relationship Impasses* (1991), Barry Duncan and Joseph Rock point out that the systemic characteristic of "mutual dependence" reflects that what one person does in a relationship influences and is at the same time dependent on what the other does (pp. 13–14).

The related systemic characteristic of "causal circularity" assumes that causation, rather than being linear and having a single identifiable beginning, is circular, and that origin is simply a matter of perceptual orientation, which punctuates an ongoing cycle of interactions at a certain point and says "this is the starting point." Causal circularity means change can be started anywhere and have an impact on everything that follows. Both mutual dependence and causal circularity provide systems arguments for the idea that "when one person makes a change, the other person will respond with a change and the relationship itself will be different, and not just in ways directly related to the specific problem that was addressed" (Duncan & Rock, 1991, p. 17).

In RPT, who is present for therapy is determined not by our theories or preferences but by negotiation with our clients. The criteria we use for who should come is simple: We want to find out (1) who thinks there is a problem to solve (is affected adversely by the situation), and (2) who is willing to work actively to solve it (is willing to take some responsibility for changing the situation). Ideally, we prefer that both partners participate in couples therapy in most cases. But, where one of the partners doesn't meet both criteria, it can be more effective to work with the partner who does. Having both individuals in the room with us makes it easier to facilitate the recreation of partnership and engage people in conversations that reinvigorate their shared *good story*. When both partners are present, we can best explore what changes would be meaningful to them individually and collectively, and we can influence people's levels of motivation to work actively in therapy for those desired changes. Naturally, like most couples therapists, we enjoy working in conjoint sessions with two highly motivated partners who both take responsibility for relationship change and are working actively and eagerly together to make therapy a success. In practice, however, this is not the most common case. We work with what we have. Sometimes there is greater potential for success working with one partner alone than in pressuring both partners to come together.

There are basically four situations in which we meet with only one partner. Each of these situations has unique characteristics, presenting the clinician with both challenges and opportunities. We begin with the situation where, during the ongoing course of couples therapy it seems useful to meet individually with one or both partners. Then we will discuss situations in which couples therapy is carried on entirely with a solo partner.

## Seeing Partners Separately in Individual Sessions during Ongoing Therapy

We sometimes meet individually with the partners of a couple we have been seeing conjointly. When a couple struggles week after week with the same complaints and goes over the same ground or when, in each session, movement toward collaboration is minimal and little or no *good story–*generating conversation occurs, one option is to suggest that the partners meet with us separately. This gives people a chance to talk with us and work on making changes outside the context of the other person's reactions and arguments.

People who are very reactive to each other in negative ways, strongly invested in blaming, or frequently view their issues from a right/wrong perspective often have a hard time working collaboratively and are either unable to acknowledge elements of the *good story* narrative in each other's presence or continually return to *bad story* material. In these cases we ask whether the couple thinks it might be helpful for us to meet alone with each of them, and they usually say yes. When we do this, we spend a good deal of time reflecting individual concerns and acknowledging and validating their experiences and points of view. Then we begin focusing on what specific changes the solo partner is willing to work for and what the individual might have to do to increase the possibility that those changes could happen. Sometimes it is easier for solo partners, in this context, to take a look at actions of their own that are not supportive of forward progress and imagine, through perspective-shifting questions, what might produce desired change on the other's part. We are working to elicit and highlight elements of the *good story* narrative in order to encourage perceptual shifts and make a foundation for further amplification of this bonding narrative when we return to conjoint sessions.

Another situation where therapy can bog down and we might suggest individual sessions is when people remain committed to incompatible goals. Perhaps one partner wants to get married and the other does not want to formalize the relationship in that way. Or one partner is questioning whether to stay in the relationship and the other is quite committed. We may suggest individual sessions in such cases if, after several conjoint sessions, no overarching, shared goal has been articulated. In our experience, when people have conflicting or incompatible goals and neither is able to modify them, continuing to meet conjointly can sometimes intensify the polarization (Weiner-Davis, 1992). Each partner may use the sessions together to marshal arguments as to why the other should give in, and any efforts on the therapist's part to redirect the process can go by the board. Taking a break from conjoint sessions and meeting with each partner alone can sometimes make a difference. The individual meetings provide a safe and less stressful context in which guarding against the other partner's point of view or attack is not necessary, and this makes it possible to explore more fully what each person wants and the meanings of those desires. Talking individually with the partners about their meta-goals, hopes for the future, and willingness to make concessions to preserve the relationship provides opportunities for constructing goals and proposals that can eventually serve as a basis for developing mutually shared solutions with the couple in later conjoint sessions. In our individual sessions in these cases we try to foster flexibility in people's thinking and a softening of their polar stances, when that is possible. When no mutual solutions are possible and the partners' goals remain incompatible, the individual sessions can become a place to explore other options, including ending the relationship. These options can then be brought into the conjoint discussions.

## Couples Therapy With the Motivated Solo Partner

In most cases, individuals wanting help with relationship problems who come to therapy alone have been working for some time without success to change the absent partner and the relationship. At the point of making the call, the motivated solo partner has decided to seek professional help in figuring out how to get the other person to change or (possibly) to decide what steps to take if change does not occur. In the first case, the solo partner usually begins by engaging in complainant/sympathizer conversation. While ultimately we intend to invite this client into customer/consultant conversation, in the beginning we take time to allow the client to tell us about his or her experiences, perceptions, and theories about the relationship problems—in other words, we listen, acknowledge, and validate this client's *bad story* narrative. Here we begin as usual by building rapport, demonstrating our interest and respect. In order to learn about the solo partner's theories of change, we listen well with that curious and not-knowing attitude we spoke of earlier. Once rapport has been established, we move toward customer/consultant conversation.

Now our goal is to help the motivated solo partner clarify (1) therapeutically well-formed goals, and (2) the potential means (what specific changes he or she might make that are most likely to promote desired changes in the other person's behavior). We use the same kinds of questions in our conversations with the solo partner that we use when both partners are in the room. However, because one of the criteria of well-formed goals is that the changes be within the client's control, our emphasis is on the changes he or she can make that will generate the possibility—without guarantees, of course—that the other partner will change as well. Additionally, we want to expand the goal framework beyond specific desired changes in the other's behavior, bringing out unarticulated meta-goals so that we can explore a variety of possible changes and actions on the partner's part that might make a difference to our client. We can also ask about recent exceptions and successes, amplifying what our client was doing in those times that might have made a difference. Once our client has begun to clarify goals and contemplate changes, perspective-shifting questions are the most helpful line of inquiry in defining the kinds of changes the other partner will respond to positively, thereby bringing about shifts in the partner's behavior or attitudes our client desires. Now it becomes a matter of trial and error as the client tries out what he or she thinks might make a difference and observes the effects at home. At the end of each session we encourage the client to pay attention to desired experiences and changes so they can provide information about ways to influence further changes and give greater weight to *good story* experiences.

For example, suppose a wife concerned about the lack of closeness in her marriage comes to therapy on her own. During goal-building conversations, she tells the therapist that one sign of more closeness would be that her husband would come home from the office earlier on weekday evenings. He would be home for dinner more often and would spend "quality time" with the family before the kids went to sleep. She says that when she has asked him to come home earlier in the past, he has replied that he can't leave early because he has deadlines to meet and because other people on his project team stay late and it would look bad if he left earlier than everyone else. Her goal, as currently defined, fails to meet the criteria of being within her control. Therefore, the therapist might begin by engaging her in meta-goal coauthoring, asking how it would make a difference to her if he did make that change—if he, at least more frequently, came home for dinner and spent evenings with the family.

Suppose she says that this would tell her that the family was at least as important to him as his work and his coworkers, that he really enjoyed and valued spending time with her and the kids, and that he and she had similar values and wanted to live the same kind of life. As she talks about these meanings, she clarifies the ways that the specific changes she has been pressing for hold personal significance for her. Now we are in a position to help her create a positive ripple effect in her relationship. Once we have helped her to clarify her meta-goals, we can proceed to help her identify what actions her husband already does that might tell her he feels this way about her and the family—things that affirm that the *good story* is sometimes already happening. At the same time, we can help her develop ideas about other changes he might make (or she might watch for) that will have the same desirable meanings. This also will help her amplify the scope and detail of her *good story* narrative and shift her perceptual lens. At this point we can begin working, through perspective-shifting and role-reversal questions, to help her develop different ways of interacting with her husband around both the disliked and preferred experiences; these changes may affect her husband's behaviors and prompt more of the kinds of experiences she has described in her meta-goals. They may even make it more likely that he will take action to do what she wanted in the first place: come home earlier.

Again, we are not interested in what she's done that didn't work. We want to help her develop a plan of action based on what has made a positive difference (exceptions and successes), or on new actions and attitudes she discovers in dialogue with us that could influence desired changes on her husband's part. What she comes up with will naturally be different from what she has done in the past, the actions that have failed to produce desired results. Sometimes, in these discussions, a client acknowledges how past behaviors or prior solution moves have been making matters worse. This is a central way that role-reversal questions and perspective-shifting conversations are effective; they help the motivated solo partner distinguish what actions might help from those that will cause things to get worse. Because she has developed a detailed list of things her husband already does that satisfy her meta-goals, her focus on this potential *good story* material encourages her to shift her perceptual orientation. When she does things differently because of the understandings these inquiries have brought out, her husband is likely to feel a shift in the relational climate and respond. When she notices the positive things he does (either because he's doing more or because she is noticing more, or both) and lets her husband know she notices, telling (or conveying to him by nonverbal signs) that what he's doing makes a positive difference to her, she will be reflecting a self-sense of her husband to him that pleases him—this naturally produces in him a more positive feeling about his wife and their relationship. The ripple effect begins to take place.

Even when a solo client agrees with the idea that both partners need to change, however, questions of who should go first or who has the real problem can come up. Rather than getting into a debate over who should initiate change or how to get the other person to admit responsibility, we want to clarify the interpersonal link between changes the solo partner can make and the changes he or she wants the other to make. We can then help our client decide to take action to set the upward change cycle in motion by doing things that are likely to trigger desired changes in the other partner. Pinpointing specific, potentially influential changes our client might make maximizes the potential for reciprocal changes. This possibility for reciprocity, when who goes first becomes an unimportant (or often moot) point, has been proven to us time and again by our clients.

Just as perceived negative actions on the part of one's partner tend to produce a like response, perceived desired actions are more likely than not to generate positive responses (Gottman, 1999; Markman, 1994). Once people decide to make their own perceptual and behavioral shifts, they often unexpectedly spark the longed-for changes in the other partner. This is why working with a solo partner is so often effective in improving relationships. As soon as reciprocity, or the ripple effect, gets started, the origin of the change is unimportant and the maintenance of change becomes mutual. However, change on the part of a single partner will go unnoticed— will be rejected as relationship-repairing—if it is not crafted so that it will be notable and make a difference to the other partner.

For example, Tobey worked with a motivated solo partner on a difficult marital issue. Chris was a graphics designer who came back to therapy on his own when he discovered that his wife, Joan, had carried on a long-term affair with a partner in her law firm. Chris and Joan had seen Tobey together several years earlier when they were trying to decide whether or not to have a second child, a decision that would impact Joan's career. Joan had left couples therapy when it became clear she did not feel ready to have another child, and though Chris wanted to move on to issues around their lack of closeness, Joan said she did not care to stay in therapy longer. Recently Chris had discovered, through one of Joan's colleagues, that she had been having an affair. Though the affair had already ended, at the behest of the other person, he was stunned by the news, and it was a tremendous shock to him to find out that it had gone on for two years, since soon after they had originally left couples therapy. Now Joan refused to come to therapy with Chris, saying she did not see how therapy could help with something like this and that she didn't think it had helped enough in the first place.

Chris was distraught. He was very hurt and angry and said he couldn't think about much of anything but the affair; his work, his sleep, and his private time were all suffering. He felt "completely messed up." He didn't think he wanted to end his marriage or break up his family at this point and felt he still loved Joan, but said he was so shocked and upset he couldn't think clearly, and he was afraid they could never recover from this. He was furious at Joan's deceit; he couldn't stop thinking, he said, about how "cruel and thoughtless she was to do this, and for years." He also said he was very angry at himself and felt there was something horribly wrong with him, because he had somehow been able to pull the wool over his own eyes and not notice that something was going on. He explained that he didn't know if he "should" love his wife anymore—maybe the fact that he still did was more evidence there was something wrong with him. Regarding therapy, he commented that he had experienced their prior work as very helpful, that he trusted Tobey, and that was why he'd come—now he really needed help.

Initially Tobey just listened to Chris talk about his pain, dismay, and jealousy. She let him know that his feelings seemed natural under the circumstances, validated the painfulness of the situation, and let his concerns guide their conversations. Then Tobey helped Chris formulate a first goal for therapy—he would develop additional goals later. The first goal entailed taking steps to reduce his confusion and feel better about himself. As they talked about this, Chris said he wanted to feel "like his own man." When Tobey asked him what would be different when he and others saw him as "his own man," he said that he would be developing his own plans about what to do about his marriage, regardless of what friends and family (and caveats he saw in broader social convention) said about how a person in his circumstances should feel and act. He said he and others would notice that he was honoring his own real feelings and taking it step by step as he figured out what to do, and when that was happening, he would be closer to developing a plan of action that would work for him. When he listened to advice that seemed to suggest that "the only thing to do in this kind of situation is leave, only a fool would stay," he began to feel desperate, because he wasn't at all sure he wanted to leave. When Tobey asked him what he would notice different about himself when he felt therapy was working, he said he would be sticking to his own plan, even when he had doubts and felt confused.

Chris and Tobey worked out what signs would tell him that particular experiences were helpful to him in achieving the goal of being "his own man" and that he was on the way to developing his own plan. One sign of this, Chris said, would be feeling good about himself and his decisions after conversations with friends, and this would be supported by telling certain friends their suggestions were not helpful, and by spending more time with people who did not focus on his marital situation. Other signs he was feeling better about himself would be getting to the gym more regularly and arriving at work on time again. A sign that he was developing his own plan would be that he would say to himself and to his wife that he was taking it one day at a time and would need time to make any decision about the future.

During the initial session, Chris also talked about how much he mistrusted his wife now, and during the next few sessions he developed and clarified another goal: to figure out whether he could trust his wife again and what the signs of his increasing trustfulness would be. He said the first signs that his trust level could increase would be that she would be willing to talk about what the affair meant to him, to tell him the truth about what happened when he asked, and to show some remorse. These, of course, are all actions on her part—behaviors over which he had no control. Using perspective-shifting and role-reversal questions, Tobey talked with him about what kinds of actions on his part might help to promote these desired behaviors on his wife's part. Chris clarified that certain of his actions had the effect of making his wife withdraw. These included cutting comments about her behavior and choices in life, angry lectures about how much and how badly she had hurt him, and giving her the cold shoulder, waiting to see if she would seek contact. During this conversation, he began to talk about the fact that he knew he had often been very critical of her—sometimes even quite nasty—in the past. In the process of answering role-reversal questions he decided that if he told her as clearly and calmly as he could how important it was to him to find out if they had a chance to make a go of it together, she might be willing to listen. If he said that he didn't want to be nasty, though he was very angry and hurt, and that what he really wanted was to see if they could talk about this and deal with it together, as partners, he would have a better chance of keeping her in the conversation and perhaps getting some of the responses he wanted.

Together, Chris and Tobey developed a list of signs on Joan's part that would show Chris she was already trying to rebuild the relationship, that she loved him, and that she honestly wanted to be with him, and to his surprise, these included a number of things Joan was already doing: coming home earlier from work to be with him, being more receptive to his point of view in conversations about their son's upbringing, and snuggling up to him in bed in ways that let him know she was open to sexual overtures. He also said that one sign that she honestly wanted to be with him is that she would call him from the office. As the weeks passed, he reported noticing that she was doing all these things more often. At home, when he tried initiating conversations in the noncombative way he had figured out during perspective-shifting inquiries, he was pleasantly surprised to find Joan didn't run away or withdraw. He reported that, over the course of several conversations, when he said how important it was to him to know whether or not she was sorry, she told him she deeply regretted hurting him, felt terrible about the consequences of the affair, and could understand how angry and hurt he was. These conversations were lengthy and intense, he reported; during them he was able to ask some questions that were very important to him, and get some answers. Joan said she had never wanted to leave; if she had, she would have done so. Chris said that his experience of their interaction during these conversation led him to begin feeling better—Joan answered his questions honestly and fully, and though sometimes this was very painful, the conversations brought them closer. In one of these conversations, Joan said she wanted them to be better friends, and he reported in therapy that this was a goal they both shared. Though he felt it would be quite a while before he was able to trust her fully again, he was beginning to see regular signs that his wife was committed to making a go of their relationship and that she wanted to be with him.

During the conversations Tobey and Chris had about trust, he developed a third goal concerning his own behavior. Having clarified that his criticality, sarcasm, and sharp comments had contributed to the difficulties in his relationship, he decided to work on ways of being warmer and more receptive to her points of view. He identified that one sign of this would be that he would not take every opportunity to refer to the affair, to his mistrust and suspicion, and to her negative qualities, but instead he would frequently let her know that he loved her and appreciated how much she was now involved in trying to make things better in their relationship. He said he needed to be honest with her when he was feeling hurt, angry, or mistrustful, but that he was learning how to do that without being cutting. Another sign of the changes he wanted to make in his own behavior, he decided, would be if he did not comment negatively on her way of doing things—the way she cleaned up after meals, how she left her clothes lying on a bedroom chair at night, whether she told him what she was thinking without his asking, etc.—but instead talked about the things she did that pleased him.

As Chris worked on these ways of moving toward his evolving goals, he reported that his relationship improved more quickly than he could ever have expected. To his surprise and pleasure, Joan and he were having good times together almost daily, and Joan seemed more eager to spend time with him than she had in years. Their sex life was actually better, he reported, than it had ever been, and he thought this was because of the new honesty and friendliness between them. She was also responding to his questions about the affair, and she did not withdraw when he wanted to talk with her about his bad days, when he felt jealous, angry, and low. Tobey used scaling questions regularly to track Chris's progress, confidence, and hope during the course of therapy, and these conversations helped Chris, who was moving up steadily in the numbers, to see that things were improving.

Chris did go through a number of emotional ups and downs. He revisited low points and feelings of self-doubt from time to time. One important juncture came some months into his work with Tobey when Joan told him she was tired of hearing about the affair from him—she felt it was time to move on. Chris reported that this made him angry, and he began to think again about how much she had hurt him—now it seemed like she was "getting away too easy." He and Tobey talked about what kind of difference it would make to him for her to understand that he needed to move more slowly on getting over this than she did, and he articulated the meta-goal of feeling that their differences, instead of driving them apart, could bring them together. On this basis, he found a way (again through perspective-shifting questions) to talk to her about their differing needs about talking about the affair, and they were able to negotiate, on their own, a balance between his needs to talk about his feelings about it and their shared need to move on and enjoy an "ordinary" and relaxed relationship. These accumulating experiences of their partnership in addressing problems helped to strengthen Chris's trust in the durability of the relationship and in the wisdom of his decision to stay and make a go of it. Though he continued to feel it would take some time to build up his trust for his wife to where he wanted it to be, he felt increasingly sure he had made the right choice. He told Tobey that when he first came to therapy he never would have believed it possible that he would feel so close to Joan again, closer, in fact, than he had ever felt before. Chris met weekly with Tobey for about eight months. When he left therapy, he felt his work to increase his trust and maintain his partnership would be ongoing and sometimes challenging, and said he felt he might need to come back at some future point if he hit a rough spot, but at the time he felt ready to leave, the *good story* narrative he and Joan shared was reviving, and now it included their mutual, challenging, and successful work to move beyond this very painful interlude.

## Couples Therapy With A Reluctant Solo Partner

The reluctant solo partner is a client who comes to therapy under some duress. He or she may have been mandated by the court or by some social service agency. In private practice, a reluctant solo partner usually comes because the other one has threatened to leave the relationship or take other unwelcome action unless this person gets therapy. Naturally, when someone has not freely decided to come to therapy, he or she rarely arrives in a positive frame of mind. When we ask how we can help, a reluctant solo partner usually begins by inviting us into visitor/host conversation (telling us there is no real problem or, if there is one, therapy is not needed) or else into complainant/sympathizer conversation (telling us that the only problem is the other partner's unreasonable insistence that he or she come to therapy).

As with any reluctant client, we begin by accepting the invitation to engage in visitor/host or complainant/sympathizer conversations. At this point, we do not assume the reluctant solo partner wants our help or that we will enter into a customer/consultant therapy relationship. We acknowledge the person's feelings about having been pressured into coming to see us and we honor the person's current belief that there is no good reason to be in therapy. This lays the groundwork for potential customer/consultant conversations. It is our job, at this point, to find out if there are any changes this person wants that could be the basis of a collaboration. The standard way we invite people to move into customer/consultant conversation is by asking, *How do you think I might be able to help you?* or *What do you think we could do together that might make some positive change in your life?* Because RPT is a collaborative approach, if reluctant clients still feel, after talking with us, that they do not want our help, we honor their decision, thank them for coming, and let them know that if things change down the road, we'll be happy to talk with them again.

However, before agreeing with a client that there is no point in continuing, we commonly ask a question (drawn from solution-focused brief therapy) that often leads the reluctant solo partner to discover a goal (Berg, 1994, pp. 64–66). Asking the reluctant client *Are you interested in getting your wife (your husband, your partner, whoever has insisted they come) off your back so she'll say you don't need to come any more?* usually provokes a positive and interested response. If the client answers this question in the affirmative, we have a starting point from which to engage in customer/consultant conversations. We think that the reluctant solo partner's desire to have the other partner abandon the demand that he or she undergo therapy is a perfectly legitimate goal. A husband's desire, for example, to "get my wife to quit bugging me constantly about how I dress and who I hang out with" or a wife's desire to get her husband to "quit telling me all the time how the way I deal with my family is screwed up" can be a fine place to begin co-constructing a set of desired future changes and a plan for making those desired changes happen. If this occurs, the reluctant solo partner becomes a motivated solo partner (Ziegler, 1998).

If the reluctant solo partner says he or she is interested in figuring out how to get out of therapy as soon as possible, we have identified another source of motivation. The next step is to find out what changes he or she might have to make to achieve that goal. It doesn't matter that the topic of conversation at the moment is how unfair and unreasonable the partner's demands are or how unnecessary therapy is. If we keep listening for what this person wants, helping him or her envision preferred future pictures (possibly with respect to the *good story* narrative the partners have lost sight of), we can help this solo partner rebuild that preferred narrative, bypassing the question of blame and responsibility.

One line of inquiry is to explore how it would make a difference if the reluctant client's partner followed through on his or her threat to leave. In such conversations, we avoid taking a position on the reasonableness of the threats or trying to get the client to examine the behaviors that have produced them (in other words, we maintain active neutrality even though only one partner is present). We simply explore what consequences the client believes will occur if the threats are carried out and ask about how the client feels about these possible outcomes. Then we can talk about what steps he or she might have to take to ward off such consequences. Using perspective-shifting questions, we listen closely for what small changes our client could make that might make a difference to the absent partner.

The following case illustrates how Phil moved back and forth from acknowledging and validating a reluctant solo partner's experiences while simultaneously helping him clarify the specific changes he might make to save his marriage. Notice how Phil uses scaling and perception-shifting questions as he continues to negotiate with Andy how to make therapy useful.

ANDY: My wife threw me out. I'm sleeping on my office floor, for Christ's sake. It's really a drag. She says if I don't do something about my temper, stop being so rude and nasty to her, there's no hope for us. According to her, I'm sitting on a ton of anger, and I'm all screwed up. But the problem's really that she's so hypersensitive. You can't say a thing to her without her taking it the wrong way.

PHIL: Hmm, sounds pretty rough. It seems like your wife has taken some pretty serious action, and things are at a bad place, painful, between you. And you're saying it feels like she takes things too much to heart, and now you've actually ended up on the verge of divorce, and she's insisting you come here, even though you don't see the need. Tell me, since it seems like you're here because your wife wants you to come, how can I help?

ANDY: I don't really know. But the truth is, I don't want our marriage to break up. I don't see how therapy can help much though.

PHIL: So if I hear you right, you're here because you don't want your wife to end the marriage. You'd rather be somewhere else.

ANDY: (*Smiles.*) Believe me.

PHIL: But neither of us can be really sure yet if there's anything we can do here that might make a difference for you and your marriage. Maybe I could ask you a question that might help us figure out whether or not we can do something together that might help?

ANDY: Okay.

PHIL: Well, okay. If I were to ask you, Andy, given the way things are right now with you and your wife, to tell me on a scale of 1 to 10, where 1 is no hope at all that your marriage will work out and 10 is all the hope you can imagine having, where would you put yourself?

ANDY: (*Looking sad*) Hmm. Shit. Excuse my French. Actually, I'd have to say it's pretty low. Probably all the way down at 1. I think she's pretty serious, that's why she made me move out. And she's not letting me come back.

PHIL: Okay. So I see, things are pretty serious. But it sounds like you're really wanting to save the relationship, is that right?

ANDY: Yes.

PHIL: Okay. Then tell me this, what do you think might move you up on that hope scale one notch, say to 2?

ANDY: (*Quickly*) That she'd let me come home.

PHIL: Wow, that would only move you up to 2? Sounds to me like that would be a pretty big sign.

ANDY: Well, yeah. I guess maybe if she said she was willing *to think* about having me come back. That would feel like something anyway. That would get me to 2.

PHIL: Hmm. Then let's see. If I were to ask her—your wife, I mean—this question, what do you think she'd say? If I asked her what first signs would tell her that you're doing things differently so she might start considering letting you come home, what would she say?

ANDY: Well, I don't think she wants me back, see.

PHIL: But are there any first signs of things you might do that would get her to start thinking about changing her mind, down the line?

ANDY: Well, maybe she'd say, if I started to listen to her more. If I respected her point of view.

Phil and Andy are now well into customer/consultant conversation. (This shift took place very rapidly, in the first 5 minutes of the initial session with a client who could be viewed as extremely resistant.) From here, Phil used further role-reversal questions to detail and amplify specific behaviors the client's wife would experience as respecting her point of view. He left it to Andy to decide whether or not he was interested in making these changes. Because he was, Phil and he went on to flesh out a *good story* narrative that both Andy and his wife might share.

Not all reluctant solo partners decide they are willing to make the changes this kind of inquiry clarifies. In these cases the work ends with the client's decision not to make the changes, and he or she leaves. Most of the time, however, we can successfully invite such clients, before the end of the initial session, to step into the other person's shoes, giving them the opportunity to develop preferred future pictures. By asking reluctant clients to imagine what their partner might say if he or she were present, we make it possible for them to use intuition and empathy to figure out exactly what changes they might make that would be meaningful and motivating to the absent partner. We also sometimes use the miracle question, emphasizing how others, principally the client's spouse, will know the miracle has happened. Asking the client to imagine how the absent partner will act differently in response to the signs of the miracle prompts the client to be on the lookout for the partner's *good story* actions. All these procedures have a narrative function, shifting the reluctant partner into an imagined, possible scenario that engenders hope and promotes agency and a partnership perspective.

# Couples Therapy (and "Uncoupling" Therapy) With the Abandoned Solo Partner

The fourth type of situation in which we conduct couples therapy with a solo partner is when one partner wants help to get a partner who has left to return to the relationship. Sometimes a client comes in after a partner has already left the relationship. Sometimes during couples therapy itself one partner decides to leave the relationship (and therapy), and at that point the abandoned partner asks if we will continue seeing him or her. In both these cases the abandoned partner's principal goal is getting the other partner back—a goal that fails to meet the criterion of being within the client's control. As in all such cases, we want to clarify how realistic this goal is. If the client acknowledges that the partner's return is unlikely, we can shift to exploring meta-goals, which may in turn reveal meaningful, desirable outcomes within his or her control. Where it becomes clear the other partner is not going to return to the relationship, goals can be developed that will help the abandoned partner cope with the loss and begin to take the first concrete steps that will tell the client and others (including and especially the abandoning partner) that he or she is beginning to move on in life. On the other hand, when the client is optimistic about winning the other partner back, we can explore what changes he or she could make that might promote the other partner's return, using perspective-shifting and role-reversal questions.

The following case is an example of an abandoned solo partner whose partner left him before he initiated therapy. Paul came into therapy saying that Liz, his fiancée, had suddenly broken off their engagement, explaining that while she loved him she could not marry him because "they weren't really soul mates." Paul was devastated. He went to see one therapist hoping to get help in figuring out how he might persuade Liz to change her mind. The therapist advised Paul to give her time—not to push her, suggesting that his only hope was to give her space to think about things. So Paul left Liz alone. He even took a three-week trip to Europe. But on his return, Liz told him that she was sure about her decision to break up. Paul grew more and more despondent; he withdrew from friends and family and was having trouble sleeping and carrying out his job responsibilities. At this point, and now somewhat reluctantly, he accepted a referral to Phil from one of Phil's former clients.

At the beginning of the initial session, Paul told Phil his story. Phil listened with interest and expressed sympathy and understanding. He normalized and validated Paul's responses. He expressed amazement that, given what had happened, Paul was doing as well as he was. Paul said he felt comforted by how Phil was responding and relieved to know that he wasn't going crazy.

At a certain point, Phil invited Paul into a potential customer/consultant conversation by asking what he might want from therapy other than reassurance that his reactions were pretty normal. Paul said he was still hoping someone could help him figure out how to win his fiancée back. Phil explained that in his experience people often kept hope alive, even if there was no basis for hope, where it might be too painful to accept the reality of a situation. He went on to say that this was in many ways a normal and healthy reaction, a way to slow down facing a difficult truth. Then Phil said he wanted to explore how realistic Paul's hope was, so that they could decide together what would be the next, best step in therapy. Phil used a variation of a scaling question. He asked Paul what percentage of his hope was protective and what percentage was a foundation for trying to win her back. Paul thought a moment and said he had not been willing to face this before, but he knew 100% that there was no reason to hope—that the relationship was over.

Paul began crying. Phil sat quietly, remaining present in the face of Paul's pain and sorrow. When Paul stopped crying, he looked up at Phil. He looked relieved. He said, "I guess I need help getting on with my life. That's what I need you to help me do, really." Now Phil and Paul were in goal-building territory. Phil asked Paul to tell him what would be the first signs—the first small things he would notice himself doing—that would tell him that "he was beginning to get on with his life." To his surprise, as he began naming indications of change and progress, Paul realized he was already doing some of these things—that he was already moving on, even though he was still in a lot of pain and was not yet completely ready to say good-bye to Liz and his dreams for a life with her.

Toward the end of the hour, Phil asked Paul to scale his progress with respect to getting on with his life, giving a 1 to where he was on the day Liz announced that the engagement was off, and a 10 to the time when this relationship was a thing of the past. Paul said, "When I first walked in today, I was probably about a 1½, but now I'd say I was at 5½, maybe even 6." He seemed both surprised and delighted. So then Phil followed up by asking what number Paul would need to reach in order to say he was confidently on his way to getting on with his life. With a broad smile, Paul quickly responded, "8," and added, "Wow, I'm not even that far!"

Phil continued this progress-scaling conversation by asking what Paul would notice different about himself that would tell him he had moved up to a solid 6 or maybe a 6½?" Paul thought for a moment this time. Then he answered, "When I wake up one morning and go out for a run instead of lying in bed feeling like crap." The hour was coming to and end and Phil wanted to end by complimenting Paul and offering him an observational task assignment. So he asked Paul to notice when he woke up feeling more like running than "lying in bed feeling like crap" and to pay attention to what he did when he was feeling more this way. (Notice Phil did not suggest that Paul push himself to go out for a run—this would have set up a possible failure. Instead he asked Paul only to observe his feelings and impulses.)

Paul came in the following week reporting that it seemed like a miracle—he had gone running almost every morning since the last session. He also reported going to a party on the weekend and having a great time, even though he was on his own. By the end of the session he scaled himself "a solid 7, even an 8." He expressed confidence that he was on his way, and so no further sessions were scheduled.

In bringing this discussion to a close we want to underscore a point we have made throughout this book—the pragmatics of couples therapy teach us that many traditional theories about its practice can shortchange the client and hamstring the clinician. With respect to working with the solo partner, it is our intention to convince readers to test out the ideas and practices presented here in the laboratory of their own clinical practices. This chapter also brings to an end our discussion of the various theoretical and technical aspects of Recreating Partnership Therapy. Here, as throughout the book, we highlight the fact that RPT is, above all else, a pragmatic, collaborative enterprise every step of the way, that all aspects of the therapy—its goals and its processes—call upon the expertise, creativity, and humanity of all participants. On the therapist's part what is required is the willingness to be open-minded and flexible—to learn continually from and be guided by our clients, whom we assume know as well or better than we do what will make a difference in their lives and what changes will set them on a course to a better relationship. Perhaps most crucial for clinicians working with challenging cases hour after hour, day after day, is the necessity of maintaining a sense of optimism about what is possible, that hidden in what we are seeing and hearing at the moment are the ways people are trying to improve their lives and relationships. The *good story* is always hovering there, waiting to emerge. Listening for and being ready to call out this narrative helps us maintain our openness and sense of possibility so we can best help clients tap resources and strengths they already possess.

# CHAPTER 12

# Coda

We are often asked certain questions by workshop participants who are just being introduced to solution-oriented, collaborative forms of therapy. Is RPT "appropriate" in one situation or another? Will it work with this or that kind of problem or when one partner has this personal characteristic or that diagnosis—say, when the husband is passive-aggressive or the wife suffers from chronic clinical depression? Can this optimistic form of couples therapy be effective with domestic violence and addictions? First, it is always important to say that couples therapy is hard and sometimes humbling work. No approach is foolproof, no therapist helps everyone, and, whatever the reason, not all couples succeed in making positive changes. But when we are asked questions like those above, questions focused on how our approach deals with problems formulated in these ways, we explain that we do not make independent, advanced assessments regarding whether RPT can be helpful with a given couple. Because our work is solution-oriented, competency-based, and collaborative, our focus in every case is to find ways of helping couples make changes specifically meaningful to them.

Another question we are frequently asked is whether RPT is effective with couples who come to us without specific complaints, problems, or conflicts. If we are solution-oriented, how can we develop solutions when the couple does not have a specific problem they need help in solving? For instance, is our approach helpful for couples who come in reporting that they no longer feel very close or affectionate—saying, for instance, that they have "just fallen out of love"—but have no specific problem or conflict?

Here again our solution-oriented approach does not require that specific problems or complaints be identified. We are interested in where people want to go, not in defining where they have been or where they are. We want to help people clarify the experiential details of what will be different when things are better, when they can say their relationship is more intimate, exciting, love-filled, joyful, or whatever other terms they use to describe what they hope to gain by coming to therapy.

A third commonly asked question—one we hope to answer by presenting the following case example—is whether our approach can be helpful for people who are dealing with specific painful and disorienting life events or overwhelming circumstances. How can a future-focused, optimistic approach like RPT make a difference when a couple, rather than presenting a relationship problem, seeks our help in trying to cope with a recent tragedy and its aftermath? Situations where people are trying to deal with the anguish of a dislocating and frightening series of events and struggling to hold their lives together naturally involve a good deal of intense emotion and some patient working through on the part of both partners as well as the therapist (Butler & Powers, 1996). Therapists working in any modality are challenged to do their best work and bring forward the best in themselves in such cases. The techniques and practices of RPT support the therapist in doing this.

By presenting the following case in some detail, we hope to help our readers stand firm in their efforts to remain solution-oriented and competency-based in all cases and resist the natural tendency to fall back on old familiar, problem-focused, theory-driven interventions when couples present difficult and painful life challenges. This case demonstrates many of the ideas and practices we have outlined throughout this book; in it we discuss an instance of our approach with a couple enduring what most of us would consider among the most painful losses of all—the death of a child. This couple experienced the loss of their newborn infant in childbirth, along with the terrifying near-death of the mother during the delivery.

We present this case for several reasons. The first and primary one is to demonstrate the emotional depth and transformative power possible in RPT. And we think it offers a particularly moving and convincing argument for what we have been saying throughout this book: that therapy can be more effective and efficient when the therapist works within the partners' models and theories of change, participates collaboratively with the couple in articulating therapeutically well-formed goals that will orient everyone participating in the therapeutic enterprise, and gently but persistently orients therapeutic conversations toward solutions and client strengths, resources, and competencies. When therapists and clients look together in the right places, they can tap the powerful and generative strengths people can muster in moving through their lives together. The *good story* narrative is not a story of untroubled life. When tragic and challenging events enter a couple's life, the *good story/bad story* dichotomy has to do with whether and how the couple, with the help of the therapist, can find and hold a sustaining partnership to meet these experiences.

Finally, we present this case to demonstrate that the therapeutic enterprise can be flexible, shifting from dyadic to individual sessions; it can stop and restart, with time for breaks between therapeutic work. Rather than indicating that something has gone wrong or that the initial therapeutic work was not adequate, clients' desire to return to therapy simply means new opportunities for change have arisen and the clients want additional help to get unstuck.

Therapy is never a matter of simply employing a set of interviewing techniques in formulaic fashion, and the cases that challenge us are the ones that best reveal the strengths and limitations of any clinical model or method of intervention as well as the personal resources of the clinician and the couple. When the two people sitting in front of you have had their lives torn apart, their dreams dashed, and their hearts broken, you realize that techniques are never enough to make a difference. In such cases, a therapist must be willing and able to be fully present with people who have come for help. We must, above all, be openhearted enough to be moved and touched—to risk sharing in some way in the pain, anger, and confusion of our clients. The techniques and practices of RPT support and enhance our ability to enter into profoundly moving relationships with couples so that we can help to provide a safe space and supportive framework for the partners to find their own way.

Dale was a software developer; his wife, Gloria, ran a small catering business near their home in Silicon Valley. In the third year of their marriage they decided to have a child, and Gloria got pregnant soon thereafter. The pregnancy itself was normal and uneventful. However, as soon as Gloria's labor began, problems developed. The delivery quickly turned into a medical emergency and, after a frightening, exhausting night of medical intervention, their newborn son died at birth. Gloria became dangerously weak from loss of blood and for some time hovered close to death as well.

When Gloria was in recovery, the hospital staff recommended a "grief counselor." The counselor explained "the stages of grief" and emphasized the importance of getting in touch with and sharing their feelings about the loss of their baby. After several sessions with her, Dale refused to go back, saying he felt things were bad enough without having to talk with and listen to some stranger who had no firsthand experience with what he and Gloria were going through. But Gloria felt they needed more help and called their family physician, who referred them to Phil. Reluctantly, Dale agreed to come once, and Gloria called to make a trial appointment.

As they entered Phil's office, Gloria and Dale looked as though their tragedy had taken place only hours before. Both had a look of shock in their eyes; they seemed exhausted and disoriented. There was little doubt that they were each living in some private, lonely hell. Sitting across from them, Phil began wondering whether he could help at all, what he could do or offer that would make any difference. How could talking to anyone, professional or otherwise, help people face such a terrible loss? He assumed they were wondering the same thing. He began in his usual way, asking what they thought the three of them might do together that could be helpful. As he asked the question, he reflected on how strange such a question must sound to this couple. How could anyone do anything that would make a difference, other than bring their baby back? In the moment of silence that followed his question, Phil recalled reading somewhere that a very high percentage of all couples who experience the death of a child break up within two years.

Rather than answer Phil's question, Dale and Gloria began taking turns telling the story of what happened in the hospital—about Gloria's sudden hemorrhaging, how frightening it was when a whole group of doctors and nurses pushing special equipment converged on the delivery room as the situation became critical. Dale talked about what it was like standing next to Gloria, holding her hand, knowing but not telling her their baby was dead, knowing and not telling her that she too might be dying. Gloria began to cry as she said she wanted more than anything to see her baby, Jamie, to hold him close. Suddenly Dale's face began to contort in rage as he spoke about hating everyone who had babies, about hating a cruel God that could let such a thing happen to them. Then he grew silent, his jaw tight and his fists clenched. Gloria sat collapsed on the couch, tears continuing to flow down her cheeks. Whenever she tried to speak, she had to stop to catch her breath. She kept losing her train of thought. All she could do was repeat Jamie's name over and over. When she was able to say more, she said that she was terrified that her baby was lost somewhere and needed her. She blamed herself for Jamie's death and wanted somehow to know his spirit was safe and protected. She explained that Dale was angry all the time and that his angry outbursts frightened her and made her feel even more alone and responsible for Jamie's death. She said Dale's anger reminded her of her father's drunken rages and all she wanted to do was to get away to be with her baby.

Although it was clear Dale was trying to control his boiling rage, he could no longer sit silently. He began shouting about how horrible it was sitting in the hospital waiting room, knowing his baby was dead and thinking his wife might die as well. How horrible life was, how he wanted to beat and smash everything and everyone in the world. Now he was also crying as he described seeing reminders of his loss everywhere—in the faces of little children, in the everyday activities of the mothers and fathers and children he saw walking or shopping, driving past in cars, playing in the park.

Phil sat silently during most of the time the couple spoke, trying to quiet and center himself, sighing sympathetically every now and then. For the time being, there was nothing to do but simply be present with the couple, allowing himself to be touched by their pain and sorrow. This was not the time to invite Dale and Gloria into other conversations, other possible worlds. For the greater part of this first session, Phil did little more than acknowledge and validate Dale's and Gloria's feelings and sit quietly in silent recognition of the loss they were having to bear. Then Gloria repeated something she hinted at earlier—that she felt her baby was lost somewhere and that she needed to die so she could find and comfort him, so he wouldn't experience terrifying loneliness.

Concerned that in her grief and confusion she might indeed harm herself and possibly take her life, Phil wanted to talk with her about this. However, he did not want to ask the typical questions about how realistic her threats were and whether she had a plan. That conversation might occur at some point, but first Phil wanted to invite Gloria into a different conversation. Assuming that taking her life was a means rather than an end, he wanted to explore with her whether there might be other, better means to accomplish her goal of comforting her baby's spirit. He began by asking what Gloria thought would happen after she died. How would she find her baby's spirit and how would she comfort him? What did Jamie need from her? What did she think Jamie needed from her most of all? As Gloria answered Phil's questions, she began articulating the need to keep baby Jamie always in her mind. This, she said, was what Jamie needed. He was watching and waiting to see if his mother forgot about him. She needed to do things Jamie could observe that would tell him she had not forgotten him. Shortly before the end of the hour, Gloria realized that if Jamie saw her keeping his spirit alive, "he could move on in peace." Phil asked her to imagine what specific things Jamie would want to see that would tell him she was keeping his spirit alive so he could move on in peace. Gloria immediately said that Jamie would want her to go to the cemetery at least three times a week. He would tell her when she could go less often, but for now it was three times a week. She added that Jamie wanted her to build a little memorial for him in their bedroom, where she could go every morning and talk with him for a while.

Suddenly, Dale became quite upset again. He said he wanted all traces of the baby removed from his life and house. He did not want any shrines around to remind him of his loss. He could not stand the pain; he wanted to forget, not remember. And if she insisted on going to the cemetery, she would have to go without him. "Jamie's dead. That's all there is to say. I don't want to think about it anymore. I can't stand it. I don't want to wake up and see reminders of him." Dale's body was shaking. There was no time to talk through Dale's feelings or to try and build a bridge between what Gloria needed and what Dale needed, for now. Phil simply said, "I can't imagine anything worse than what you two are going through." At that, Dale broke down again and began to cry, his body still shaking. Gloria took him in her arms.

Sitting again in silence, watching Gloria hold and comfort Dale, Phil thought about the birth of his own son: how, at one point during labor a medical team rushed in concerned about fetal stress and told Phil he would have to wait outside the labor room. Phil, standing in the hall, watched nurses push a fetal heart monitor into the room. He remembered standing alone, leaning against a wall, wondering if his baby was okay, if it would be healthy, if it would be born alive. What would he do—what would they do—if they lost the baby? He remembered the flashes of panic, the unthinkable thought that kept pressing into his consciousness, a terrifying possibility that had become reality for Dale and Gloria.

The session had to come to an end. Phil again expressed his sorrow over the loss of baby Jamie. He admitted that for the time being he had no answers, but that Gloria seemed to have developed a plan for helping and comforting Jamie. He asked if, before they met again, Dale and Gloria could begin working out a plan that would shield Dale from evidence of the loss for the time being but would allow Gloria to show baby Jamie that "she was keeping his spirit alive." Both Dale and Gloria thanked Phil and said they wanted to come back. They said they appreciated that Phil didn't offer pat formulas or false comfort, and they agreed to try and come up with a plan.

When they returned the following week, Dale seemed noticeably more relaxed. Both appeared to have gotten some rest. Gloria had gone to the cemetery three times, as planned, and had chosen to build a little shrine for Jamie in their guest bedroom, where she went each morning before Dale woke up. There she talked to Jamie, telling him how much she loved him and that some day they would be together. Dale reported that he felt calmer and more able to deal with his own feelings now that Gloria seemed to be doing better. He went on to say he had been concerned about her statements about wanting to be with Jamie, and he was relieved to see she was finding ways to comfort Jamie's spirit and herself. Both Gloria and Dale acknowledged that it was going to take a long time to get back to normal life.

Gloria and Dale continued meeting with Phil weekly for about seven months. During that time they found creative ways to move forward individually and as a couple. Dale found it helpful to throw himself back into his work. In the sessions, he also talked about his feelings of grief and anger in a time and rhythm quite different from Gloria's, and eventually those feelings became less intense. Gloria continued her dialogues with Jamie at home and used the sessions to explore and express the depth of her loss. They both explained to Phil that by using the therapy hours in this way, Gloria could do what she needed to do and Dale could comfort her and experience his own feelings in his own time. At home they were beginning to be able to tend to other aspects of their lives. They were finding ways to honor their loss while moving forward. Eventually, Dale began going to the cemetery with Gloria, but not every time. Gloria continued her private conversations with baby Jamie, but they were more occasional and she was sure Jamie's spirit was at peace. Dale and Gloria occasionally mentioned a desire to try having another child, but agreed they needed more time.

During a session in the seventh month, when Phil asked them to scale progress, both said they were at about a 9 and were feeling ready to cut back the frequency of the sessions. Gloria, Dale, and Phil met about four more times, spread out over the next four months. Near the anniversary of their first meeting, Dale and Gloria announced that they felt ready to end therapy, and they and Phil shared a warm and tearful good-bye.

About three months later, Gloria called Phil to say she wanted to come in for a few sessions on her own to work on her "self-confidence issues." When she came in she said there were times when she was very insecure and worried unreasonably that Dale would leave her or take up with another woman. She explained these were feelings that had troubled her in other relationships and also in the early part of her relationship with Dale; now that she knew Phil could be helpful, she wanted to tackle this issue. She knew her fears about Dale were ungrounded but they still haunted her, driving her to seek constant reassurance from him. Her anxieties also were causing her to do things that drove a wedge between them. She wanted to feel more trusting of Dale and more confident in herself and in his love for her.

Phil saw Gloria this time for a total of four sessions. In the first session, he helped her develop and clarify a set of well-formed goals in the form of video pictures of how she would be acting differently when she was "more confident in herself and trusting of Dale and his love." Among the signs of difference would be that she would give Dale a kiss good-bye when he went out in the evenings and tell him to have a good time. She also described seeing herself smiling, looking relaxed and absorbed, as she worked on a sewing project on the evenings she was alone. In another preferred future picture she saw herself calling some of her friends, making dates to do things together, and actually going out in the evenings with them.

Phil and Gloria began talking about the steps that might bring some of these desired changes about. During this conversation, Gloria said—somewhat shyly at first—that she believed she had a kind of guardian angel to whom she sometimes turned. In fact, her guardian angel sometimes brought her messages from Jamie and told her that Jamie was happy. Gloria said that there was also a sort of "mean person" inside her head that made her feel bad about herself and caused her to become insecure and doubt Dale's love. This "mean person" would make up stories about Dale's meeting some beautiful, sexy woman and running off with her. Gloria would then become very frightened. She would try to keep her fears to herself, but when she withdrew from Dale he would question her, and eventually she would admit her fears. He would then reassure her that he would always be faithful to her, that he loved her very much. But he also told her how much it bothered him that she was so insecure and untrusting.

Phil asked Gloria if there were times her guardian angel came to her defense and reminded her how much Dale loved her. She said there were, but it was hard for her to stay in touch with her guardian angel and the angel's message when she was under the influence of the "mean person." Phil asked her if she thought it would make a difference if she were able to draw strength from her guardian angel even when the "mean person" was doing its worst—if there were ways she could keep the "mean person" from keeping her apart from her guardian angel so she and her angel could work together to keep the "mean person" from making trouble between her and Dale. Gloria thought for a while and suddenly lit up with the most wonderful smile. She said she knew exactly what to do, but didn't want to share it with Phil. She wanted to keep it a secret because if she said it out loud it might not work as well. Phil said he trusted that Gloria knew best, and there was no reason for her to tell him her plan. By the end of the session, Gloria said she wanted to try out her idea and come back once or twice more to make sure it was working.

Gloria returned the following week. She was very excited to report that, while there were times the "mean person" really got to her, she and her guardian angel were working well together. Her guardian angel had even told her that she noticed that Gloria was getting much stronger. Gloria wanted to make sure, as she did get stronger and more self-confident, that her guardian angel would not leave her. She reported that the angel reassured her that she would always be there, even as Gloria became more and more confident. Gloria said at this point she felt ready to stop therapy, but she wanted two more sessions just to be sure. She did come two more times, and in the last session she said there was something she wanted to share with Phil before leaving: She and Dale were trying to get pregnant again. She wanted to know if the family could all come in together after the baby was born, even if she and Dale didn't have any problems. Phil said he would love that.

About a year later, Gloria called to make an appointment. When Phil came out to the waiting room, he was greeted by Gloria, Dale, and a gorgeous little three-week old baby boy who was introduced to Phil as Tyler. They spent an hour together in joyful reunion with Phil holding, feeding, and playing with Tyler while Gloria and Dale filled him in on all the exciting events of the year. After the family left, Phil asked himself, as he often does, how he could be lucky enough to get paid for this kind of work.

# References

Anderson, H. (1997). *Conversation, language and possibilities: A postmodern approach to therapy*. New York: Basic.

Anderson, H., & Goolishian, H. (1992). The client is the expert: A not-knowing approach to therapy. In S. McNamee & K. Gergen (Eds.), *Therapy as social construction* (pp. 25–39). Newbury Park, CA: Sage.

Bader, E., & Pearson, P. (1988). *In quest of the mythical mate: A developmental approach to diagnosis and treatment in couples therapy*. New York: Brunner/Mazel.

Berg, I. K. (1994). *Family-based services: A solution-focused approach*. New York: W. W. Norton.

Berg, I. K. (1995). Solution-focused brief therapy with substance abusers. In A. Washton (Ed.), *Psychotherapy and substance abuse: A practitioner's handbook* (pp. 223–242). New York: Guilford.

Berg, I. K., & de Shazer, S. (1993). Making numbers talk: Language in therapy. In S. Friedman (Ed.), *The new language of change* (pp. 5–24). New York: Guilford.

Berg, I. K., & Kelly, S. (2000). *Building solutions in child protective services*. New York: W. W. Norton.

Berg, I. K., & Miller, S. (1992). *Working with the problem drinker: A solution-focused approach*. New York: W. W. Norton.

Blumstein, P., & Schwartz, P. (1983). *American couples*. New York: William Morrow.

Boscolo, L., Cecchin, G., Hoffman, L., & Penn, P. (1987). *Milan systemic family therapy: Conversations in theory and practice*. New York: Basic.

Bray, J. H., & Jouriles, E. N. (1995). Treatment of marital conflict and prevention of divorce. *Journal of Marital and Family Therapy, 21*(4), 461–473.

Budman, S. H., & Gurman, A. S. (1988). *Theory and practice of brief therapy*. New York: Guilford.

Butler, W. R., & Powers K. V. (1996). Solution-focused grief therapy. In S. D. Miller, M. A. Hubble, & B. L. Duncan (Eds.), *Handbook of brief solution-focused therapy* (pp. 228–247). San Francisco: Jossey-Bass.

Cade, B., & O'Hanlon, B. (1993). *A brief guide to brief therapy.* New York: W. W. Norton.

De Jong, P., & Berg, I. K. (1998). *Interviewing for solutions.* Monterey, CA: Brooks-Cole.

De Jong, P., & Miller, S. D. (1995). How to interview for client strengths. *Social Work, 40*(6), 729–735.

Deluca, P. (1996). *The solo partner: Repairing your relationship on your own.* Point Roberts, WA: Hartley & Marks.

de Shazer, S. (1984). The death of resistance. *Family Process, 23*(1), 79–93.

de Shazer, S. (1985). *Keys to solution in brief therapy.* New York: W. W. Norton.

de Shazer, S. (1988). *Clues: Investigating solutions in brief therapy.* New York: W. W. Norton.

de Shazer, S. (1990). What is it about brief therapy that works? In J. K. Zeig & S. Gilligan (Eds.), *Brief therapy: Myths, methods and metaphors* (pp. 90–99). New York: Brunner/Mazel.

de Shazer, S. (1991). *Putting difference to work.* New York: W. W. Norton.

de Shazer, S. (1993). Commentary: de Shazer & White: Vive la différence. In S. Gilligan & R. Price (Eds.), *Therapeutic conversations* (pp. 112–120). New York: W. W. Norton.

de Shazer, S. (1994). *Words were originally magic.* New York: W. W. Norton.

de Shazer, S., & Berg, I. K. (1985). A part is not apart: Working with only one of the partners present. In A. S. Gurman (Ed.), *Casebook of marital therapy* (pp. 97–110). New York: Guilford.

de Shazer, S. Berg, I. K., Lipchik, E., Nunnally, E., Molnar, A., Gingerich, W., & Weiner-Davis, M. (1986). Brief therapy: Focused solution development. *Family Process, 25*(3), 207–221.

DiClemente, C. C. (1991). Motivational interviewing and the stages of change. In W. R. Miller & S. Rollnick (Eds.), *Motivational interviewing: Preparing people to change addictive behaviors* (pp. 191–202). New York: Guilford.

Duncan, B., Hubble, M. A., & Miller, S. D. (1997). *Psychotherapy with impossible cases: The efficient treatment of therapy veterans.* New York: W. W. Norton.

Duncan, B. L., & Miller, S. D. (2000). *The heroic client: Doing client-directed, outcome informed therapy.* San Francisco: Jossey-Bass.

Duncan, B. L., & Rock, J. W. (1991). *Overcoming relationship impasses: Ways to initiate change when your partner won't help.* New York: Plenum.

Duncan, B., Solovey, A., & Rusk, G. (1992). *Changing the rules: A client-directed approach to therapy.* New York: Guilford.

Durrant, M. (1993). *Residential treatment: A cooperative, competency-based approach.* New York: W. W. Norton.

Epston, D. (1993). Internalizing other questions with couples: The New Zealand version. In S. Gilligan & R. Price (Eds.), *Therapeutic conversations* (pp. 183–196). New York: W. W. Norton.

Eron, J. B., & Lund, T. W. (1996). *Narrative solutions in brief therapy.* New York: Guilford.

Eron, J. B., & Lund, T. W. (1999). Narrative solutions in brief couple therapy. In J. M. Donovan (Ed.), *Short-term couple therapy* (pp. 291–324). New York: Guilford.

Fisch, R., Weakland, J., & Segal, L. (1982). *Tactics of change: Doing therapy briefly*. San Francisco: Jossey-Bass.

Follette, V. M., & Jacobson, N. S. (1990). Treating communications problems from a behavioral perspective. In R. Chasin, H. Grunebaum, & M. Herzig (Eds.), *One couple, four realities: Multiple perspectives on couples therapy* (pp. 229–245). New York: Guilford.

Freedman, J., & Combs, G. (1996). *Narrative therapy: The social construction of preferred realities*. New York: W. W. Norton.

Friedman, S. (1996). Couples therapy: Changing conversations. In H. Rosen & K. T. Kuehlwein (Eds.), *Constructing realities: Meaning making perspectives for psychotherapists* (pp. 413–453). San Francisco: Jossey-Bass.

Friedman, S., & Lipchick, E. (1999). A time-effective, solution-focused approach to couple therapy. In J. M. Donovan (Ed.), *Short-term couple therapy* (pp. 325–359). New York: Guilford.

Furman, B., & Ahola, T. (1992). *Solution talk: Hosting therapeutic conversations*. New York: W. W. Norton.

Gergen, K. (1991). *The saturated self: Dilemmas of identity in contemporary life*. New York: Basic.

Gergen, K. (1994). *Realities and relationships: Soundings in social construction*. Cambridge, MA: Harvard University Press.

Gergen, K., & Gergen, M. (1991). Toward reflexive methodologies. In F. Steir (Ed.), *Research and reflexivity* (pp. 76–95). Newbury Park, CA: Sage.

Gergen, K., & Kaye, J. (1992). Beyond narrative in the negotiation of therapeutic meaning. In S. McNamee & K. Gergen (Eds.), *Therapy as social construction* (pp. 166–185). Newbury Park, CA: Sage.

Gergen, K., & McNamee, S. (Eds.). (1992). *Therapy as social construction*. Newbury Park, CA: Sage.

Gilligan, S., & Price, R. (Eds.). (1993). *Therapeutic conversations*. New York: W. W. Norton.

Gottman, J. (1994). *Why marriages succeed or fail . . . and how you can make yours last*. New York: Fireside.

Gottman, J. M. (1999). *The marriage clinic: A scientifically-based marital therapy*. New York: W. W. Norton.

Greenberg, L. S., & Johnson, S. M. (1998). *Emotionally focused therapy for couples*. New York: Guilford.

Haley, J. (1976). *Problem-solving therapy: New strategies for effective family therapy*. San Francisco: Jossey-Bass.

Heitler, S. (1990). *From conflict to resolution: Skills and strategies for individual, couple and family therapy*. New York: W. W. Norton.

Held, B. S. (1995). *Back to reality: A critique of postmodern theory in psychotherapy*. New York: W. W. Norton.

Hendrix, H. (1988). *Getting the love you want: A guide for couples*. New York: Holt.

Hoffman, L. (1993). *Exchanging voices: A collaborative approach to family therapy.* London: Karnac.

Holtzworth-Monroe, A., Beatty, S. B., & Anglin, K. (1995). The assessment and treatment of marital violence: An introduction for the marital therapist. In N. S. Jacobson & A. S Gurman (Eds.), *Clinical handbook of couple therapy* (pp. 317–339). New York: Guilford.

Hoyt, M. F. (Ed.). (1994). *Constructive therapies* (Vol. 1). New York: Guilford.

Hoyt, M. F. (Ed.). (1996). *Constructive therapies* (Vol. 2). New York: Guilford.

Hoyt, M. F. (Ed.). (1998). *The handbook of constructive therapies: Innovative approaches from leading practitioners.* San Francisco: Jossey-Bass.

Hoyt, M. F. (2000). *Some stories are better than others: Doing what works in brief therapy and managed care.* New York: Brunner/Mazel.

Hoyt, M. F. (In press). Solution-focused couple therapy. In A. S. Gurman (Ed.), *Clinical Handbook of Couple Therapy* (3rd ed.). New York: Guilford.

Hoyt, M. F., & Berg, I. K. (1998). Solution-focused couple therapy: Helping clients construct self-fulfilling realities. In M. Hoyt (Ed.), *The handbook of constructive therapies: Innovative approaches from leading practitioners* (pp. 314–340). San Francisco: Jossey-Bass.

Hudson, P. O., & O'Hanlon, W. H. (1992). *Re-writing love stories: Brief marital therapy.* New York: W. W. Norton.

Jacobson, N. S., & Christensen, A. (1996). *Integrative couple therapy.* New York: W. W. Norton.

Jacobson, N. S., & Gurman, A. (Eds.). (1995). *Clinical handbook of couple therapy.* New York: Guilford.

Jacobson, N. S., & Margolin, G. (1979). *Marital therapy: Strategies based on social learning and behavior exchange principles.* New York: Brunner/Mazel.

Johnson, C. E., & Goldman, J. (1996). Taking safety home: A solution-focused approach to domestic violence. In M. Hoyt (Ed.), *Constructive* therapies (Vol. 2, pp. 184–196). New York: Guilford.

Johnson, L. D. (1995). *Psychotherapy in the age of accountability.* New York: W. W. Norton.

Johnson, S. M. (1996). *The practice of emotionally focused marital therapy: Creating connection.* New York: Brunner/Mazel.

Keim, J. (1999). Brief strategic marital therapy. In J. M. Donovan (Ed.), *Short-term couple therapy* (pp. 265–290). New York: Guilford.

Klar, H., & Berg, I. K. (1999). Solution-focused brief therapy. In D. M. Lawson & F. F. Prevatt (Eds.), *Casebook in family therapy* (pp. 232–258). Belmont: CA: Wadsworth.

Lambert, M. J. (1992). Implications of outcome research for psychotherapy integration. In J. C. Norcross & M. R. Goldfried (Eds.), *Handbook of psychotherapy integration* (pp. 94–129). New York: Basic.

Lambert, M. J., & Bergin, A. E. (1994). The effectiveness of psychotherapy. In A. J. Bergin & S. L. Garfield (Eds.), *Handbook of psychotherapy and behavior change* (4th ed., pp. 143–189). New York: Wiley.

Lipchick, E., & Kubicki, A. D. (1996). Solution-focused domestic violence issues: Bridges toward a new reality in couples therapy. In S. Miller, M. Hubble, & B. Duncan (Eds.), *Handbook of solution-focused brief therapy* (pp. 65–98). San Francisco: Jossey-Bass.

Madanes, C. (1981). *Strategic family therapy*. San Francisco: Jossey-Bass.

Madanes, C. (1990). *Sex, love and violence: Strategies for transformation*. New York: W. W. Norton.

Madanes, C., Keim, J., & Smelser, D. (1995). *The violence of men*. San Francisco: Jossey-Bass.

Markman, H., Stanley, S., & Blumberg, S. (1994). *Fighting for your marriage: Positive steps for preventing divorce and preserving a lasting love*. San Francisco: Jossey-Bass.

McKeel, A. J. (1996). A clinician's guide to research on solution-focused brief therapy. In S. D. Miller, M. A. Hubble, & B. L. Duncan (Eds.), *Handbook of solution-focused brief therapy* (pp. 251–271). San Francisco: Jossey-Bass.

McKeel, A. J. (1999). *A selected review of research of solution-focused brief therapy*. Unpublished manuscript.

Miller, G. (1997). *Becoming miracle workers: Language and meaning in brief therapy*. Hawthorne, NY: Aldine de Gruyter.

Miller, S. D., Duncan, B. L., & Hubble, M. A. (1997). *Escape from Babel: Towards a unifying language of psychotherapy practice*. New York: W. W. Norton.

Miller, W. R., & Rollnick, S. (1991). *Motivational interviewing: Preparing people to change addictive behavior*. New York: Guilford.

Neimeyer, R. A., & Mahoney, M. J. (Eds.). (1995). *Constructivism in psychotherapy*. Washington, DC: American Psychological Association.

Notarius, C., & Markman, H. (1993). *We can work it out: How to solve conflicts, save your marriage, and strengthen your love for each other*. New York: Perigee.

Nyland, D., & Corsiglia, V. (1994). Becoming solution forced in brief therapy: Remembering something important we already knew. *Journal of Systemic Therapies, 13*(1), 5–11.

O'Hanlon, W. H. (1998). Possibility therapy: An inclusive, collaborative, solution-based model of psychotherapy. In M. F. Hoyt (Ed.), *The handbook of constructive therapies* (pp. 137–158). San Francisco: Jossey-Bass.

O'Hanlon, W. H., & Weiner-Davis, M. (1989). *In search of solutions: A new direction in psychotherapy*. New York: W. W. Norton.

Parry, A., & Doan, R. E. (1994). *Story revisions: Narrative therapy in the postmodern world*. New York: W. W. Norton.

Prochaska, J. O., Norcross, J. C., & DiClemente, C. C. (1994). *Changing for good*. New York: Morrow.

Robinson, E. A., & Price, M. G. (1980). Pleasurable behavior in marital interaction: An observational study. *Journal of Consulting and Clinical Psychology, 48*, 117–118.

Rogers, C. R. (1951). *Client-centered therapy: Its current practice, implications and theory*. Boston: Houghton Mifflin.

Rosenblatt, P. C. (1994). *Metaphors of family systems theory: Toward new constructions*. New York: Guilford.

Saleebey, D. (1997). *The Strengths perspective in social work practice* (2nd ed.). White Plains, NY: Longman.

Schwartz, P. (1994). *Love between equals: How peer marriage really works.* New York: Free.

Shoham, V., Rohrbaugh, M., & Patterson, J. (1995). Problem- and solution-focused couple therapies: The MRI and Milwaukee Models. In N. S. Jacobson & A. S. Gurman (Eds.), *Clinical handbook of couple therapy* (pp. 142–163). New York: Guilford.

Sokal, A., & Bricmont, J. (1998). *Fashionable nonsense: Postmodern intellectuals' abuse of science.* New York: Picador.

Solomon, M. (1989). *Narcissism and intimacy: Love and marriage in an age of confusion.* New York: W. W. Norton.

Stuart, R. (1980). *Helping couples change: A social learning approach to marital therapy.* New York: Guilford.

Thomas, F., & Cockburn, J. (1998). *Competency-based counseling: Building on client strengths.* Minneapolis, MN: Fortress.

Tolstoy, L. (1965). *Anna Karenina* (Constance Garnett translation, revised and edited by L. J. Kent & N. Berberova). New York: Random House.

Tomm, K. (1987). Interventive Interviewing: Part II, Reflexive questioning as a means to enable self-healing. *Family Process, 26*(4), 167–183.

Tomm, K. (1988). Interventive interviewing: Part III, Intending to ask lineal, circular, strategic, or reflexive questions? *Family Process, 27*(1), 1–15.

Tomm, K. (1993). The courage to protest: A commentary on Michael White's work. In S. Gilligan & R. Price (Eds.), *Therapeutic conversations* (pp. 62–80). New York: W. W. Norton.

Turnell, A., & Edwards, S. (1999). *Signs of safety: A solution- and safety-oriented approach to child protection case work.* New York: W. W. Norton.

Wall, M., Kleckner, T., Amendt, J., & Bryant, D. (1989). Therapeutic compliments: Setting the stage for successful therapy. *Journal of Marital and Family Therapy, 15,* 159–167.

Walter, J. L., & Peller, J. E. (1988). Going beyond the attempted solution: A couple's meta-solution. *Family Therapy Case Studies, 3*(1), 41–45.

Walter, J. L., & Peller, J. E. (1992). *Becoming solution-focused in brief therapy.* New York: Brunner/Mazel.

Walter, J. L., & Peller, J. E. (1994). "On track" in solution-focused brief therapy. In M. Hoyt (Ed.), *Constructive therapies* (Vol. 1, pp. 111–125). New York: Guilford.

Walter, J. L., & Peller, J. E. (1996). Rethinking our assumptions: Assuming anew in a postmodern world. In S. D. Miller, M. A. Hubble, & B. L. Duncan (Eds.), *Handbook of solution-focused brief therapy* (pp. 9–26). San Francisco: Jossey-Bass.

Walter, J. L., & Peller, J. E. (2000). *Recreating brief therapy: Preferences and possibilities.* New York: W. W. Norton.

Watzlawick, P. (Ed.). (1984). *The invented reality.* New York: W. W. Norton.

Watzlawick, P., Weakland, J., & Fisch, R. (1974). *Change: Principles of problem formation and problem resolution.* New York: W. W. Norton.

Weiner-Davis, M. (1992). *Divorce busting: A revolutionary and rapid program for staying together.* New York: Fireside.

Weiner–Davis, M., de Shazer, S., & Gingerich, W. (1987). Building on pretreatment change to construct the therapeutic solution: An exploratory study. *Journal of Marital and Family Therapy, 13*(4), 359–363.

White, M., & Epston, D. (1990). *Narrative means to therapeutic ends.* New York: W. W. Norton.

Ziegler, P. (1998). Solution-focused therapy for the not-so-brief clinician. *Journal of Collaborative Therapies, 6*(1), 22–25.

Zimmerman, J. L., & Dickerson, V. C. (1996). *If problems talked: Narrative therapy in action.* New York: Guilford.

# Notes

## Introduction

1. When we use the term *couple*, we mean to include all intimate dyadic relationship between adults, whether they are married or not, heterosexual or homosexual.

2. By way of comparison, readers are referred to the outcome research demonstrating the effectiveness of solution-focused therapy with individuals, couples, and families, in particular the studies conducted by McKeel (1996, 1999).

3. Readers interested in gaining a general overview of constructionist approaches to therapy are referred to the following edited works: Gilligan & Price, 1993; Hoyt, 1994, 1996; Neimeyer & Mahoney, 1995.

## Chapter 1

1. As Michael Hoyt notes in the title of his book (Hoyt, 2000), "Some stories are better than others."

2. These co-constructed narratives may be shared or differing in detail. Co-construction is the process in which people mutually reinforce or transform each other's (and their own) perceptions. Even divisive narratives are to some degree co-constructed, in that each partner contributes action, meaning, and reaction to the interactive process.

3. Of course, this discussion of the kinds of stories couples build together is culture-specific. The terms and elements of marriage stories vary widely from culture to culture, group to group, generation to generation, and country to country.

4. Both Kenneth Gergen and Karl Tomm have written about the social construction of the self and related issues of language and narrative (Gergen, 1991, 1994; Gergen & McNamee, 1992). Tomm's concept of the "distributed self," a term we heard him use in a workshop in 1997, is relevant here (Tomm, 1987, 1988).

5. These past successes are also called exceptions in solution-focused brief therapy (de Shazer, 1991, 1994; De Jong & Berg, 1998) and unique outcomes or "sparkling moments" in narrative therapy (White & Epston, 1990; Freedman & Combs, 1996). Successes, exceptions, and unique outcomes are discussed more fully in chapter 6.

# Chapter 2

1. While a number of constructionist therapy developers (Hoyt, 1994, 1996, 1998) view their ideas as "postmodernist," we don't like to apply that term to our ideas and practices. This is not the place (nor are we competent) to make a lengthy critique of postmodernism's cluster of ideas and their effects in various spheres of the cultural milieu (Held, 1995; Sokal & Bricmont, 1998). Suffice it to say that, regarding human social behavior, constructivist and constructionist thought has had a leavening and often creative effect and made a substantive contribution to the practice of psychotherapy. We think, in the long run, that basing psychological theories and clinical models on the ideology of "post-modernism" is unnecessary and may in some cases weaken the case for construc-tionist therapies.

2. There is a spectrum regarding theories of change within these approaches, too. Narrative therapists (Freedman & Combs, 1996; White & Epston, 1990), for instance, begin with very specific political ideas about the nature of the difficulties individuals and couples face, and these ideas direct their therapeutic attention. In contrast, collaborative language system therapists (Andersen, 1997) enter with no particular expectations about the nature of problems and rely on the free flow of open dialogue to produce solutions, change, or positive developments for the couple.

3. These working assumptions are just that—working assumptions. Because RPT's overriding principle is that therapy be collaborative, we are continually taking cues and direction from our clients. This means that, in any given case, we may abandon a particular assumption because, above all else, we assume that what clients tell us is helpful and not helpful is the ultimate guide.

4. Psychodrama, Tobey's earliest field of study, strongly favors the notion that the imagined future is salient to the experience of the present. A technique called the "future projection" is frequently used to help a protagonist (patient) devise ways of dealing with current difficulties. In this method, the protagonist, exploring and detailing an imagined successful future "picture," enacts a pre-ferred self and post-solution state of being. This technique serves a function similar to de Shazer's "miracle question," which we will discuss later.

5. Scott Miller first directed our attention to the importance of an awareness of the client's theory of change and of working as much as possible within that framework to help clients find ways to solve their problems (Duncan et al., 1997; Duncan & Miller, 2000).

# Chapter 3

1. Having observed films of Rogers and read transcripts of his interviews with clients, we notice that many times he goes outside the parameters of his model,

saying and asking things that seem more directive and solution-oriented than his model prescribes.

2. The externalizing of problems is addressed more fully in the next chapter.

3. In chapter 7 we will discuss ways of creating safety in relationships where domestic violence is an existing or potential issue.

4. It should be noted that at the successful end of therapy with Phil, the father said that the therapists they had seen before Phil blamed him for the family's troubles and recommended that he go back into individual therapy to deal with his issues. He told Phil that while he always knew he had to deal with his vulnerability, the other therapists' comments and suggestions felt like attacks and made him feel even more isolated and shamed. As a consequence, he dropped out of those therapies without accomplishing any change.

# Chapter 4

1. The Brief Therapy Center of the Mental Research Institute in Palo Alto and the Brief Family Therapy Center in Milwaukee use the terms *visitor, complainant,* and *customer* to refer to types of client-therapist relationships. They emphasize that these labels refer to the therapeutic relationship and are not meant to label the client. We prefer the two-term names, using them to characterize conversation because they emphasize the interpersonal role relationship in any given conversation and point to the fluid nature of dialogue.

2. We discuss working with the reluctant solo partner in more detail in chapter 11.

3. Of course solution-focused therapists recognize that problem talk may be necessary in establishing rapport with clients.

4. In *Putting Difference to Work*, de Shazer (1991, p. 64) describes an intriguing case where reframing played a central role in solving a couple's problem. A couple reported that the wife had turned into a "nymphomaniac"—that recently she began requiring sex at least once a day before going to sleep. As the therapist inquired about this "sex problem," the husband made an offhand remark that this was a "sleep problem." The therapist quickly picked up on this normalizing reframe (it is easier to solve a "sleep problem" than cure "nymphomania"). For the rest of the session, all conversation focused on ways to solve this "sleep problem." At the end of the hour, the therapist presented several strategic-type task assignments to the wife based on this redefinition of the problem (one was, for instance, that she should, as an experiment, quit exercising for now, another that, if insomniac, she should get up and do disliked household chores). Two weeks later, the wife sent a note saying the problem had been solved and thanking the therapist and the observing team for helping her "see her insatiable need for sex" was simply "a symptom of insomnia." No mention was made in the note as to whether she and her husband had tried any of the suggestions. Two things stand out for us in this case discussion. The first is that the reframing came out of something the husband said and was not originally an idea generated by the therapist or the observing team. Secondly, as de Shazer himself notes, "Perhaps the new name, with its attached meanings, was enough to solve the client's problem and the suggestions were unnecessary."

5. Also, we do not generally view ourselves as experts on the most appropriate or healthful political and cultural attitudes. Narrative therapists are interested in introducing into the therapeutic dialogue progressive, egalitarian, and culturally diverse ways of thinking about human relationships in order to alter the more or less automatic patriarchal and oppressive terms of much intimate and familial life. While we generally share the progressive political views of the narrative therapists, we do not feel, in most cases, that it is our role to introduce these ideas as a matter of course into the therapeutic dialogue. Attitudinal change takes place frequently in RPT, but it is by and large on the basis of goals of intimacy and partnership developed by the couples we work with.

6. We've taken the summary of findings and conclusions that provide the basis for this intervention from Gottman's work (1994, 1999). It is sometimes difficult to summarize Gottman's work precisely, since a careful reading of his work suggests slightly different formulations of his findings at various times, so what we say in these conversations with couples is a presentation of his findings and conclusions in this particular area as we understand them. Note that we present this "expert" information in a collaborative way. Once the couple agrees this information can be useful to them, we do not move on to teach them conflict management skills. Rather, we use goal-building and exceptions conversations to clarify and amplify what the partners already do that is experienced as positive, so that they can find ways to use these successful activities more of the time.

8. Not quite as enjoyable a sparring team at home, apparently, as the couple in the film *Adam's Rib*, with Katherine Hepburn and Spencer Tracey.

# Chapter 5

1. In the 1970s, when Tobey was doing psychodrama groups with psychiatric patients at Mt. Zion Hospital in San Francisco, she used future projections (enacted future pictures) to embody and explore clients' sense of self and possibility. Because clients' pictures of themselves and the future were often negative or defeating, she began experimenting with the use of alternative future projections, one negative, one positive. In this way, she helped people look back from an achieved future and detail the steps leading from the present to that future. Doing this, she discovered how well and how often people could name concrete steps they had taken and specific attitudes they had fostered in themselves to get to these varying futures. This work is one antecedent of the work we are doing now.

2. In developing scenarios of change, it is often helpful to start with signs of change or difference in the speaker, rather than signs of change or difference in the partner (which is usually how dissatisfied partners have imagined difference up to now.) We often start with questions about what will be different about the person imagining the preferred scenario, rather than what will be different about the partner. It is also possible, of course, to ask direct questions about what a partner will be doing differently in a future picture, but generally that line of inquiry is more useful later. At this point asking the wife what her

husband will be doing differently will only remind her of her dissatisfactions, encourage her to say things that will arouse his defensiveness, and turn conversation toward the *bad story* territory.

3. A caveat here: It is important not to confuse the criterion that a well-formed goal must be within the client's control with the process for developing agency (discussed in chapter 6).

4. While we usually begin goal-building by talking about people's imagined preferred futures, there are times when we begin the process by asking what has happened recently that people would like to have happen more in the future. In other words, we ask people to look back to the recent past for successes and exceptions to their problems as a way to engage them in developing therapeutically well-formed goals. We will explore the use of exceptions to develop goals more fully in the next chapter.

# Chapter 6

1. We want to point out that we are doubtful whether, in human affairs, it is possible to identify what causes what to happen, since factors contributing to particular consequences are always multiple. This is one reason that we do not think it useful to spend time searching for possible past causes of current problems. At the same time, we do not believe one can say with certainty that actions people took concurrently with preferred experiences necessarily caused those experiences. There is no doubt, however, that partners influence each other and their own perceptions of experience, both by behavioral acts and perceptual shifts, and so developing causal stories with respect to successes and exceptions usually leads to desirable therapeutic ends.

2. This is a technique Tobey uses in psychodramatic group work.

# Chapter 7

1. Note that de Shazer and Berg use a scale of 0 to 10. While there may be no practical difference, we prefer to use a scale of 1 to 10. All the examples and transcripts reflect this difference.

2. We discuss how to guide such conversations between the partners more fully in chapter 9.

3. In a study released in 1990, Straus and Gelles found that one out of six married American couples (16%) experienced at least one act of violence during the year of the study. This led them to estimate that 8.7 million couples experience marital violence each year and 3.4 million of those couples experience severe violence carrying a high risk of injury (cited in Holtzworth-Monroe et al., 1995, p. 317).

4. De Shazer views the formula first-session task as a sort of skeleton key (de Shazer, 1985, p. 137) that can serve to open a number of different locks. Such task assignments, discussed more fully in chapter 10, open perceptual exits from the *bad story* narrative and often result in experiential changes for the partners.

# Chapter 9

1. Once again, we remind readers that RPT is not carried out in cookbook fashion. We present general guidelines and describe what we usually do toward the end of sessions. But, as always, the context and requirements of the moment, not our adherence to a fixed formula, dictate what we do as sessions come to a close.

2. Duncan and Miller are quick to point out that this finding does not support the idea that all therapy should be brief or that, unless changes take place in the first few sessions, continuing treatment will be a waste of time and money. The issue is not whether therapy should be of short or long duration, but how to ensure that the initial sessions serve as a positive foundation so that treatment, whatever the duration, can continue toward desired outcomes.

3. We might have covered this second type of couples conversation in our discussion of goal-building in chapter 5. We chose to discuss this process here because we wanted to talk in one place about how we facilitate partner-to-partner conversations.

4. We know several solution-focused brief therapists who swear by the value of this end-of-session break. Readers who want to learn more about the use of the break should explore the solution-focused brief therapy literature (De Jong & Berg, 1998; Walter & Peller, 1992).

5. There is a common misunderstanding among those who have only a cursory knowledge of these brief strategic models that the therapist designs assignments which themselves are intended as solutions. A closer reading of the literature reveals that in these approach the assignments, which must be framed and offered in ways that convince people to carry them out, disrupt and thereby change the interpersonal field of problem-solving, and it is this disruption/change that frees the individual, couple, or family to find their own solutions in a new contextual and meaning-generating social environment.

6. In their book *The Heroic Client* (2000), Duncan and Miller advocate the use of both postsession and posttreatment outcome instruments to determine the efficacy of therapy for clients. They are interested in substantiating how and when therapy is helpful on the basis of client report. We think this effort is significant and commendable, and, though we do not use these types of written outcome questionnaires, their work has made us think more about ways to make sure we are getting and understanding client feedback.

# Chapter 10

1. We do not believe solution-focused brief therapy encourages practitioners to force solution talk on clients. However, because the approach is usually presented with a heavy emphasis on the idea that solution talk, not problem talk, leads to solutions, it is easy for those learning this approach to prevent clients from talking about their concerns and troubles. We have never heard or read anything in the solution-focused brief therapy literature that suggests clients should be forced to talk only about positive things. Watching de Shazer

and Berg on videotapes, we have always noted their respectful attitudes and their skillful ways of "leading from behind."

2. As we began developing the practices of RPT, we noticed that many couples completed successful therapies much faster than before. This was initially somewhat disturbing: more open hours appeared in our schedules, and this meant our incomes decreased. We began wondering whether becoming solution-focused was such a good idea. In good conscience, however, we couldn't turn back. Now, primarily because we have worked with so many couples who were pleased both with their success and the relative brevity of the therapy, our caseloads remain full despite the more rapid comings and going of many of our clients.

# Chapter 11

1. We want to point out that the systems metaphor and theory have evolved since its earliest formulations. Lynn Hoffman (1993), in distinguishing first-order and second-order cybernetics, identifies the former as based on information-exchange systems that function to maintain stasis and the latter as based on organic systems that function to make generative and adaptive change possible.

# Index

When you examine both concepts, it becomes clear that "mandatory" programs are the real problem.

Some lawmakers want to raise individual income taxes on the "wealthy" to reduce the federal deficit. But aside from the fact that Tea Party members are almost universally opposed to tax increases, what would such an increase accomplish?

The projected federal deficit in the 2012 budget is $1.1 trillion. This is significantly lower than the deficit of 2011, which the 2012 budget estimates will wind up as $1.6 trillion. Let us assume that the progressive/liberal dream could be accomplished with a snap of the fingers, and income taxes on everyone doubled without affecting the economy. Even if the entire individual income tax were doubled, the projected deficit could not be bridged.

Obviously, the damage to the economy would be catastrophic. Consumer spending would plummet, businesses would collapse, unemployment would skyrocket, and the economy would plunge into chaos. Of course, assumptions about tax revenues would have to be revised, because so many people would be out of work. So if we can't double everyone's income taxes, how about just raising them on the rich?

If we use 2008 IRS data, this would roughly be the result: In 2008, the top 1 percent of all earners in America (those making more than about $380,000 a year) paid approximately 38 percent of all individual income taxes. This tax revenue to the federal government was $392 billion. So if taxes on these individuals were doubled, only $400 billion in new revenue might be raised. With a $1.6-trillion deficit, this is clearly not enough to solve the deficit problem, let alone pay off our existing debt.

When we take it down to the next level, the top 5 percent of all income earners (those making about $159,000 a year or more) are responsible for the payment of 59 percent of income taxes. This results in revenues of about $600 billion. Many of those people, while financially well off, certainly aren't hugely wealthy. However, even if taxes on these "rich fat-cats" were doubled, an additional $600 billion could be raised. Still not enough to make a dent in that $1.6-trillion deficit.

But for the purposes of economic matters, the short answer is: disband the Department of Education and put that money toward actually educating our children, or, better, give it back to parents so they can choose the education options that are best for their children.

## MONETARY POLICY

*I believe that banking institutions are more dangerous to our liberties than standing armies. Already they have raised up a monied aristocracy that has set the government at defiance. The issuing power (of money) should be taken away from the banks and restored to the people to whom it properly belongs.*

—Thomas Jefferson

*Every effort has been made by the Fed to conceal its power but the truth is, the Fed has usurped the government. It controls everything here and it controls all our foreign relations. It makes and breaks governments at will.*

—Congressman Louis T. McFadden, 1933, chairman, Banking and Currency Committee

### AUDIT OF THE FEDERAL RESERVE

The U.S. Federal Reserve System (aka *the Fed*) describes itself as "the central bank of the United States" with a mandate to "provide the nation with a safer, more flexible, and more stable monetary and financial system" and notes, in a flourish of understatement, "Over the years, its role in banking and the economy has expanded."

Yes. It has.

Its duties today, according to its own documentation, are to regulate banking institutions, author and control the nation's monetary policy, and create stability in the financial system. It also provides a variety of services to depository institutions, the U.S. government, and a multitude of international entities.

Lately, the Fed's main job has been to print money, which has debased U.S. currency, driven up inflation, and caused the world to seriously reconsider decoupling itself from the U.S. dollar. And the Fed has been doing all this beyond the reach of the people's representatives. The Fed has consistently taken the position that it operates outside the supervisory purview of both the legislative and executive branches. However, its authority is granted by the U.S. Congress, and it is supposed to be subject to congressional oversight. But the Fed is strenuously resistant to an audit of its operations, stating that a true accounting would restrict its independence and autonomy.

Stated another way: the entity that controls our money supply, sets our interest rates, and creates inflation or deflation at its whim doesn't even have to comply with the basic principles of accounting oversight that any company has to observe to be listed on a stock exchange. Most people find this fact stunning. And 75 percent of Americans, according to a 2009 Rasmussen poll, want the Fed audited. We, the Tea Party Patriots, agree with 75 percent of Americans: the time to audit the Fed is now.

## OUT-OF-CONTROL SPENDING

*The multiplication of public offices, increase of expense beyond income, growth and entailment of a public debt, are indications soliciting the employment of the pruning knife.*

—THOMAS JEFFERSON,
letter to Spencer Roane, March 9, 1821

*Government is like a baby. An alimentary canal with a big appetite at one end and no sense of responsibility at the other.*

—RONALD REAGAN

All levels of government have grown in size and scope. Even in the time of Thomas Jefferson, way back in 1821, people were concerned about national debt. And today we keep going deeper and deeper into a black hole of government debt.

The 2012 budget offered by President Obama in January 2011 showed a projected $1.6 trillion deficit for fiscal 2011. The current debt owed by the U.S. government is $14.7 trillion (but will be substantially more by the time this book is in print). That comes out to over $47,000 per citizen. That's right, every child born in America today will face a $47,000 debt. And that's just at the federal level. If you live in a fiscally irresponsible state like California or New Jersey, every baby will be burdened by another $10,000. For those children born in New York, add an extra $15,000. (If you have the stomach for it, you can watch the debt grow minute by minute at http://www.usdebtclock.org.) That is the gift our politicians are bequeathing to future generations.

So what can we do? The answer is simple. Stop overspending. We don't have a revenue problem; we have a spending problem. Spending, whether politicians call it *discretionary* or *mandatory*, is really *all* discretionary. Every law can be repealed or amended, and every program can be revised or scrapped. The question is not really whether something can be done; the question is whether our politicians have the political will to act.

We have to accept some basic facts about America's deficit before we can hold any reasonable discussion:

- The tax base is too small to solve the problem.
- Discretionary spending is too small to solve the problem.
- Mandatory entitlement programs are the *real* problem.

The scale of the problem can be assessed like this:

- Even if *all* discretionary spending were cut 50 percent, there would still be a $1-trillion deficit in 2011.
- Even if *all* current taxes were increased by 50 percent, there would still be a $1-trillion deficit in 2011.

Let's take it down one more step. If taxes on the top 25 percent of all taxpayers were doubled, an additional $809 billion could be raised (assuming that it wouldn't just crater the economy and destroy America's tax base). Now we have to double income taxes on everyone earning over $67,000 per year. Ouch. That really hurts. And it *still* doesn't cover the deficit. And because the top 25 percent of all taxpayers paid 86 percent of all income taxes, their income tax would result, more or less, in the same harmful impact as doubling taxes for everyone.

We could run through the same analysis for corporate income taxes, but we would get the same results. No matter how much we tax, there is simply not enough revenue to cover the deficit or pay off our long-term debt. This leaves cutting government spending as the only way to control deficits.

## GOVERNMENT SPENDING—DISCRETIONARY VERSUS MANDATORY

The biggest obstacle to reducing government spending is the fact that the majority of it goes to entitlement programs, where the spending is "mandated" by federal laws. If any citizen meets the appropriate set of criteria, the government must make the payments.

The biggest of these programs is Social Security, followed by Medicare and Medicaid. Medicare and Medicaid are quickly approaching bankruptcy, and Social Security is not far behind.

These entitlement programs must be reformed if we are to avoid fiscal calamity. For those not currently in these programs, and who have enough time to plan, we must reduce promised benefits and even eliminate some programs altogether. Younger people need to sacrifice more to make sure we honor the promises we as a nation have made to older people who are depending on us.

We, the coauthors of this book, travel around the nation and have the privilege of speaking with literally thousands of Tea Party Patriots. Sometimes we are at events with thousands of people, and sometimes just sitting around a table at a coffee shop. But wherever we go, we always talk to people about the issue of entitlement spending. We always ask if they are willing to make the personal sacrifices necessary to save the nation. The answer is always a resounding yes.

Recently, we have been hearing more and more people suggest that maybe younger Americans should give up the thought of receiving *anything* from Social Security, Medicare, or Medicaid. Folks have suggested they would still be willing to pay into those systems to protect our current seniors and to save our country for our children and grandchildren.

This is the real spirit of the Tea Party. We can look out for ourselves and for each other. We don't need or want the government to do it for us. We have seen where the "big government" approach takes us: impossible promises and a future mortgaged beyond the lifetimes of our children's children.

Doing the right thing isn't always easy, but it's always right. The real solution is fiscal discipline and entitlement reform. The big question is whether the politicians have the will to put their careers on the line to get it done. In the next chapter we'll talk about our broken political system and offer some Tea Party thoughts on how to fix it.

## ★ 4 ★

# The Tea Party's Interactions with Our Political System

*We base all our experiments on the capacity of mankind for self-government.*

—James Madison

IN PREVIOUS CHAPTERS, we've seen that the greatest threat to our economic success today comes not from abroad but from our elected officials. And it is through changing the behavior of those elected officials—and making sure that those whose behavior doesn't change don't stay in their jobs—that the Tea Party movement plans to exercise its influence.

The elections of November 2010 were a watershed moment for us. Some even started referring to the event as the Tea Party's "great victory."

In the spirit of our revolutionary forefathers, millions of Tea Partiers from across the nation had worked within the system to stand up to a distant unresponsive government. And we won. If it had been a Hollywood movie, the Tea Party Patriots' story would end here. Mission accomplished. Roll the credits. Our work here is done.

But the thing about America is that our work here is never done—particularly with the political process. It takes constant effort to build and maintain the national grassroots movement that will restore America, and constant effort to withstand the worst from the media and special interest groups—and even occasionally from our friends and allies. And it also takes constant effort to persevere under brutal attacks from the president of the United States, from the vice president, the Speaker of the House, and the Senate majority leader.

Yet none of that vigilance prepared us for what we would face on November 3, the day after our "great victory." We quickly learned that we would have to fight another battle—this time against some of the very politicians whose victories we had helped secure.

In the 1980s, Ronald Reagan achieved his landslide electoral victories by building a "three-legged stool" coalition that was composed of fiscal conservatives, social conservatives, and defense hawks. Part of Reagan's success came from his ability to unite both the country and the Republican Party, the former with his cheerful optimism and vision of American exceptionalism, the latter through preaching the "Eleventh Commandment," a hard-and-fast rule that one should never speak ill of one's philosophical allies.

But within a week of the 2010 midterm elections, the conservative chattering class had already broken the Eleventh Commandment (and at least one of the original ten) by openly deriding the Tea Party movement. All three legs of Reagan's coalition—along with a few extra—were broken off and aimed directly at us.

The group that turned on us faster and harder than any other was the old guard of the GOP: the Republican Beltway establishment. That's right, we were surprised to find that our biggest detractors were, in fact, the very same pork-barrel politicians we had restored to the majority.

As Peggy Noonan wrote in the *Wall Street Journal*, on October 22, 2010, "The tea party saved the Republican Party. In a broad sense, the tea party rescued it from being the fat, unhappy, querulous creature it had become, a party that didn't remember anymore why it existed, or what its historical purpose was. The tea party, with its energy and earnestness, restored the GOP to itself. In a practical sense, the tea party saved the Republican Party in this cycle by not going third-party."

She was right. We could have. But we chose not to.

While the Democratic and Republican parties are made up of loose coalitions of special interest groups held together by sometimes tenuous ties around the shared desire to win and seize power, the Tea Party movement makes its decisions through the lens of its core values of fiscal responsibility, constitutionally limited government, and free markets.

Given these principles, the 2010 election presented the Tea Party movement with a Hobson's choice. Seven years earlier, Republicans had created a massive unfunded government health-care scheme to provide prescription drugs for seniors, a program that was neither fiscally responsible, within its constitutional authority, nor respectful of free-market values. Worse, it opened the door to Obamacare.

And Republicans brought in not one but *eight* rounds of outrageously expensive and utterly unsuccessful stimuli in 2008 before the Democrats took over and ratcheted up that regime by nearly $2 trillion more—all of it unfunded—in less than two years.

To the Tea Party movement, the idea of supporting Republicans was only moderately less distasteful than supporting Democrats. But we knew that if we had "gone rogue" and launched a third-party challenge, we would have split the conservative vote and handed perpetual power to the Democratic Party, at a time when that party's most radical members already had full control over Congress and the presidency, and were using their power to erode America's founding principles like never before.

So Tea Partiers did something that was remarkably difficult. In 2010, Tea Partiers chose the lesser of two evils and supported a slate of Republican candidates, many of whom had pledged allegiance to our core Tea Party values.

We didn't pretend that Republicans are honorable, principled, or worthy of our trust, any more than Democrats. We knew that we would have to be eternally vigilant with them, too. What we didn't know was how quickly they would turn against us.

Before the helium had drained from the GOP victory balloons, the national Republican Party apparatus was already distancing itself from the Tea Party movement, taking credit for the historic number of election victories—and blaming us for its tiny handful of defeats.

The National Republican Congressional Committee (NRCC)

trumpeted—of course—the NRCC's role in the victories as "crucial" and crowed that "the fact is, our candidates would not have won without [our] . . . help."

The influential blogger Robert Stacy McCain had a different view: "That the GOP won the House is some kind of miracle, considering the total ineptitude of Pete Sessions and his crew of bumbling dingbats at the NRCC," he posted on November 10, 2010.

On November 6, 2010, the *Telegraph*,\* a UK newspaper, wrote of a "complacent Washington consensus that the Tea Party failed" and went on to explain the truth: "Never mind that [t]his grassroots anti-tax, small-government 'constitutional conservatism' movement provided the energy and momentum behind the biggest congressional election victory in 62 years."

On November 2, 2010, Timothy Carney, senior political columnist for the *Washington Examiner*,† had the same perspective as the Republican Party. "Among the old guard of the GOP caucus, there's no notion that Republicans need to abandon their standard operating procedure." The paper went on to reveal that there was "open warfare" with the "Tea Party groups on one side, against the National Republican Senatorial Committee, Minority Leader Mitch McConnell, and the GOP's K Street kingpins" on the other.

The bloggers, the British, and the new media were right. And the first battle of this war would be over a particular kind of government spending called *earmarks*.

∿

The driving force that gave birth to the Tea Party movement, the glue that held it together and energized it, and the central issue of the 2010 midterm elections, were the same: namely, the desire of Americans across the political spectrum to stop the runaway government spending. And the most egregious spending of all, the lowest-hanging type

---

\* http://www.telegraph.co.uk/news/worldnews/barackobama/8114548/Barack-Obama
-becomes-the-Relevant-Progressive-President.htm/.
† http://www.washingtonexaminer.com/news/2010/11/gops-k-street-wing-ready
-insurgent-challenge#izz14J268stk.

of pork-barrel spending that everyone agreed should go, was *earmarks*, spending for special projects often paid to a congressman's campaign supporters.

Well, almost everyone. Senator Mitch McConnell and the GOP Beltway establishment were opposed, even though earmark spending is unconstitutional. It's the kind of spending the government does without, and sometimes *against*, the will of the people.

Before the U.S. government can pass an appropriations bill—meaning, before Washington can pass a new law to spend more of your hard-earned money—it must have your consent to do so. Under the American system of government, the consent of the people is expressed through the votes of the people's representatives. We elect Congress to uphold and defend the Constitution, and each member takes the following oath: "I do solemnly swear that I will support and defend the Constitution of the United States against all enemies, foreign and domestic; that I will bear true faith and allegiance to the same; that I take this obligation freely, without any mental reservation or purpose of evasion; and that I will well and faithfully discharge the duties of the office on which I am about to enter: So help me God."

When our representatives break that oath, or fail to vote according to the people who elected them, it becomes our responsibility to reassert our will. That is what Abraham Lincoln meant when he resolved that "government of the people, by the people, and for the people, shall not perish from the earth."

And when governments spend our money without our consent by simply "writing in" funding for various projects that are not the province of the federal government, they break their oath and start to destroy self-governance. The inevitable result of shifting power away from the people in the case of earmarks is that politicians then spend our money not according to our will, but according to the whims of the special interests.

The amount of $50 million of your hard-earned dollars were "earmarked" and spent on an indoor rain forest in Iowa. $500,000 went to a teapot museum in North Carolina; $25,000 was spent to study mariachi music; and $100,000 went to the Tiger Woods Foundation. In addition, $1.8 million of your money was earmarked and spent, without your consent, to study why pigs stink.

> *I'm sure that David Letterman will probably be talking about it and Jay Leno will be talking about it; we've got $1.8 million to study why pigs smell.*
>
> —SENATOR TOM HARKIN,
> March 4, 2009

You can see why, fresh on the heels of a massive election victory, we thought that eliminating earmarks would be the easiest thing in the world to accomplish. Surely the politicians in Washington wouldn't go against the clearly expressed will of the voters so soon after an election! But the ensuing fight highlighted for us just how far we have gotten away from the principle that each individual should be engaged in the governing of the country on a daily basis, and how such a thing could happen.

Let's take a look at just one of the specific earmarks we mentioned: the Sparta, North Carolina, Teapot Museum, which received $500,000 of government largesse. Chances are, if you heard about that earmark, it made your blood boil. But did you do anything about it, other than shake your head at how badly Washington was caring for your hard-earned tax dollars? Probably not. The cost to you, personally, of that one earmark was tiny. From a purely economic perspective, spread over the entire population of our nation, each individual's proportionate share of that $500,000 was less than one cent. If you wrote a letter to one of your members of Congress protesting this outrage, you would have spent more money on the postage stamp than on the museum.

On the other hand, the people who had paying jobs at that museum had quite a large incentive to spend as much time and money as possible to maintain that earmark. This is the classic problem with centralized spending: the benefits of that spending go to a few fortunate recipients, and the costs are spread over a much larger segment of the population. When benefits are concentrated, and costs diffused, the recipients of those benefits will do anything they can to maintain their fortunate status. They'll raise funds for lawmakers who promise to keep spending money on them, they'll hire powerful lobbyists with access to decision makers, and they'll form pressure groups to "educate" the public about the "benefits" of whatever pork-barrel project they wish to maintain.

The Founders understood this dynamic and, as a result, created a system of government that pushed spending decisions down the political ladder. They made it very clear, particularly through the Tenth Amendment, that whatever powers weren't specifically granted to the federal government in the Constitution were reserved to the states or to the people themselves.

What happens to earmarks as the decisions are made closer to home? What happens when you try to fund a project like the teapot museum at the state level? There are a little more than 9 million citizens in North Carolina. Spending $500,000 would cost each of them about five cents. Again, to the average citizen of North Carolina, it wouldn't be worth a postage stamp to protest. (And, in fact, the state of North Carolina did spend $400,000 of its taxpayers' money on that very same boondoggle.)

But let's take it one step farther. What might have happened if the mayor of Sparta, North Carolina, decided that spending $500,000 on a teapot museum was a good idea? There are about eighteen hundred residents of Sparta. That comes out to $277 per resident. Now, all of a sudden, each individual citizen has a significant incentive to make sure that his or her money is being spent wisely.

It's possible that the citizens of Sparta would have been delighted to see a few hundred dollars of their hard-earned money go to a teapot museum. But, in reality, they weren't. When the only way to keep the teapot museum open was by spending their own money, the good Spartans refused, forcing the museum to cease operations in January 2010.

The moral of the story, of course, is that when politics and political decisions are made locally, each individual has more power to affect the outcome, leading to better overall choices. People are naturally more careful with their own money than when they're spending dollars that come from some anonymous strangers.

When it comes down to it, we're *all* that anonymous stranger. And what we've done with Tea Party Patriots is create a structure through which the millions of us who are tired of being treated like piggy banks for some politician's pork-barrel projects can stand up and make our voices heard as loudly as the special interests who benefit from eating at the public trough.

When politicians need public support to do the right thing, we must be there for them. Ideally, of course, our elected officials should have the courage to do the right thing on their own; but when they lack the courage to do the right thing, it's up to us to give them the moral, political, and vocal support to stand up and do what's right.

On the issue of earmarks, we didn't think that we would be starting by battling two Republican senators, but Mitch McConnell and James Inhofe initially came out in favor of this odious practice. They suggested that we just didn't "understand" the earmark issue. That if we would just listen to the wisdom of the Senate leadership, everything would be OK. After all, the amount of money earmarked was just a drop in the bucket—a mere $16 billion. So why did we even care about what amounted to a rounding error in the federal budget?

We explained that to those of us who work for a living, $16 billion sure sounded like a lot of money. So much, in fact, that it would cover the average American's mortgage payments for nearly nine hundred thousand years.

At that point, the senators changed their tactics and tried to convince us that national security was at stake, and that without earmarks, the Defense Department wouldn't be able to defend the country. (An ironic argument, given that the Defense Department is one of the most competent branches of our federal government and is closest to playing the role the Founders intended it to play. It may spend too much money accomplishing its mission, but the cure for that problem is more vigorous oversight, not earmarks.)

And then a funny thing happened. Senator McConnell went on

TV and admitted that he'd been wrong. That regardless of what he thought, the American people had sent a clear message that they didn't want earmarks. McConnell explained that he didn't want to be a hypocrite, and after criticizing the Democrats for ignoring the will of the people, he was equally wrong to do so himself.

So he stopped. We won. Perhaps the hundreds of thousands of phone calls from Tea Partiers around the country had something to do with the senator's epiphany. (Perhaps not; he still spent 75 percent of his "concession" speech on earmarks saying how wonderful he thought they were and citing all of the lovely things he'd been able to do with them over his years in the Senate.)

∽

While the fight over earmarks was still going on in November of 2010, another critical battle was also taking place in Washington, D.C.: the struggle over who would influence the freshmen members of Congress we had just helped to elect before the GOP establishment and K Street lobbyists poisoned their hearts and minds.

As the political author and commentator Dick Morris observed, the first few days after an election are "all about brainwashing the new members. That's why it is vital to get to them first. When a freshman enters the Congress, he or she is subject to an intense storm of absurd projections, false assumptions, phony numbers, and artificial choices foisted on them by the establishment. Freshmen are dangerous [to the status quo] since they have not [yet] been brainwashed and may inject common sense into some of Washington's deliberations."

This was our most important task: to reach the new members before they were corrupted by the Washington establishment.

Within forty-eight hours of election day we began planning our first-ever orientation session. It was an audacious goal for us—a group of untrained citizen-activists—to think that we could gather dozens of newly minted congressmen and -women in the Ronald Reagan Building in Washington, D.C., and pull it all off with a volunteer staff in less than nine days. But it was no less audacious than what we had pulled off at the beginning of the movement.

Before our first session, we found ourselves under assault from the Republican Party, the conservative leadership, social conservatives, lobbyists, a major conservative think tank, and even Fox News. First we were attacked for being too conservative. Then we were attacked for not being conservative enough. We were attacked for caring too much about social issues (which, as an organization, Tea Party Patriots doesn't get involved in) and finally for not caring about social issues *enough*.

But despite this, we put together a remarkably successful event. We were able to tell the freshman members of Congress that they were going to face unimaginable pressure to do the wrong thing. That they would be pressured to go along to get along. That leadership would dangle everything from committee assignments to parking spaces in front of them, as incentives to avoid change. Then we explained that we planned to keep up the praise and tell the whole world when they were doing something right, especially when a position was difficult to maintain.

The first test of whether Tea Party Patriots would keep its promise came less than one month later.

On December 14, 2010, lame-duck Democrats in the Senate introduced a nearly two-thousand-page omnibus spending bill that, if it had passed, would have prevented Congress from making any cuts in spending until 2012. In complete contravention of the will of the voters, who had taken away their majority in the House of Representatives and dealt them a series of stinging electoral blows in the Senate, these Democrats proposed a bill that would spend more than half a billion dollars *per page* of the written legislation.

Some Republican senators turned out to be allies in the fight against this ridiculous attempt to get around the will of American voters. GOP senator Jim DeMint stated: "President Obama and Democrats have apparently learned nothing from this November's election. This nearly 2,000-page omnibus filled with thousands of earmarks shows they are still determined to ram through as much big-government spending as they can in this lame duck session. Americans loudly demanded an end to the runaway spending, but Democrats are intent on raiding every taxpayer dollar that they can grab from the Treasury on their way out of power."

Senator McConnell again saw the error of his previous positions and said on the Senate floor: "Americans told Democrats last month to stop what they've been doing: bigger government, 2,000-page bills jammed through on Christmas Eve, wasteful spending. The bill is a monument to all three." (It's amazing what effect a few hundred thousand phone calls can have on a politician.)

Other Republican senators, however, saw no problem with the bill. Outgoing Utah senator Bob Bennett, whom the Tea Party movement had targeted for defeat because of his votes in favor of TARP (Troubled Asset Relief Program) and his introduction of a plainly unconstitutional bill to mandate individual insurance coverage, announced his intention to vote with the Democrats: "It will be tough for some, but not for me," he said.

Once again we melted the phone lines to Capitol Hill and provided support to those senators who, either due to a desire to do the right thing or out of fear of suffering the same fate as Senator Bennett, stood in opposition.

And once again, the Tea Party movement won. Two days later, Senator Harry Reid withdrew the bill.

∼

The specifics of what happens to our elected representatives once they're co-opted by the Washington, D.C., establishment can be horrific. But we have to understand, as the Founders did, that it's basic human nature for people to want to accumulate more power. The genius of the Constitution is that it recognizes that tendency and clearly limits the authority of the federal government.

At the end of the day, the one core issue when it comes to the political process is this: who decides? Where can an individual's voice be heard most clearly, at the state and local levels or in Washington, D.C.? The argument over where important decisions should be made is going on right now over the battle to cut spending in 2011 and beyond. And congressional memories have proved themselves to be as short as ever.

In 2010, the federal government spent about $3.5 trillion of your money. Many Republican congressional candidates (most of them not incumbents) structured their campaigns around one very important promise: to cut $100 billion from the budget their first year in office.

The Tea Party Patriots completely supported that goal but thought it didn't go anywhere near far enough. In a $3.5-trillion budget, $100 billion is just a tiny fraction of a reduction. In fact, in 2009, federal spending increased by *six times* that amount.

Before the election, all these candidates wanted to do was to reduce spending by one-sixth of the gigantic Bush/Obama stimulus. What could be easier? Bolstered by the Tea Party movement, which was able to rally millions of people all around the country to support the principle of fiscal responsibility, and fresh on the heels of a political victory against the lame-duck omnibus spending bill, Congress should have had all it needed to cut costs.

But here's what really happened. We were told by the congressional leadership that although so many members ran on cutting at least $100 billion from the federal budget their first year in office, those members really meant that they would cut $100 billion in the government's first *fiscal* year. What had been a drop in the bucket of federal spending had now dwindled to a fraction of a mere drop in the gigantic bucket that is the U.S. government's federal budget.

But we did not give up and say "Thank you, Congress, for agreeing to put a tiny little Band-Aid on the gigantic gaping wound that is the federal budget." Instead, we jammed their phone lines and stuffed their e-mail boxes with tens of thousands of comments from Tea Partiers, telling them to stand up to their word.

And we made progress. Some in Congress knew why they were elected and had begun to listen. While not all kept their promises, the Republican Study Committee (the supposed watchdog of conservative principles in the Republican caucus) came out with a plan to cut the full $100 billion in the current year.

Unfortunately, the House Republican leadership refused to listen, and refused to press for the full amount of promised cuts. They explained that we just "didn't understand" what they had meant by their promise of $100 billion in cuts. In D.C., apparently $100 billion doesn't mean $100 billion. As usual, they defaulted to the ruling elite position that we were just too simple to understand Washington, D.C.'s unique accounting practices. We were disappointed, but not surprised.

Just prior to the historic 2010 election, we met with then minority leader Boehner in his large, ornate Capitol Hill office. Members of the Tea Party Patriots had asked us to meet with him to let him know what was expected if and when the Republicans took the majority. Surrounded by multiple staffers with pens and pads at the ready, we sat down with Boehner and delivered a very simple message from the Tea Party Patriots.

Our members had voted and they expected "bold" and immediate leadership on the budget. They wanted an immediate return to fiscal responsibility. They wanted the soon-to-be Speaker to propose a return to the spending levels of the last budget under President Clinton, a time when the budget was balanced and there was a surplus.

Upon hearing this plan, Boehner threw his head back and laughed a deep and resounding laugh. As he regained his breath, he smiled a condescending smile, took a deep draw off of his cigarette, and with the smoke wafting out of his mouth, said, "Well, that sure is bold!" We knew at that moment exactly what to expect from the incoming Republican majority leadership.

Unlike John Boehner, who at the time was in his tenth term in Congress, we were not amused. We went on to articulate the position of the Tea Party movement: if he and the rest of our elected officials couldn't find a way to be bold in moving the country toward fiscal responsibility in 2011, in 2012, we'd find people who could.

The outcome of the 2011 budget battle doesn't particularly matter. What matters is that the Tea Party movement is learning how to best affect the political process. We're getting more savvy every day. We refuse to let deeply entrenched politicians continue to drive our once-strong economy off a cliff.

How did these politicians forget why they were elected in the first place?

For one thing, politics has become a career path, rather than a duty to serve, the way the Founders intended it to be. Our elected and appointed officials treat their positions as cushy sinecures that will ultimately lead to lucrative lobbying jobs, persuading their former colleagues to give special favors to those who can afford their $25,000-a-month retainer fees. Sclerosis has set in. Politics has become like the mafia in more ways than one: once you're in, you can never leave.

So it's up to us—all of us—to change things. How can we do that?

Through a three-part plan. Over the next two years, the Tea Party movement's strategy includes three *p*'s: (1) prod, (2) pressure, and (3) primary.

What do we mean by this?

First, as citizens, it's our responsibility to petition our government to do the right thing. We need to make our voice heard loud and clear and make sure that the politicians can't ever claim that they didn't know what the Tea Party thought on any given issue. They knew we considered anything less than $100 billion in budget cuts a sellout. Like cowboys herding cattle, we have to prod the herd in the right direction.

Second, when politicians of any party act against our interests, it's up to us to call attention to their failures, immediately, loudly, and as publicly as possible. By working together, the Tea Party movement has a much greater impact collectively on our politicians than any of us working alone.

Ginni Rapini, the coordinator of the NorCal Tea Party Patriots, tells a story about a competition among draft horses at a county fair. Every year, for thirty years, organizers staged a contest to see which horse could pull the most weight. One year, the winning horse pulled a record-breaking 4,500 pounds. The second-place horse didn't do much worse; it was able to pull 4,300 pounds.

But that year, the judges tried a little experiment. They hitched the two top horses together, to see how much they could pull as a team. They were expecting the team might be able to pull a load of 8,800 or

9,000 pounds. To their amazement, together the two horses were able to pull 12,000 pounds—an increase of 30 percent more than what the horses could have done alone! Teamwork is a force multiplier; a thousand calls to a member of Congress aren't just a thousand times more effective than one call—they're priceless. And Tea Party Patriots now has the ability to generate not just thousands, but hundreds of thousands of phone calls.

Third, when all else fails, the Tea Party movement has shown it knows how to use the power of direct democracy to replace lawmakers who don't support its core values of fiscal responsibility, constitutionally limited government, and free markets.

We know that if we wait until the November 2012 general elections, we'll lose the battle. Because of the way congressional districts are drawn (in many cases, by the Republican and Democratic parties themselves), representatives have very safe seats. Even given the turmoil of the 2010 elections, almost 90 percent of incumbent members of Congress were reelected. But the country got an idea of what's possible. We want to remind each elected official that he or she could be the next Senator Bob Bennett, who lost his 2010 primary because he failed to listen to the voters who sent him to D.C. in the first place.

So the third pillar of the Tea Party strategy to keep our elected officials in line is to make sure that those representatives who don't respond to prodding and pressuring face strong primary opponents. We don't care whether they're Republicans or Democrats. All we care about is whether they believe in our three core values. And given that those are three of the core values of America, we'll have no problem finding qualified citizens to take on their party establishment.

Right now, there are 435 members of the House of Representatives and 33 senators who will have to stand for election in 2012. Some may think their seats are safe. They're wrong. Those who have voted for fiscally irresponsible budgets, resolutions, and policies should be particularly worried.

To those members, though, we tell them that they still have a chance. It's not too late for them to do the right thing. Restore fiscal responsibility, adhere to the Constitution, and embrace the free market, and we'll be your biggest advocates. But if you don't, this is what we will do to you:

First, we're going to melt your phones. Remember that the Tea Party has access to many millions of activists, most of whom are just itching to tell their members of Congress what they're doing wrong.

But it's not just your constituents we can activate. Former Speaker of the House Tip O'Neill once quipped that "all politics is local." With the tools we Tea Partiers now have at our disposal, we've turned that maxim on its head.

Yes, we've got members in every congressional district and over 3,500 affiliated state and local groups. But that's not all. When members of Congress aren't properly representing their districts and aren't governing according to constitutional, fiscally responsible principles, with the push of a button, we can make any congressional race in the country a national referendum on the size and scope of government.

Consider the 2010 Senate race in Delaware. Virtually everyone who was paying attention probably still remembers Christine O'Donnell. In an amazing primary victory, she soundly beat veteran establishment politician Mike Castle, 53 to 47 percent. Though she lost in the general election, we'd be willing to wager that more people can now name the loser of that race than the winner. Why? Some might argue that it was because of the Republican candidate's personal foibles. But the reality is that the Delaware Senate race went national. The Tea Party stepped in and told the GOP establishment that business as usual wasn't going to work anymore, and that the people who cared about our Constitution weren't going to let a career politician with a terrible record get elected. At the end of the day, the election results were secondary; far more important was the message we sent to the establishment: the political world has changed.

Politicians who think that they only represent one state or one small area of that state are just wrong. While they need to be strong advocates for the views of their constituents, they also have a responsibility to the United States of America as a whole. Politics should no longer be about the people from Delaware taking money from the taxpayers of Massachusetts, or the farmers of Iowa getting subsidized by the manufacturers of Michigan.

We understand that some politicians will be reluctant to abandon their Washington-knows-best ways—in part because they're surrounded by the culture of corruption that exists inside the Beltway. But after we raise the profile on their races, our next step is to send activists to members' district offices. A hundred Tea Party activists at a strip mall in Sheboygan can go a long way toward making sure the voice of liberty is heard.

Next comes local advertising. Billboards. Direct mail. Training local citizens to be experts in pointing out which members are ignoring the will of the people and how, then sending them to knock on doors and stand in front of supermarkets to explain why a particular member of Congress is failing the country.

Law professor and Instapundit blogger Glen Reynolds titled his book *An Army of Davids*. It's subtitled, *How Markets and Technology Empower Ordinary People to Beat Big Media, Big Government and Other Goliaths*. This perfectly describes the Tea Party movement, which through a combination of technology, passion, and patriotism can bring down the Goliaths in government who refuse to hear our message. The Davids of the Tea Party movement know that it's time to restore America to greatness, and they understand that they are the ones who will make it happen.

We have at our disposal tools that no other mass movement has ever had. We can do tele-town hall meetings, where dozens, or hundreds, or thousands of activists come together to learn about what our government is doing, to educate each other and to make plans. We can use Twitter, and Facebook, and LinkedIn to instantly share the truth with our activists. We have Flip cameras that for less than a hundred dollars will allow virtually anyone to shoot professional-quality video, so that citizens can see for themselves what politicians, lobbyists, and special interests are doing, and decide whose side they're on.

In the past, with their paid staff, their free mail, and their access to the mainstream media, professional politicians had a huge advantage over We the People. That era is over. Politicians, take note: lying is no longer a viable reelection strategy. Sooner or later—and in most cases, it will be much, much sooner—people will know the truth.

When Democratic state legislators in Wisconsin fled to Illinois in an attempt to allow unions to hold the public hostage through the collective bargaining process, Tea Partiers made their whereabouts public within hours. And when a member of Congress accused peaceful protestors of uttering reprehensible racial slurs, individuals could watch the video of the event from multiple sources and make up their own minds without any ideological filter.

In politics, sunshine truly is the best disinfectant. As we saw with the fight over Obamacare, the only way that legislation passed was by hiding what was in it from the general public. In the past, congressional leadership could slip in as many "Cornhusker Kickbacks" and "Louisiana Purchases" as they thought necessary to pass some monstrosity of federal legislation. That's no longer the case.

It's no exaggeration to suggest that as soon as important pieces of legislation are introduced, hundreds or thousands of Tea Partiers will be reading the bills line by line to see what the politicians are actually trying to push through. Politicians like Nancy Pelosi will no longer be able to hide their actions from the general public. As we saw in the 2010 elections in the House of Representatives, the longest they can manipulate the public without paying an electoral price is two years.

We've sent the message loud and clear: any bill that Congress "has to pass" so that the general public "can see what is in it" will result in catastrophic consequences for any member who votes in the affirmative.

In short, the Tea Party is a perpetual pressure group. We're millions strong, and we work for free, because we care about this country and want to see America do the right thing. If you're a member of Congress remember this: when you're sleeping, when your staff is on vacation, while you're at your fund-raiser, some Tea Party member will be holding you accountable.

And that's why we're going to win.

In the next chapter, we'll talk about some of the specific reforms we'd like to see in order to begin to take power away from Washington and restore it to the people of America.

# ★ 5 ★

# The Political Pathway to Liberty

*If ever time should come, when vain and aspiring men
shall possess the highest seats in Government, our
country will stand in need of its experienced patriots to
prevent its ruin.*

—SAMUEL ADAMS

ON SEPTEMBER 17, 1787, at the Pennsylvania statehouse in Philadelphia, the delegates to the Constitutional Convention affixed their
signatures to the document that would create the greatest nation in
the world. As Benjamin Franklin left the statehouse, one of the anxious citizens assembled outside, a Mrs. Powel of Philadelphia, asked
him what sort of government those assembled inside had decided
upon. "A Republic," replied Franklin, "if you can keep it."

America is indeed a Republic, and a unique one at that. According
to our Constitution, the people themselves retain sovereignty over
their government, and while the people can delegate power to elected
officials, those officials must make political decisions within rigidly
circumscribed guidelines. All powers not specifically granted to the
federal government are reserved to the states and the people.

The Founding Fathers understood the vagaries of human nature
and designed a structure for our government that would protect the
citizens of America not only from the unchecked power exercised by
a king or a queen, but also from the tyranny of pure majority rule,
which is the result of pure democracy.

In theory, the Constitution is such a powerful document that we could elect a hundred Al Frankens to the Senate, and 435 Nancy Pelosis to the House of Representatives, and they wouldn't be able to do much permanent damage. In practice, however, humans always tend to want more power for themselves. So we ignore the original intent of the Founders at great risk. Some departures, of course, have served only to adapt to a world the Founders never envisioned. Those changes and the amendments that empowered more citizens to participate in the political process have been purely good.

Others, however, specifically those that ceded more power to the government, that altered the fundamental balance between the federal government and the states, or that undermined the principle of *one person, one vote* have served only to undermine the principle that government should be a servant of the people, not its master.

As we look into the future, it is important never to lose sight of mistakes we made in the past. And at no time in American history did we make more mistakes to upset the delicate balance of power between the people and their government than in 1913.

In that year, the country made three critical mistakes that have had repercussions for nearly a hundred years. First, it ratified the Sixteenth Amendment to the Constitution. Second, it ratified the Seventeenth Amendment. And third, it departed from one critical practice that had served us well for the previous 120 years of American history and fixed the number of U.S. representatives at 435. In this chapter we'll look at these three mistakes, explain why they were so bad for America, and then lay out our vision for *how* America should make political decisions over the next forty years.

## THE FIRST MISTAKE OF 1913
### (THE SIXTEENTH AMENDMENT)

The first great mistake of 1913 consists of only one line of text, but what a line: "The Congress shall have power to lay and collect taxes on incomes, from whatever source derived, without apportionment among the several States, and without regard to any census or enumeration."

That's right. In 1913, the Constitution was changed to allow the federal government to institute a permanent individual income tax. If you're reading this book, you don't need any more explanation on this point. As John Marshall, chief justice of the Supreme Court, said succinctly in 1819, the power to tax truly does involve the power to destroy. Importantly, along with the Seventeenth Amendment, this gave the federal government a complete and direct relationship with its citizens, bypassing the states and breaking the fragile balance of power created by the framers.

## THE SECOND MISTAKE OF 1913
### (THE SEVENTEENTH AMENDMENT)

James Madison, who would go on to become the fourth president of our nation, ultimately wasn't too concerned about the number of representatives in the House leading to a dangerous concentration of power. Writing again in Federalist 55, he said: "The true question to be decided then is, whether the smallness of the number [of representatives], as a temporary regulation, be dangerous to the public liberty . . . ? [J]udging from the circumstances now before us, and from the probable state of them within a moderate period of time, I must pronounce that the liberties of America cannot be unsafe in the number of hands proposed by the federal Constitution."

Was this a misjudgment on his part? Or were there other factors at play? Madison relied on two key factors in ultimately deciding that the number of legislators wasn't particularly important.

First, he relied on his faith in the American people. Madison found it difficult to believe that the American people would elect—and then reelect—any number of politicians who would be inclined toward "tyranny or treachery" or that any member of Congress would "betray the solemn trust committed to them." (Madison had obviously never met Nancy Pelosi, Arlen Specter, or Bob Bennett.)

But more important than the goodwill of Americans, Madison relied upon the balance of power between the federal government and the states themselves in making this assessment: "I am unable to conceive that the State legislatures, which must feel so many motives to watch, and which possess so many means of counteracting, the federal legislature, would fail either to detect or to defeat a conspiracy of the latter against the liberties of their common constituents."

Unfortunately, the primary mechanism through which the state legislatures could serve as a check on the power of the federal government changed—in 1913. In that year, the Seventeenth Amendment to the U.S. Constitution was ratified, forever tipping the balance of power toward Washington, and leading to a hundred-year march toward federal tyranny.

For those of you who, as Rush Limbaugh says, went to public school, let us explain (and don't feel bad, this was news to us as well): The Seventeenth Amendment provided for the direct election of U.S. senators by the people of each state. Prior to that year, each state legislature was responsible for selecting U.S. senators. The effect of such selection was powerful; the Senate, fully half of the legislative branch, had a great incentive to ensure that as much power as possible continued to be exercised at the state level. Senators were sent to Washington, D.C., to protect the states' interest from overreach and intrusion by the federal government. And in the event the senators failed to do so, or acted against the interest of their own state, they were unceremoniously called home and replaced by someone who would work on behalf of the state.

Since 1913, however, rather than protecting the states from the influence of the federal government, the Senate has had a vested interest in accumulating more and more power for itself, and for Washington. In practice, we've seen numerous senators—most recently (and egregiously) Chuck Schumer and Harry Reid—who press for policies that will harm their constituents and potentially bankrupt their state governments, as long as those policies have a tendency to increase their own or their political party's power.

Changes that subjugate state governments to the will of Washington, D.C., impose unconstitutional mandates on the states, and increase the power of the federal government are bad things for the Republic.

Much of American progress has depended on the dynamism that has come from the introduction of new and better ideas, which are dramatically more likely to arise and be tried at the state level. (And in an ideal world—one in which politicians listen to the electorate—the ones that prove to be disastrous failures, like Massachusetts' health insurance experiment, are less likely to be implemented nationwide.) Much of this state autonomy was lost when senators began to stand for direct election.

We believe it's critical to allow the states to be the laboratories of democracy that the Supreme Court justice Louis Brandeis envisioned them to be (though Brandeis himself was no Tea Partier). The notion that ideas can be tried at the state level, and if they work, be incorporated into the source code of the American system, is integral to the progress of American democracy, and one of the first and strongest examples of open-source politics to appear in the world.

Another great example of the importance of the fifty-state laboratory is in education. Education initiatives vary greatly by state, though the federal Department of Education is hard at work spending tax dollars to make sure all our schools are equally terrible. Currently there is a great diversity of results among state education systems. Spending, structure, parental choice, charter schools; all are inherently local or state issues and offer a chance for us to examine what works and doesn't work in practice.

The centralized programs and standards pushed upon the states by the Department of Education have done nothing to improve the educational outcomes of our children. In fact, the more education authority has become centralized in this vast D.C. bureaucracy, the worse the measurable results have become.

According to the HSLDA (Home School Legal Defense Association):

Since the 1979 inception of the U.S. Department of Education, its spending has grown astronomically. Excluding expenditures on loans such as higher education loans, the Department spent $14,612 million in 1980, one year after its inception. By 1989, the ED's budget had increased to $18,145 million and grew to $25,832 [million] by 1992. Today, the Department of Ed's outlays continue to grow, reaching $32 billion in 1999 and an estimated $36 billion for the year 2000. The Department's yearly outlay is expected to reach over $47 billion by the year 2005.*

With an annual budget now approaching $36 billion, the ED employs over 5,100 people (89.4% of whom were deemed nonessential during the November 1995 government shutdown). Furthermore, the education-spending rate since the Department's founding has risen three times as fast as non-defense discretionary programs (29.5% versus 7.9%).

Despite the fact that no positive correlation between spending and student performance has been found, Congress continues to fund the Department of Education. And the Department of Education itself represents only 52 percent of federal education funding. Billions of dollars in taxpayer money are wasted through a multitude of other federal agencies and departments as well (see the chart on page 87).

We recognize that some problems appear just too big to be solved at the local level or even the individual state level. In some cases, economies of scale might suggest that a problem should be dealt with on a wider basis. However, such temptation should be avoided at all costs. If it's not constitutional, it shouldn't be done, no matter how tempting. In the case of federal involvement in education, there is no support in the Constitution for such intervention. And coincidentally, the results (total failure despite massive and growing expenditures) also weigh against a vast federal government education bureaucracy.

We hold firm in our opposition to allowing the federal government to take authority over any of these spheres, first because it's against the law. The Constitution *is* the law, contrary to what many politicians would have us believe. And as we've seen time and again, the federal

* http://www.hslda.org/docs/nche.00000270.asp.

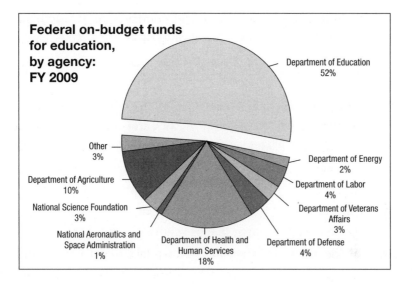

Federal on-budget funds for education, by agency: FY 2009

- Department of Education 52%
- Department of Energy 2%
- Department of Labor 4%
- Department of Veterans Affairs 3%
- Department of Defense 4%
- Department of Health and Human Services 18%
- National Aeronautics and Space Administration 1%
- National Science Foundation 3%
- Department of Agriculture 10%
- Other 3%

government is addicted to power and taxpayer money. Give it an inch, and it will surely take a mile.

## THE THIRD MISTAKE OF 1913

### (THE APPORTIONMENT ACT OF 1913)

The Tea Party movement is a direct response to what seemed to be an inexorable accumulation of power in the hands of our federal government, at the expense of We the People. One president, 100 hundred senators, and 435 members of Congress have more control over our everyday lives than the Founders ever intended, and far more than the American people should stand for. In purely economic terms, the phenomenon is staggering; for years now, Americans have paid more in taxes at all levels than they pay for food, clothing, and shelter—combined!

How did all this power get concentrated in the hands of so few people, and what can we do about it? The Founders understood how important it is to dole out political power to a large number of people. In Federalist 55, for example, James Madison suggested that the provision of the Constitution that dealt with how many members of the House of Representatives there should be was, arguably, *the* most important issue in the entire constitutional debate.

> The number of which the House of Representatives is to consist, forms another and a very interesting point of view, under which this branch of the federal legislature may be contemplated. Scarce any article, indeed, in the whole Constitution seems to be rendered more worthy of attention, by the weight of character and the apparent force of argument with which it has been assailed. The charges exhibited against it are, first, that so small a number of representatives will be an unsafe depositary of the public interests; secondly, that they will not possess a proper knowledge of the local circumstances of their numerous constituents; thirdly, that they will be taken from that class of citizens which will sympathize least with the feelings of the mass of the people, and be most likely to aim at a permanent elevation of the few on the depression of the many; fourthly, that defective as the number will be in the first instance, it will be more and more disproportionate, by the increase of the people, and the obstacles which will prevent a correspondent increase of the representatives.

Any Tea Partier would understand Madison's fears, because they are current reality. On February 13, 1788, the framers of the Constitution worried that Congress would eventually be made up of a small number of elitists who would be entirely divorced from the problems their constituents faced back at home. In 2011, their fears have come to pass. Madison, it seems, was in possession of a crystal ball.

We dealt with this very real threat by increasing the total number of congressional districts every ten years after the census from 1793 to 1913. But since 1913, based on congressional passage of the Apportionment Act of 1913, the number of congressional districts has remained fixed at 435, where it still is today. The population of the United States, on the other hand, has increased by more than 200 million people! As a result, we've gone from a system where, at the founding, each member of the House represented 30,000 constituents to one in which, today, the average congressional district numbers nearly 700,000—and the largest is home to more than 900,000.

One lonely voice, crying out among 700,000, is difficult to hear. The expansion of suffrage since the founding, while absolutely critical and the right thing to do, has compounded the mathematical issues that were considered by the framers of the Constitution. Since so many more people are now eligible to vote, each individual voter's voice in electing his or her member of Congress is, proportionally, even harder to hear. The power of the many has been diluted on the ground and concentrated in so few elected officials that it's frightening.

It has become almost impossible for our elected representatives to accurately reflect the wishes of their constituents. Everyone who has ever been to a committee meeting knows how hard it can be for even a small group to agree on something as trivial as the color of party invitations. How can 700,000 people be expected to agree on the sorts of issues Congress is tasked with deciding? The expansion of congressional districts led to the creation of a mushy middle in American politics; only those candidates with largely mild and inoffensive views will be able to attract enough votes to get elected.

As a consequence, the House of Representatives is now populated with the kinds of milquetoasts who are afraid to take the difficult positions necessary to save our country from the impending fiscal catastrophe. We've gone so far as to create a legislative body in which those who believe that we should reduce federal spending by a mere 2.5 percent are looked at as "extremists"! Unless we change that dynamic, and change it quickly, we're heading for insolvency.

We've also set up a system that requires legislators to spend so much time raising money and campaigning for reelection that they have no time to fully debate the consequences of their actions (or, as we've seen in so many cases, actually even *read* legislation before they vote on it). The solution to this problem isn't, as so many on the political left suggest, some kind of campaign finance reform that will, invariably, either trample the First Amendment or further drive us into debt.

The Tea Party knows the reason there is so much money in politics is that there is *so much money* in politics. So we strongly support the most effective form of campaign finance reform there is: a dramatic reduction in the federal budget.

Think about it: when was the last time someone spent thousands of dollars just to be in the same room with you? Unless you're a rock star or one of Eliot Spitzer's "lady friends," it's unlikely that's *ever* happened. Your freezer probably isn't stuffed with $90,000 in cash the way Louisiana congressman William Jefferson's was. Nor is it likely that someone bought your house for $700,000 more than it was worth, offered you a Rolls-Royce, or let you use their yacht for free—all of which happened to California congressman Randy "Duke" Cunningham.

But then again, you didn't have the power to send millions—or billions—of other people's money someone's way. The numbers, once again, are staggering. Under President Obama's 2011 budget proposal, the U.S. government would spend nearly $9 billion for each member of the House of Representatives. That's $9,000 *million* ($9,000,000,000) per congressman. With those kinds of numbers floating around, it's amazing every single one of them isn't crooked.

So what can we do to remedy all of these problems? First, we can, and should, increase the number of congressional districts, which would once again allow individuals to have more of a say in the election of their representatives.

But we don't think that goes far enough. We think the best way to avoid further concentration of power in Washington, D.C., is simple: avoid concentrating power in Washington, D.C. In order to return power to the people, we want to force our representatives to return to the people. That's right. We want to kick Congress out of Washington, D.C.

At the time of the first American Revolution, it's perfectly understandable why Congress had to meet under one roof. Real-time debate and exchange of ideas are essential to the work of efficient government. But in the context of the second American Revolution, there's no longer any need for every member of Congress to be in the Capitol building to participate in debate or to cast a vote. (Plus, if we significantly expand the number of representatives, from a purely logistical perspective not every representative will even be able to fit!)

Instead, we propose a system in which senators and representatives live and work most of the time in their home districts and travel to Washington, D.C., only infrequently—at most once or twice a year. The technology exists to allow everything that a representative currently does in Washington to be done equally well from his or her home district. There's no need for a twenty-first-century legislature to be constrained by eighteenth-century technology.

If tens of millions of Americans can telecommute, there's no reason why members of Congress can't attend committee and subcommittee meetings by videoconference. And in a world where we entrust the security of our bank accounts to small plastic cards and four-digit PINs, congressional votes can surely be taken over the Internet. Biometric technology exists to verify anyone's identity regardless of geographic location. And even in the event of some sort of fraud, a member of Congress can look at the posted record of his or her vote on any given bill and say, "Wait a minute—I didn't vote yes on funding for that teapot museum!"

Instituting a virtual Congress will have a variety of benefits. First, senators and representatives will be able to spend more time in the communities they represent. They'll be surrounded by skeptical constituents, rather than fawning supplicants. And they'll continually have to justify any political decision they make that's contrary to the will of the voters. In the recent past, we've seen cowardly lawmakers do everything in their power short of joining the federal Witness Protection Program to avoid listening to us.

In 2003, Texas Democratic state legislators fled to Oklahoma to prevent the legislature from voting on a redistricting plan that they opposed, and on which they were going to be outvoted. In 2011, Indiana Democratic state legislators fled the state to Illinois, to prevent the legislature from reaching a quorum to vote on legislation unfavorable to public employee unions (who, not coincidentally, happened to be some of their biggest donors). And, most famously, also in 2011, a group of fourteen Wisconsin Democratic legislators fled the state (also to Illinois) to avoid a legislative quorum for a vote on newly elected Republican governor Walker's Budget Repair Plan, also opposed by the public employee unions. All of these legislators, fleeing their states to prevent the legislature from enacting the will of the people as expressed by duly elected representatives, represent a disturbing trend.

And in the summer of 2009, as the Tea Party movement was really coming to a boil, as the "Outside the Beltway" blog put it, Democratic lawmakers avoided constituents outraged at their support of Obamacare by . . . simply avoiding their constituents. Members of Congress eschewed traditional town-hall-style meetings for carefully planned and scripted photo-ops with no question-and-answer sessions, afraid that Tea Partiers with Flip cameras would expose their hypocrisy on YouTube for all the world to see. Those who did hold town hall meetings often removed the schedules from their congressional Web pages, thus attempting to hold "private" or "secret" town halls. They were generally outed by angry Tea Partiers, but the intent of the elected officials was obvious: avoid their constituents at all costs. This behavior continues, with representatives holding a record low number of town hall events during their August 2011 recess. Not exactly the picture of "representation" intended by the Founders.

To borrow a phrase from the protestors in Madison, Wisconsin, this is *not* what democracy looks like! But members of a virtual or eCongress who spend the majority of their time living and working in their districts in West Windsor, New Jersey, or Troy, Ohio, or Newton, Massachusetts, can't hide from their constituents forever. Sooner or later, they'll go to their churches, synagogues, or mosques, or to the grocery store, or to the gas station—and they should be prepared to get either an earful or a "way to go!" The Founders and all early members of the House of Representatives were closely connected to and integrated within their own, small communities. They spent the majority of their time living and working in their districts, close to the people and concerns they would be representing in Congress.

That's the nature of being a representative; being closely tied to the people and their concerns. It's an important piece intended as a safeguard by the Founders, and it has unfortunately been stripped from our government.

The virtual Congress will have countless other benefits as well. Given the precarious financial straits our country is in, it's likely to save money. Members won't have to travel between their home districts and Washington, D.C., as much; nor will they have to maintain two separate staffs. They won't have to maintain two separate residences, either. We look forward to giving them a pay cut that takes all of this into account.

But the two biggest benefits of a virtual Congress are structural. No longer will our nation's lawmakers be a captive audience for lobbyists and special interests. The way it stands now, every trade association, labor union, and interest group can plunk its headquarters down in Washington, D.C., and be assured nearly full-time access to our politicians. If you, on the other hand, want to express your concerns directly, you have to drive or fly a long distance (unless you live in the District of Columbia or close to it) and make it past a phalanx of staff, lobbyists, and big-money donors—provided you can get a meeting with your senator or congressional representative at all.

It's time to once again level the playing field. *Constituents* should be the ones with full-time access to their members of Congress, and lobbyists should be the ones forced to stand with their hats in their hands in order to gain access. Without access to our representatives, democracy does not work. The problem is even worse than you imagine. If you've ever tried to attend a congressional committee meeting in Washington, D.C., when controversial legislation was being debated, it's likely you came away disappointed. You probably couldn't even get in the door because the room was packed with lawyers and lobbyists.

How did those lobbyists get in the room? Did they get there early and wear out the leather of their Gucci loafers like teenagers standing in line to buy tickets for a rock concert? Of course not. Washington, D.C., lobbyists are too important to stand in line.

They pay people to do that for them. Really.

We know how absurd this sounds to people who live in the real world, but the Washington, D.C., standing-in-line industry is growing by leaps and bounds. (In fact, it might be one of the only bright spots in our dreadful economy.) The going price for line standers? About $40 an hour. But that's peanuts to lobbyists who charge $1,000 an hour or $25,000-a-month retainers to beg Congress for millions of your tax dollars.

More important than reducing the influence of special interests, though, is the effect that allowing elected officials to work closer to home would have on the pool of people who might be willing to run for office. At present, many of those who are drawn to politics are those who appreciate the glitz, the glitter, and the power that's concentrated in Washington, D.C. ("They're paying to stand in line to hear me talk about tax policy!")

Many regular folks like us would make fantastic public servants yet wouldn't serve if their lives depended on it. But if we allow them to stay in their neighborhoods, close to their friends and their families, surrounded by people who share the values they were raised with, we're likely to see candidates who share *our* views.

It's time for power to come back to the people.

If you think the idea of a virtual Congress is far-fetched, you might be surprised to know that it already has support in the current Congress. The freshman congressman Steve Pearce from New Mexico introduced just such a proposal in 2010. He highlights all of the above benefits and raises two other excellent points. Under a virtual Congress system, cash-strapped local newspapers could afford to "attend" critical debates and votes, and report the news in a manner consistent with their community values. In addition, congressional policy staffers are almost exclusively located in Washington and rarely come from the districts they are hired to represent. With a virtual Congress, policy staffers could be hired who reside in the district and who have ties to the district. As the legislative process has become more and more complicated, members of Congress have been forced to rely heavily on these staffers to make key decisions on legislation. The way things stand now, they're more or less a permanent Washington fixture, who spend much more time meeting with lobbyists than with constituents. As the longtime conservative activist and patriot Morton Blackwell, president and founder of the Leadership Institute, is often fond of pointing out, "Personnel *is* policy"; replacing Washington staff with smart, local staff will once again tilt the balance of power to individuals.

The machinery for implementing a virtual Congress is already in the works.

## INTERSTATE COMPACTS

In addition to having the senators appointed by the state legislatures, the Founders had another mechanism for allowing the states to control their own destinies: *interstate compacts*. An interstate compact is any agreement that's entered into between two or more states. A compact is equivalent to a contract that's made between individuals, where each party has its own responsibilities and benefits accordingly.

These compacts are actually older than the U.S. Constitution. There were nine compacts in effect before the thirteen colonies became the United States of America, and four more were part of the Articles of Confederation. The Constitution itself recognizes the concept; according to Article I, Section 10, "No State shall, without the Consent of Congress . . . enter into any Agreement of Compact with another State."

The law with regard to compacts has evolved since the passage of the Constitution, and the Supreme Court now agrees that states may enter into compacts even without the approval of Congress, as long as they don't infringe upon an area over which the federal government clearly has supremacy.

On issues as diverse as transportation infrastructure and environmental protection, we believe that rather than allowing the federal government to take over, states, working together, can better address these problems. The closer that decisions can be made to the people, the better those decisions will be. And when the people making decisions are close to home, they are more accountable for the decisions they make. Interstate compacts bring decision making home to the people.

Until now, interstate compacts have been used for a variety of purposes, from regulating water rights and waterways to the interstate transfer of prisoners and foster children. Few had heard of them until the recent creation and promotion of the Health Care Compact. With the advent of Obamacare, and the federal government's continuing push to centralize and control health care, we realized that we needed a creative way to return to the people the authority over their health-care decisions.

There's no area where the federal government has so egregiously outstripped its authority more than health care. It's clear, from reading the Constitution that the federal government doesn't have the authority to regulate health care at all. So how should we deal with this issue?

We believe that an issue as large as health care is best addressed through interstate compacts. That's why we support the Health Care Compact, which returns the authority over health care (and the money) to the states, so that states can craft their own solution, giving us the brilliant, fifty-state laboratory to find out what really works.

Interstate compacts have the potential to return power to the states in a variety of areas—such as education and environmental regulation—where the federal government has usurped state authority. And fundamentally, interstate compacts are about who decides. We believe that it's better for the people to decide as locally as possible.

We also believe that interstate compacts are an idea whose time has once again come for several reasons. First, and most important, they allow for the enforcement of governmental authority where it legally resides, instead of unconstitutionally in the federal government. Second, compacts are, by nature, less rigid and bureaucratic than other governmental structures. If a state is having a problem with a particular provision of a compact, it can change the way it implements that provision without first obtaining the approval of its compact partners.

As the Cleveland Tea Party Patriots point out in their Frequently Asked Questions about health-care compacts: Who's better at providing effective transportation infrastructure? Your state department of transportation or Amtrak?

Devolving power to lower levels of government adds accountability to the process. Many a mayor has seen his or her reelection threatened by an inadequate response to a snowstorm. (Just think about what would happen if the federal Department of Transportation were responsible for snow removal in New York City.) Why do some people think that our schools should be controlled by the Department of Education? Local education managed by a bureaucrat in Washington, D.C., lacks local accountability.

Health care, in particular, is the perfect subject to be addressed by an interstate compact. Any industry that represents one-sixth of the American economy is simply too large for bureaucrats in Washington to oversee effectively. In the same way that centralized planners in Japan, or China, or the Soviet Union were unable to direct large swaths of their economies effectively, so, too, is the federal government unable to manage a problem as complex as the health-care problem in America today.

Health-care compacts themselves don't impose a one-size-fits-all approach on any state. They allow each individual state to choose what solution it believes is best for its citizens. Will some states implement systems that aren't compatible with the Tea Party movement's core values of fiscal responsibility, free markets, and constitutionally limited government? Of course. Are we okay with that? Absolutely. Power to the people.

Legislators and governors who have no sense of fiscal responsibility or faith in free markets will likely use these interstate compacts as an excuse to expand their power in the way the legislatures in Massachusetts and Tennessee have already done. But given that the alternative is the very real prospect of the socialization of the nation's health-care system at a national level, we do not believe that the citizens of fiscally responsible states who value the free market should continue to be held hostage by the Nancy Pelosis, Harry Reids, and Barack Obamas of the world.

What might the results of the passage of the Health Care Compact look like in individual states?

Some states may choose to implement a European-style, single-payer health-care system, where that state either utilizes its existing tax revenues or institutes a new tax and uses the subsequent proceeds to cover the cost of medical care for all of its citizens, taking private insurance companies out of the equation entirely.

Other states could decide to more or less fully privatize health care for their citizens, creating some hybrid system of health savings accounts, traditional insurance, and everything in between. Under this scenario, it's likely the states or the interstate compact authority itself will provide some level of catastrophic-care insurance for those citizens whose medical needs are far above average. Otherwise, individuals would be allowed to choose what sort of medical care is appropriate for themselves. Some might choose to pay for all of their medical expenses directly out of pocket. Others might choose to purchase high-deductible insurance plans and pay for routine care directly. Some risk-averse families and individuals might choose to pay more for plans that are similar to prepaid health care than what is traditionally thought of as insurance. It's likely that under this scenario, the states that have entered into the compact will provide some level of subsidized care for the poor or indigent, perhaps by providing "health stamps" that function in the health-care arena the way food stamps function to meet basic nutritional needs for low-income recipients.

Some states may contract all health care out to HMOs (health maintenance organizations) or ACOs (accountable care organizations), either for low-income residents or for the elderly, in a system that would effectively replace Medicare and Medicaid.

Other compacts may choose a solution that looks nothing like any of the above.

The point is that imposing the same health-care solution on states as diverse as New York, West Virginia, California, and Texas is likely to have catastrophic results. Under these compacts, however, the people of Texas can determine what kind of health care they would like—

and are willing to pay for—and the people of New York can do the same. And in the event one state's system seems to be working much better or costing much less to achieve the same results, we guarantee that the mechanisms of open-source politics will make sure that voters in states that are facing higher costs or worse results know about it, and can pressure their politicians to reform business as usual, leave the compact they're in and enter into a more successful compact, or try another solution that seems likely to achieve better results.

Though many thought the idea of using an interstate compact to free the states to manage their own health care was somehow "fringe" or "radical," through the collective wisdom of the Tea Party movement across the country, we knew better. As of this writing four states have now passed the Health Care Compact: Georgia, Oklahoma, Missouri, and Texas. It has support and is working its way through the legislatures of many more states. Once enough states pass the compact so that it reaches critical mass (between 20 to 30), we'll move to the next phase, which is presenting it to Congress for approval (though it's legally debatable whether such approval is even necessary).

We anticipate that when the Health Care Compact is in place, it will be easier for Americans to vote with their feet. If one state is so beholden to special interests that it uses the issue of health care to redistribute wealth or enrich favored constituencies at the expense of the general public, citizens can move to another state much more easily than they could move to another country.

If you are interested in learning more about the Health Care Compact, you can do so at http://www.heathcarecompact.org.

## WHAT HAPPENED TO CHECKS AND BALANCES?

The three mistakes of 1913 have served to undermine the strongest principle the Founders put into place to restrain the government's natural tendencies to expand its own power: the system of checks and balances.

While most of us are familiar with the concept of checks and balances from our high school civics lessons, the Founders would be shocked at the extent to which each branch of government—executive, legislative, and judicial—has overstepped its role as dictated both in law and in our founding documents. In chapter 8, we'll talk more about how the courts in particular have exceeded their authority, but for now, it's important to remember what powers are supposed to be wielded by the president and the executive branch, and which are specifically the province of Congress.

According to the Constitution, the president holds all the executive power; that is, he is ultimately responsible for implementing the laws that Congress passes. The president serves as commander in chief of the armed forces, has the power to sign treaties with foreign nations (but only after they are approved by a supermajority of the Senate), appoints judicial officials (who, again, must be confirmed by the Senate), and provides the ultimate check against the abuse of the judiciary's authority in criminal matters by having the authority to pardon anyone convicted of a federal crime.

Congress, in contrast, has the power to tax, and to spend, and is the *only* body in the federal government that, by law, is responsible for making laws (though the president has the authority to veto them; in which case a two-thirds majority vote of both houses can still impose any constitutional law it chooses, even over the president's objection). Congress also is the only branch of government that has the ability to declare war on another country, to impeach federal officials (including the president), and to try officials who are impeached. In addition, it oversees the executive branch to ensure that its operations are lawful and proper.

It's easy to see how the executive and legislative branches of government have exceeded their constitutional role, particularly over the past fifty years. In particular, the president has accumulated more and more power, overriding several critical congressional functions and taking power even farther away from the people.

This phenomenon has taken place most strikingly in two broad areas.

First, Congress has all but ceded its exclusive power to declare war to the executive branch. Legislators have entered into a "wink-and-a-nod" relationship with the president that absolves them of any responsibility for making decisions over when our troops are to be sent in harm's way. For members of Congress, it's a no-lose proposition: If military action goes well, they can take the credit for not standing in the president's way. If military action goes poorly, it becomes a weapon for opposition members of Congress to wield against the administration. This practice must stop. Congress must once again regain its role as the only branch of government that can declare war against another sovereign nation, regardless of what impact making that decision has on individual members' political fortunes.

Second, in entirely too many areas, Congress has ceded its ability to make laws to independent agencies of the federal government. And the problem is getting worse each year.

While the first independent agency, the Interstate Commerce Commission, was not created until 1887, the number of these bodies began to expand in the early part of the twentieth century, when the Federal Reserve System (established in, yes, 1913), the Food and Drug Administration, and the Federal Trade Commission were created. Then the Securities and Exchange Commission, the National Labor Relations Board, and the Federal Communications Commission came into being during the presidency of Franklin Roosevelt. And in the 1970s, another set of independent agencies was named: specifically, the Occupational Safety and Health Administration, the Environmental Protection Agency, the Consumer Product Safety Commission, and the Federal Energy Regulatory Commission.

The greatest threat to free markets and constitutionally limited government now comes from these agencies. The rules they make (we know them as *regulations*) have the force of federal law. Rather than allowing the Constitution to function the way it was intended, where the executive and legislative branches serve as a check on each other's power, these independent agencies have become stealthy mechanisms for increasing the power of the government to intrude in the everyday lives of individuals and businesses. By delegating legislative authority to these agencies, Congress can avoid going on the record about critical issues.

Recent presidents (specifically George W. Bush and Barack Obama) have used the independent agencies as a way to implement a legislative agenda in the face of congressional opposition. Nearly every agency has put forth a major policy proposal that would dramatically reduce our liberty. For instance:

- Despite Congress clearly rejecting the idea, the Environmental Protection Agency is trying to foist President Obama's cap-and-trade carbon tax on the American People.
- The Federal Communications Commission has, in violation of its statutory authority, attempted to impose so-called net neutrality rules on the Internet.
- The National Labor Relations Board is currently trying to undo decades of democratic tradition in union elections by imposing "card-check" provisions for certifying labor unions and changing the way votes are counted in union elections.

The newest independent agency is among the most frightening of them all. The Bureau of Consumer Protection was created by 2010's Dodd-Frank "financial reform" bill. It is a vehicle to exercise nearly unchecked authority over our nation's financial industry.

In short, these independent agencies have evolved into unaccountable bureaucracies that are taking over our nation's political decision-making process. When we ask, "Who decides?" the answer should always be, first and foremost, "the people." No decision critical to our country's future should be made by faceless government officials beholden to no one.

How can we solve this problem?

In the long term, the solution lies with the courts. We must ensure that the federal judiciary exercises its power to stop the executive and legislative branches from overstepping their constitutionally delegated authority. In the near future, we must exercise our power at the ballot box to vote out members of Congress who propose new and unnecessary bureaucracies. There's also a good structural solution that will allow us to force our politicians to be accountable for more of their decisions.

The REINS (Regulations from the Executive in Need of Scrutiny) Act, introduced by Senator Jim DeMint in the Senate, and by Congressman Geoff Davis in the House, would require an up-or-down vote by Congress on any rule made by an agency that (a) is likely to have an annual impact on the economy of $100 million or more; (b) will result in a major increase in costs or prices to consumers; or (c) will have a significant impact on the economy. At the time of this writing, the REINS Act, like most things in D.C. based on common sense, appears to be stuck in committees.

Passing this legislation would put members of Congress on notice that the voters are watching them, and will bring decision making one step closer to the people. Members of Congress will have to stand up and support or oppose every major decision that has the force of law, so that their constituents can applaud them for it—or punish them at the ballot box.

∾

These are just some of the suggestions Tea Party members have come up with on how to implement structural changes to our government that will facilitate a return to the core values of free markets, fiscal responsibility, and constitutionally limited government. We urge you to share your best ideas with us on the Web at www.teapartypatriots .org/40yearplan.

Other Tea Partiers are hard at work thinking about these issues. Dick Morris, political commentator and strategist, was kind enough to share the following suggestions in the final section of this chapter; we hope you find them inspirational.

# PROTECTING FREEDOM:
# STRUCTURAL CHANGES FOR
# AMERICAN GOVERNMENT

## BY DICK MORRIS

Except for presidential term limits and specifications of what to do in the event of presidential disability, the U.S. Constitution has remained essentially unchanged for one hundred years. Ever since the four amendments of the early twentieth century (income tax, women's suffrage, direct election of senators, and prohibition), it has not been altered significantly.

But as we have watched the federal government grow in size to become the behemoth it is, we must admit that our governing charter is not doing a good job of fulfilling the original intent of its framers: to limit the power of the central government. Instead, the interstate commerce clause has been so expanded and the Tenth Amendment and the contract clause so shrunken that virtually anything Congress wants to do is constitutionally permissible.

Certainly structural changes are needed if we are to strengthen the foundation of our democracy and limit the growth of government power. Some of these changes are constitutional and some statutory, and still others relate to changes in the very process of amending our Constitution.

## TERM LIMITS FOR BUREAUCRATS

The leading threat to our freedom in the world today is not communism or even Islamic extremism. It is bureaucratism—the rule of appointed officials over our lives.

Japan and Europe are totally run by appointed bureaucrats who have virtually unlimited control over all aspects of their economies. Global entities like the International Monetary Fund (IMF) and the G-20 group of nations aspire to exert similar sway over our own economy. But here at home, the power of the regulator—the entrenched bureaucrat—is increasingly exercising an almost dictatorial power over every aspect of our commerce and our lives.

The very concept of government by experts has come to replace governance by democratically elected officials as the desideratum of public administration. Wars are left to the generals. The economy is run by the Federal Reserve. Every aspect of our lives is controlled by the interpretations and actions of agents of the Internal Revenue Service. OSHA, EPA, the NLRB, the FCC, the FAA, the FTC, and the FDA exercise life-and-death power over their respective industries and, more and more, over all of us.

Bureaucracies become inbred, hidebound, rigid, and self-perpetuating. They lose touch with the fabric of the areas they regulate and march only to the beat of their own institutional drummer.

The Congress should pass a law establishing term limits for all federal employees earning more than $100,000 per year (adjusted for inflation). No appointed official should be permitted to serve at that level for more than eight years. This law should apply, as well, to congressional and committee staffs.

We need to preserve the turnover vital to venting these agencies with the breeze of new people and new ideas from outside their offices and halls. Such term limits must, of course, be accompanied by strict prohibitions against lobbying their former agencies for at least three years so that term limits for bureaucrats do not invite a revolving door between the regulator and the regulated.

## SINGLE-ISSUE CONSTITUTIONAL CONVENTIONS

The framers no more intended for Congress to control the amending process for the Constitution than they meant for the Continental Congress to control the ratification procedure for the document they wrote. They specified that Congress and the state legislatures control only one gateway to amending our basic document. They intended that a constitutional convention—without the participation of Congress—also be able to amend the Constitution. The constitutional convention was intended as a check and balance on the power of Congress, just as the exclusion of the president from the amending process was seen as a limitation on executive power.

But no amendment has ever been passed through a convention. Those who have considered such an approach are rightly fearful that an open-ended convention could produce changes that would alter the very framework that guarantees us freedom. Who wants a group of politicians to have the power to repeal the First Amendment? Or to mess with our system of elected representation?

More likely, any convention would get so tangled up in such issues as abortion, gay marriage, and gun control that it would never be able to address anything else.

So we need a constitutional amendment to change the process of amending the constitution to permit single-issue constitutional conventions to be called where only certain topics may be considered. For example, we clearly need to limit the terms of our congressional representatives and senators. While the vast majority of our country has called for such a change, the vested interests of the incumbents of both houses of Congress have frustrated it. A new amending procedure would allow voters to bypass Congress and hold conventions without fearing damage to the fundamental fabric of our governing institutions.

## EMPOWER STATE LEGISLATURES

The men who wrote our Constitution were clearly deeply concerned to protect the power of states from encroachment by Washington. While federal supremacy was essential to uniting the states into one country, the framers checked and balanced it by specifying that the Senate would be chosen by state legislatures while only the House of Representatives would be elected directly by the voters. The Seventeenth Amendment changed that by requiring that the Senate, as well as the House, be directly elected. This change threw away a key check and balance in the original document and left state governments powerless to limit the growth of federal power.

It would be a serious mistake to repeal the Seventeenth Amendment and return the power to choose the Senate to the state legislatures. We need more democracy in our nation, not less. We deliberate long and hard over senatorial elections, but most of us don't even know who our state senators and house members are. We need to continue direct election.

But we do need to vindicate the desires of the framers to bolster the power of states in the face of an ever-growing federal government. Just list all the powers that Washington has taken away from the states: bank regulation, pension protection, usury limitations, environmental protections, labor standards, food and drug purity, to name a few. A parallel system of federal criminal justice and courts has arisen more powerful than its state counterparts.

We need to restore the balance intended by the original Constitution. We need a constitutional amendment providing that if three-quarters of the states pass a law repealing or modifying a federal statute, their change is binding on the federal government. A three-quarters majority is difficult to achieve. It would require thirty-seven governors and seventy-four legislative chambers (unless we include Nebraska, which has but one) to agree on a policy. But if they feel strongly enough about the law in question, they should be able to change or repeal it.

## MODIFY THE FILIBUSTER

In the nineteenth and twentieth centuries, the right of unlimited debate in the U.S. Senate was regularly used by racist southern senators to deny rights to African Americans and others, protecting a legal system of American apartheid. Liberals and fair-minded people modified the power of the filibuster by reducing the requirement for cloture—to end debate and force a vote—from the original two-thirds majority to a mere sixty votes. This change made it possible to pass vital civil rights legislation in 1964 and 1965 that ended our domestic apartheid.

But as the partisanship of the last thirty years has asserted itself, the filibuster has become a routine part of the legislative process. The requirement for passing a law is a majority of the House, 60 percent of the Senate, and approval of the president. It is perilous to depart from the fundamental idea of majority rule, vital to any democracy. Courts and constitutions exist to protect the rights of the minority, and supermajorities should only be required for the most important pieces of legislation.

The following changes would restrict the power of the filibuster and restore the principle of majority rule to our government.

- No filibuster should be permitted for judicial nominations below the level of the Supreme Court. We cannot allow petty partisan politics to paralyze our federal courts by keeping them perpetually short of judges because one side or the other wants to block confirmation in the hopes of winning the next election.
- When a group of senators undertake a filibuster, make them carry it through. The current system is one of the virtual filibuster. If the majority leader doesn't have sixty votes, he doesn't call up the bill. This makes the filibuster routine. Instead, anyone who wants to block legislation from consideration and passage by the majority should be required to stand on his or her feet and debate the bill 24/7. The physical toll of such a requirement would guarantee its use only in important cases.
- While the filibuster is in progress, no other legislation should be considered. The buildup of other legislative business and the spectacle of limitless debate will increasingly galvanize the public to oppose the filibuster and demand that Congress move on and do the people's business. But where the filibuster enjoys real popular support, voters will be patient and back the cause.

### REQUIRE SUPERMAJORITIES TO RAISE TAXES

But in some cases, the power of the legislative minority needs to be protected and strengthened. Legislation to raise taxes should require a two-thirds vote of Congress. More than sixty votes should be necessary before we levy taxes on Americans.

As tax credits have multiplied and tax rates for lower-income Americans have dropped, a majority of our citizens pay no income taxes. The refundable child-care credit, the Earned Income Tax Credit, and the expanded personal deduction have all combined with lower tax rates to exempt more than half of us from paying taxes.

On the other end of the political spectrum, 1 percent of us pay 41 percent of the income taxes, and 20 percent of us pay 80 percent.

What is to stop a majority that pays no taxes from endlessly raising taxes on the minority that does? A supermajority requirement would protect us against this economic despotism by those with lower incomes.

## A BALANCED BUDGET AMENDMENT

Every state government is required to balance its budget each year. Only the federal government is allowed to run deficits. As these deficits have grown, so that 40 percent of federal spending is now financed through borrowing, it has fundamentally distorted the U.S. economy and threatens to create a situation in which debt service consumes an unsupportable portion of the federal budget. Only the current environment of near zero interest rates has stopped it from becoming such a burden today. But the global scarcity of capital heralds the day when interest rates return to historic norms. When that happens, Americans will become like the subprime mortgage family, suddenly living in a home they can't afford.

We need an amendment to the Constitution requiring a balanced budget. The amendment should make exceptions for wartime or for other national emergencies. But it should limit the number of consecutive years during which the government may operate at a deficit to ensure that the exemptions are not abused.

Some argue that there is a need for deficit spending during economic downturns. But the abject failure of Keynesian economics to halt the current economic recession demonstrates the fallacy of this approach. We need to require a balanced budget.

## THE LINE-ITEM VETO AND IMPOUNDMENT
## AND EARMARKING

Presidents, nominally in charge of the executive branch of government, have been hampered in exercising their administrative duties by Congress's usurpation of the budgeting process. By not letting presidents veto individual spending items or impound—refuse to spend—sums voted by Congress, we do not let the president run the executive branch. We encourage profligate spending guided by local political needs and the desire for patronage rather than the public good.

We need three changes.

1. Presidents should have the line-item veto to kill specific appropriations passed by Congress.
2. The chief executive should have the authority to impound sums voted by Congress, refusing to spend the money.
3. Earmarks inserted by congressmen and senators should be banned.

These changes will help to restore fiscal responsibility to the federal government and rein in parochial interest group politics.

Together the changes suggested above will give us a more democratic government with greater control at the local and state levels. We will vindicate the vision of the Founders and curb the galloping growth of the federal government.

～

Dick Morris is one among millions of Tea Partiers with a passion for preserving liberty for future generations. While we don't necessarily endorse all of his suggestions, we appreciate his contribution and hope you do as well.

# ★ 6 ★

## The Educational Tea Party

*It is in the interest of tyrants to reduce the people to ignorance and vice. For they cannot live in any country where virtue and knowledge prevail.*

—Samuel Adams

*I say [to my students] what about important people who spoke out about the taxes? A voice says hesitantly, "Samuel Adams?" Another voice counters, "No, John Adams. Sam Adams is the name on my Dad's beer."*

—AMERICAN ELEMENTARY
SCHOOL TEACHER

SOME PEOPLE LOOK at underperforming schools in low-income neighborhoods like Harlem and see poverty. Or skin color. Or broken families. Or worse: statistics.

We see the next generation of Tea Partiers.

This may come as a surprise to the politicians, media, and special interest groups who fixate on race. The irony is that while they falsely paint Tea Partiers as racist, they are practicing a quiet racism of their own, by peddling false notions that children in places like Harlem are "not the same kids, and the families are really troubled, and these young people are dealing with so many issues in their life, we really can't expect them to be able to compete with other children who are growing up in better circumstances."* (As told to Madeleine Sackler, director/producer of "The Lottery" about Harlem charter schools.)

That way of looking at children is worse than racist. It is un-American. And it is precisely that view which has robbed generations of inner-city youth of their right, and opportunity, to pursue the American dream. If we could build the world's greatest nation on other countries' "wretched refuse," we can certainly ensure that every child born within our borders can enjoy a good education.

When the Tea Party movement looks at our fellow Americans—in Harlem or anywhere else in this country—we see historically unique individuals who are endowed by their Creator with the unalienable right to liberty.

Another word for *liberty* is *choice*.

*Choice* has become a loaded word in America. To some, it means the choice to terminate a pregnancy: a choice that is fiercely defended by judges, governments, and in our media and culture. To others, *choice* means parents' right to choose the best education for their children. Yet when parents try to exercise *that* kind of choice, they are fiercely opposed by American judges, state governments, the media, the culture—and, most of all, by the education establishment: the unions, and the politicians they endorse, bankroll, and help elect.

We are focusing on Harlem because Harlem has become the battle-ground for an educational Tea Party.

The district stands at the intersection between some of the great-est *challenges* in American education and some of the greatest *chal-lengers* to the status quo.

First, the challenges.

Of Harlem's twenty-three zoned schools, nineteen have fewer than 50 percent of their students reading at grade level. Some fall as low as 20 percent. As one Harlem educator observed, "The overwhelming majority of [Harlem] schools are abysmal academic failures."

Some blame race. Others blame poverty. The truly cynical will peddle

---

* Madeleine Sackler, director/producer, "The Lottery." Program transcript from Q&A on CSPAN; http://www.c-spanvideo.org/videoLibrary/clip-php?appid-598379721.

half-baked theories wrapped in the false language of caring and empathy. They say that some children have too many challenges at home, or
that some parents don't care, or worse: that some kids just can't learn.

None of this is an excuse for failing to educate America's children.

We know that at the same time Harlem's traditional schools have
been failing, a new generation of educators (in charter schools like
Harlem Success Academy) are effectively educating the same kids, from
the same neighborhoods—and sometimes even from the same families.

As one Harlem Success Academy parent said, "I've got a child in the
third grade, in regular public school, and my five-year-old (from Harlem Success charter school) teaches her how to say the words out."
Another Harlem Success parent stated, "My thirteen-year-old just got
put in the eighth grade, and my five-year-old (from Harlem Success
charter school) is teaching her to read."

Same neighborhood. Same poverty. Same upbringing. Even the
same families. And yet one child learns, and the other child does not.
What is the key difference? Why does one approach fail and the other
succeed?

The answer is: choice.

It is not just about better schools. It is about a parent's ability to
*choose* better schools. In the case of these two parents in Harlem, they
did not have the choice to send their older children to charter schools,
and so these kids wound up as illiterate casualties of Harlem's failing
public schools. When parents did have a choice for their younger children, they did what any parent would do: they sent their children to
the best school possible (in this case, Harlem Success Academy). The
results were stunning: their five-year-old children wound up teaching their eight-year-old and thirteen-year-old siblings how to read.

According to Eva Moskowitz, the founder of Harlem Success
Academy: "There is a myth that parents in certain neighborhoods don't
really care about education. I have never believed that to be true, and
all of my experience has indicated that that is not the case. The problem in less-affluent communities is that parents don't have the choices
that middle- and upper-middle-class parents have. They can't buy an
apartment in the P.S. 6 zone; they can't move to Westchester. Those

are not options. It doesn't mean, because they don't have those options, that they don't want alternatives. The problem is not the parents, the problem is not the children, the problem is a system that protects academic failure and *limits* the *choices* that parents have."

For *choices*, we can substitute *liberty*. These parents in Harlem are fighting for their liberty against a controlling and power-hungry government. They are Tea Partiers, just like us. Liberty is the inalienable birthright of every American. It is protected by the Constitution. In America, the people are sovereign. That is what sets us apart as Americans.

To the extent that parents in Harlem—and parents across America—can choose which school is best for their children, they overwhelmingly abandon the failing public schools. Instead, they choose charter schools, homeschooling, and private schools through vouchers. As of February 2011, "more than 190,000 students are enrolled in school choice programs in the United States, a growth of nearly 100 percent since 2004–05."*

When school choice programs grow by nearly 100 percent, it means these parents want *more choice*. Which is their right as American citizens. When governments fight back against parents, kill school choice programs, and pour 300 percent more money into failing public schools,† it means that government does not want parents to have that choice, and takes away their liberty.

As the CATO scholar Andrew Coulson reminded Congress, "The federal government is not empowered by the Constitution to create [an education] program on a national level. Indeed the Constitution delegates to the federal government no national education policy powers, reserving them, under the 10th Amendment, to the states and the people."

Remember, in America, We the People are sovereign. And yet that has not stopped the federal government from breaking through its constitutional restraints and seizing parents' rights to choose what is best for their children.

* Alliance for School Choice, press release, February 9, 2011.
† "Kids Deserve Better," Heritage Foundation.

This trend began in 1958 with the National Defense Education Act (NDEA), which was sold to the American people as a reaction to the Soviet Union's successful launch of the world's first Earth-orbiting satellite: Sputnik. Like so many government intrusions, it was sold to the American people by hyping an external threat and using it to transfer more power from the people to the state—an approach that would have made the Communist Soviet Union proud.

> *The crisis was a sham, sold to the American public by politicians who knew it was a sham. Many legislators for years had wanted to expand federal control over education, and they saw in Sputnik an opportunity to package such expanded federal controls as a response to a "national defense crisis." Members of Congress openly discussed the purported national emergency as a "better sales argument" to secure passage of the legislation. Shortly after the bill's passage, Representative Frank Thompson referred to the NDEA as "a bill having a gimmick in it, namely the tie to the national defense."*
>
> —PROFESSOR CHARLOTTE A. TWIGHT,
> "Origins of Federal Control Over
> Education," the *Freeman*, December 1994

NDEA was the satellite government education program that launched a thousand federal incursions into classrooms. Then the real federal takeover began in 1965, as part of President Lyndon Johnson's *war on poverty* with the Elementary and Secondary Education Act (ESEA). While NDEA used Sputnik as an excuse to seize power, the ESEA used the emotional reaction to the words *poor children*. And, more often than not, *poor children of color*.

President Johnson branded his government takeover of education "a major program of assistance to public elementary and secondary schools serving children of low-income families," citing "Negroes" who were "trapped . . . in inherited, gateless poverty," vowing to "attack these evils through our poverty program, through our education program," and promising that "we will increase, and we will accelerate, and we will broaden this attack in years to come."

In the years that followed, government's attack on liberty—through our classrooms—broadened and accelerated.

In 1965, the ESEA was around thirty pages long. Today (under its current name, No Child Left Behind), this unconstitutional federal overreach dictates almost every aspect of public education with nearly six hundred pages of rules and regulations—each one an infringement on the liberty of local principals, teachers, parents, and students.

Like most government programs, it did not simply grow in complexity; it also increased in cost. Since 1965, federal education spending per pupil has more than tripled. If money were the answer, or if federal government controls were the answer, surely the federal government would have had enough time in the past forty-six years to achieve some results.

That has not happened.

The chart directly below shows government spending per pupil,

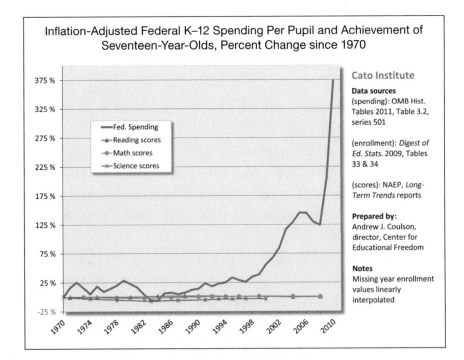

since the federal government first took control of the education system, compared to the achievement of the students it purports to serve.

While federal per-student spending has skyrocketed, students' reading and math scores have stagnated, and science scores have actually gone down.

Some might argue that focusing on "per-student" spending or "federal" spending cloaks some hidden reductions in *overall* spending on education. Not true. The chart below shows overall government spending on education, compared to the achievement of the students it claims to serve:

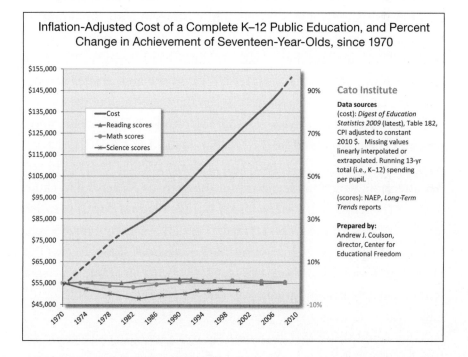

Inflation-Adjusted Cost of a Complete K–12 Public Education, and Percent Change in Achievement of Seventeen-Year-Olds, since 1970

As Andrew J. Coulson testified, U.S. government expenditures nationwide on public education in 2009 were "nearly three times as much as we spent on the graduating class of 1970, adjusting for inflation ... To sum up, we have little to show for the $2 trillion in federal education spending of the past half century ... public schooling has suffered a massive productivity collapse—it now costs three times as much to provide essentially the same education as we provided in 1970."

And it costs even more in Washington, D.C.

For years, the District of Columbia was the highest-funded public school district in the country as well as the nation's worst school district. To produce an education system that ranked fifty-first in the nation, Washington, D.C., spends $28,000 per pupil.

So what would happen if we spent less than a third of that money and gave parents the liberty to choose what is best for their children?

That is precisely what was tried in 2004.

The D.C. Opportunity Scholarship Program (D.C. OSP) was the first federally funded voucher program in America. It gave low-income parents $7,500 a year to choose the best education for their children. It transformed parents and students into customers with the power to exercise choice. And, like most customers, these parents shopped around. They exercised their choice. And it worked. As in Harlem, kids who failed in public schools succeeded in private and charter schools that were chosen by their parents—at less than one-third of the cost.

In the words of an eleven-year-old D.C. student: "In my old public school, people screamed at the teacher, walked out (of) the school door in class, hurt me and made fun of all my friends. People did not pay attention, which made it hard for me to focus. When I first came to (my private) school, I made lots of friends the first day. It is easier for me to focus. In the second quarter I got all 'A's, except for French, (in) which I got a 'B.'" This young student was not alone. Across the District of Columbia, "those who used a voucher to attend a private school had a 91 percent graduation rate. In DC Public Schools, graduation rates stand at just 49 percent."[*]

One would think that if something was generating success in its own backyard, the U.S. government would support it.

Wrong.

Instead of supporting the D.C. Opportunity Scholarship Program, the federal government eliminated funding for new students who wanted to enter the program. "The Obama Administration and the

---

[*] "National School Choice Week: It's Personal," Heritage Foundation, January 22, 2011.

democratic majority prevented siblings and other new students from joining the OSP [Opportunity Scholarship Program], effectively ending the program."* When the Republicans took over the House of Representatives and tried to reinstate the D.C. Opportunity Scholarship Program in 2011, former Speaker of the House Nancy Pelosi slammed it as an "ideological" scheme to "privatize public education in the District of Columbia," and the president of the United States himself, in an official statement through the Office of Management and Budget, said, "The administration strongly opposes expanding the D.C. Opportunity Scholarship Program and opening it to new students."

The federal government has actually taken the position that students who are currently in the program, and graduating at a rate of 91 percent, can continue their chosen education which has been proven to work, but their younger brothers and sisters will not be given the same choice and will be forced back into failing public schools where only 49 percent of students graduate.

Fortunately, on March 30, 2011, a Republican-sponsored bill to restore and enhance the D.C. Opportunity Scholarship Program passed—over the objections of the White House and the Democratic Party—by a vote of 225 to 195. But, as reported in the *Washington Post*, "legislation opposed by the administration sometimes carries a warning, either that the president would veto the bill if it reached his desk, or at least that the president's advisors would recommend that he veto it."† Ultimately, funding for the program was included in the 2011 long-term Continuing Resolution, which resulted in a five-year reauthorization of the program.

～

In Harlem, a little farther beyond the reach of the veto pen of the federal government, a miracle is happening. The challengers to the educational

---

* D.C. Parents for School Choice, "The D.C. Opportunities Scholarship Is Making a Difference."

† Ben Pershing, *Washington Post*, March 29, 2011.

status quo, against overwhelming obstacles, are changing schools to the benefit of students.

As Harlem Success Academy teacher Candice Fryer said, "Every child can learn. We, as the educators, are there to give them the resources. If they don't make it to college, then the system has failed them, not the other way around." And Geoffrey Canada, the president and CEO of Harlem Children's Zone, noted that "one of the great things" about a charter school is that "it is totally accountable. If you don't run a decent school, you will not get your charter renewed and, essentially, your school will be closed. And we think that's fair. In the end, if you take money to do this kind of work, you have to deliver for children."

That kind of personal accountability led to such a dramatic turn-around in Harlem that parents are now clamoring to get their children into these schools. Indeed, demand is so high that the schools are forced to hold "lotteries" to assign the few available spaces.

It is heartbreaking to watch thousands of desperately hopeful parents crowd into auditoriums to see their children's future being decided by the luck of the draw. It is even sadder to know that fewer than one in ten of these students will "win" and get into a good school. The size of the crowds, and the need for these lotteries, are testaments to the desire of parents—in Harlem and elsewhere—to break free from government control and to give their children the best future possible.

After the first "Sputnik" moment trapped generations of American children in underperforming government-controlled schools, President Obama doubled down in his 2011 State of the Union speech and called for "our generation's Sputnik moment," as he touted a new big-government education program called Race to the Top as the most meaningful reform of our public schools in a generation.

He is right. It represents the greatest federal incursion into American education in a generation. It centralizes power in Washington, D.C., like never before. Some call it Race to the Takeover, noting that it cede[s] sovereignty of the states' rights to educate . . . to the federal government. Race to the Top is, by far, the biggest assault on parental liberty in U.S. history. It takes power away from teachers, parents, and principals and concentrates it in Washington, D.C., through *standards*. A national *standard* is the opposite of local *choice*. It is the death of choice. Worse still, it causes educators to turn away from children, and to focus on their new customer: the federal government. The federal government is the source of their funds, rules, and marching orders, so educators must turn to government to be told what they can, and cannot do, for the money they receive. That is why educators spend so much time interfacing with government, writing "grant applications total[ing] hundreds of pages," and sending "representatives to Washington to give presentations on why their state deserved the additional funding."

According to Jennifer Marshall, "Florida's Race to the Top application, for example, totaled 327 pages and included a 606-page appendix. Illinois' application was 187 pages plus a 644-page appendix, and California submitted an application totaling 131 pages in length with a 475-page appendix."*

Imagine if all that time and energy were focused on teaching our kids. Fortunately, we don't just have to imagine. Because it is happening right now all across the country. It's happening in the inner city (as seen in the documentary "The Lottery" about a charter school in Harlem) and in charter schools and private schools all across the country.

If our education system focused on students, the way teachers prefer to focus on students when they are allowed to educate in the way they know how, then America would deliver the kind of results that many charter schools deliver without so much intervention and control by self-serving bureaucracies.

But America's education system is not focused on students. The problem is not the kids. The problem is the adults. The problem is the massive education bureaucracy, from the federal level on down. The system is so top-heavy with bureaucrats and administrators that many adults have

---

* Testimony before House Education Subcommittee on Early Childhood, Elementary and Secondary Education, U.S. House of Representatives, March 15, 2011.

turned their focus away from the real aim of the education system, which is educating our children.

Why is that?

Education demagogues work overtime to recast any criticism of the education system as an attack on teachers. They know that almost everyone loves teachers. A recent Gallup poll rated grade-school teachers higher on people's list of esteemed professions than doctors, police officers, or even the clergy. By wrapping themselves in the positive sentiments associated with teachers, demagogic defenders of the education status quo arm themselves with what professional communicators call a *one-step argument*.

Legitimate criticism of the education system takes two or three steps to identify as well as explain the problem, plus several caveats to reassure people that we love teachers, too. Demagogues slam those who want to improve the education system as Hitler-like thugs, and if that sounds too extreme and unbelievable to you, here is some photographic evidence from the Wisconsin teachers' union protests of early 2011.

Defenders of the failed American education system use emotion to shift our focus away from the real problems in the system. Note: we said *system*, not *teachers*. Because the teachers are not the problem. The broken, bureaucratic, union-controlled education *system* is the problem.

How do we know that teachers are not the problem? The same way we learned that parents in Harlem are not the problem. By tracing the path of teachers who have escaped the unaccountable, government-run, union-controlled, top-down, public education system for the freedom and choice and accountability of independent schools that have been shown to work.

Teacher Jessica Reid said it best: "For two years, I taught at P.S. 121 in the Bronx as a fifth-grade teacher. My experience was incredibly disheartening. Most days I felt like I was running into a brick wall. My fifth graders were functioning far below grade level. For example—right now, in my first-grade class (at an independent school) almost all of my students are reading at or above grade level. In my fifth-grade classroom (back in the old system), I had the majority of my students not even able to read a second-grade text."

Same teacher. Same passion for teaching kids. And yet, when she was trapped in a system that forcibly removed choice and accountability, this teacher failed to teach her children. Two years later, in a charter school, she succeeded in teaching students who were younger, poorer, and more challenged.

It bears repeating: The teachers are not the problem. The kids are not the problem. The parents are not the problem. The system is the problem.

The government-run, union-controlled education system systematically removes choice from the system. The teachers' union contract in New York is six hundred pages long, and it dictates almost every aspect of schooling—not just what teachers and schools *can* do, but specifically what teachers and schools *cannot* do. Any variation from the top-down standardized master plan is forbidden. Another word for *variation* is *innovation*.

In the centralized-control world of public education, if a teacher discovers a more effective way to educate, she is contractually forbidden from acting on it. And so, over time, new and good ideas are never instituted. Not only are innovations not rewarded; they are viewed as threats. And when this system is threatened by anything resembling change—even good change that helps kids—the system violently opposes new ideas, as we've witnessed in Wisconsin and anyplace else where the people, politicians, teachers, and students try to change the system to benefit kids.

To the administrators, bureaucrats, and union bosses, the union contract is sacred. More sacred than their purported mission, which presumably is to educate kids. "If you're a politician who decides that we should look at the contract," said Eva Moskowitz, "that's considered the 'third rail.' You're not supposed to speak about the contract. The only people who can speak about the contract are the leadership of the teachers' union."

When people challenge the status quo, the unions react violently. It was true in Wisconsin, and it is true in Harlem. "They also use tactics that are quite thuggish," said Moskowitz. "So, if you cross them, it will not be a very pleasant experience. I've certainly experienced that personally. I think if you ask any democratically elected official who has ever done something that the teachers' union doesn't like, they come after you. They told me they will put me six feet under. It's really Godfather-like tactics that are being used."

When they don't threaten, they storm and occupy government buildings, as they did in Wisconsin. Or they protest against newspapers that dare to report the truth about America's education system, or that are involved in private education, as they did against the *Washington Post*. Or, as in California, they vow to shut down roads, co-opt fire drills, "target the businesses of legislators in their home districts," and take over the state capitol. All of this they do purportedly in order to "educate, energize and organize members [and] educate and outreach to community" to their cause. Apparently their "cause" is to shovel more money into their failed education system.

That is a lot of effort to protect a closed, broken system from the mortal "threat" of choice and innovation.

The opposite of a closed system is an open system. Or, as we like to call it, *open source*.

What ails our education system is the same thing that ails our political system. There is a stark contrast between what works and what doesn't. In a battle between individual choice and central control, choice always wins. When we're confronted with a system that imposes national standards versus one that allows for local flexibility, the people choose flexibility.

⁓

No component of our civic lives is ultimately more important to a thriving free society than education. If we expect the people to be sovereign, and to make good decisions consistent with running our nation, we should have the greatest educational system in the world. Yet it's difficult to think of any area of American life in which we've gotten farther away from the Tea Party movement's core values of fiscal responsibility, constitutionally limited government, and free markets.

As the Center for American Progress (CAP), a heavily Democratic think tank, points out in its January 2011 white paper on educational costs, the United States of America spends more to educate its students than almost any other developed country. (Only Luxembourg spends more.) If we were getting what we paid for, the investment might be worth it. But we get approximately the same results as countries like Poland and Estonia—and we spend an incredible $60,000 more per student to do so.*

There is virtually no correlation between the amount of money we spend on education and the results we achieve. Even in similar locations, with similar populations, the disparities are staggering. In addition to providing a wealth of data (though some analysis reflects its political leanings), the CAP report presents a fascinating comparison of two Wisconsin towns, Oshkosh and Eau Claire, explains how much each spends on education, and then reveals what sorts of results they achieve.

The towns are remarkably similar; both have about ten thousand students, and their demographics are almost identical. Their students' test results were almost exactly the same in 2008; in both districts, 83 percent of fourth-grade students scored proficient or above in reading skills. But there's one important difference: in 2008, Eau

* http://www.americanprogress.org/issues/2010/04/pdf/dww_education.pdf.

Claire spent over *$8 million* more for its students to achieve the same results in math and reading as Oshkosh. We imagine that the taxpayers of Eau Claire will react to this news with some dismay.

The extra dollars spent went almost entirely to administrators in Eau Claire—but for the purposes of this discussion, the whys are irrelevant. It's clearly not fiscally responsible when some of our school districts spend millions of dollars more with nothing to show for it.

"We actually think that education spending should go up a little bit," declared President Barack Obama, whose proposed 2012 budget would have increased federal spending on education by 21 percent, to $71 billion. Yet increasing the amount of money we spend on education without commensurate results is the height of fiscal irresponsibility. It's only possible because the government has a virtual monopoly on our elementary education system. If the free market were allowed to operate, as we'll demonstrate in the next chapter, parents would have more and better choices of schools for their children, and we could reduce the amount of money we spend on education overall, while increasing its quality.

And, of course, as we've seen in this chapter, as Washington takes a bigger and bigger role in education, we're getting farther and farther away from what the Founders intended the federal government to do with respect to educating our population: nothing.

America was built on an inherent distrust of centralized power and control. The reason the states agreed to unite and form a federal government was that they were guaranteed that they would maintain their "states' rights." The powers of the central government were few and enumerated. The real power was vested in the people, as declared in our nation's founding document: the Declaration of Independence. And the idea that government of the people, by the people, and for the people was the historically unique idea that made America so great.

Over time, the people have been nudged farther and farther away from our founding principles by politicians who either scare us into the welcoming arms of government with external threats (Sputnik moments) or manipulate our emotional instincts to appear to side with poor and needy children in order to get us to cede more of our control, more of our choice, and more of our liberty to a government that is sworn to uphold our unalienable right to liberty.

The reason why parents in Harlem are standing up to their failed schools is the same reason why Tea Partiers are standing up to our failed government. Because centralized control fails every time it is tried. It is true in our classrooms, and it is true in our country. We offer the last two and a half centuries of American history as proof. When power is vested in the hands of the people, America succeeds like no other nation ever has. When governments centralize power and control, America slips into decline as it did during the Great Depression, the dark days of the late 1970s, and today, with our nation teetering on economic collapse and insolvency.

∼

Before we offer the Tea Party Patriots' Path to Educational Liberty in the next chapter, here are the philosophical foundations upon which our practical ideas will stand. We the People believe that:

Parents should be able to choose the best educational options for their children.

The federal government should not exercise control over local schools.

Teachers should have the freedom to opt into, or out of, choice-limiting union contracts.

Principals should have the liberty to set their own curricula.

Parents should have the freedom to homeschool their children.

All teaching methods—including homeschooling—should be measured and made freely available so that parents can choose the best options for their children.

Failing schools should be shut down.

Failing teachers should be fired.

Collective bargaining should end in schools.

Union contracts that limit choice in education should be broken.

# ★ 7 ★

## *The Educational Pathway
to Liberty*

**HOW WOULD YOU** like to have Lance Armstrong as your fitness teacher? Or Tony Robbins as your success coach? Or learn chess from Garry Kasparov?

What if you could have access to the wisdom and experience of the world's greatest thinkers and teachers—right now?

The truth is, thanks to the free market, you already do.

Lance Armstrong charges about $275,000 to speak to you in person about fitness and cancer survival. But for around $20, you can learn many of the same lessons from his books. Or you could get yourself fit with one of the online fitness trackers and calorie counters at Armstrong's Web site—for free.*

Tony Robbins charges millions of dollars for personal success coaching, and his waiting list is years long. But you can learn from Tony at a public event for only a few hundred dollars. Or you could buy one of his books right now for less than $10.

Garry Kasparov as your chess teacher? He charges $60,000 for rapid-fire chess with a group of twenty, followed by dinner and a speech. True, it's hard to learn much about chess from a single game, even from a grandmaster, but you could always learn from one of Kas-

* http://www.livestrong.org.

parov's guidebooks. Or, for a more hands-on experience, you could learn by playing against one of Garry Kasparov's many computerized chess programs.

Right now, even if you don't have much money, you have access to the knowledge and teachings of the world's greatest cyclist, success coach, and chess master.

So why don't you or your school-age children have access to the world's greatest teachers? The world's greatest historians? Or the world's greatest engineers, mathematicians, and physicists?

We, the Tea Party Patriots, believe school-age children should. That is why a key part of our Pathway to Educational Liberty is to expand *teacher-based learning* and treat superstar teachers the same way we treat superstar cyclists, success coaches, and chess players. But even though many students and parents would jump at the opportunity, this option—and several others—are not currently available to millions of American parents and students because, in many parts of the country, two key elements are missing from our education system: *exceptionalism* and *liberty*.

## EXCEPTIONALISM

Make no mistake: we believe the desire for exceptionalism lives within the heart of every American teacher and student. Unfortunately, America's school *system*—along with its unions and educrats—systematically destroys the path to creating extraordinary students.

How do we know that Garry Kasparov was the best chess player? Because Kasparov entered tournaments and played against the best of the best—even computers—and beat them. Chess players are measured by ratings numbers. Kasparov achieved the highest rating in history (2851), and he was the world's number one–ranked chess player for 255 months—nearly three times longer than anyone else.

Tony Robbins? He made a name for himself on television, curing people of lifelong phobias and inspiring people to walk across beds of hot coals. If he had failed, we would have heard about it by now.

Instead, he has racked up thirty years of success by helping millions of people embrace their personal power and exceptionalism.

How do we know that Lance Armstrong was a great cyclist? Because he won the Tour de France seven times—two times more than anyone else.

But how do you know which math teacher is best? Right now, you probably don't.

When New York City tried to release *value-added* evaluation data that ranks teachers against their peers, the teachers' union fought to keep that information hidden. "The United Federation of Teachers filed a lawsuit in state court saying that data reports did not qualify as something that needed to be released under the freedom-of-information laws. It argued that the data reports are often unreliable and if released would 'cause the public to form unsupported conclusions as to teacher quality' and 'irreparably harm the professional reputations of educators.'"*

Let's look at the previous paragraph point by point.

1. *The teachers' union went to the court to suppress freedom of information.* Aren't teachers in the business of *sharing* information?
2. *They argued that test data is unreliable.* Then why do they test students if test data is unreliable?
3. *They said that if this test data was released, it would "cause the public to form unsupported conclusions as to teacher quality."* Not necessarily. Perhaps it would allow the public, for the first time, to form *supported* conclusions as to teacher quality. Right now, the public has no choice but to guess.
4. *They argued that if people knew how bad certain teachers are, it could "irreparably harm the professional reputations of educators."* Exactly! That's the whole point. A bad teacher's professional reputation *should* be ruined if he or she is a bad teacher.

---

*http://www.csmonitor.com/USA/Education/2010/1021/New-York-City-spat-over-publishing-teacher-rankings-reaches-brief-truce.

Right now, a bad teacher's professional standing is not harmed by the fact that he or she is a bad teacher, because that fact is withheld from the public by a system that does not test itself, and by unions that fight, including in court, to prevent any attempt to bring the facts about poor teachers to light, thus robbing parents and students of the ability to make informed decisions on something as critical to a child's life as his or her education.

When Lance Armstrong failed to win the Tour de France in 1993 and 1995, did he try to stop you from finding out about his loss by dragging the race's organizers into court and arguing that the release of such information could "irreparably harm" him? No. Instead, he worked harder, became a better cyclist, and won the Tour each year from 1999 to 2005. If Lance Armstrong had filed a grievance back in the early 1990s, or blamed the timekeeper for being "unreliable," or even blamed his cancer and just gave up, he would have never achieved those historic victories.

Exceptionalism. What is missing from America's education system is a culture that measures, recognizes, values, and rewards exceptionalism, and has the courage to weed out the bad apples.

Right now, only two school districts in America even *have* value-added teacher performance ratings: Los Angeles and New York. In Los Angeles, in "another example of the teachers unions protecting their members at the cost of a good education for students,"* the teachers' union actually picketed the *Los Angeles Times* building to protest the release of teacher rankings to the public. In case you missed that: American teachers picketed a newspaper, whose right to publish teacher rankings is protected by the First Amendment, and the picketers themselves were people whose chosen profession was to freely share information with the public, and whose salaries are paid by taxpayers.

---

* Don Irvine, "LA Unified & Education Reform," Accuracy in Academia, http://www .academia.org/la-unified-education-reform/.

If you're not angry, you're not paying attention.

What about New York? "The statistical model that New York City uses to calculate value-added scores takes more than 30 factors into account including the students' ethnicity and whether they are poor enough to qualify for free lunch."* That's right. The New York teacher test even accounted for all the wrongheaded, soft-bigotry excuses made by educrats, and yet they still they complained about being tested. Which means: what they were actually complaining about was being tested at all.

Without measures of excellence and exceptionalism—for teachers, students, or schools—parents will never be able to tell good from bad and will end up with precisely the education system that America now has, in which mediocrity is the norm, excellence is punished, and failure is rewarded.

So the first necessary ingredient for parents to be able to choose the best schools, the best teachers, or the best programs is an honest and objective measure of their quality. Before we can *choose* what is best, we have to *know* what is best. What are the best methods of teaching? What tests adequately measure mastery of subjects? How should principals manage their instructional staff to maximize student achievement?

Right now, we don't know what's exceptional because the system doesn't reward exceptionalism. The best teachers in most schools make exactly the same amount of money as the worst, assuming they've got the same college degrees and have been teaching for the same amount of time.

How many readers have ever heard the name Chris Redman? Redman entered his chosen profession in the year 2000, shortly after graduating from college. He was a promising newcomer in his field, and his first employer held out great hopes for him. He performed modestly, never the worst employee, never the best. He worked in his first job for four years—long enough, had he been a professional schoolteacher, to

---

* Karen Matthews, Associated Press, December 7, 2010, *Minnesota Star Tribune*, http://www .startribune.com/templates/Print-This-Story?sid=111455364.

qualify for lifetime tenure in many school districts. But Chris Redman isn't a schoolteacher. He's an NFL quarterback. And unlike public school teachers, NFL quarterbacks don't get tenure. To be fair, Redman got a deal most Americans wouldn't complain about; reportedly he made almost $3 million in the 2010–2011 football season.

Why do we bring up Chris Redman in this context? To highlight how performance is compensated in other areas of American life. The same year that Chris Redman started his professional football career, another quarterback entered the NFL. In the beginning, nobody expected that other quarterback to perform anywhere near as well as Redman; in fact, he was drafted three rounds later. The other guy, however, wasn't just any old football player. He was Tom Brady, perhaps the greatest quarterback to ever play in the NFL. Brady's compensation last football season? Close to $30 million—*ten times* Chris Redman's.

Of course, had Tom Brady and Chris Redman been teachers working for the same school district, because they have the same educational credentials and the same length of service in their jobs, they would be making the same amount of money.

No other country in the world can come close to competing with the United States of America in football. But our nation is in the middle of the pack when it comes to education. Perhaps it's time to start paying our top-performing teachers like professional athletes—based on merit, not tenure—and making sure that the worst performers get cut from the team.

## LIBERTY

The second key ingredient to a great education is liberty. Because knowing which option is best means nothing without the liberty to choose what is best. For years, government educrats trapped generations of children by giving them no other choice but to spend their formative years in so-called dropout factories. According to the Alliance for Excellent Education, America's "nearly 2,000 dropout factories turn out 51 percent of the nation's dropouts. They produce 81 percent of all Native American dropouts, 73 percent of all African American dropouts, and 66 percent of all Hispanic dropouts."

Generations of American parents had no choice but to feed their precious children into these failing schools, knowing full well that there was a near 50 percent chance that their children wouldn't graduate.

> *Every parent wants to see their child succeed. It's mind-boggling . . . that in the United States, we are not giving parents this option.*
>
> —Tyron Young, charter school graduate, quoted in the *Washington Examiner,* January 19, 2011

*Choice,* otherwise known as *liberty,* is the rallying cry that can unite millions of Americans of all political stripes and from all parts of the country to give our children a better education. When New Jersey governor Chris Christie went on the *Oprah Winfrey Show* to accept a $100-million check from Facebook founder Mark Zuckerberg to revamp New Jersey's schools, it was mere days after Oprah embraced the documentary *Waiting for "Superman,"* which advocates choice. And when House Speaker John Boehner, comedian Bill Cosby, and the Tea Party Patriots are all pulling in the same direction for school choice, it is a clear signal that we are at a historical moment of true bipartisanship.

That is not to say that all American parents currently have the liberty to choose the best education for their children. Far from it. But we are at a historically unique moment—right now—to make American education great the same way we made America great: by seating power in the hands of the people and giving them the liberty to choose what is best.

The Alliance for School Choice annual yearbook tracks school choice options throughout the country. At the time of this writing, only twelve U.S. states, plus D.C., have private school choice programs, and only 190,811 students are able to exercise this choice. That is less than one half of one percent of all American students. More than 75 percent of U.S. states have no choice at all.

### 2010–11 School Choice Data at a Glance

| | |
|---|---|
| **Overall: States with private school choice programs** | **12+D.C.** |
| States with voucher programs | 7+D.C. |
| States with scholarship tax credit programs | 7 |
| States with special needs scholarship programs | 7 |
| **Overall: Number of private school choice programs** | **20** |
| Number of voucher programs | 11 |
| Number of scholarship tax credit programs | 9 |
| Number of special needs scholarship programs (vouchers and tax credits) | 7 |
| **Overall: Number of students in private school choice programs** | **190,811** |
| Number of students in voucher programs | 67,267 |
| Number of students in scholarship tax credit programs | 123,544 |
| Number of students in special needs scholarship programs (vouchers and tax credits) | 26,055 |

Alliance for School Choice, School Choice Yearbook 2010–11, p. 24; http://www.alliance forschoolchoice.org/UploadedFiles/Home/School%20Choice%20Yearbook%202010-11.pdf.

Of course, our argument only applies for poor and middle-class parents. Wealthy parents have all sorts of choices. If you can afford $5,000, or $10,000, or $30,000 a year to send your child to a private school, you can. The rest of us, however, aren't so fortunate.

So our first job is to increase the amount of educational choice across the country for *all* parents. Parents and students who do have choice—in Florida, Pennsylvania, Arizona, Wisconsin, Ohio, Iowa, Georgia, Louisiana, Washington, D.C., Utah, Rhode Island, Indiana, and Oklahoma—are seeing tremendous results. Now it is time for parents in all U.S. states to have the same liberty to choose the best education options for their children.

One way to increase the amount of choice in America's education system is to demand more choice from our politicians. This is where the Tea Party Patriots' model of grassroots activism can be deployed to effect change in America's education system, the same way we are effecting change in America's political system.

## ACTIVISM FOR EDUCATION

### HOLD RALLIES

In March 2010, 5,500 school-choice supporters marched in Florida to demand more choice in education. Not bad, even by Tea Party standards. Florida's then-governor, Charlie Crist—who was seeking a new mandate as a U.S. senator—saw the powerful winds of change and choice that were sweeping through Florida and decided to join the march and speak at the rally. During his remarks, Governor Crist emphasized the importance of school choice that "provides parents an invaluable opportunity to choose a learning environment that gives their children the best chance for success."*

On March 22, 2011, the state capitol in Atlanta, Georgia, was swarming with children and parents as a rally was held in favor of a variety of school choice options. From tax breaks for corporations who donate to private schools to promoting online virtual schools, they were there to rally express support for the concept of educational choice. Senate Majority leader Chip Rogers said, "Parents need to be able to choose from public and private schools to find the right setting for each child's unique skills and challenges."†

Only one day later, in Columbus, Ohio, more than 1,100 parents, children, and other advocates of school choice rallied at the state capitol for more options. Supporters of school choice were seeking "more tax-funded tuition vouchers that parents can use to send their children to private schools, removal of the cap on privately operated charter schools, and a new scholarship program for special-needs

---

* Press release from Governor Crist's office, as reported by *WCTV News;* http://www.wctv
.tv/news/headlines/89058027.html.
† http://www.onlineathens.com/stories/032211/new_803509263.shtml.

children." "We believe parents should have options," Lieutenant Governor Mary Taylor told the crowd.*

All across the country, in states as geographically and culturally diverse as Ohio, New Jersey, Georgia, Pennsylvania, Indiana, Virginia, Oklahoma, Oregon, and even Washington, D.C., parents and students are rallying in favor of school choice. The trend has been accelerating, and if results are any indication, it will continue to do so.

## MELT THE PHONES

Ask any politician who has been on the receiving end of Tea Party Patriots' phone campaigns the following question: would you rather have your phones melted by the Tea Party Patriots or simply do the right thing and have this group on your side? No doubt the answer would be to do the right thing. Indeed, it is in every politician's job description to represent the will of the electorate. But sometimes

*http://www.dispatchpolitics.com/live/content/local_news/stories/2011/03/23/copy/
school-choice-options-advocated-at-rally.html?adsec=politics&sid=101.

their self-interests are better served by lobbyists or unions. For years, politicians who chose the will of lobbyists and unions over the will of the people suffered no consequences.

We can, and will, end their free ride by deploying our grassroots tactics to remind politicians that if they don't serve We the People, they will be voted out of office.

### ADVERTISE

The Tea Party Patriots is a grassroots organization, operating almost entirely on volunteer power, and so it hasn't yet engaged in large advertising campaigns. Notice we said *yet*. If every Tea Party Patriot donated a dollar, we could mount one of the largest political action advertising campaigns in American history. And a good place to start such a campaign would be in the noble, bipartisan, and unifying cause of giving parents the choice in how their children are educated.

How do we know this will work? Because it already has, in an ad campaign against the most powerful man in the world (President Barack Obama).

When D.C. Parents for School Choice ran a series of television ads

calling on President Obama to give D.C. parents the same educational opportunities that his children have, by not canceling the D.C. Opportunities Scholarship Program, it shocked many observers. African American parents were asking the first African American president, "Whose side are you on?"

The president never moved from his position. But these ads, and the efforts of D.C. parents and activists, helped frame the debate and gave Congress the political cover it needed to do the right thing. On April 18, 2011, Congress voted against the will of the president—225 to 195—to reauthorize the D.C. Opportunity Scholarship Program. And ultimately, even though it was opposed by the president, the program was renewed for a five-year term.

That ad could easily have had a Tea Party Patriots logo at the end. Or perhaps we could simply forward an ad like this to one million of our closest friends on Facebook. Or ask our fellow patriots to donate five dollars to personalize the ad for Congressman X or Senator Y and air it in their districts. These options remain available.

## ELECT POLITICIANS WHO WILL HONOR YOUR RIGHT TO LIBERTY

The April 18, 2011, vote to reauthorize the D.C. Opportunity Scholarship Fund would not have been won had the Tea Party movement not helped elect a new generation of like-minded politicians in November 2010. Without all of our hard work leading up to the November 2010 midterms to elect a Tea Party caucus, the balance of power in Congress would have remained on the side of the president.

No politician is perfect. But it is critically important to have more politicians in Congress who respect their oaths to uphold our liberty. So one of the most important ways that we, the Tea Party Patriots, can work to empower American parents of schoolchildren with more choice is to elect more politicians who understand and respect the proper role of government, as articulated by our Founders, which is to "secure the Blessings of Liberty to ourselves and our Posterity (our children)."

## WHAT TO CHOOSE?

*We got into this movement because we thought fighting for parental choice was the right thing to do. And sometimes in politics, you just have to do the right thing.*

Oklahoma representative
JABAR SHUMATE (D-Tulsa)

*Who in their right mind would oppose giving parents such a choice? School choice takes many forms— vouchers, tax credits, charters, student scholarships,*

*and transfers to better schools . . . I support whatever*
*works, depending on the needs of the community.*

—Louisiana governor BOBBY JINDAL,
*Leadership and Crisis*, 2010

Which school choice option is best? Don't ask us. Ask yourself or your child. The right education option for your child is not for us to decide. It should also not be the federal government's decision. You, the parent, should be empowered to choose whichever education options work best for your child. We, the Tea Party Patriots, will fight for your right to control your child's education. Once this right has been restored, you can pick from the following short, and by no means exhaustive, list of possible education options.

## TEACHER-BASED LEARNING
## (SUPERSTAR TEACHERS)

Right now, you can go to http://www.elance.com, type in the words *Spanish translation*, and choose from nearly ten thousand providers of translation services. These translators are rated by those who have used their services. They do not protest against being rated—they welcome it. Elance has not been picketed or taken to the court to prevent it from displaying the ratings of its service providers. In fact, the ratings on Elance are prominently displayed because they are the most important determining factor that customers use when choosing providers. Each translator is rated by his or her customers in six areas: quality, expertise, cost, schedule, response, and professionalism. In addition, customers are encouraged to write editorial reviews describing the services provided by these professionals. Did they deliver what they promised? Did they stay on budget and on schedule? Were their services exceptional? One bad review could affect a provider's rating forever and cause other potential customers to move along to the next provider. That's a powerful incentive to do an excellent job each and every time.

If we have the technology to deliver that level of excellence, cost-effectiveness, and accountability in document translation, surely we can do it for something as important as the education of our children.

You may not get Garry Kasparov to personally teach your child chess, but someday you could get a five-star math teacher to teach your child algebra—graphically and immersively—on a computer screen, or perhaps on a backseat monitor in the family car during a long drive. Maybe you and your child could sit down in front of a computer screen and learn together. Superstar teachers would attract more and more students, which would reward the top teachers, and incentivize less stellar teachers to improve their skills and build up their ratings so that they, too, could someday be number one. It worked for America, and it can work for America's teachers.

Or what if a software company—like the one that makes popular games like Super Monkey Ball—made a 3-D game to teach your child theoretical physics? America's education budget is a staggering $972 billion. In 2010, Sega, the company that brought us Super Monkey Ball 3D, just turned a profit for the first time in four years, making $34 million. That's three one-thousandths of one percent of the U.S. education budget. Doubling Sega's profits would be a fraction of a percentage of a one-week rounding error at the U.S. Department of Education. Would the prospect of doubling Sega's profits, with just one educational game, be enough incentive to get Sega to pick up the phone and call Stephen Hawking or Lee Smolin to create a 3-D game that would teach America's children quantum physics in fun and immersive ways?

Why don't we find out?

## VOUCHERS

One choice-based education option that is working right now for schoolchildren in twelve states and the District of Columbia is what is commonly referred to as a *voucher program*. The Alliance for School

Choice describes the programs as giving "children (at present, usually low-income children, children in failing schools, or children with special needs) greater access to high-quality private schools." Education dollars "follow the child," and parents select private schools and receive state-funded scholarships to pay tuition.

The debate over whether vouchers work is effectively over. They do. They may not work for teachers' unions or the entrenched educational bureaucracies of municipal school systems, but they're tremendously effective for students.

But we think it's important to reflect for a moment on *why* vouchers work, and to bring up a side of the argument that rarely sees the light of day. The demand side of the equation is easy to understand. By giving parents more educational purchasing power, we enable them to serve as consumers and exercise their demand for better schools. The demand-side results are immediate—when parents get to choose between sending their kids to failing local schools or succeeding local schools, they obviously choose the ones that succeed. One of two things happens to the unsuccessful schools—either they get better, or they close—and each is a perfectly acceptable option.

But most arguments against vouchers fail to mention the *supply-side* benefits to schools. If all American parents had vouchers to send their children to the schools of their choice, it's likely that a lot of those kids would be going to schools that don't even exist today. Giving vouchers to only a few students would be like giving parents vouchers to spend on newspapers. Right now, parents in Harlem, for instance, could choose among the *New York Times*, the *Wall Street Journal*, the *New York Post*, the *New York Daily News*, and a few other smaller newspapers. But in the long term, entrepreneurs would be drawn to all the money to be made in newspaper vouchers, and there would be a cornucopia of choice.

If you give one child a voucher that allows her to move from a failing school to a school that is succeeding, you help that child. But if you give a million vouchers to a million children, you unlock one of the most powerful forces in the world: the American entrepreneurial mind. Today, vouchers ask parents to choose the best horse for their children. But if the money is there, sooner or later, someone *will* invent the educational equivalent of the automobile.

## SCHOLARSHIP TAX CREDIT PROGRAMS

Scholarship tax credit programs unleash the power of the most generous people in the world: Americans. These programs give companies and individuals tax credits to provide scholarships for children to attend private schools. Instead of being run by inefficient government bureaucracies, these programs are designed and operated by nonprofit organizations operating as educational charities. The scholarships are not funded by public agencies, but rather from private charitable donations made under provisions of the tax code.

These programs bypass government funding almost entirely (tax credits are government funding after the fact). Companies and individual Americans give scholarship funds directly to students. What may sound like an interesting idea that would appeal only to a handful of donors has grown remarkably over the past decade in the handful of states that allow them tax credits, empowering 123,544 students— nearly double the number of kids currently in voucher programs—to attend private schools. In other words, the American people are nearly twice as generous as the American government when it comes to educating our kids.

## PUBLIC CHARTER SCHOOLS

As described in the previous chapter, public charter schools operate free of government bureaucracy and lesson-planning. They are beyond the reach of teachers' unions and their proscriptive rules and limitations, and exist solely to deliver the best possible education for children. They are funded by the government, just like public schools, but after that they are on their own and free from the tentacles of governments and unions. The only measure is success. If they do well (for their students), they get to keep their charter and stay in business. If they fail to deliver for their students, they lose their charter and go out of business.

## HOMESCHOOLING

Many American parents take control of their child's education by teaching their children themselves. According to the National Home Education Research Institute, there were "2.04 million homeschool students in the United States in 2010." It is understandable why parents would choose such an option. Americans love liberty and have a well-earned and historical distrust of government. No wonder, when it comes to something as important as educating their children, more and more Americans are choosing to take matters into their own hands and into their own homes.

For the most part, it works. "In most studies, the homeschooled have scored, on average, at the 65th to 80th percentile on standardized achievement tests, compared to the national school average of the 50th percentile (which is largely based on public schools)."*

One of the reasons for these remarkably high test scores is that homeschoolers tend to be self-selecting. If a parent cares enough about her child's education to stay at home and teach that child herself, she is clearly heavily invested in making sure that child gets the best education possible. If all teachers and schools, unions and governments, were equally invested in a child's education, . . . well, there would be no problems at all in the public education system.

But since no one will ever care for a child as much as that child's parent, homeschooling is likely here to stay.

∽

---

*Brian D. Ray, Academic Achievement and Demographic Traits of Homeschool Students: A Nationwide Study, Academic Leadership—The Online Journal, Volume 8, Issue 1 (Winter 2010), posted on Wednesday, February 3, 2010, 03:01:38.

The list of education options discussed in this chapter is by no means complete. In fact, we encourage you to come up with new ideas of your own and put them to the test—as we do with all ideas at the Tea Party Patriots—by opening them up to the floor, in a demonstration of true democracy, and kicking the tires to see if they work, then refining those concepts through hands-on experience. That is how we, in the Tea Party movement, created and refined many of the ideas and techniques that have helped our movement grow into one of the most powerful political forces in the country in less than two years. America's education system has been trying to get it right since Sputnik.

## FINAL THOUGHTS—ITEMS FOR DISCUSSION

Here are a handful of new ideas, suggested by grassroots Tea Party Patriots, which we now open up to the group at: http://www.teapar typatriots.org/40yearplan.

- *Zero-based budgeting for all schools.* Meaning: every school, every year or two, must prove its value and effectiveness for students before getting more funds to continue operating for the next year.
- *Defund the Department of Education and/or the National Education Association.* Ronald Reagan tried but failed. Many politicians propose the idea, and many more American citizens want it. But is it possible? Is it desirable? Let's discuss.
- *Education tax opt-outs.* Allow taxpayers to opt out of property taxes for local schools that do not perform. This would certainly introduce the concept of *consequences for bad behavior* into the education system.
- *Textbooks.* All of these "school-choice" options won't amount to much if the lessons in our children's textbooks run counter to America's founding principles. If a child is sent to a high-performing school whose textbooks teach that American excep-

tionalism is a farce, and that America is a force for evil in the world (both of which are regularly taught in American universities), then the only way for a student to get high test scores would be to write essays on why America is not exceptional and why America is a force for evil in the world.

No! We must teach our children the truth, as evidenced by the last two hundred–plus years of history, proving that America is the greatest nation in history. Yes, America has its imperfections. But instead of focusing almost entirely on the nation's imperfections, we must reveal the country's exceptionalism. There's a saying that history is written by the victors. As a victorious nation, America should not artificially paint itself as a villain and a loser.

- *Teach basic economic literacy.* One need look no farther than the U.S. Congress, the White House, and countless government agencies—all filled with highly educated people—to know that economic literacy is not well taught by America's education system. The basic fact that you cannot spend more than you take in is completely missing from America's highly educated corridors of power.

  We need to teach our students how to balance a checkbook and how to run a lemonade stand. We need to teach capitalism. And we must teach it in an honest way, not as the cartoonish, mustache-twisting caricature as it is so often painted by teachers, the media, and elected officials. Instead of, or in addition to, making children read *Heather Has Two Mommies*, why not have American schoolchildren read *Heather Has Two Income Streams*? Or economics textbooks written by Thomas Sowell or Walter E. Williams? Let's open this discussion up to the group.

- *Teach comparative government.* First and foremost, we need to teach the Constitution. Kids need to understand why the American system of government, based on freedom, liberty, and God-given rights, is demonstrably better than any other. The facts are indisputable. America is number one. Other systems of government are not. Therefore, our children should be taught not only that our system is the best, but also that other systems—like socialism or communism—are not the best and, in fact, are not even good. American children should be taught that those systems of government are bad at best and evil at worst. And the fact that that sounds even remotely controversial proves how far American education has drifted from the truth.

# ★ 8 ★

## *The Tea Party Goes to Court:*
## *What We Believe*
## *about the Judiciary*

*This Constitution, and the Laws of the United States which shall be made in pursuance thereof; and all treaties made, or which shall be made, under the authority of the United States, shall be the supreme law of the land; and the judges in every state shall be bound thereby, anything in the Constitution or laws of any state to the contrary notwithstanding.*

—SUPREMACY CLAUSE OF THE
U.S. CONSTITUTION,
ARTICLE VI, CLAUSE 2

*The judiciary of the United States is the subtle corps of sappers and miners constantly working under ground to undermine the foundations of our confederated fabric. They are construing our constitution from a co-ordination of a general and special government to a general and supreme one alone.*

—THOMAS JEFFERSON,
letter to Thomas Ritchie, December 25, 1820

**TEA PARTIERS ACROSS** the nation have told us that America's judicial system is disconnected from society and no longer reflects the values judges are tasked to protect. The rulings from the U.S. circuit courts and the Supreme Court often run counter to the original intent of America's Founders as expressed through the Constitution. Even at the local level, where judges are often elected by We the People, courts reflect a great and growing disconnect in America between the judges and the judged.

## THE JUDICIARY VERSUS THE PEOPLE'S INTERESTS

Pick an issue that you care about deeply. Now imagine that some judge ruled against your interests. What can you do? In a democratic republic the people have the power of the ballot. So imagine putting forth a ballot initiative to see if your fellow citizens support it. And suppose you win at the polls. Does that mean your initiative will become law?

Not if you live in Oklahoma.

In 2010 citizens of Oklahoma overwhelmingly approved Question 755, which clarified the separation between church and state enshrined in the First Amendment by an overwhelming 70 percent of the vote. This initiative should have prohibited state courts from considering either international law or Islamic sharia in state judicial decisions. Even though Oklahoma voters supported the new law separating church and state, Judge Vicki Miles-LaGrange issued a permanent injunction in the U.S. Federal Court in the Western District of Oklahoma overruling the will of the people. That ruling has yet to be finally decided, leaving voters in Oklahoma wondering just who is in charge of their state laws; the millions of people who voted, or a single judge.

Thomas Jefferson wrote, "One single object . . . [will merit] the endless gratitude of the society; that of restraining the judges from usurping legislation."* What would Jefferson say about judges today who overturn legislation directly initiated and voted upon by We the People?

* Thomas Jefferson, letter to Edward Livingston, March 25, 1825.

At the Supreme Court level, a hundred years of jurisprudence have warped the interpretation of the Constitution's Commerce Clause to the point where it would be unrecognizable to America's Founders.

According to the Constitution, the federal government has the power to "regulate Commerce . . . among the several States," and also to "make all Laws which shall be necessary and proper" to do so. But in the last century and a half, the U.S. Supreme Court has authorized the expansion of government power into areas the Constitution never intended.

Most citizens have a pretty good understanding of what *commerce* means. *The Oxford English Dictionary* defines it as the activity of buying and selling, especially on a large scale. That seems to make sense, doesn't it? Apparently not to the Supreme Court.

Over time, the Supreme Court has expanded the law to include any activity that "substantially affects" commerce among the states, even if that activity is noncommercial in nature. Since virtually any activity on a large scale can be said to "substantially affect" interstate commerce, the federal government obtains almost infinite regulatory authority. Is this what the Founders intended when they carefully crafted a form of government with checks and balances specifically designed to limit the power and reach of the federal government? Of course not.

It is bad enough when the government seizes power over our everyday activities. But now the administration is trying to extend its control even farther. The so-called constitutional justification for the requirement under Obamacare that every individual purchase health insurance is that the "nonactivity" of not buying health insurance is actually "commerce." If you agree with that last sentence, you've got a great future as a federal official.

If, on the other hand, you think the idea sounds like nonsense, you are in good company. The majority of American citizens believe that this kind of craziness is best left to Marx. Groucho Marx. Doesn't it remind you of the following scene in the Marx Brothers' 1930 film *Animal Crackers*?

MRS. RITTENHOUSE: You are one of the musicians? But you were not due until tomorrow.

RAVELLI: Couldn't come tomorrow, that's too quick.

SPAULDING: Say, you're lucky they didn't come yesterday!

RAVELLI: We were busy yesterday, but we charge just the same.

SPAULDING: This is better than exploring! What do you fellows get an hour?

RAVELLI: Oh, for playing we getta ten dollars an hour.

SPAULDING: I see . . . What do you get for not playing?

RAVELLI: Twelve dollars an hour.

SPAULDING: Well, clip me off a piece of that.

RAVELLI: Now, for rehearsing we make special rate. Thatsa fifteen dollars an hour.

SPAULDING: That's for rehearsing?

RAVELLI: Thatsa for rehearsing.

SPAULDING: And what do you get for not rehearsing?

RAVELLI: You couldn't afford it . . . Heh . . . you see, if we don't rehearse, we don't play . . . And, if we don't play . . . That runs into money . . . Yesterday, we didn't come. You remember, yesterday we didn't come?

SPAULDING: Oh, I remember . . .

RAVELLI: Yeah, that's three-hundred dollars.

SPAULDING: Yesterday you didn't come, that's three-hundred dollars?

RAVELLI: That's three-hundred dollars.

SPAULDING: Well, that's reasonable. I can see that alright.

RAVELLI: Now . . . today, we *did* come. That's uh . . .

SPAULDING: That's a hundred you owe us.

RAVELLI: Say, I bet I'm gonna lose on the deal . . . Tomorrow, we leave. That's worth about . . .

SPAULDING: A million dollars!

The judiciary's interpretation of government authority may please politicians looking to expand their power, but to the average citizen of the United States it seems absurd. And it's not just the Commerce Clause that is being distorted. Our Supreme Court has recently begun to reinterpret the Bill of Rights to favor powerful corporations or individuals with government officials in their pockets.

Take, for example, the Supreme Court's revision of the Fifth Amendment in its 2005 decision on the case of *Kelo v. City of New London*. The Constitution states: "No person shall . . . be deprived of life, liberty, or property, without due process of law; nor shall private property be taken for public use, without just compensation."

But in 1998, the city of New London, Connecticut, seized the property of home owner Suzette Kelo for what it considered a "public purpose." Had that public purpose been to build a highway or a public school, the case would probably not have raised many eyebrows. Suzette Kelo's property, however, was seized and given to a private entity that claimed it would create more economic growth in the area than Kelo. (The land was ostensibly taken to build a hotel and offices to enhance the value of a campus for Pfizer Pharmaceuticals.) That's right—the government seized property from one private landowner and gave it to another. And the Supreme Court, in a 5–4 decision, said that was OK.

Justice Sandra Day O'Connor, however, was scathing in her dissent: "The specter of condemnation hangs over all property," she wrote. "Nothing is to prevent the state from replacing any Motel 6 with a Ritz Carlton, any home with a shopping mall, or any farm with a factory."

To add insult to injury, the projected economic development never took place. After spending $78 million, the project flopped and the thousands of new jobs and tax revenue projected by the government never materialized. Worse still, in 2010 Pfizer closed the facility that was at the center of the controversy, just before tax breaks given to it by the city would have expired, raising its tax bill by 400 percent.

Our citizens are disconnected from the judiciary, disenchanted, and distrustful. The people feel that they are no longer sovereign. So what are we to do?

The first thing we must do is educate ourselves. History is a great teacher, and the Tea Party Patriots are lucky to have Eugene Meyer (president of the Federalist Society for Law and Public Policy Studies) and Nelson Lund (Patrick Henry Professor of Constitutional Law and the Second Amendment at George Mason University School of Law) provide us with some perspective for this book.*

## THE FOUNDATIONS OF THE U.S. JUDICIARY

### BY EUGENE MEYER AND NELSON LUND*

The most basic principle underlying our Constitution is the sovereignty of the people. That principle, which justified our revolt against the British monarchy, was respected in every state constitution adopted after our Revolution, and it has never been seriously questioned since that time. As history had shown, however, popular or democratic governments (including our early state governments) had very seldom proved in practice to be *good* governments. What was needed was a theory of government that would respect the principle of popular sovereignty while putting checks on the tendency of democracies to be swept up in shortsighted enthusiasms and exploitative attacks by self-interested majorities on the rights of minorities.

In Federalist 51, James Madison framed the theoretical problem with unsurpassed clarity.

> It may be a reflection on human nature that [certain] devices should be necessary to control the abuses of government. But what is government itself but the greatest of all reflections on human nature? If men were angels, no government would be necessary. If angels were to govern men, neither external nor internal controls on government would be necessary. In framing a government which is to be administered by men over men, the great difficulty lies in this: you must first enable the government to control the governed; and in the next place oblige it to control itself. A dependence on the

---

* The views expressed in the following section are those of Meyer and Lund and are not necessarily those of the institutions with which they are affiliated.

people is, no doubt, the primary control on the government; but experience has taught mankind the necessity of auxiliary precautions.

Madison also offered a succinct theoretical principle according to which these auxiliary precautions should be designed: "Ambition must be made to counteract ambition."

We are all familiar with the practical scheme based on this theory. We call it checks and balances, or separation of powers and federalism. For the most part, the key is to make each official and each institution *dependent* on others, so that it is difficult for any individual or special interest group to use the government to oppress other citizens.

Enacting a law, for example, requires the agreement of the House and the Senate, and usually the president as well. The president takes many actions by himself, but almost all of them require either congressional authorization or congressional appropriations, or both. And all of these officials are dependent on elections by the people for their continuance in office.

There is, however, one institution that the framers went to some lengths to *insulate* from dependence on others. In a number of ways, the Constitution protects the judiciary from being influenced by the president, the Congress, and even the people themselves. The primary device for accomplishing this was the institution of life tenure for federal judges.

The main reason for protecting the judges' independence was to enable them to be faithful to the law in the performance of their duty, and especially to the Constitution's limitations on governmental power and protections for minority rights. As Hamilton explained:

> [Protections for individual rights] can be preserved in practice no other way than through the medium of courts of justice, whose duty it must be to declare all acts contrary to the manifest tenor of the Constitution void. Without this, all the reservations of particular rights or privileges would amount to nothing . . . This indepen-

dence of the judges is equally requisite to guard the Constitution and the rights of individuals from the effects of those ill humors, which the arts of designing men, or the influence of particular conjunctures, sometimes disseminate among the people themselves, and which, though they speedily give place to better information, and more deliberate reflection, have a tendency, in the meantime, to occasion dangerous innovations in the government, and serious oppressions of the minor party in the community.

The Constitution's provisions regarding the federal judiciary did not provoke major controversies during the framing period. Nonetheless, they did worry a few of the most thoughtful skeptics about the proposed new Constitution. Because the Constitution is a species of law, and one that takes precedence over ordinary statutes, these skeptics correctly assumed that the new Supreme Court would have the power both to strike down unconstitutional statutes and to interpret statutes to make them consistent with the Constitution. They feared that the Supreme Court would be tempted to misuse this power by basing its decisions on "the spirit of the Constitution," which would turn out to be whatever the justices personally favored as a matter of policy.

If this were to happen, unelected life-tenured federal judges could become a kind of oligarchy, contrary to the principle of popular sovereignty. Whoever gets the last word is the effectual supreme ruler, and the Supreme Court has the last word on the meaning of the law on cases within its jurisdiction.

In *The Federalist Papers*, Alexander Hamilton responded to this objection at some length. The core of his response boiled down to this: somebody has to have the final word on the meaning of the Constitution and the laws, and the judiciary is the least dangerous place to put that power.

What made the judiciary the least dangerous branch? The best-known explanation is in Federalist 78, where Hamilton says:

The judiciary [unlike the executive or the legislature] has no influence over either the sword or the purse; no direction either of the

strength or of the wealth of the society, and can take no active resolution whatever. It may truly be said to have neither force nor will
but merely judgment; and must ultimately depend upon the aid of
the executive arm even for the efficacy of its judgments.

History has shown, however, that the Supreme Court can exercise
considerable power, effectively commandeering both the strength
and the wealth of the society in aid of its own policy preferences.
Typically, the justices have done this in just the way that was originally feared, by finding whatever they wanted to find in the "spirit of
the Constitution." In so doing, especially in areas where journalistic
and academic elites agree with them, they have too often substituted
laws that they like for the ones adopted by our elected representatives.

What may be at least as bad is that in many instances the Supreme
Court's independence has not prevented it from *upholding* congressional enactments that are *unconstitutional*. That kind of irresponsibility can have tremendous and long-lasting consequences. The power
of government swells beyond constitutional limits, the legitimate
rights of individuals are trampled, and the principal reason for instituting life tenure and judicial independence in the first place is lost.

It is important to keep this last point in mind, especially when
thinking about what is called *judicial activism*. This judicial vice
comes in two forms, and it is every bit as improper for courts to
uphold unconstitutional laws as it is to strike down or misinterpret
laws that are within a legislature's constitutional power. The double
nature of judicial activism should also serve as a warning against
simplistic solutions to the problems of the courts. Judicial restraint,
which certainly is a virtue, should emphatically not mean passivity in
the face of constitutional violations by Congress, or the president, or
indeed the state governments.

Hamilton was hardly naive, and he did not rely entirely on the
inherent institutional weakness of courts. There is another theme in
his defense of the independent judiciary that is less well known, but
which may have been more significant for his audience.

When our Constitution was drafted, the nation was heir to a tradition of judicial integrity that had developed in Great Britain over the course of many centuries. That tradition placed a heavy emphasis on the judicial duty to *follow the law in every case*, even when the judge considered the law unjust or ill-advised. British and American courts celebrated and vigorously defended a judicial ideal that required judges to apply the law, and only the law, in every judicial decision. Judges recognized that this is a lot harder than it may seem. It is not always easy to figure out exactly what a written law means, and it is frequently tempting to cook up an "interpretation" that fits what the judge thinks the law should be, or one that distorts the law to fit the judge's own views of justice or sound policy. And it can be very hard to resist political or popular pressure, especially when the judge is sympathetic to the views of those who want him to ignore or bend the law.

Nobody could have thought that judges had been, or ever would be, entirely successful in resisting these temptations. To a remarkable extent, however, British and American courts had succeeded in creating a culture in which this ideal of fidelity to the law was taken very seriously by judges, and recognized and respected by the wider public. In his defense of an independent judiciary, Hamilton alluded to the special qualities of integrity, learnedness, and modesty that judges were expected to possess. His audience knew what he was talking about, and they could reasonably believe that the awesome power to determine what the law is would be less dangerous in hands like these than in those of elected politicians.

This ideal of judicial duty has not been lost in our culture, even though it came under sustained attack, especially in academic circles, throughout much of the twentieth century. As popular attention has increasingly focused on this question over the past decade, opinion polls consistently show that substantial majorities believe that Supreme Court justices should base their decisions on what is written in the Constitution and legal precedents and not on their own sense of fairness and justice. In turn, the past four Supreme Court nominees—Democrats and Republicans alike—have pledged absolute fidelity to exactly this understanding of the judicial role. All nominees now say that they aspire to nothing higher than to be humble servants of the law. All of them say that they have no political or policy agendas of any kind. None of them claims authority to override the law in the name of their particular vision of justice, or promises to rule on the basis of their personal sympathies or their ethnic backgrounds. This is as it should be, for this is what the nation was promised by the framers of our Constitution. The challenge for the future will be to figure out which candidates for judicial office mean what they say, and will stick to it after they get their life-tenured appointments.

This is the end of the contribution by Eugene Meyer and Nelson Lund. We thank them for contributing their expertise on the judiciary.

∼

Eugene Meyer and Nelson Lund are both great patriots among the millions in the movement who have ideas about what has gone wrong and how to steer the country back onto the path they believe was envisioned by the Founders. While inclusion in this book doesn't necessarily mean that Tea Party Patriots endorses all of their views as expressed above, we appreciate standing shoulder to shoulder with them in the fight to return the nation to its founding principles.

## JUDICIAL DRIFT

The fundamental problem is that some American judges, to put it generously, interpret their mandates too broadly. They seem to place themselves above the law and view themselves as ultimate arbiters of right and wrong, regardless of the intent of the Constitution or of the will of the people. This problem seems to have become endemic from local counties to the marble halls of the U.S. Supreme Court.

How have our courts veered so far from the ideals set forth by the framers?

According to Edwin S. Corwin, author of *The Constitution of the United States, Annotated* (an official government publication), the Supreme Court has passed through four distinct phases in its history.

During John Marshall's term (1801–1835), the Constitution was primarily used to establish national supremacy. *The Federalist Papers* and the words of the Founders were almost the exclusive reference materials used to interpret the law during this period. When Thomas Jefferson became president, he said: "The Constitution on which our Union rests shall be administered by me according to the safe and honest meaning contemplated by the plain understanding of the people of the United States at the time of its adoption—a meaning to be found in the explanations of those who advocated, not those who opposed it . . . These explanations are preserved in the publications of the time."

Look at how far we have drifted from the days when the principal author and defender of the Declaration of Independence was our president. Jefferson respected the sovereignty of the people, but today the White House uses the courts to force people to buy health insurance against their will.

The second phase in the Supreme Court's drift from strict interpretation toward activism began with the appointment of Chief Justice Roger B. Taney in 1835 and lasted until roughly 1895. In this period, while the Court adhered to the philosophy of the Founders, it rarely quoted *The Federalist Papers* or the Founders themselves.

The third phase began around 1895 when the Supreme Court began replacing the idea of constitutional supremacy with "judicial" supremacy. The Court no longer respected the intent of our Founders. Instead, it began to interpret the Constitution according to its own views. Around this time, New York governor Charles Evan Hughes (who later ascended to the bench and ultimately became chief justice) said, "We are under a Constitution, but the Constitution is what the judges say it is."

Finally, we come to the current phase of judicial drift away from "originalism." From the local county courts, to our once-vaunted appellate system, on up to the Supreme Court, the people have lost faith in the "justice" system.

## SHORT-TERM SOLUTIONS

So what can we do? In the short term, knowledge is power. We must help people understand how the judiciary was designed to work. This is rudimentary civics education, which most of us never received in school. Once people learn what the Founders wrote, they can make judgments about how their courts are functioning. In cooperation with the National Center for Constitutional Studies (http://www .nccs.net), the Tea Party Patriots is committed to educating Americans about their Constitution and is including as part of that education the structure, history, and current state of our court system.

As we approach the elections of 2012, We the People need better information about local candidates for positions on the bench. At the local level, how many Americans have voted for judges when they know little or nothing about them? Have you? Faced with a slate of names you know nothing about, do you vote on the basis of gender, party affiliation (if allowed), or simply because you like or dislike a name? Part of the blame for casting such uninformed votes is ours. The rest is the result of a system that is not designed to give us the critical information we need in order to vote intelligently.

That is where the Tea Party Patriots comes in.

Currently there is no system for methodically analyzing judicial candidates at the local level. In many places campaigning for judicial elections is prohibited. So we are left to rely upon candidate-prepared biographies, newspaper clippings, and occasionally statements of a friend or family member. What we really need is a system of questionnaires that would allow us to adequately analyze judicial candidates' suitability for office. At a minimum, the questionnaires would include the following:

- Professional qualifications
- Judicial philosophy (simple categories should be created— activist, orginalist, etc.)
- Legal history (type of practice, cases handled as an attorney, etc.)

- Judicial history (citizen committees should be established to review the judicial record of a candidate up for reelection)

Such a system would allow the average voter to learn how each candidate would perform if elected. And bear in mind that lower-court judges make decisions that affect our communities and our friends and neighbors every day.

Importantly, local judges ultimately get elevated to higher positions on the bench. We need the same analytical system for all levels of the judiciary, nationwide. By working with Tea Party chapters nationwide, and reaching out to our membership and other organizations, Tea Party Patriots is developing the standards necessary to create such a system, online across the country.

As we move into the 2012 electoral season, basic education on our court system and effective candidate vetting are important first steps toward reforming our judiciary.

In the next chapter, we will discuss potential long-term solutions.

# ★ 9 ★

## *The Judicial Pathway to Liberty*

> *We, the people are the rightful masters of both Congress and the courts, not to overthrow the Constitution, but to overthrow men who pervert the Constitution.*
>
> —ABRAHAM LINCOLN

IN THIS CHAPTER, we will discuss some long-term proposals to fix our broken judicial system, starting at the local level and working our way up to the Supreme Court.

### TORT REFORM

The abuse of America's legal system by greedy or unscrupulous lawyers and plaintiffs has led many Americans—inside and outside of the Tea Party movement—to call for *tort reform*. What is a *tort* and why should it be reformed? A tort is a type of civil case that can be filed after someone suffers an injury, presumably due to the negligence of a company or an individual. *Slip-and-fall lawyers* and *ambulance chasers* are the intentionally derogatory terms for lawyers who specialize in helping wronged parties sue for damages. While we support verdicts providing reasonable damages, we are opposed to those that award penalties totally out of line with the injury inflicted.

One of the most famous cases of unreasonable damages was the "McDonald's hot coffee" incident in 1992. A woman scalded herself with McDonald's hot coffee and then sued the company for serving her a drink that was too hot. She was awarded nearly $3 million in damages by a jury (later reduced to $450,000). Ever since then, the rest of us (who are able to figure out on our own that coffee is hot) have witnessed an explosion of idiotic warning labels and signs—not necessarily designed to protect us from harm—but designed to protect businesses from potential lawsuits. Here are some of the more notable warning labels.

REMOVE CHILD BEFORE FOLDING (baby stroller)

THIS PRODUCT MOVES WHEN USED (child's scooter)

DO NOT EAT TONER (laser printer cartridge)

CAUTION—RISK OF FIRE (fireplace log)

IF YOU DO NOT UNDERSTAND, OR CANNOT READ, ALL DIRECTIONS, CAUTIONS AND WARNINGS, DO NOT USE THIS PRODUCT (drain cleaner)

This infantilization of the American public is not the only cost of such lawsuits. The companies that issue these silly warnings do so because the silly lawsuits filed by greedy lawyers cost American businesses and doctors—and, through them, the American public— billions of wasted dollars each year.

According to the Heritage Foundation, "Over the past 50 years, tort liability has increased more than a hundredfold, while the GDP has increased by a factor of only 37." "The total estimated cost for 2007 was $252 billion—almost $1,000 for every person in the country." But that is not the only cost. "Tort risks are the second most important factor when a company decides where to relocate or expand operations or build a new plant or introduce a new product." That means: for almost every item that you and your family buy, "built into every price is a component to pay for liability insurance and lawsuit defense." That costs each American approximately $2,000 per year in hidden fees.*

But there is yet another cost: that of stifled innovation, due to fear of punitive class-action lawsuits.

* Quotes in this paragraph taken from http://www.heritage.org/research/lecture/tort-reform
-in-the-states-protecting-consumers-and-enhancing-economic-growth.

Imagine that the polio epidemic was still with us, affecting 20,000 to 50,000 Americans each year as it did back in the 1950s. Would Jonas Salk try to develop his vaccine, or would today's constant threat of punitive lawsuits drive him out of the lab?

The first fact to consider is that the polio vaccine actually *caused* polio in approximately one out of every one million people who received the shot. Every life is priceless. But, in the eyes of certain trial lawyers, every life has a price. If Salk knew that there was a multimillion dollar judgment against him lurking behind every one-in-a-million casualty, would he have pursued the vaccine? Would he even be able to test it today?

Judge for yourself whether anything like the following would be allowed to happen in today's litigious society.

- "Jonas Salk first tested his polio vaccine on humans in July 1952 when he inoculated thirty children at the D. T. Watson Home for Crippled Children near Pittsburgh, Pennsylvania."
- "Salk then vaccinated children at the 'Polk State School for the Retarded and Feeble Minded.'"
- On April 26, 1954, "the largest public health experiment in American history" began at Franklin Sherman Elementary School, where six-year-old Randy Kerr "received the first inoculation of the 1954 volunteer polio vaccine field trials." Instead of recoiling in horror at six-year-old first-graders being used for medical experiments, the nation celebrated young Randy Kerr and the vaccination trials, which then went national.
- "The trial's study population, then, targeted some 1.8 million children in the first three grades of elementary school at 215 test sites. In the double-blind experiment, 650,000 children received vaccine, 750,000 received a placebo (a solution made to look like vaccine, but containing no virus), and 430,000 served as controls and had neither."

These 1.8 million American children were not cast as victims by the media, and they were not considered potential paychecks by greedy lawyers. Instead, they were called "Polio Pioneers" and were rewarded with a certificate and a piece of candy. Today, Jonas Salk would be the target of multiple class-action lawsuits for conducting such experimental trials on

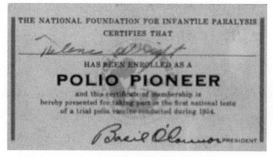

schoolchildren, and whoever gave these children candy would be sued for contributing to childhood obesity.

*In the midst of our litigious society, with the constant threat of huge class-action settlements, is it any wonder why only twenty-one new drugs were approved by the FDA in 2010?*

There is yet another cost to today's litigious atmosphere, which proponents of tort reform hope to clear up: the devastating cost to America's health-care system due to the unnecessarily large number of tests ordered by doctors who live under the daily threat of malpractice claims. The name for this phenomenon is Defensive Medicine, and it describes how doctors today are forced to order "unnecessary tests and treatments to avoid potential lawsuits. This literally adds hundreds of billions of dollars to the cost of health care every year."*

Obamacare would make it worse. Nowhere in its thousands of pages of legislation, or scores of offshoot regulations, is there any mention of tort reform. Unfortunately for patients, doctors, and the American citizens who have to pay for all of this litigiousness—"tort lawyers are one of the biggest sources of campaign funding for Democrats. In a very candid moment, Howard Dean admitted that the reason there was nothing in Obamacare on tort reform was 'because the people who wrote it did not want to take on the trial lawyers . . . And that's the plain and simple truth.'"

---

* Hans von Spakowsky, "The State of Medical Malpractice Reform in the Union." *The Foundry*, January 26, 2011; http://www.blog.heritage.org/2011/01/26/the-state-of-medical -malpractice-reform-in-the-union/.

*The Tea Party Patriots are willing to take on the trial lawyers on a state-by-state basis. And we are not alone.*

After roughly a decade of serious reform efforts, in 2003 the Texas legislature enacted the strongest tort reform legislation in the nation. The state passed the country's most effective asbestos and silica litigation reforms two years later. These victories came in a state long known as a plaintiff lawyer's paradise. They proved that, with a concentrated and sustained effort, such reforms could be achieved. Texans for Lawsuit Reform (TLR) deserves the majority of the credit for these reforms and provides a model the rest of the nation should follow.

According to TLR, success must be achieved on two battlefields: electoral politics and legislative advocacy. Without political strength, no organization is likely to be effective in delivering tort reform. Reform is a political process, and only by engaging local groups who support local candidates can we expect to achieve real reform.

Local Tea Party groups are uniquely suited for this role. Having already proved their efficacy in the 2010 elections, local Tea Party groups can engage all political candidates on the issue of tort reform. And after elections, these groups can pressure legislatures to deliver on their promises. In partnership with other like-minded groups, the Tea Party movement has already shown that it can change legislative debates on local, state, and national levels. We Tea Partiers can deploy our expertise on a state-by-state basis and finally deliver what politicians have been promising for years, and what the majority of Americans* say they want: tort reform.

Based on our experience, we recommend that in each state, Tea Partiers model their efforts on those of Texans for Lawsuit Reform (TLR). TLR has successfully accomplished the most effective lawsuit reform effort in the nation, and openly shares its methodologies.†

---

\* AP poll: Americans want medical malpractice reform, November 19, 2009.
† TLR can be found online at http://www.tortreform.com.

## JUDGING THE JUDGES

In the previous chapter we discussed the idea of reviewing the performance of sitting judges who are standing for reelection. One of the more robust online models for achieving this goal is called Judgepedia, which fashions itself like Wikipedia and offers one of the biggest databases on judges and courts. But there's a catch. The problem with "wikis" is that they often overweight the beliefs of their contributors. This results in some rather curious postings and omissions on Judgepedia.

To illustrate, let's consider the (tarnished) gold standard for judicial activism in America: the U.S. Court of Appeals for the Ninth Circuit, which is irreverently referred to as the Ninth Circus. The San Francisco–based court is the fountainhead of judicial activism and overreach. When a case is sent to the Ninth Circus, it is a safe bet that the verdict will reflect its leftist views, be at odds with America's founding principles, and stand a darn good chance of being overturned as unconstitutional. The Ninth Circuit has ruled:

- "It's Legal to Abet Terrorists."*
- The Pledge of Allegiance is "unconstitutional."
- Felons should be allowed to vote.
- Arizona should not be allowed to enforce federal law.
- Illegals should be allowed to vote without ID.
- Threatening to assassinate President George W. Bush (while saying "long live bin Laden") is "protected speech."

The result of such rulings is that the Ninth Circuit is the "most overturned court in the United States" "responsible for more than a third (35%, or 8 of 23) of the High (Supreme) Court's unanimous reversals." The San Francisco court accounted for more reversals in the 2009–2010 term than all the state courts across the country combined and

* Newsmax, December 4, 2003.

represented nearly half of the overturned judgments (45 percent) of the federal appellate courts.*

Yet nowhere on the Judgepedia site does it mention *why* the Ninth Circuit's decisions continually get overturned: because they are activist, hard leftist, and do not reflect the limits of our Constitution. Judgepedia actually goes out of its way to direct its readers to "a persuasive empirical argument that the Ninth Circuit is *not* liberal leaning."

So it is important, when seeking opinions on judges, to always seek a second opinion. Here are a few other places to look.

In California, Craig Huey of the Judge Voter Guide (http://www.judgevoterguide.com) researches as many candidates for judicial office as possible. Utilizing in-person or telephone interviews, he attempts to speak with them all. Judges are evaluated based on their rulings, who appointed them (if they were appointed to their first term), their endorsements, and other criteria.

Each candidate is thoroughly evaluated and the results posted on the Judge Voter Guide Web site before each election. The guide uses the following scale system to rate candidates.

## QUALIFICATIONS

To rate qualifications, the guide takes into account: experience, reputation, integrity, and American Bar Association ratings.

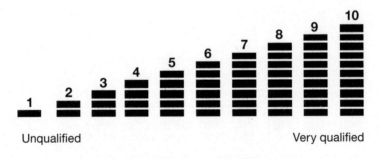

Unqualified | Very qualified

* http://www.judgepedia.org/index.php/United_States_Court_of_Appeals_for_the_Ninth_Circuit.

## JUDICIAL INDEX AVERAGE

This rating is determined by looking at the judicial candidate's positions, contributions, rulings, and statements.

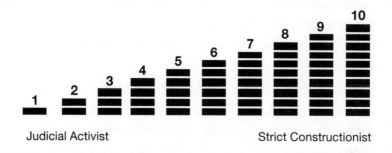

Judicial Activist                            Strict Constructionist

In Colorado, an organization called Clear the Bench Colorado (http://www.clearthebenchcolorado.org) is helping to bring transparency to that state's courtrooms and a constructionist approach to judging judges. According to its Web site, its mission is to:

1. Educate Colorado voters on the importance of judges observing principles of the "rule of law" in deciding cases;
2. Educate Colorado voters on their right to non-retain judges who do not follow these principles;
3. Advocate for the non-retention of justices statewide who demonstrate a consistent pattern of deciding cases in contravention of the Colorado Constitution, established statutory law, legal precedent, & "rule of law" principles (naming judges as necessary to educate voters).

And in Washington State, Voting for Judges* has a similar mission: "**VotingforJudges** is a nonpartisan, impartial source of information about judicial elections in the state of Washington. The site was established in 2006 to provide information to voters in connection with the judicial candidates running for election that year."

---

* http://www.VotingforJudges.com.

Judge for yourself which system is best. At the time of this writing, there is no comprehensive system to help Americans judge their judges (and judicial candidates) on whether or not they support the original intent of America's Founding Fathers.

A good grassroots template for such a system can be found at http://www.RobeProbe.com, which allows the American people who find themselves on the receiving end of justice (litigants and lawyers) to rate the judges and comment on their findings. Books, such as the one you are now reading, have been subject to online reviews for years, and we saw how schoolteachers in Los Angeles and New York are starting to be rated by those they serve. Therefore, it is not too much to hope that someday Americans will be able to go online and learn about the judges who preside over the laws of the land, and those who are seeking election to the bench. This is a project that has been suggested for adoption by many grassroots Tea Party Patriots.

All across the country citizens are rising up against a judiciary out of control. In the long run our nation will need committed activists in each state, dedicated to effecting the sort of judicial analysis and vetting now being done by a handful of small but committed activists. Tea Party Patriots wants to assist in these efforts on a national scale, by setting up a national support system for existing local organizations, helping to create them in states where they do not exist, and supplying research and vital information to national groups that seek to empower the American people to make informed decisions about their judges.

Only by knowing the candidates and their records and voting accordingly can we begin to restore the judiciary to its original and proper role in America.

## RESTRAINING THE SUPREME COURT

Even in the earliest days of the Supreme Court, our Founders knew that the Supreme Court was composed of fallible human beings, who have lifetime tenures, and who are accountable to no higher authority than themselves. This means they could pose great dangers to America should they ever forget that they are ultimately accountable to the U.S. Constitution.

Thomas Jefferson warned about "public ruin" at the hands of Supreme Court justices who are answerable to no one, an admonishment that was prescient. The Supreme Court has expanded its power well beyond its original mandate. Even Alexander Hamilton, who had an expansive view of federal power, would have blushed at the modern Supreme Court's interpretations of the Constitution.

## CONSTITUTIONAL AMENDMENT PROPOSED
## BY THOMAS JEFFERSON

Jefferson proposed an amendment to the Constitution that would have allowed Congress or the state legislatures (or possibly both) to have veto power, or removal power, over the Supreme Court. Recognizing that the framers had failed to place any safeguards against a High Court run amok, Jefferson believed that such a structure might provide the people with much-needed checks and balances. Unfortunately, this amendment never saw the light of day.

Say what you want about the "overreaches" of the presidency—at least every U.S. president is accountable to American voters every four years, and accountable to Congress for every bill that passes, and subject to impeachment should he or she stray too far from the constitutional mandate of the office.

Supreme Court justices are not subject to any of these checks and balances beyond impeachment, which is problematic because these justices wield power from the bench that can even supersede the power of our elected president. That amount of unchecked power is doubly disturbing when we consider that this is the same judicial body that once ruled that black slaves were property (*Dred Scott v. Sandford*, 1857) and more recently ruled against free speech (*McConnell v. Federal Election Commission*, 2003) and property rights (*Kelo v. City of New London*, 2005, "eminent domain").

# REPEAL AMENDMENT PROPOSED BY GRASSROOTS TEA PARTIERS

Today, people within the Tea Party movement are proposing a way to restrain the Supreme Court. It's called the Repeal Amendment, and it would restore the balance of power between the states and the federal government.

According to the grassroots folks at http://www.repealamendment .org, a fully vetted proposed amendment reads as follows: "Any provision of law or regulation of the United States may be repealed by the several states, and such repeal shall be effective when the legislatures of two-thirds of the several states approve resolutions for this purpose that particularly describes the same provision or provisions of law or regulation to be repealed."

This proposed amendment was drafted with the guidance of Randy Barnett, a law professor and constitutional law expert at Georgetown University. Initially adopted and promoted by members of the Virginia Tea Party Patriots Federation, the proposal has wide support in the Tea Party movement. It also has the support of many senators, congressional representatives, and other notable public figures.

Prior to the Tea Party movement, such an amendment would have been considered impossible. Yet on May 13, 2011, it was introduced by Bob Bishop (a Utah Republican in the U.S. House of Representatives) and Mike Enzi (a Wyoming Republican in the U.S. Senate), reflecting public sentiment in their stated belief that over the past several decades, the balance of power between the federal government and state governments has been upset. They expressed hope that this amendment would help to reverse this trend. "The Repeal Amendment would provide states with a powerful tool to return power and rights back to the states and to the people respectively, just as our Founding Fathers intended," Bishop said. "It is my hope that this joint resolution will inspire a new way of thinking in Washington, serving as a reminder to lawmakers and bureaucrats that policies that reflect the will of the people most often originate at the local and state levels, and not in Washington, D.C."

In effect, the amendment would allow two-thirds of the states, acting in concert, to repeal federal legislation or federal regulations. The two-thirds requirement prevents a simple majority from overriding the other states and ensures that only legislation that is opposed by the vast majority of citizens is overturned. Motivated by Tea Party activists, politicians are working to ensure the right of the states to overrule the Supreme Court when the Court rules a government action constitutional but a majority of citizens believe it is not.

Passing such an amendment takes time, often years, but structural changes are part of our long-term solution for the reform of the judiciary.

## SUPREME AND APPELLATE COURT JUDICIAL SELECTIONS

We must never forget that the president has the authority to appoint both Appellate and Supreme Court justices. This power cannot be underestimated. When used as a tool to implement a particular view of society, as has been done to dramatic effect under the Obama administration, it is a more powerful tool than any other the president wields.

President Obama has placed two justices on the Supreme Court: Sonia Sotomayor and Elena Kagan. Both have radical views regarding the role of judges and the way they should decide cases.

Justice Sotomayor, in a remarkably race-based opinion that had been a staple of her public speeches before being appointed to the bench, famously said, "I would hope that a wise Latina woman with the richness of her experiences would more often than not reach a better conclusion than a white male who hasn't lived that life." Instead of ruling on laws based on constitutional issues, Justice Sotomayor has openly expressed that race, sex, and the "richness of her experiences" are among the guiding principles she will bring to her rulings.

Before her appointment to the Court, Justice Kagan had never served on the bench and had very few writings that could be analyzed in order to determine her philosophy. However, the following excerpt from an article by Charmaine Yoest identifies Kagan's judicial heroes and thereby makes her approach clear.

> According to Human Events, "The President's nominee to the Supreme Court, Elena Kagan, called Aharon Barak "my judicial hero. He is the judge who has best advanced democracy, human rights, the rule of law, and justice."
>
> One of the troubling things about Kagan's 2006 statement is her assumption that the role of judges is to "advance" abstract concepts and values, rather than faithfully apply the law that they have been given by the people through the Constitution or statutes passed by legislatures.
>
> So who is Aharon Barak? Barak is the retired chief judge of the Supreme Court of Israel, and is considered one of the most liberal activist judges in the entire world, according to leading judges across the political spectrum.
>
> Kagan's admiration for Barak should be no surprise, since she worked for Abner Mikva, one of the most liberal activist judges in American history.
>
> Kagan is so admiring of judicial activists that she sought to silence congressional critics of activist judges. While dean of Harvard Law School in May 2005, Kagan joined a letter by law school deans that rebuked members of Congress as "irresponsible" and asserting that their criticism of activist judges was "harmful to our constitutional system and to the value of a judiciary."
>
> Apparently, no matter how political judges get, they should be beyond criticism. But it's precisely when judges begin to act like politicians that they should be subject to the same open criticism that politicians are.*

Although presidents are supposed to nominate the most qualified jurists available, in recent years, this standard has all but been aban-

---

* Charmaine Yoest, Human Events, May 11, 2010, http://www.humanevents.com/article.php?id=36932.

doned. Citizens must demand that presidents go back to appointing judges who believe in "original intent" and who will apply that standard when judging the constitutionality of challenged laws.

## ADVICE AND CONSENT OF THE SENATE

Article II, Section 2, of the Constitution requires the president to seek the "advice" and obtain the "consent" of the Senate regarding his appointment of all federal judges and other "officers" of the United States. Historically, the Senate has rejected approximately 20 percent of nominees to the Supreme Court, with the first rejection taking place in 1795 when the Senate refused to affirm President Washington's nomination of John Rutledge.

Recently, the most controversial rejection of a Supreme Court nominee was that of Judge Robert Bork, nominated by Ronald Reagan. Bork was an avowed "originalist" and as such a serious threat to those who pursue judicial activism. His confirmation was narrowly defeated in the Senate, where conservatives missed the opportunity to return the Court to the application of "original intent" and judicial restraint.

These fights take place at the appellate-court level as well. A recent example occurred on May 19, 2011, when the Senate refused to confirm the radical activist judge Goodwin Liu to the Ninth Circuit Court of Appeals. Liu was finally forced to withdraw from consideration. This was an important victory in the fight to preserve the originalist view of the Constitution.

In a 2008 article, Liu wrote: "The problem for courts is to determine, at the moment of decision, whether our collective values on a given issue have converged to a degree that they can be persuasively crystallized and credibly absorbed into legal doctrine. This difficult task requires keen attention to the trajectory of social norms reflected in public policies, institutions, and practices, as well as predictive judgment as to how a judicial decision may help forge or frustrate a social consensus.*

---

* Goodwin Liu, "Rethinking Constitutional Welfare Rights," *Stanford Law Review* 61, no. 2 (2008): 254.

As a *Washington Times* editorial charged, "Mr. Liu's goal was to create a judicially enforceable, constitutional right to welfare."

The Senate's refusal to confirm a radical judicial activist like Liu is a good sign. With millions of Tea Party activists reviewing nominations to the appellate and Supreme Courts, we can help bring the country back in line with its founding principles.

It is a long road, but for the sake of our children and grandchildren, we have no choice but to be eternally vigilant.

# ★ 10 ★

## The Tea Party on Television: What's Happened to Our Popular Culture?

*We hold these truths to be self-evident, that all men are created equal, that they are endowed by their Creator with certain unalienable Rights, that among these are Life, Liberty and the pursuit of Happiness.*

—The Declaration of Independence

**IN THE ORIGINAL,** 1962 film version of the novelist Richard Condon's *The Manchurian Candidate*, Frank Sinatra gives a virtuoso performance as the U.S. Army major Bennett Marco, a patriotic soldier whose platoon is captured by the Soviets and secretly taken to China during the Korean War. The Americans are brainwashed, and Staff Sergeant Raymond Shaw is programmed to assassinate a U.S. presidential candidate as part of a plot to bring the United States under Communist control.

The movie was released during the Cuban missile crisis and captured the American spirit at the height of the Cold War: "We are right, and they are wrong." The film portrays the Soviet Union, in words that Ronald Reagan would use twenty years later during a speech to the National Association of Evangelicals, as an *evil empire*, bent on uniting the world under totalitarian rule. And, predictably, at the end of the movie, as at the end of the Cold War, the good guys win. (For the benefit of those readers whose only experience with

American culture came after the mid-1960s, the good guys are the Americans.)

In the 2004 remake of *The Manchurian Candidate*, however, the moral landscape is very different. Given the setting of the movie, it would have been easy for the filmmaker Jonathan Demme to cast Saddam Hussein and the Baathist government of Iraq in the role originally occupied by the Communists. But the director made a different choice, casting America as a villain. Rather than painting the United States as the guardian of freedom, our nation is portrayed as a xenophobic dystopia governed by martial law and the perpetrator of all sorts of reprehensible behavior—perhaps the worst of which is its lack of respect for . . . the environment.

In the remake, though, America is only cast as a minor villain. The true bad guy, in what has become a cinematic cliché in recent years, is a greedy corporation. The "candidate" in this 2004 version is being controlled not by a foreign power, but by the Manchurian Global Corporation, bent on worldwide domination in the pursuit of profit.

In recent years, "greedy" capitalists have taken over as the villains of choice in popular culture. Take James Cameron's *Avatar*, the top-grossing movie of all time. The villain in *Avatar* is the RDA Corporation, which, while strip-mining a moon, starts killing the native species, a band of peaceful, environmentally sensitive pantheists. Predictably, the mainstream media and the Hollywood Academy swooned over the film. Somewhat less predictably, so did Evo Morales, the Socialist president-of-Bolivia-turned-movie-critic, who praised the film for its "profound show of resistance to capitalism and the struggle for the defense of nature." (Morales perhaps conveniently neglected to include as part of his movie review the fact that per capita GDP in Bolivia is less than $5,000 per person, perhaps due to that country's own "profound show of resistance to capitalism.")

While it is just fine to portray free-market capitalists as villains, it is no longer acceptable to do the same for religious terrorists. Tom Clancy's 1991 novel, *The Sum of All Fears*, for example, features Muslim extremists destroying Baltimore with a nuclear bomb. The 2002 film version casts South African neo-Nazis as the bad guys. And, of course, it has almost become a cliché in recent years for movies to demonize American soldiers and veterans. Brian de Palma's 2007 film *Redacted* focuses on five American soldiers who rape and kill a young Iraqi girl and her family. In the 1999 film *Three Kings*, U.S. soldiers are portrayed as thieves bent on stealing Saddam Hussein's hidden gold.

> *Every single one of our soldiers signed up or re-signed up after 9/11. The term, the longest one was 6 years, so every single one signed up after 9/11, every single one knew where he was going, what was going to happen to him, and has an idea of why it's the right thing to do. Those guys cannot appear in the movies. And you know, it wouldn't bother me so much, the movies that Hollywood makes never bother me so much as the movies they don't make. If there were eight films attacking our troops, I would still despise them for making them during wartime. But if there were eight films supporting our troops, I know that those films would win out with the audience, and I know their arguments would be better, and I know the depiction of life would be more realistic.*

—screenwriter and novelist ANDREW KLAVAN

What has happened to American culture? How did it become OK to trash the values that made America great? And what can we do, once again, to applaud America as a force for good in the world, so that our traditional heroes are celebrated, not demonized?

Do not misunderstand: we do not think that corporations, the military, or even the United States of America are above criticism. We the People are hardly perfect. Our Founders understood this. All humans make mistakes, and when they do, we believe, as patriots, that it is the duty of all citizens to call attention to those errors and to build "a more perfect union." As you can see in the Tea Party move-ment, we do not shy away from criticizing any and all leaders.

Nor do we suggest that Americans should be praised simply for existing. Such praise is often cringe-worthy:

> *Obama's finest speeches do not excite. They do not inform. They don't even really inspire. They elevate. They enmesh you in a grander moment, as if history has stopped flowing passively by, and, just for an instant, contracted around you, made you aware of its presence, and your role in it. He is not the Word made flesh, but the triumph of word over flesh, over color, over despair. The other great leaders I've heard guide us towards a better politics, but Obama is, at his best, able to call us back to our highest selves, to the place where America exists as a glittering ideal, and where we, its honored inhabitants, seem capable of achieving it, and thus of sharing in its meaning and transcendence.*
>
> —*Washington Post* blogger EZRA KLEIN
> in *The American Prospect*

There is a strong relationship between entertainment and a cul-ture's overall values. Movies, music, and books are a leading indicator of where a society is going, or a reaction to what a society has become. There is a definite correlation between how we portray ourselves and the values we hold.

> Art is the indispensable medium for the communi-cation of a moral ideal . . . *This does not mean that art is a substitute for philosophical thought: without a conceptual theory of ethics, an artist would not be able successfully to concretize an image of the ideal. But without the assistance of art, ethics remains in the posi-tion of theoretical engineering: art is the model-builder.*
>
> —AYN RAND, *The Romantic Manifesto*

In the past fifty years, there has been a decided shift in our culture against the idea of American exceptionalism. Today, rather than offering reasoned and appropriate criticism of America for its mistakes, and encouragement to live up to its highest ideals, the media instead lash out at the values and founding principles that made America exceptional. Currently, the dominant face of popular culture is critical of America for its power and success. Much of our culture celebrates our weaknesses and apologizes for our strengths. And it delights in our misfortunes and roots for us to fail.

Even when we are confronted with pure evil, many Americans are quick to blame America first. Conflict in the Middle East? It's America's fault for supporting the region's only democracy. Starvation in Cuba? America's fault for imposing a unilateral embargo. American civilians killed by religious extremists? America's fault.

The humorist and commentator Andy Rooney had this to say: "Might be better if we figured out how to behave as a nation in a way that wouldn't make so many people in the world want to kill us." It's ironic that these words should come from Rooney, who experienced firsthand the horrors of World War II. Perhaps he thinks that America was responsible for that war, as well.

The actress Susan Sarandon once proclaimed, "The United States is a land that has raped every area of the world." The director Robert Altman sneered, "When I see an American flag flying, it's a joke." Perhaps misunderstanding what the word *terrorist* means, the actress Sandra Bernhard suggested that "the real terrorist threats are George W. Bush and his brown-shirted thugs." The litany continues. "When the Communist USSR was a superpower, the world was better off," claims the actress Janeane Garofalo (unless, of course, you happened to be one of the millions murdered by the Soviet government or its puppet states). "Have we gone to war yet?" asked the musician Chrissie Hynde? "We fuc#ing deserve to get bombed."

We, the Tea Party Patriots, disagree. We believe that truth, justice, and the American way *are* what is needed today, not just in America, but all over the world. And we question what leads so many

Americans—particularly those in the media—to disagree. What is the root cause of this cultural phenomenon? How did we go from American exceptionalism to a deep sense of self-loathing in only two generations?

The author Michael Prell, who is a political strategist and an adviser to Tea Party Patriots (and who, in the way of full disclosure, has been instrumental in the writing of this book), identified part of the phenomenon and gave it a name: Underdogma, which he defines as "the reflexive belief that those who have less power are good—*because* they have less power, and that those who have more power are bad—*because* they have more power." As long as America continues to be the most powerful nation in the world, we will suffer the slings and arrows of Underdogma. The only way to satisfy those at home and abroad who hate America for being powerful is for America to become weak. And while our current leaders in Washington, D.C., believe it is their job to bow down and apologize for America's strength, to preside over America's orderly and "managed decline," and to "lead from behind," we know that it is our job as Tea Party Patriots to champion American greatness, power, and exceptionalism, and to keep the "shining city upon a hill" shining brightly as a beacon to the world.

≈

At the birth of our nation, the Founders emphasized equality of opportunity over equality of outcome. The principles of the American Revolution differed in that way from other revolutions—particularly the French. While it is ingrained in the American source code that we are all created equal, the Founders expected that we would not end up in the same place. We the People believe that those who work hard, take prudent risks, and defer gratification by investing rather than consuming should eventually get to enjoy the fruits of their decisions. The corollary is the belief that those who fail must suffer the consequences of their failure.

When Jefferson wrote the Declaration of Independence, he was precise in his language. "We are endowed by our Creator with certain unalienable rights—life, liberty and the pursuit of happiness." Our founding principles don't promise happiness; they promise the *pursuit* of happiness.

The Founders emphasized the protection of the individual and the family against the excesses of a repressive central government. Our experiences settling the continent further reinforced those values. At the beginning of the American experiment, our forefathers only had their friends, family, church, and rifle to provide for themselves and to protect them against misfortune.

But as our institutions began to expand, government increasingly began devising ways to redistribute wealth, rather than protecting the liberties—or even championing the virtues—of those Americans who create wealth.

> *I do think at a certain point you've made enough money.*
> —BARACK OBAMA

Many Americans don't even realize how wealth is actually created. Our culture claims that companies are evil, and that wealth either is something stolen by cigar-chomping CEOs or is a fund to be redistributed to the needy by some benevolent government agency. We are told that the way to end a recession is by borrowing and spending more money rather than by creating more wealth. We hear that flooding the market with more dollar bills will increase our collective wealth. We are taught that everything produced in this country belongs to all of us, and that it's only by the grace of the government that we should be allowed to keep any of it.

This is the kind of "thinking" that our culture produces today. It fosters an entitlement mentality, rather than one that encourages hard work and excellence. A substantial portion of our country believes that the only way the government can keep its promises is by playing a game of musical chairs that divorces the process of creating wealth from the process of consumption. But when the music stops—as it did in 2008—those false promises are revealed. Sooner or later, as Margaret Thatcher pointed out, "the problem with socialism is that you run out of other people's money." We cannot ultimately consume more than we produce.

The consequences of such practices demonize those who have succeeded at the expense of those who have not. But when you don't realize how much effort goes into creating something, you don't value it. When you don't value something, you don't celebrate it. And that's where we are in our popular culture today. We've rejected the traditional values of sacrifice and investment in favor of immediate gratification; after all, many of our politicians tell us that we're entitled to it. Buy a house you can't afford, then expect "the government" to pay for it when you default on your mortgage. Make a bad investment with your shareholders' money, and when it fails, expect "the government" to bail you out.

Too many believe they "deserve" what they "want," when they want it. The city of New York is considering imposing a $1,000 fine on those who purchase counterfeit goods, a law meant to protect the valuable designs of companies that make high-end, quality consumer goods. But we've gotten to the point where people believe that it's a "right" for them to carry around a designer handbag. One Brooklyn teacher shrugged at the backlash against the fine, suggesting that she knew it was wrong to buy knockoffs but couldn't resist. "Everyone steals," she told the *New York Post*. This woman is an elementary school teacher. In America. No wonder our culture is adrift.

People are also learning these warped lessons from pop culture. Whether it's from scripted programs or reality TV, the message is clear. Consider *The Honeymooners*. In that 1950s TV series, Ralph and Alice Kramden's two-room, walk-up Brooklyn apartment looked like what a real New York City bus driver and his homemaker wife could afford at the time. They dressed and lived a typical blue-collar life. Now contrast *The Honeymooners* with more recent NYC sitcoms like *Friends* and *Sex and the City*, where unemployed actors live in multimillion-dollar apartments, and newspaper columnists wear thousand-dollar shoes.

Some may argue that these things don't matter, and that throughout American history, each generation has always questioned the entertainment choices of their children and grandchildren. At one point, some people thought Elvis Presley might be the greatest threat to the Union. Say what you want about Elvis, he sang and danced for his dinner, served in the army, and belted out "America the Beautiful." Many of today's celebrities sit around the house all day in muscle shirts or go on television and bray about "America the real terrorist." Each generation may push the envelope as to what is acceptable, but something is wrong when hating your own country is celebrated.

Nobody could better articulate why it's important for our culture to support American values than, well, one Hollywood actor, who had this to say:

> Are we doing a good enough job teaching our children what America is and what she represents in the long history of the world? Those of us who are over 35 or so years of age grew up in a different America. We were taught, very directly, what it means to be an American. And we absorbed, almost in the air, a love of country and an appreciation of its institutions. If you didn't get these things from your family you got them from the neighborhood, from the father down the street who fought in Korea or the family who lost someone at Anzio. Or you could get a sense of patriotism from school. And if all else failed you could get a sense of patriotism from the popular culture. The movies celebrated democratic values and implicitly reinforced the idea that America was special. TV was like that, too, through the mid-sixties.
>
> But now . . . some things have changed. Younger parents aren't sure that an unambivalent appreciation of America is the right thing to teach modern children. And as for those who create the popular culture, well-grounded patriotism is no longer the style. Our spirit is back, but we haven't reinstitutionalized it. We've got to do a better job of getting across that America is freedom—freedom of speech, freedom of religion, freedom of enterprise. And freedom is special and rare. It's fragile; it needs protection . . .
>
> And let me offer lesson number one about America: All great change in America begins at the dinner table. So, tomorrow night

in the kitchen I hope the talking begins. And children, if your parents haven't been teaching you what it means to be an American, let 'em know and nail 'em on it. That would be a very American thing to do.

The actor responsible for those words was Ronald Reagan, in his farewell address to the nation in 1989. His warnings still ring with truth.

So what can we, as patriots, do to repair our culture in addition to talking to our children at the dinner table? The screenwriter Andrew Klavan pointed out, "For the last three decades or so, the usual conservative approach to the arts has been threefold: We complain about what's being produced; we fret about the influence it will have; then we give up with a shrug."*

The Tea Party movement believes that the area of American culture is too important to cede to those who apologize for America's greatness and the values that got us here. Books, movies, music, theater, visual arts, and the environment in which these cultural touchstones are created have such a huge impact on the ideals of a society that they should not be left to chance; nor should they be left solely in the hands of those who hate the very country that gives them the freedom and financial support to be in the business of culture.

Often, some of our most talented creators—particularly those who hold the values that are America's source code—are lured away from the arts and into business by the promise that they can make more money in other endeavors. We need to come together to provide incentives to young people to pursue careers in the arts. If we fail to do so, we risk losing our position as the world's leader in the creation of intellectual property.

Accordingly, we propose the creation of a massive public effort to encourage creativity, through the creation of an ambitious grant program to be administered through a new organization, the National

---

* http://www.nationalreview.com/articles/255296/can-conservatives-win-back-arts
-andrew-klavan.

Endowment for Patriotism in the Arts, or NEPA. The organization would be responsible for working to identify promising young artists who glorify America, provide seed funding for raw materials and living expenses for those artists, and help them to find markets for their work. NEPA would be nothing short of a new Manhattan Project for the arts—an all-out effort to ensure that we advance our national goals and repair America's tarnished image.

As an independent agency, NEPA would start with a small budget—perhaps $250 million annually—a sum that would cost each individual American less than a dollar a year; far less than we spend on our military, our State Department, or foreign aid. We hope NEPA will eventually grow into the equivalent of an artistic Peace Corps, spreading the ideals of capitalism and American patriotism around the world at a very small cost to taxpayers.

The agency would be run by a bipartisan board of directors, composed of influential artists, public servants, and cultural critics from both sides of the aisle. From the Democratic side, figures like Tipper Gore, cofounder of the Parents Music Resource Center, and Senator Joe Lieberman of Connecticut, whose work on preventing children from seeing violence in video games, and who is known for his staunch support of our troops, would be appropriate founding members. On the conservative side, the actor Stephen Baldwin, game-show host Pat Sajak, and the novelist and television personality Glenn Beck would all provide valuable guidance on how we, as a society, can encourage patriotism in literature, as well as in the visual and performing arts.

Of course, since one of the Tea Party movement's core values is fiscal responsibility, we would make sure that such an initiative was fully funded through new revenue sources. A penny tax on tickets to R-rated movies, music downloads of songs with parental advisory labels, or "Mature"-rated video games not only would fully fund NEPA but could contribute to closing the deficit as well.

∼

If you've been paying attention for the last nine chapters, you'll realize that, although the goal may be laudable, creating a federal agency to promote "patriotism in the arts" is a terrible idea and that the last several paragraphs are meant as sarcasm. Sadly, however, it's much easier to propose a new government program or the expansion of an existing program than it is to actually solve problems in any area of American society. Spending hundreds of millions of taxpayer dollars on a propaganda program (particularly one run by the likes of Tipper Gore and Stephen Baldwin) is no more likely to actually foster patriotism than the National Endowment for the Arts ($167 million in taxpayer dollars in fiscal year 2010) can achieve its stated mission of "advancing artistic excellence, innovation, and creativity."

Take another arts-related federal agency, the National Endowment for the Humanities. Its mission is to "serve and strengthen our Republic by promoting excellence in the humanities" and to teach the lessons of history to all Americans. It spent $171 million to achieve this mission in 2010 on such projects as: the purchase of a coffee farm in Hawaii; a traveling exhibit of circus posters from 1879 to 1939; educational programs on Africa's human and ecological diversity; an international symposium on the sculptures of Xiangtangshan caves in China; a Web site on the history and culture of the Yoruba people in Nigeria; and an interactive, trilingual exhibition on the Children of Hangzhou, China, that will be displayed in Ontario, Canada.

In the next chapter, as part of the Cultural Pathway to Liberty, we'll propose some specific ideas on what Americans can do to encourage the creation of art and entertainment that is consistent with our core values: fiscal responsibility, constitutionally limited government, and free markets.

And in the meantime, we'll remind you of the words of the novelist George Orwell, whose works *1984* and *Animal Farm* are two of the most important books ever written in the fight against collectivism: "Who controls the past controls the future; who controls the present controls the past." The key to the control of the present is popular culture.

# ★ 11 ★

## The Cultural Pathway to Liberty

**Popular culture** . . . *is the totality of ideas, perspectives, attitudes, images and other phenomena that are deemed preferred through an informal consensus within the mainstream of a given society. Popular culture is heavily influenced by the mass media and permeates the everyday life of many people.*

—Entry in Wikipedia (itself a form
of popular culture)

**OVER THE PAST** forty years in America, we conservatives have largely abdicated any serious role in defining pop culture. We complain that it does not reflect our values, and instead of doing anything proactive about it, many of us retreat into the past. We introduce our kids to the clear representations of right and wrong portrayed in John Wayne movies and the "old" musicals like *The Music Man,* for fear they will emulate the disrespectful "cult heroes" of today. We try to share with our kids the joys of *Father Knows Best* and *Leave It to Beaver,* rather than letting them watch the dysfunctional families on Nickelodeon and the Disney Channel.

Musically, we do our best to embrace current trends while trying to introduce our kids to bands that share our cultural values. At the very least, we do our best to keep our children away from the misogynistic, cop-killing songs popular today.

But in the end, these are all defensive measures. They do nothing to foster a culture that celebrates or even supports our values. We are like keepers of an old flame, rather than builders of a new fire. Surrounded by a culture that denigrates American ideals, we have retreated. And while this may serve the immediate needs of our families, it fails the needs of our country. At best, we are holding the line while never advancing our beliefs. At worst, we are losing the culture war without joining the battle, and ceding victory to those who view us patriots as their cultural enemies.

As we discussed, popular culture in the United States has devolved from celebrating American values to largely vilifying them. While movies once glorified the men and women in our military, today's films, with the notable exception of the Academy Award–winning film *The Hurt Locker*, tend to paint our soldiers as genocidal murderers. While movies and literature once widely celebrated American achievement, ingenuity, and industry (a set of values that used to be called the American dream), today's achievers are attacked as "fat-cat" villains painted in less flattering hues than terrorists. What went wrong?

In the 1960s, America and American ideals came under attack from the *counterculture*. This was the first generation to come of age when America was a superpower. And when it came time for that generation to rebel, they attacked the power structures and values of their own country. They took stands ranging from "free speech" to ending the war in Vietnam. They fought everything "the man" stood for. Even if something directly benefited the 1960s activists, they didn't care. They opposed our national leaders and "dropped out." Unlike today's Tea Party protesters, the youth of the 1960s attacked what came before them, regardless of its value or efficacy.

Our Founders believed that a good revolution is sometimes necessary. As Thomas Jefferson said, "I like a little rebellion now and then. It is like a storm in the atmosphere." The Declaration of Independence itself was a revolutionary document that began with the rebellious statement "when in the course of human events it becomes necessary for one people to dissolve the political bands which have connected them with another . . ." In the eighteenth century our citizens actually were oppressed. King George III limited the freedom and creative spirit of our forefathers who forged a new union, built on new principles. The protesters of the 1960s were rebels without a cause, or rebels with a new cause every week. They reflexively fought virtually every aspect of our society.

Unlike our Founding Fathers, or the Tea Partiers of today, the 1960s cultural revolutionaries did not rationally examine history to find what works best. They reflexively rejected what had been proved to work best, and began to tear down everything that made America exceptional. Through music, visual arts, poetry, and film, they attacked the very fabric of American society.

By the end of the 1960s, drugs, promiscuity, secularism, and a general disdain for everything their parents stood for migrated from the counterculture to the mainstream. Lest you think Tea Partiers believe this was all bad, remember that many of us came of age in this era. Many who consider themselves part of the Tea Party movement also rejected the norms of the day back then, pushing back against excessive government and societal interference in our private lives in the hopes of creating a country in which all of us, regardless of race, gender, or ethnicity, truly were equal in the eyes of the law.

But there is a fundamental difference between the upheavals of the 1960s and today's Tea Party movement. While the 1960s led to a period in which our youth turned away from morality, religion, and our Founders' legacy, the Tea Party movement embraces these values. In many ways, we are part of a movement that wants to return our culture to the time when American power—and the principles that gave rise to that power—were seen as a beacon of liberty and freedom. We want to go back to the time when honesty, integrity, and a good work ethic were celebrated; today's culture, by contrast, rewards depravity and bad behavior with "fifteen minutes of fame."

What can the Tea Party movement do to make a difference in our culture now? First we must engage with our culture rather than abandon it to those who aim to tear it down.

## INDIVIDUAL ACTIONS MATTER

Even though the Tea Party movement is relatively young, it has already encouraged a renaissance of books, music, art, television, and films that represent the values that we hold dear. We patriots are a "niche" market that Fox News founder Roger Ailes once famously described as "half the country." With only 21 percent of Americans identifying themselves as "liberal," smart producers and creators are realizing that the potential audience for books, music, art, television, and films that embrace what is great about America is far bigger than the audience that is already well served (or perhaps overserved) by a plethora of entertainment that denigrates American values.

This does not mean that we want to fill America's cineplexes with flag-waving propaganda, or even to stop anti-American movies from being made. All we are saying is: we are a big audience, we are drastically underserved, and it is simply bad business to ignore us.

> *Your ideas about who you are don't just come from inside you. They come from the culture. And, in this culture, they come especially from the movies.*
>
> —RICHARD DYER, film historian

> *They're our storytelling. They are the fabric of our lives. They show us what is glorious and tragic and wonderful and funny about the day-to-day experiences that we all share. And, when you're [not] reflected, in any way, ever, in the movies—you begin to feel that something truly is wrong.*
>
> —ARMISTEAD MAUPIN, writer

> *You feel invisible. You feel like a ghost, and . . . a ghost that nobody believes in. There's this sense of isolation.*
>
> —SUSIE BRIGHT, writer

*Join the club. It's a whole group that is not represented.*
—WHOOPI GOLDBERG, actor

*There are lots of needs for art. The greatest one is "the mirror" of our own lives and our own existence.*
—HARVEY FIERSTEIN, actor/screenwriter

The preceding quotes are not from Tea Partiers. They are from the 1995 documentary *The Celluloid Closet*, which is about the ways that Hollywood traditionally depicted, and often ignored, homosexuals. Change a few words, or perhaps no words at all, and they could just as easily be speaking about the way patriots are treated by Hollywood today. Hollywood will not appreciate this comparison.

In the years since *The Celluloid Closet* was released, American culture has more openly embraced gay characters and themes. If catering to an audience that self-identifies as only 10 percent of the country is good business, surely it would make sense for producers to portray the values of the vast number of Americans who describe themselves as patriots. The gay cowboy movie *Brokeback Mountain* earned $178 million in six years. The traditional cowboy movie *True Grit* (2010) made $249 million in just six months. We are not telling anyone to stop making movies that appeal to any American subculture. We are merely suggesting that it might make sense to make movies that appeal to a niche group of patriotic Americans, otherwise known as at least "half the country." The time has come for all patriots in Hollywood to come out of the closet.

Again, we are not suggesting that all movies must be political or patriotic for Tea Partiers to embrace them. A film that applauds our values will find an audience with Americans who share and respect the same values.

For example, take the film *Secretariat* (2010). In this film, hard work, honesty, integrity, and a willingness to stand and fight for what one believes (in the face of great obstacles) were all represented as positive values. Tellingly, even though *Secretariat* contained no direct political references, the film was attacked by the Left. A Salon review slammed *Secretariat* for "presenting a honey-dipped fantasy vision of the American past as the Tea Party would like to imagine it, loaded with uplift and glory" and maligned it as "a work of creepy, half-hilarious master-race propaganda almost worthy of [Nazi propagandist] Leni Riefenstahl." That's right. A movie about a horse that ran faster than other horses, and the woman who believed in that horse, was—in the eyes of the Left—comparable to Nazism. We in the Tea Party ignored shrill demagoguery, and went to the movie with our kids and our grandkids. We spent our hard-earned dollars on a film that reflected our values on-screen. If we want more films to reflect our values, we must support the films that do. Fortunately, the success of films is measured by box-office receipts, not reviewers. *Secretariat* took in more than $60 million at the box office and turned a healthy $24-million profit. By comparison, the latest Michael Moore attack on American values (*Capitalism: A Love Story*) took in only $14 million at the box office, $6 million less than its $20-million production budget. Which goes to show: it is never good business to bite the hand that feeds you.

Other films that embrace American values and were box-office hits include *The Incredibles, Groundhog Day, We Were Soldiers, Rocky, Cinderella Man, United 93, Braveheart, The Dark Knight, 300, Forrest Gump,* and others.

When it comes to books, it is no secret that books embracing our core values already dominate the nonfiction bestseller lists. Tea Partiers have come out in droves to support nonfiction books from Mark Levin, Dick Morris, Sarah Palin, Rush Limbaugh, Sean Hannity, Glenn Beck, and countless others. We Tea Partiers are big readers, and when we get behind books, they become bestsellers. But, rather than embrace us as potential paying customers, the *New York Times* and other liberal newspapers do their best to ignore us. In 2009, the Huffington Post asked the question "Should The New York Times create a separate bestseller list for conservative blockbusters?" Apparently, too many Fox News contributors are crowding the hardcover bestseller lists.

And if we like reading nonfiction books, is it too much of a stretch to imagine that we would read fiction as well? *Atlas Shrugged* is one of the bestselling American novels in history and—more than fifty years after it was published—continues to sell more copies each year than most of the books signed to please the personal taste of editors, rather than the tastes of a hungry and starved reading public. How many Vince Flynns, Brad Thors, Daniel Silva, and even Glenn Becks need to put out blockbuster conservative novels before more New York publishers realize that there is an untapped market out there called "half the country"?

At the time of this writing, Simon & Schuster has chosen to release a novel by Danielle Santiago called *Allure of the Game*, which is described by the publisher as a "streetwise novel about an all-female drug cartel." If there is a market for this, there must be at least as big a market, or perhaps an even bigger market, for novels that are not about all-female drug cartels. Simon & Schuster is doing a great job catering to the all-female drug cartel market. But surely, if this publisher has the time and resources to promote a book with a small target audience, it could promote a novel that appeals to 50 percent of the country. True, we Tea Partiers are not as "streetwise" as Danielle Santiago, but when it comes to spreading the word about, we would gladly put our roughly 850,000 Facebook fans up against Santiago's 659 fans any day (or even Simon & Schuster's 14,734 fans, which is only 2 percent of ours).

In the visual arts we are lucky to have artists like Steve Penley. (You can see his work now at http://www.stevepenley.com.) Penley is one of the finest painters working today, and he is creating inspirational American art that reflects our values. Mixing bold colors and a modernist approach to classic subject matter, Penley appeals to a new generation of art lovers with his patriotic interpretations of American history and historical figures. Tea Party Patriots promotes Penley's work and has featured him at its events. We view it as part of our responsibility to support and promote those who support and promote our shared goals.

Each of us is responsible for supporting artists like Penley. When we see a piece of art that reflects our values, we should put our money on the table and proudly hang it in our homes. They are speaking for us. They are helping to create a culture in which we will be more comfortable raising our children and our grandchildren. But they cannot do it without our support. While artists who trash American values are being fed with American taxpayer dollars through the National Endowment for the Arts, it is up to us to support those artists who do not disparage the hand that feeds them. Do it now. Buy a painting, or a sculpture, or a collage, or a fine-art photograph that supports your values. It will make you feel good every time it catches your eye.

The Tea Party movement has also spawned an incredible variety of music that speaks to our values. At Dartmouth College, two members of the basketball team, who were fed up with the prevailing anti-American music on campus, formed the Young Cons rap duo (http://www.theyoungcons.com). Celebrating conservative values, utilizing a contemporary music format, they have developed a large fan base, along with a who's-who list of conservative endorsers, including Mike Huckabee, Michelle Malkin, Bill O'Reilly, and Mark Steyn.

Rock-and-roll musicians like Jeremy Dodge and Jeremy Hoop are creating new music for the new culture. Both Hoop and Dodge have written what many consider to be the anthems of the Tea Party movement (Dodge with "Stand Up" and Hoop with "Rise Up"). Dodge, aiming at a somewhat younger audience, writes edgy rock and roll and has also recorded the youth anthem "We Are Americans." Jeremy Hoop, an openhearted recording artist, writes uplifting songs about America. It goes without saying that he has yet to be "discovered" and signed to a lucrative record deal. Which makes him even more remarkable. Jeremy Hoop is a self-produced singer and songwriter (http://www.jeremyhoop.com). So is Jeremy Dodge (http://www.jeremydodge.com). So are the Young Cons. So is the patriotic pop singer Krista Branch (http://www.kristabranch.com). And Chris Cassone, who makes folk-rock-style songs like "Take It Back" (http://www.chriscassone.com). And on the country side, where the music has always tended toward conservative values, Steve Vaus has recorded "Tea Party" and "We Must Take America Back" (http://www.stevevaus.com). If you support these singers and songwriters today, their success will inspire the next generation who share our values to produce more great songs that will enrich our culture.

Each of these artists, and many more, can be found on the Tea Party Patriots Web site (http://www.teapartypatriots.org). They are doing their part to restore America's culture, but we have a role to play as well. We hear over and over about the difference it makes to these artists if we simply go to iTunes or to Amazon or BN.com or wherever we buy music and purchase a few of their songs. At roughly ninety-nine cents each, it is not much to ask. If you can afford to spend a couple of dollars each week, you will get great music that will inspire you to fight the battles we face. And you will be supporting the artists who are helping to reshape the culture in a way that promotes the values we hold dear. Go ahead—log on to your favorite music store and buy a song now.

## ORGANIZATIONS MATTER TOO

You can make a difference not only as an individual (simply by being a consumer of culture that reflects your values) but also by supporting organizations that encourage the creation of this type of art or music.

Bill Whittle is a conservative commentator who first came to notoriety on PJTV, a conservative alternative online news and opinion channel launched during the early days of the Tea Party movement. As PJTV has grown, so has Whittle's popularity. In addition to being one of the most sought-after conservative commentators, Whittle has now ventured into movie production.

Called Declaration Entertainment, and located at http://www.declarationentertainment.com, Whittle's venture gives individuals a chance to contribute to the production of movies that reflect their views of a healthy culture for America. Declaration describes itself as "a grass-roots film-financing movement that turns you, the audience, into Citizen Producers to reclaim American values. Declaration

Entertainment is dedicated to making the kinds of movies that made Hollywood successful—Movies about Freedom and Sacrifice, Hard-Work and Self-Reliance, Faith and Family." Instead of passively waiting for movies like *Secretariat*, you can join Declaration for $9.99 a month and actually fund the next generation of films that will reflect your beliefs. As an individual, you might not be able to raise millions of dollars to make a film, but if millions of us put our money where our mouths are, we'll get the kind of quality entertainment we want.

We cannot wait for Hollywood to wake up and realize that it is leaving millions on the table. It is up to us in the Tea Party movement to embrace people like Bill Whittle, and unique companies like Declaration Entertainment, that are trying to bring back the kind of culture that we say we want. We don't have access to the National Endowment for the Arts, nor do we want it. We don't have access to the Hollywood studio system. But we do have access to millions of patriotic Americans. You know what to do. Support those who support your values.

Another important organization in the culture war is the Media Research Center (MRC).* Founded in 1987 by Brent Bozell, MRC was created "to not only prove—through sound scientific research—that liberal bias in the media does exist and undermines traditional American values, but also to neutralize its impact on the American political scene." What began as a handful of employees with a black-and-white TV and a rented computer has now grown into "the largest, most comprehensive media monitoring operation in the world [that] serves as the checks and balances on the Fourth Estate. Through its divisions, programs, and a marketing effort that never rests, the Media Research Center has become an institutionalized machine on the issue of balance in the press."

In addition to his regular opinion columns in major newspapers, Bozell and his staff are regular commentators on news programs across the political spectrum. MRC has amassed the largest collection on Earth of documented liberal media bias. By exposing the lies of the Left, MRC is slowly disinfecting the media of their most virulent

* http://www.mediaresearchcenter.org.

strains of bias and contributing to a healthier, more informed, and more media-savvy culture in America.

MRC's annual gala—called the Media Research Center Dishonor Awards—is roundly considered the most amusing of D.C.'s many annual events. A panel of distinguished judges reviews the most outrageously biased media statements of the year and then presents each of the finalists with a Dishonor Award. In 2011, the authors of this book were invited to accept the "Tea Party from Hell" Dishonor Award on behalf of Tavis Smiley, the host of a National Public Radio show that bears his name. On the nation's taxpayer-funded, and government-regulated, airwaves, Smiley conducted the following interview with the wonderfully courageous author Ayaan Hirsi Ali on the subject of radical Muslims.

ALI: Somehow, the idea got into their minds that to kill other people is a great thing to do and that they would be rewarded in the hereafter.

HOST TAVIS SMILEY: But Christians do that every single day in this country.

ALI: Do they blow people up every day?

SMILEY: Yes. Oh, Christians, every day, people walk into post offices, they walk into schools, that's what Columbine is—I could do this all day long . . . There are folk in the Tea Party, for example, every day who are being recently arrested for making threats against elected officials, for calling people "nigger" as they walk into Capitol Hill, for spitting on people. That's within the political—that's within the body politic of this country.

Despite the fact that such accusations are outrageous and have been conclusively proved to be unfounded, liberals continue their slander of everything Tea Party. While having fun, the MRC also points out the absurdity and dishonesty of the progressive Left. The authors of this book were honored to have been asked to participate in exposing the dishonesty of the Left in its coverage of our movement.

By supporting ventures like Bill Whittle's Declaration Entertainment, Media Research Center, and others, Tea Partiers support a long-term investment in the creation and improvement of our popular culture that will serve as a multigenerational foundation for the rebirth of a fundamental belief in American exceptionalism.

The Tea Party Patriots would like to host a series of artist retreats, workshops, networking, and training as a direct way for the organization to play a role in the ongoing culture war. We are currently seeking funding for this type of ongoing arts program. Please visit http://www.teapartypatriots.org to learn how you can contribute to, or receive, this funding.

One more thing. If you're a publisher, film producer, record label, or musician, and you think your book, movie, or music would be of interest to Tea Party Patriots, drop us an e-mail at Culture@TeaParty Patriots.org, and if we agree, we'll help you get the word out.

# ★ 12 ★

## The Tea Party Patriots' Forty-Year Plan for America's Future

**WE LIVE IN** a high-speed, high-stress, and instant-gratification world. A long-term approach to almost anything in America is rare these days. Many of us do not plan beyond the next few days or weeks. Fewer plan for the next year, and even fewer plan for the next decade. Planning for the next generation is one of the last things on our minds. Yet that is precisely what we must do as Americans and as Tea Party Patriots.

Generations of politicians have focused first on their own reelections. Constantly driven by their need to attract votes, their policies and positions are often crafted to serve the needs of their election cycles, not the long-term needs of the country. That sets up a near-irresistible paradigm: make promises today, take credit today, and let someone else worry about paying for it tomorrow.

This "consequence-free" way of thinking is the root cause of many of the ills that plague our country. It is also an affront to the giants who sacrificed all to build this nation for future generations. The spirit of our Founders is precisely the opposite of the shortsighted, cloistered disdain today's "leaders" have for their responsibility to the people. Thomas Jefferson warned us specifically about this danger: "The principle of spending money to be paid by posterity, under the name of funding, is but swindling futurity on a large scale."

Today, politicians are swindling the future on a large scale. Why?

Because they have been allowed to create a system that rewards them immediately with power, fame, adoration, and wealth while pushing responsibility for reckless spending and unfunded promises onto future generations. If every one of them was given no choice but to pay for all of their promises in real time—the way We the People have to pay for our gas and groceries in real time—politicians would not be able to promise what they cannot afford to deliver. Unfortunately, those who should serve their country seem to have forgotten their obligation to future generations. The unfunded promises they make about Social Security, Medicare, and Medicaid will not come home to roost until long after they are retired. Meanwhile, real plans to sustain our nation are perpetually put on hold.

But the free ride is about to come to an end. America is speeding toward a fiscal brick wall. With a national debt exceeding $14 trillion, and with government at all levels going bankrupt, a crisis is imminent. Americans of all political stripes are reevaluating the way we look at our political future. The promises of our politicians have run smack into economic reality. But the collision, if it does not destroy us, will give us an opportunity to make America stronger.

While politicians continue to ignore the impending crisis, the vast majority of Americans know exactly where we are headed and exactly what must be done. And they are prepared to make the difficult decisions to put America back on track. They understand that our fiscal problems run deep, that these problems are the fault of both major political parties, and that only We the People can return our country to a sustainable path.

Tea Partiers know exactly where to look for answers. The wisdom of America is found both in our history and in the hearts and minds of its average citizens, not in the so-called geniuses of the ruling elite. Why should we trust the folks in D.C., who got us into this trouble in the first place, to get us out—when the only tools in their toolbox seem to be: tax, spend, and government control?

The answer is that we should not. If they were worthy of our trust, they would not have brought the greatest nation in world history to the brink of collapse. We must rely upon ourselves, as Americans have always done in times of crisis. As President Reagan famously said, "Government is not the solution to our problems, government is the problem."

It took generations of irresponsibility to bring America to this point. We will not be able to repair generations of damage immediately, nor can we reinfuse America's founding principles into the system overnight. It will take decades of vigilance. This is true economically, politically, and culturally. It will take time to restore our educational system and our judicial system. The Tea Party movement is dedicated to this cause. The focus of the movement is not solely on winning elections in the short term but also on returning the nation to the fundamental principles that made American exceptional. The battle is long term, and it is societal and cultural as well as political.

## DEVELOPING THE FORTY-YEAR PLAN

The outline for Tea Party Patriots' Forty-Year Plan came from the grass roots through an open and democratic process. Although our names are on this book, we are not the authors of this movement any more than we are authors of this plan. Our ideas originate at the local level and rise up through consensus. (Indeed, this kind of active participation in our democracy is not just our right but our duty as American citizens who believe in the concept of self-governance.) The Tea Party Patriots has fully embraced its role as a driving force in the long-term planning for America's future.

The outline for this plan was developed from suggestions put forth by Tea Partiers since February 20, 2009. It is not a static plan. It is not a top-down plan. It is a grassroots plan that returns power to the people. Therefore, it is forever subject to oversight, refinement, and improvement by our citizens.

Along with this book, we have launched a new section on our Web site to continue developing the Forty-Year Plan (http://www.teapar typatriots.org/40yearplan). It is a forum for all those who care about our country to come together around our shared goal of restoring

America. The genius of our citizens will shine as their ideas are submitted, debated, refined, and ultimately adopted as integral parts of the Forty-Year Plan.

In addition to input from the grass roots, we encourage suggestions from economists, educators, commentators, philosophers, artists, jurists, and others with expertise in their fields. Their comments will be open for you to challenge, embrace, refine, and eventually vote up or down. The framework for the plan is based on the Five Pathways to Liberty outlined in this book (comprising economics, politics, education, the judiciary, and the culture), but the final product—like every idea in the Tea Party movement—will be tailored the people's way. We will work together to finalize the Forty-Year Plan, which we plan to deliver to the public, to the presidential candidates, and to all candidates for Congress, the Senate, and state Houses across America in the months before the November 2012 elections.

What will the final plan look like? One thing we can tell you from experience is that it will be far better, and wiser, than anything that any one of us can imagine right now. When the creativity, ingenuity, and genius of the American people are unleashed, wonderful things happen. We Tea Partiers see evidence of this phenomenon every day. It is the reason that our movement in less than three years has become one of the most potent political forces in American history.

What will ultimately be in the plan is for the people to decide. It will be based on our three core principles, and in the end it will be drafted by We the People. The people are sovereign in this country. And the people will control this process. Just as the Founders intended.

It is up to all of us to develop the Forty-Year Plan, utilizing the Five Pathways to Liberty, if we are to return our nation to its founding principles and brighten its fading glory.

## AN AUDACIOUS PLAN

We, the authors of this book, realize that it's audacious to propose the creation of a Forty-Year Plan. We've seen the politicians roll their eyes and heard the ruling elites snicker when we suggest it. We've seen journalists left speechless when we talk about it. Walking the marble halls of congressional office buildings and statehouses, we've been told "you just don't understand how it's done" so many times, that we've lost count.

Yes, we understand that it's audacious, but this is not the "Audacity of Hope" spouted by a candidate for office. Unlike politicians who believe that we are too stupid to decide for ourselves, we have faith in the American people. Of course, we have an unfair advantage over Washington, D.C. We are not part of the exclusive club that is the ruling elite. We've spent the last two years traveling around the nation listening to and learning from other Tea Partiers. We've been on literally thousands of phone calls with local Tea Party leaders from across the nation. Almost every Monday night since February of 2009 we've been on a National Leadership Council conference call with local Tea Party coordinators from all over the country. Between us, we've read hundreds of thousands of e-mails. We understand that the answers are out there, and that you have them.

Yes, we know the idea of a Forty-Year Plan is audacious, but we have faith because we know who the American people are and what the American people are capable of. Most likely, if you are reading this book, you are already a "Tea Partier." Or maybe this is a new realization for you because you've learned that the Tea Party movement is not what the media tell you. You may never have attended a tea party. You may not have joined a local group. You may not have joined the Tea Party Patriots (http://www.teapartypatriots.org). And you may never refer to yourself as a Tea Partier. Forty-three percent of American citizens don't even bother to vote. Engaged in their own lives, living out their God-given right to "pursue happiness," they view it as someone else's job to secure our liberties, someone else's job to govern.

But if you are like most Americans, you feel some affinity with our core principles of fiscal responsibility, constitutionally limited government, and free markets. Those principles cut across party lines, socioeconomic status, education level, race, religion, and gender.

They are the principles upon which this nation was built. And they are principles that will guide us back onto the path of exceptionalism.

## WALKING IN THE SHOES OF
## THE ORIGINAL PATRIOTS

The Founders recognized power should rest with the people. That is a blessing, but it is also a responsibility. One of the challenges of our system is that it requires "eternal vigilance." As John Adams wrote in 1808, "Our obligations to our country never cease but with our lives."

For many Americans today, their obligations to America end after they vote once every four years. For 43 percent of Americans, their obligations to their country do not even approach that low bar, because life has become relatively easy, thanks to the sacrifices of our forefathers. Many of us are too busy enjoying the blessings of liberty to ever think about paying the price.

But that is not true of all Americans. Some dedicate their lives to securing and defending our liberty through the armed forces. Some give their last full measure with their lives.

Although we believe in our Founders' ideas, the Tea Party movement does not overly romanticize the America of the past. After the Revolution, and in the years leading up to the ratification of the Constitution, America had serious, existential problems. England and Spain expected the United States to collapse. Both sought to profit from the turmoil.

There was internal revolt taking place as well. Soldiers protested against the federal government's failure to pay them. The nation suffered from a paralyzing financial depression, caused by severe inflation. During the war, Congress had gone deeply into debt and dramatically increased the money supply. State governments tried to solve the problem through price fixing, leading only to further economic troubles. These were dark times. And we can draw many parallels with the problems our country faces today.

On November 5, 1786, almost a year before the Constitution was signed, George Washington wrote to James Madison, "No day was ever more clouded than the present . . . We are fast verging on anarchy and confusion . . . How melancholy is the reflection." Washington was weary from years of war, personal ill health, and the death of his children. But he refused to give up. He was called "the indispensable man." And his indispensable heirs now form the backbone of our movement.

Francis Corbin, a delegate to the Constitutional Convention from Virginia, had this to say during the ratification debates at the Virginia convention on June 7, 1788:

> The honorable gentleman must be well acquainted with the debts due by the United States, and how much is due to foreign nations . . . No part of the principal is paid to those nations, nor has even the interest been paid as honorably and punctually as it ought. Nay, we were obliged to borrow money last year to pay the interest. What! Borrow money to discharge the interest of what was borrowed, and continually augment the amount of the public debt! Such a plan would destroy the richest country on earth.

Sound familiar? It is true today. To preserve the nation means that each of us must take a stand against these timeless pressures.

Tea Partiers walk in the shoes of indispensable patriots like Washington, Jefferson, Madison, and Adams. With our nation at stake, the Tea Party movement—like the Sons of Liberty of yesteryear—is stoking the fires of a new revolution to preserve our liberty. We are not seeking to forge a new union. We seek only to illuminate the path back to the founding principles that made this nation great. Without a concerted and sustained effort by millions of committed citizens, this great nation as we know it will cease to exist.

Throughout history, great nations rise and fall. Just because you grew up when America was a superpower and a beacon of liberty does not mean that your grandchildren, or even your children, will live in the same place.

If the survival of this nation, and the realization of human potential that it represents, is not worth fighting for, what is?

We know you are busy. We understand that your daily commitments make it hard to get involved in politics. You have families, jobs, and responsibilities that make it hard to do more than vote on Election Day. We get it. But you *must* get involved, and you *must* get involved now. It is our solemn responsibility as American citizens to preserve this nation for our children and their children. As President Ronald Reagan famously said in his second inaugural address on January 21, 1985, "If not us, who? And if not now, when?"

You already know the answer to those questions. And you understand what happens when we leave our country in the hands of distant and unrepresentative governments. Elected officials steal our liberty, steal our money, and steal our children's and grandchildren's inheritance. If those who are destroying America are not stopped now—if you do not stand up and control them—they will rob the world of the liberty that is America, or, as Ronald Reagan called our country, the last place in the world to escape to.

You are the sons and daughters of revolutionaries. Never forget that. Americans are not weaklings who trade liberty and independence for safety and comfort. We fought bloody battles to build this nation and establish our freedom from such control.

> *They that can give up essential liberty to obtain a little temporary safety deserve neither liberty nor safety.*
>
> —BENJAMIN FRANKLIN

> *The only thing necessary for the triumph of evil is for good men to do nothing.*
>
> —EDMUND BURKE

> *It is not the function of our government to keep the citizen from falling into error; it is the function of the*

*citizen to keep the government from falling into error.*

—Supreme Court Justice ROBERT H. JACKSON

*Extremism in the defense of liberty is no vice . . . moderation in the pursuit of justice is no virtue.*

—Senator BARRY GOLDWATER

We are often told that we cannot make a difference; that the system is stacked against us. Yet the Tea Party movement has already accomplished what many thought was impossible. Just a few short years ago, some people called us radical, or "fringe." Our doubters said we would vanish into the dustbin of history. Yet we are still here. While our elected officials disdained us, We the People joined together and brought about the largest turnover in Congress since 1938. We changed the debate from "How much money should we spend?" to "How much must we cut to save the nation?"

We altered the debate so profoundly that, while politicians and the media were telling us the world would end if we did not raise America's debt ceiling, we said no and forced every Republican and eighty-two Democrats to vote against the very thing the president and his administration had spent months telling us we must do or the world would end. We fought back, and we won, even if only temporarily. The world did not end. But that was just one small victory. They will try again. Next week, next month, and next year, there will be another battle, and we will be there to fight those too. We'll also be present for every election—city, county, state, Senate, Congress, judges, sheriffs, dog catchers—even the White House—and all of the nomination processes along the way.

Tea Party principles are now the defining issues in almost every political race in the country. Do not give in to the political elites and commentators who tell you that you cannot make a difference. They are terrified that you *are* making a difference, which threatens their way of life—the way of life that leaches the greatness from America. Never let them discourage you. You *are* making a difference. Millions of us, standing shoulder to shoulder, *are* making a difference—and we will continue to do so for however long it takes to restore America.

We look to America's first revolutionaries for guidance and inspiration. Our children and grandchildren will look to us. This is our moment. This is your moment. This is your right, your duty, your privilege, and your blessing as an American.

The second great American Revolution has begun. Join now and keep America exceptional.

# *Epilogue*

IF THIS BOOK has inspired you to do your part for America, please start by helping to shape our Forty-Year Plan. Your opinions, ideas, and passions will matter. You can be part of the solution.

Start by going online to http://www.teapartypatriots.org/40year plan. You will be able to give your input, submit your ideas, and enter into the great American debate about the future of the country.

If you want to do more, you can join our national conference calls on the plan, attend a Tea Party rally, or start your own local Tea Party Patriots group. There are nearly four thousand groups across the country, each one started by someone just like you.

Our liberty is at stake, and not for the first time. Every time our way of life has been threatened, Americans have risen to the challenge. Today, our challenges come from within. Together we must again step up, contribute our skills and passion, and create and commit to the Forty-Year Plan to restore America.

You must decide now: do you want to be remembered as someone who let liberty slip through our fingers, or as a patriot who saved America from the jaws of tyranny?

The Forty-Year Plan begins today. Will you help shape it? Will you help write it? When the time comes, will you be there to put your "John Hancock" on the new Declaration of Independence? The choice is yours. It is up to you. Join the next American Revolution now.

# *Acknowledgments*

This book and all of my life experiences would not be possible without God, who has given me strength and discernment and so much when I have needed it the most. Thank you, God, for blessing my life.

Thank you so much Scott Hoffman and Michael Prell for having faith in Mark and me. You made this book come to fruition. What we have learned from you is priceless. Thank you for being our mentors and our friends. Thank you also to Pat Eisemann, Francesca Giacco, Maggie Richards, Lauren Culley, and Stephen Rubin. We are learning so much about the publishing process from you and are grateful to you for your faith in this book.

Rick Santelli had a rant that was heard around the world and started a movement. So many other things could have happened differently in this country but I am convinced that as long as Congress passed TARP and the Stimulus bill and Rick Santelli had his spontaneous rant, this movement would have started. Without his rant, I do not know if there would be a modern day Tea Party movement. Rick, you will never know how much the words you spoke that day and especially the mention of "your neighbors' houses with more bathrooms" affected my husband's and my life and the course of this country. Thank you!

Special thanks to Eric Odom who started #dontgo, Stacy Mott and

Teri Christoph who founded Smart Girl Politics, and Michael Patrick Leahy and Rob Neppell who started Top Conservatives on Twitter. You laid the groundwork that turned Rick Santelli's rant into action. This movement would not be here without the time and effort you gave in 2008 to lay that groundwork and your wisdom and leadership to visualize a need for these online social communities.

TPP's national coordinator, support team, board, advisors, and friends: Debbie and Phillip, Sally and Steve, Diana and Don, Dawn and Geoff; Ernest, Ken, and Ginni; Richard and Vickie, JD and Rebecca, Scott, Scot, Keli, Phillip, Leanne, Jamie, Tim, Jody, Ben, Darcy, Luke, Joanne, Debby and Darcy, Kenny, Bob, Foster, Steve, Don, Ray, Eric, Tim, Leo, Mike, Pritchett, and the State Coordinator Team, and all the local coordinators on our weekly National Leadership Council webinar. Each of you in your own way has contributed to the success of the organization that is Tea Party Patriots. There is no way to list every single one. You have made the movement what it is and have made Tea Party Patriots the grassroots organization it is today. Without your contributions, there would be no book about the Tea Party movement.

Thank you my Mom and Daddy James and Jo Mooneyhan and to my in-laws Lee and Linda Martin and Charlie and Beverly Roseberry. Thank you also to Linda and Ken, Charlice and Mike, Sean and Kate, Derek and Cheri, Kevin, and Karen. You have each supported Lee and the family, while I have been on the front line growing the movement and writing this book.

There has hardly been a day in my adult life, when Lee Martin has not been there for me. Thank you for being my husband, my best friend, the father of my children, and my greatest champion. You have been there every step of the way since we first met over twenty years ago and certainly every step of the way during the writing of this book. Thank you to our children who have had to learn more about economics and personal finances from our successes and our personal failures than any children should have to learn so young. They love this country and are my favorite Tea Party Patriots.

Finally, and most importantly, to every person who has come to a protest, picked up a sign, sent a letter, e-mail, or fax to Congress, picked up the phone to make a call, or answered the call to run for office, you have my deepest gratitude. You are serving our country by adhering to our Constitution and calling for a return to our core values. Together, we can, and will, empower our fellow citizens to self-govern once again.

—Jenny Beth

The first and most important acknowledgment goes to God, for allowing all of us the privilege to endeavor to make a difference with our lives. Next, there are many people who were instrumental in the writing of this book. First thanks go to my parents, Stan and Elaine, for raising me to believe the things that compel me to fight the principled fight. More than thanks, eternal gratitude goes to my wife and guiding light, Patty, and to my children, Jacob and Lucy; their love and support through late nights and long travel are more than I could ever expect or hope for. Next, thanks goes to the Tea Party Patriots National Coordinator Team, Dawn Wildman, Diana Reimer, Debbie Dooley, Sally Oljar, and my cofounder, Jenny Beth Martin. Without them there would be no Tea Party Patriots. They are true heroes. A thank-you is also owed to all the local Tea Party Patriots Coordinators out there. They are there on the ground, fighting the fight, every day, and this movement belongs to them. A special thanks goes to our agent, Scott Hoffman, and our personal writing mentor, Michael Prell. Without their help, support, and guidance, the actual writing of this book would have been impossible. Writing a book is much harder than I ever knew. And finally, to the millions of Tea Party Patriots across the country who have pledged their lives, their fortunes, and their sacred honor to save the nation, I salute you, and I am constantly humbled by your intelligence, your commitment, and your personal strength. I'm privileged to stand shoulder to shoulder with you in this fight.

—Mark

# Index

Page numbers in *italics* refer to illustrations.